I AM
JACKIE CHAN

I AM
JACKIE CHAN
MY LIFE IN ACTION

JACKIE CHAN
with Jeff Yang

PAN BOOKS

First published in the United States of America in 1998
by Ballantine Publishing Group, a division of Random House, Inc.

First published in Great Britain 1999 by Pan Books
an imprint of Pan Macmillan Ltd
Pan Macmillan, 20 New Wharf Road, London N1 9RR
Basingstoke and Oxford
Associated companies throughout the world
www.panmacmillan.com

Associated companies throughout the world

ISBN 0 330 37590 3

9

A CIP catalogue record for this book is available from
the British Library.

Photographs courtesy of Jackie Chan Kong Sang

Special thanks to Media Asia Distribution for their support in providing certain
film photographs, and to Richard Cooper of *Screen Power* for his support

Text design by BTD/Ann Obringer
Typeset by Creative Graphics, Inc.
Printed and bound in Great Britain by
Mackays of Chatham plc, Chatham, Kent

To my mother and father,
who brought me into the world,
and
to all my colleagues, friends, and fans,
without whose love and support,
I could not possibly be where I am today.

I AM
JACKIE CHAN

PROLOGUE: TAKING FLIGHT

I'm standing in the sky on the roof of a glass and steel office tower in Rotterdam, Holland. There are twenty-one floors of air between me and the concrete pavement below. I am about to do what I do best.

I am about to jump.

My stuntmen tell me that the fall is safe—well, not safe, but maybe a little less than deadly. Of course, *they've* only tried the jump from the sixteenth floor . . . and, as I watched the test footage late last night, alone in our production offices, I realized that a sixteen-floor fall was too predictable.

Too . . . *possible.*

After all, my producer has been bragging to reporters that this will be the world's most dangerous stunt. And who would I be if I didn't live up to my press?

Not Jackie Chan.

So, against the advice of my director and my costars and the executives at the studio, I have decided to add five stories to the stunt.

That's sixty more feet of very thin air through which my forty-five-year-old body will be sliding.

A few more seconds of excitement for the cameras.

A few more screams from an audience starving for adrenaline.

The formula is simple: *The more terrified my friends and family are, the more satisfied my fans will be.* And they mean everything to me. They come to the theaters hungry for a hero, for someone who can laugh at disaster, who can make funny faces at death. Someone who can show them for real that the only thing to fear is fear itself.

But whoever said that never stood on a roof in Rotterdam. He never looked down over the edge of a skyscraper to see a foam target 250 feet below. From here, the mattress looks like a postage stamp. When I hold out both hands in front of my face, I can just about cover it entirely.

Sorry to contradict you, Mr. Whoever, but the only things to fear are fear itself, *and* hitting the ground at one hundred miles per hour with nothing between you and the emergency room but a few inches of foam rubber.

I'm tired.

My heart feels like a rock in my chest.

My body screams at me about the abuse I've put it through over the last four decades. Parts of me I can't even *pronounce* are complaining about how badly I've treated them. And despite the mob of extras milling around the base of the building—hundreds of Dutch marines and fire-fighters and police, looking nervously up at the sky—I think to myself: *Is this jump really necessary?*

But the answer is there as soon as I ask the question: *Yes.*

Because this jump is special.

It isn't just for the fans and the critics and the box office charts.

This one is for the man who made it possible for me to stand here to-day, aching and shivering in the spotlight.

This is for my master, Yu Jim-yuen, who was buried a week ago in Los Angeles.

My trip from Holland to California for the funeral brought produc-tion to a grinding stop, costing Golden Harvest nearly a quarter of a mil-lion dollars. They knew better than to tell me not to go, even if for them every wasted dollar is like a drop of spilled blood.

I remember a frightened seven-year-old walking into the dark and musty halls of the China Drama Academy, holding his father's hand. Inside, he sees young boys and girls leaping and tumbling and screaming. Paradise—

"How long do you want to stay here, Jackie?"

"Forever!" answers the boy, his eyes bright and wide. And he lets go of his father to clutch at the hem of his master's robe. . . .

For the next ten years, I sweated and cried and bled under Master's hands. I cursed his name when I went to sleep at night, and I swallowed my fear and hatred of him when I woke in the morning. He asked for every-thing we had, and we gave it to him, under pain of injury, or even death.

But when we came of age, we realized he'd given it all back. With interest.

It was Master Yu Jim-yuen who created Jackie Chan, and I do what I do today—*I am what I am today*—because of him. And so this leap is in his memory, a final act of gratitude. A last gesture of defiance.

Someone slaps me on the back, asks me if I'm ready. I nod, barely un-derstanding. Another voice calls for quiet on the set, and suddenly the only sound is the wind and the blood rushing in my ears and my heart be-ginning to pound like a giant drum.

"Camera!"

"Rolling!"

"Action!"

And I suck in my churning stomach. Launch myself into the sky.

I fly.

I remember. . . .

THE YOUNG MASTER

I was born on April 7, 1954, the only son of Charles and Lee-lee Chan. They named me Chan Kong-sang, which means "Born in Hong Kong" Chan.

I guess my parents weren't very original when it came to names. Or maybe they just wanted to celebrate their relief at making it to Hong Kong, as survivors of a breathless escape from the turmoil of the mainland. Hong Kong was the promised land, a place that offered safety and prosperity. A place where new lives could begin.

By the Chinese calendar, 1954 was the Year of the Horse.

According to superstition, the Horse is a sign of energy, ambition, and success. It's a good year to be born in if you're a boy—not such a good one if you're a girl, because tradition says that a female Horse will have trouble finding a proper husband—and my parents were happy that I came into the world under such a fortunate sign. Of course, my arrival in the Year of the Horse was hardly a coincidence; actually, it took an awful lot of stubbornness on my part to pull it off! Most babies are born nine months after being conceived. I, on the other hand, stuck around an extra three months, until my mother was forced to go to a surgeon to bring me into the world, kicking and screaming, by caesarean section.

Maybe it was my rebellious streak that made me refuse to join my parents on time, or maybe it was a premonition of what my future would hold. After all, while comfortably inside my mother, I had privacy, sleep, and all the food I could ever ask for, without having to fight or work or suffer. In fact, I can honestly say that those three extra months were the easiest time of my life.

Nothing like that waited for me in the world outside. Hong Kong in the '50s was a hard and restless place, and my family's position there was at the very bottom of the social ladder, among the thousands of destitute migrants who'd fled to the British colony after the mainland's Communist Revolution. Still, as poor as we were, we felt lucky to have survived China's civil war, and especially grateful that my parents had good jobs in the strange new society of the island. Many of our fellow refugees had arrived in Hong Kong with nothing but the clothes on their back and the memories of what they'd left behind. They lived in shacks in the island's crowded ghettos, making paper flowers and cheap trinkets to survive, or turning to less socially accepted—and more dangerous—pursuits.

It was a bad time to be poor. (But then again, when is it ever a good time to be poor?) As the crowds of new immigrants grew, the colony's swelling population divided itself into two groups: the determined and the desperate. On the one hand, there were those who embraced the city's unspoken philosophy: Work hard and you'll survive, do well, maybe even get rich. But meanwhile, in the lower parts of the city, the lives of many of our fellow newcomers were filled with hunger, crime, and fear.

We belonged to the first group—the lucky ones. Soon after coming to the island, my father and mother had found employment with the French ambassador to Hong Kong, a kind gentleman with a warm and caring family. Dad became the ambassador's cook and handyman; my mother was the housekeeper. And so, when I was born, I found myself not on the tough streets of lower Hong Kong, but in a mansion on the exclusive slopes of Victoria Peak—the home of the wealthy, the famous, the powerful. And me.

I don't recall the house itself too well.

It was big, I remember, and very grand. In the front rooms, well-dressed Westerners (and sometimes Chinese) would chat and take tea or listen to music; upstairs, the ambassador's family had their quarters, huge rooms with high ceilings and windows that opened out onto the lights of the city below. But I didn't see these parts of the house very often. This was a different world from the one in which my family lived.

Our place was the rear of the mansion, divided from the air and light of the front by a small door.

If you were to open that door and pass through, you'd find yourself in a long, narrow hall that ran along the length of the house—the highway of our world. It was usually dark in that corridor, except when meals were being served, so it might be easier to find your way around by smell and sound than by sight.

Here's a quick tour of our world.

To your right, the first door off the corridor: the noise of chopping and sizzling, an occasional curse; the aroma of roasting meat and vegetables simmering in fragrant peanut oil. That would be the kitchen, where my father spent his mornings and afternoons preparing food for the ambassador's family. Farther down the corridor: the soft *slush-slush* of trickling water, and the sweet melody of a hummed folk song—the laundry room, where my mother washed mountains of fluffy white linens and the family's fine, beautiful clothing. And then: the smell of incense and wool and dried-grass matting, the gentle noise of an infant's breathing. This would be our family's bedroom, where my mother and father and I all slept together.

Our room was tiny, and it was not what you would probably consider comfortable. There were no windows, and the walls and floor were clean, but bare. The furniture had all been made by my father's hands, and there wasn't much of it: a bunk bed, some benches, and a storage trunk. My parents slept together in the top bunk of the bed, and I slept in the bottom one. From the top bunk, you could reach up and touch the ceiling; four long steps would take you from wall to wall.

This was all the home I knew for the first six years of my life, and I was happy there, despite the cramped quarters and the simple furnishings. Actually, I didn't know at the time just how good I had it.

The next place I'd call home would make our small room seem like a palace.

But I haven't finished the tour. Follow the corridor to its end, and you'd hear the buzz of flies, and your nose would wrinkle at the pungent odors of mold and aging food. This alcove at the end of the hall would be the rubbish room, where the household garbage was stored during the day, to be disposed of at night.

By the time I was a small child, I'd get to know this room very well. More on why later.

I mentioned that I'd started giving trouble to my parents even before I was born. Of all the crazy stunts I've done, in my opinion, nothing compares to my mom's achievement—surviving nearly an entire year of pregnancy, then giving birth to a healthy baby who weighed *twelve pounds* at delivery. Both my parents were shocked when I finally arrived. My father said he'd never seen such a big baby in his life—he and Mom nicknamed me Pao-pao, which is Chinese for "cannonball." And I'm sure my mother was glad that she didn't have to give birth to me naturally. . . .

There was a price to pay for my safe and sound arrival, of course. The bill for my mother's surgery came to HK$500 (about U.S.$26), and my parents' savings didn't come close to covering that cost. But the lady doctor who performed the surgery must have been impressed by me too, because afterward she approached my nervous father with a deal. She had no kids of her own, she explained to him, and she knew he and my mother had no money. If my father would allow her to "adopt" me, she would be willing to pay for the costs of the surgery and my mother's hospital stay, and even give my parents an additional adoption fee of HK$1,500.

I'm not angry about the fact that my father thought long and hard about the offer. Two thousand Hong Kong dollars was a lot of money back then, and poor children were regularly given to wealthier friends and relatives to bring up in those days. Maybe it would have even been for the best, because the lady doctor would have brought me up in style.

But I was my parents' only son. I was a symbol of their new start in

Hong Kong. I was born under a lucky sign, and I was big and healthy. My father went home and talked about the doctor's offer with some of his friends, who all said the same thing: there was something special about me, the twelve-month, twelve-pound baby, and if I grew up to be a great man, my father would always regret giving me up. Dad's friends lent him the money to pay off the hospital debt, and (after thanking the doctor for her skillful surgery and generous offer), he took my mother and me home, to the big house on the Peak.

FAMILY STORIES

That's the story of how I was born.

Or at least that's the one my dad told me all my life, anyway.

But inside every story hides another one, and over the years, I found out a little more about our *secret* history—about what my parents left behind in China when they came to Hong Kong, and the real reason I was too special to give away.

If you were to look at pictures of my father as a young man, your first impression would be that this is a man of great strength and enormous pride. And of course, you'd be right. Dad was born in China's Shandong province, the land of the famous North Clan and the birthplace of many legendary warriors and martial artists. His family was a very respected one, and even as a small child, he was expected to go on to great things.

Now, back then, Shanghai was the style capital of Asia. All of the finest things and people in China could be found in this one city, where art, fashion, philosophy, and society reached their height of sophistication. The Chans brought their promising son there at the age of three, grooming him to become one of society's leaders. When he came into adulthood, he was married to the daughter of another respectable family.

I don't know if he was happy then, but I have to assume he was. My father and his wife lived together, with the approval of their clans. They shared a roof and a household. And they had children.

I found this out just a few years ago. I knew my father always sent money back home to relatives in China—sometimes he'd say it was for his brother, other times, his sister. I'd never met any other member of his family, so I didn't have any reason to ask him any further questions. And really, I don't have that much curiosity in my personality.

But then something happened that made me curious in spite of myself. The mail had just arrived, and I was going through it. Nothing interesting: bills, invitations to events . . . and an unsigned letter from the mainland, addressed to my dad. He wasn't at home, and suddenly, I realized that I wanted to know more about this mystery—all those unasked, unanswered questions about my family. So I opened the envelope.

"Dearest father . . ." *Dearest father!?* I knew *I* hadn't sent the letter. I looked at the envelope again; it was sent to my house, in my dad's name.

And inside the envelope, something else. A photograph of three old men. "We miss you . . ." continued the letter.

My brothers. My dad's sons. And I'd never seen them before in my life. When my father came home, I waved the letter in his face. "What's this?" I shouted. "Who are these guys?"

His face went stiff. Like stone. "You don't need to know, Jackie," he said quietly. "You don't need to know." And he took the letter and photograph away.

We never talked about it again.

That's how I found out about my half brothers.

The rest of his story isn't very clear. I know that it involved the Japanese. When the armies invaded China, they turned the nation upside down. Chinese were fighting Chinese, and Shanghai—the city they called the Jewel of the East—became a place of fear. My father's family had to abandon everything it owned. And even more: my father was forced to leave behind him his sons and his wife. I don't think she survived the war.

At this time, my mother was also in Shanghai. She was from a very poor background, so she had none of the advantages of my father's upbringing. Like my father, she was married. And, like my father, in the turmoil of the war, she had to leave her husband and family behind.

She escaped the terror by hiding from Japanese troops, scavenging food, and making a dangerous journey on foot to the coast. It was in Shandong—my ancestral home—that she met my dad. Despite the difference in their backgrounds, the war had turned them into equals: two refugees, still mourning the loss of their loved ones. Somehow, Dad managed to bring her with him on the boat that smuggled him out of the mainland. They got married soon after safely reaching Hong Kong. And not long after that, I was on my way.

All through my childhood, they always told me that I was an only child, their special son. This is part of the reason why I was so shocked to find out about my brothers. But that shock was just the beginning.

My mother is very old now, and even though my wife has always helped to take care of her, some years ago it became clear that she needed someone to be with her all the time, to live with her in my parents' house in Australia.

One day, when I went to visit them, the person who answered the door was a strange older woman. She didn't introduce herself as she brought me in to see my mother, but somehow, she seemed familiar. "Hey, Mom, who's the new housekeeper?" I asked. My mother looked at me in silence for a few moments. "She isn't a housekeeper," she said finally. "Son, meet your sister."

Even today, I don't know everything. I don't think I want to know. My mother told my manager Willie the whole story once, and he came running over to tell me that it would make a fantastic movie. I told him that even if it would, I didn't want to make it. I don't want to find out that I have more brothers or sisters, or that my father isn't my real father, or that my mother isn't my real mother.

Our secret history belongs where it is now: in the past.

Still, I guess you can see why my parents were reluctant to give me up. There might have been other children lost in the branches of the family tree, but who knew at the time if they'd survived the war? And besides, I was the only child they *shared*: the only son of Charles and Lee-lee Chan.

Sometimes I wonder what it would have been like to have known my half brothers and sisters growing up. But being an only child had its advantages, too—most of which had to do with my mother. Without any competition from siblings, I had all of my mom's attention—which of course is exactly what I demanded.

As a toddler, I remember watching my mother do the chores that filled her waking hours. A large part of her day was spent in the laundry room, washing, ironing, and folding, and I would crawl around her feet, pulling down sheets, putting soap chips in my mouth, and nearly tripping her as she carried hot water from the running tap to the scrub basin. Eventually, Mom did what she always did when she needed a little bit of peace: she filled a big tub with warm water and put me inside, letting me splash and play. I wasn't any easier to take care of when evening arrived, either; restless in my lower bunk, I would scream and cry throughout the night. The noise would not only keep up my hardworking parents, it would sometimes filter upstairs to the ambassador's bedroom, waking his patient—but light-sleeping—wife. I can only imagine my parents' embarrassment when the wife of their employer came down in her nightgown and robe to the servants' quarters, asking them (very politely) to quiet their obnoxious child!

When this happened, my mother would pick me up and bring me outside to the mansion's back garden, cradling me in her arms and gently shooing the mosquitoes away with a straw fan. While she held me, she would hum a soft melody without words, until finally I went to sleep.

Every child thinks his mother is the best in the world, but my mom really *is* the greatest. She had no education, no opportunities in her life; she's a very traditional Chinese woman who devoted her entire life to her husband and her son. I never remember her going out, and never saw her in makeup or fancy clothing. I don't even remember her spending money on herself: everything was for the family. Even now, when I can afford to buy her anything, the things she chooses to wear are things she bought forty years ago. I remember one day, when I was in Australia visiting her, all of a sudden she turned to me and said, "Son, can you give me one hundred twenty dollars?"

It was a strange request. "Why such a weird amount?"

"If you give me one hundred twenty dollars," she said, "I'll turn it into one thousand."

That made me blink. "How?" I asked. My mother is a wonderful woman, but she's no magician—or financial wizard.

She smiled. "I'll show you."

I followed her as she left the living room and walked down the corridor to her bedroom. "Reach up and get that bag, Jackie," she said. I stood on my toes and grunted as I pulled down the suitcase. It was almost brand-new, one of the ones I'd bought her; she never used them when she traveled, preferring the old, battered bags she'd had since my parents lived in Hong Kong. Inside the suitcase were clothes she no longer wore, but couldn't bear to throw away. Lifting out and setting aside some old sweaters, she pulled out a huge bundle of wrinkled, faded bills. I looked at it in shock. Not a single one of the bills was in a denomination greater than twenty dollars. There were hundreds of ones and fives and tens. And it all added up to $880.

This was the money she'd saved from over twenty years of keeping house: tips from ambassadors and presidents and members of parliament, all of the people she'd cleaned up for and straightened up after.

"Mom, give me the money, and I'll give you ten thousand dollars in Australian cash."

So we traded. And you know what? We had dinner with friends that night, and we spent her whole stack. Twenty years of my mother's life, and boom—we ate it in one meal.

I said before that there are advantages to being an only child. Well, there are also disadvantages—most of which had to do with my father. How much easier would my childhood have been, if only I'd had siblings to share the burden of my father's expectations?

You see, Dad, like his Shandong ancestors, was a warrior at heart—a man of great courage and determination. He was proud that he had managed to overcome everything fate had thrown his way, all the tragedy and suffering and years of backbreaking labor. "The Japanese army conquered China," he would often boast, "but they could never conquer the Chinese! That is why our civilization has survived for thousands of years. To a Chinese man, suffering is like rice: it only makes us stronger."

From this followed a scary kind of logic: pain gives you discipline. Discipline is at the root of manhood. And so, to be a real man, one must suffer as much as possible.

Because bringing me into the world was so expensive, Dad was especially adamant about raising me up as a properly disciplined man, even if he had to knock me sideways to do it. Each morning, he'd rise when dawn was just a hair-thin line of light on the horizon, leaving my mother still dozing. Leaping to the ground from his bunk as softly as possible, he'd shake me roughly awake. "Ah Pao, it's morning. Up, up, up."

If I complained too much or rolled away, he'd just grab me by the waist and pull me out of bed in a tangle of sheets and arms. When I was lucky, I'd get my feet under me before the rest of me hit the floor. When I wasn't, well, at least I learned how to take a fall. A good lesson for the future.

Once we were both more or less awake, we went to the laundry area and splashed water on our faces and chests. The water was always freezing cold, and in the chill of the early morning it raised goose bumps on my skin. But the chill wouldn't last long. Like any survivor, my father was a jack-of-all-trades, an accomplished amateur carpenter and handyman. Out of stray pieces of wood and recycled rubbish—rice sacks, rope, and large cans that still smelled faintly of cooking oil—he'd made a makeshift gym, and we would greet sunrise with a workout that left me breathless and soaked with perspiration. We would run, lift bags filled with sand, do military-style push-ups—and spend hours practicing martial arts. Though I was just four or five years old, already my father was teaching me the basics of Northern-style kung fu.

It may seem strange that such a young child would be learning how to fight. You have to remember, though, that to us Chinese, kung fu isn't just a means of self-defense. In some ways, the history of kung fu is the history of China.

Legend says that kung fu was invented by Bodhidharma, the monk who traveled from India to China to spread Buddha's teachings. When he arrived at the great temple of Shaolin, Bodhidharma was turned away by the skeptical Shaolin brothers. He then took up residence in a small cave near the temple, and meditated there for nearly a decade. Over the years, the Shaolin monks watched in awe as Bodhidharma stared intently, without sleeping or even blinking, at the wall of his cave. After nine years, the power of the stare bore a hole through the wall into the daylight.

This display of discipline led the monks to embrace Bodhidharma as a great teacher. "How can we learn how to be like you?" they asked. And so Bodhidharma taught them about the greater wisdom of Buddhism and the power of meditation, but found that, no matter how the monks tried, they were not strong enough to resist sleep and other temptations. As a result, he wrote a manual called *The Classic of Muscle Change*, blueprinting a series of exercises to toughen the body and mind.

Over time, the Shaolin monks adapted these exercises into Chinese kung fu.

Kung fu translates loosely into English as "skill," but by the time of the Tang dynasty, which they call China's heroic age, kung fu had diverged into *many* different skills: the Southern styles, which emphasize strong defensive postures and powerful fist techniques, and the Northern, which are flowing, acrobatic, and focused on dynamic, spinning kicks. When the Tang emperor Wang Shih-ch'ung faced a revolt in the countryside, it was warrior monks from the Shaolin Temple who defeated the rebels—spreading the legend of their boxing abilities, and turning kung fu into something every gentleman of quality should know.

Although skills with the sword, the spear, and the staff were always an important part of Chinese martial arts, it was the unarmed techniques that were most admired. A master of Chinese boxing was deadly even when alone and armed only with his iron fists and lightning legs. When the Manchu invaders conquered China in the seventeenth century, study of martial arts was outlawed. But the spirit of kung fu could not die. Rebels loyal to the true emperor gathered in underground societies called "Triads," developing the art of kung fu in secret.

By the turn of the century, the Triads had turned into an extensive network of revolutionaries committed to driving out the Manchus and their Western allies, and restoring Chinese rule. The arrival of the year 1900 triggered the Boxer Rebellion, an uprising by Triads convinced that their mysterious skills would protect them from the bullets of the hated foreigners.

Unfortunately, they were wrong.

Thousands of Triad members were killed, and the rest were driven into hiding in Hong Kong, in Taiwan, and even in the West.

In China, kung fu was suppressed for generations, its masters dead or in exile, while the disgraced and broken Triads degenerated into brutal criminal gangs. But the crackdown on kung fu in China only led to its spread throughout the world. Now, the techniques of kung fu are practiced everywhere by those who realize that it builds the character traits that lead to greatness: strength, patience, courage, and subtlety.

My father believed this more than anyone. To him, learning kung fu was the same as learning how to be a man.

And frankly, I was a big disappointment. Lazy and impatient by nature, at first I practiced under his watchful eye only out of the fear that if I didn't, he'd demonstrate his techniques on me, his useless son. Worse yet, when I finally realized that his training was making me strong, tough, and a fearsome opponent for any kid stupid enough to get in my way, I brought my dad's worst nightmare to life: I went from being a brat, to being a brawler.

I found out quickly that fighting was fun—when you won, anyway—and it soon became one of my favorite hobbies, next to eating. (Well, nothing really compared to eating. Even now, I guess I'd have to say that nothing comes close to the pleasure of a good, hearty meal.)

But, in my own defense, I never got into fights without good reason. Or at least a reason that seemed good at the time. I mentioned that the ambassador's family was always very nice to us, but you couldn't say the same for some of our neighbors. We were poor Chinese, living as servants in the home of a rich and important Westerner. The other Western kids thought it a shame that the ambassador's wife encouraged her children to play with me. These bullies made it their hobby to pick on me, which was okay, and on my friends . . . which was not.

Don't mess with my friends. Ever. That's a lesson I'm always willing to teach with my fists. My closest companion in the world at the time was the ambassador's youngest daughter, a beautiful little girl who called me her boyfriend. I accepted the role with pride, and anyone who dared to make her cry would soon find himself on the ground, with me and all my chubby weight on top.

Unfortunately, my dad didn't care about my chivalrous efforts to defend my young friend's honor. The first time he found me seated on the screaming body of one of the neighboring boys, bruised but crowing victory, he grabbed me by the scruff of my neck and pulled me into the house.

"Dad, I won!" I shouted, causing my mother to peek her head out of the laundry room in alarm. "Daaaaaad, ow!"

I was more scared of my father when he was silent than when he was shouting. When he yelled at me, I knew I'd get a spanking at the very worst. Pain never bothered me much. After all, it went away eventually, and at least after a spanking I'd be free to do whatever I wanted. But when my dad was quiet, I had no idea what he would do next.

Except that I wouldn't enjoy it.

My mother watched as my father pulled me down the corridor, past our room, where spankings usually took place, and into the alcove where trash was stored.

"What's wrong, Dad? I *won!*" I said, my voice trembling. His eyes flashed, and I flinched away from him.

"I did not teach you kung fu so you could beat up your friends," he said, ice dripping from his words. "I am teaching you how to fight so that you will never have to fight at *all.*"

"Well, he wasn't my friend," I countered.

My dad turned bright red. Without another word, he pushed me into the alcove, which was full and stinking with the day's garbage. I stumbled to my knees, and heard the door being slammed and locked behind me. In the corridor, my mother said something to my father, who barked back a response, before both voices disappeared into the distance.

I looked around at my surroundings. The alcove was tiny and crowded. I could reach out with both of my arms and touch both walls, or at least I could have if the walls hadn't been lined with bins and bags of trash. There was no roof to the alcove, allowing the dimming light of the sun to trickle into the space. I suspected that I would be there long after the moon took over. Gingerly sitting down on the floor and resting my back against the locked door, I made myself as comfortable as possible, and tried to take a nap.

I didn't care what my dad said. When I jumped on that bully, my little friend had looked at me like I was a hero. If a hero's place was out with the trash, well, I'd take it as an honor. Too bad I was going to miss dinner.

A faint tapping roused me from my dozing. I realized that my stomach was rumbling with hunger—even as a boy, my body always demanded food on a regular and sizable basis.

"Pao-pao?" said my mother in a whisper from behind the door. "Look up."

The doorway to the alcove had a narrow space above for ventilation. My mom is a small woman, but by reaching up with both arms and standing on her tiptoes she could just place her fingertips into the crack. As I raised my head, a crisp white paper package fell from the ventilation space into my lap, pushed through by my loving mother's hands. Inside the wrapping was a sandwich, made of warm, soft bread and roast meat.

Without even thanking my mom, I began gobbling the food, only half listening to the padding sound of my mother's feet walking back down the corridor to our family's bedroom.

As I said, my mom is the best mom in the whole wide world.

The next morning, I was rudely awakened by the opening of the door against which I was leaning. I fell backward into the corridor, blinking up at the expressionless face of my father.

"Ah Pao, it's morning. Time to get up," he said, and instructed me to help him move the heavy bins of trash out for collection. By the time that was done, dawn had arrived, and it was time to greet the sun with our morning workout.

SCHOOL DAYS

Thinking back to those few years living on the Peak, I'd have to say I was happy. I could have been content spending the rest of my life in that house, helping my mom fold clothes, watching my dad curse as he chopped vegetables, and explaining the world as I saw it to my friend the ambassador's daughter. Even the early morning workouts, as painful as they were, had a beautiful side: as the sun rose up over the mountain, it painted the city and the bay below in gold, like a giant chest of treasure.

So it came as a nasty surprise when my father told me my days of innocence were coming to an end.

"School?" I shouted, stomping my foot in rage. School was the place where the neighbors' kids wasted all the best parts of the day. It meant dressing up in sissy clothes, spending hours in a stifling classroom, and learning things that were of no use to anyone. I could learn everything I needed to right here at home. Probably more.

Of course, like other arguments I had with my father, this one was a complete waste of time, and so a few days later I found myself taking my first bus ride down the Peak to the Nan Hua Elementary Academy. On my way down, I ate my lunch, even though I'd just finished breakfast.

Nan Hua was a very good school, one of the best in the area, and I was extremely lucky to have a chance to go there. The teachers were patient, the classrooms were spacious and brightly lit, and the students were all from well-bred families.

I hated it from the instant I walked through the schoolyard gates.

Every minute I spent there was torture (except for lunch hour, and occasionally, gym). Trapped in a classroom with nothing to do but puzzle at the words in my texts or listen to the droning voice of the teacher, I almost missed the aches and pains of my father's morning regimen—a sore body was better than a numb brain any day. The boredom forced me to find ways of amusing myself. I'd make faces at other students, or thump rhythms on the desk with my palms, or fall out of my chair by accident . . . over and over again.

After a few noisy but enjoyable disruptions, the teacher would usually drag me out into the hall.

"Chan Kong-sang, you'll never amount to *anything*!" she'd tell me, her face stretched out in anger. It would be all I could do to avoid breaking into laughter. (It really was a very funny expression.)

In those days, teachers could be creative with their punishments. Usually I'd have to stand for the rest of the period holding a desk over my head. Sometimes I'd have to wear a sign around my neck, explaining the nature of my crime. Like, "This is a noisy, ill-behaved boy." Or, "This boy lost all of his books." Or, "This boy has not done his homework." Sometimes it would just say, in a couple of characters, "Useless!" To be honest, I couldn't read very well back then, so I'd have to take my teacher's word as to what they said.

Standing out in the hall was peaceful, at least. And if no one was looking, I'd gently put the desk down, lean against the wall, and catch a few winks. Learning how to sleep standing up was probably the most useful thing school ever taught me.

Actually, now I regret not having paid more attention in school. You can't ever go back again, and I'll never know the pleasures of the classics, or higher mathematics, or the great lessons of history. Once in a while, I wonder what would have happened if I had taken the other path, the one that led to high school, and college, and a respectable career in business. Or maybe law, or medicine.

I could have been the world's most famous doctor.

Instead of the world's most famous patient.

I never did get the hang of being a student. Each morning, before I left, my mother would give me money for the bus ride home—not wanting me to take the long hike up the Peak in the evening. Well, I'd usually use the money to buy snacks, and then rely on the kindness of strangers to get a ride home. It's surprising how many strangers were willing to pick up a small, ragged-looking Chinese boy walking up the side of a mountain.

If I had no luck hitchhiking, I'd walk home, which would take hours. To save time, I'd usually take a shortcut the last couple of hundred feet, a scramble up the side of a cliff that would put me in our backyard. With any luck, I'd be able to sneak in the rear entrance and find my mom before my dad found me.

When I wasn't lucky, which was often enough, at the top of the climb the first thing I'd see were my father's work shoes. Looking up, I'd see the rest of my dad, his face rigid with rage. Without a word, he'd grab my arms and haul me up, marching me into the house, down the hall, and into the garbage room, not even letting me change out of my school clothes first.

Dad wasn't the only obstacle I'd have to get past in my daily trip back home. As I dragged myself up the cliff, sweaty and annoyed, I'd hear braying laughter—*Hyah hah hanh!* Like a pack of hyenas.

"Hey, guys, look—there're monkeys on this mountain!"

The neighborhood bullies who'd tormented my friend the ambassador's daughter were rich enough to have drivers take them up and down the mountain. So by the time I'd gotten back home, they'd already be there—waiting for me.

"What's the matter, boy? Lose your bus money?"

"Or are you too *poor* for the bus?"

"Hey, what do you expect? His parents are just servants, anyway."

I'd be tired, my shirttails hanging out, my face smudged, but a second later, I'd be making the biggest of the bullies eat a dirt sandwich.

Those fights weren't like in the movies.

There isn't anything pretty or graceful about a fight between two young kids. Everything is arms and legs, poked eyes and ripped clothing and sharp gravel stuck in awkward places. Even the winner ends up looking like an avalanche survivor. And I wasn't always the winner.

I remember one fight when this wealthy little brat I was pounding on grabbed me by the legs and pulled me off balance. I went down, and he went down on top of me. My body hit the hard ground. My head hit an even harder rock. Everything went dark.

The boy I was fighting with was the son of another ambassador—I don't remember what country—and as soon as he saw me, stiff and motionless on the ground, he ran to find his father. The other kids scattered.

When his dad came over, he turned white with horror. If I died, there'd surely be a scandal. This was an international incident in the making. (These days, maybe I would have sued them, but at the time, I couldn't do anything.)

Anyway, I woke up in my bed in the dark, a huge bump on my head, feeling nauseated. Little flashes of light, like tiny comets, seemed to shoot through the blackness. And my entire skull hurt. I was floating in a bath of pain.

The door opened and my father walked in. "Ah Pao," he said. "This is from your friend." I lifted my head with effort and saw a parcel in his arms—a large, fancy box of chocolates. I think they were French, even.

Dad brought it over and set it down next to the bed, and quietly left to go cook dinner.

Even though I was sick to my stomach, I was also hungry. Well, I was *always* hungry.

That box of chocolates, the entire box, didn't even last an hour. I crawled back into bed trying hard not to throw up—after all, they were *French chocolates*, and I didn't want to waste them. Getting hit in the head had turned into the best thing that had happened to me in a long time.

That didn't last long. When my father came back, smelling of scallions and sesame oil, he saw the crumpled tissue paper scattered around the bed and the sweet smear of chocolate around my mouth and exploded.

"You ate the whole box?" he shouted.

"Ooh . . ." I said, caramel rising in my throat.

Without another word, he pulled me out of bed and gave me a sound spanking. If I was well enough to eat four dozen milk chocolates—some with cherry liqueur centers—I was well enough to take my medicine.

If it wasn't one thing, it was another. I never did any homework. I'd tear my good school clothes in fights or in scrambles up my special shortcut. I'd throw my books and schoolbag off the Peak, giving no thought to the fact that my parents would only have to buy me new ones. Each time, I'd face the music—lectures, spankings, a night in the trash room—with a shrug and a smirk.

I ended up being told I'd have to repeat the first year of primary school, and even if I wasn't learning anything, my parents were: they were beginning to realize that their son was not the scholarly type.

My parents pulled me out of school and I went back to my old routine of following my mom around and getting under my dad's skin.

And that was the end of my academic career.

I guess I thought I was pretty smart, getting out of school that way. I'd watch the rich kids driving down the mountain to a fresh day of hell, laughing to myself as I looked forward to another warm afternoon on my own. The last laugh would be on me.

I imagine the conversation as having happened something like this. My mother and my father ran into one another in the corridor that dominated our world.

"Lee-lee, we have to talk about Ah Pao."

My mother, afraid of what was coming next, remained silent, but reluctantly nodded.

"That boy is out of control," my father said. "He has no direction, no self-respect."

"He's a good boy. . . ." she said in my defense, sounding tentative.

"He needs to learn how to be a man."

Then they talked about the future and about the painful subject of money. The post with the French ambassador had been a lifesaver, but it was not allowing them to save anything else. My father's cooking and my mother's housekeeping had impressed the ambassador's friends to no end. Other job offers had come. Some of them were too good to ignore. One of them was too good to pass up: a job as head cook for the American embassy . . . in Australia.

Not only would the job pay more money, it would also give us the chance to get Australian residency, maybe even a chance someday to move to the United States. Even back then, there was uncertainty about the mainland, and my father had learned from personal experience that in uncertainty lay danger.

But taking the job in Australia would mean leaving the family behind, at least for the time being. And while my mom was a strong woman, I was too big now to be put in a washbasin and left to splash around.

Finally, Dad, a guy's guy to the bone, went back to the traditional source of advice for men all over the world: his drinking buddies. They'd helped him decide to keep me, even lending my dad money to pay for my mom's operation. Now they suggested a way of getting rid of me—for my own good.

"It's a hard life, but a good one."

"He'll get some discipline."

"Maybe he'll even become a star."

And they all shared a hearty laugh. But the decision was made. My dad would take me to the place that would become my home for the next decade of my life:

Yu Jim-yuen's China Drama Academy.

PEKING OPERA BLUES

There was no warning at all.

    Not even that sense of impending doom I frequently got when my dad approached, punishment in mind, or the tickling sensation of danger I felt when about to do something risky . . . and fun.

It just happened.

One day, after our morning workout, my dad told me we were going out on a trip. I was just seven years old, and my father had never taken me on an outing before, so the prospect of spending the afternoon away with him was a Big Event—especially since, for a change, he didn't seem the slightest bit angry.

Shouting at the top of my lungs, I ran back to our bedroom and changed into my best outfit: a Western cowboy costume, complete with ten-gallon hat and plastic six-shooters, that had been my parents' birthday gift, with a little help from the ambassador and his family. Dressed to kill (or at least to rustle cattle), I waved excitedly to my mom as I walked with my father down to the bus stop, then took the twisting journey down to the base of Victoria Peak.

I'd never been down to the lower city before, though I'd seen it from above all of my life. It was dirtier and more crowded and louder than anything I'd ever seen in my life, and I loved it.

"Watch where you're going!"

"Very cheap . . . For you, I'll make it half price."

"Screw off—!"

"Move along, move along."

"Screw you!"

"Fine sweet buns, fresh this morning—"

"Hey!"

"—Half price!"

The Peak, with its clear air and open streets, suddenly seemed like a blank, unpainted canvas. This, on the other hand, was a picture of life in glorious color, stinking greens and foulmouthed browns and angry reds and sweet and satisfying blues and yellows. How could I go back?

"Sweet buns, Dad!" I tugged at his arm, pointing toward the shouting vendor. I knew my father would just snort and pull me away, telling me that money shouldn't be wasted on snacks. But it never hurt to try.

Well, *sometimes* it hurt.

Instead, my father turned, smiled benevolently, and pulled out some coins. Bowing his head, the vendor gave us a brown paper bag full of steamed buns, so hot and soft that the white fluffy dough stuck to my fingers when I reached in to poke at them. The street scene receded into the background as I grabbed a bun and pushed it into my mouth, gasping as the rush of cooked vapor burned my tongue. The red bean paste inside was thick and sugary, and utterly delicious. The two of us ate buns all the way to the harbor, all the way to the pier where the Star Ferry embarks for Kowloon.

For those of you who've never been there, the city of Hong Kong is stretched across a set of small islands, the biggest of which is also called Hong Kong. Hong Kong Island isn't much bigger than Manhattan. The smaller ones, Lantau and Lamma, are lovely, scenic places, full of fishing villages and little open-air markets.

And then there's Kowloon.

Kowloon isn't an island; it's the bottom tip of a peninsula that hangs down from the mainland, part of a land grant that the British squeezed out of China in 1860 after a series of border squabbles.

Hong Kong, a city that began as a haven for pirates and smugglers, has always been a place where opportunists have hopped back and forth across the line of law, where the devout and the diabolical have tipped their hats to one another when passing in the street. Nowhere in Hong Kong is this more apparent than in Kowloon: the heart of new Hong Kong, the turbocharged engine of the city's nightlife, its underworld, and its artistic community.

In Kowloon, it's said, everything's for sale, and everyone has his price. Or hers. In the hot streets of Tsim Sha Tsui, gamblers smoke thin black cigarettes and throw bundles of currency on rolls of felt; dance-hall vixens drape themselves on the shoulders of sugar daddies while scanning the clubs for fatter meal tickets to come; money changes hands everywhere, and lives are constantly shattered and remade.

Kowloon's alleys are always full of smells: fresh cut flowers, skewers of roasting meat, perfume, nervous perspiration. And sounds—squeals and laughter, the music of streetside crooners and itinerant tunesmiths, heated conversation, soft, secret whispers.

The Star Ferry is the gateway to this other world, bringing the honest and hardworking people of the Hong Kong side to their weekend haunts, businessmen to their mistresses, students to their bars and basement clubs. Then back again at dawn, to start the cycle over.

I'd never been to Kowloon, and I'd never been on the sea, not even the placid waters of Victoria Harbour. I stared in fascination at the people emerging from the ferry terminal, some satisfied, others frustrated, all exhausted. All of them turned their faces away upon noticing the plump little boy in the cowboy costume, and one even spat a rude word in my direction, until my father pushed me by the shoulders over to a wooden bench, which I clambered onto, swinging my legs back and forth. In one hand, I held the last sweet bean bun, still warm, and half forgotten.

"Where are we going, Dad?" I said, suddenly curious.

"Somewhere special," he grunted, and shoved his hands into his pockets. An old man sitting next to me looked longingly at my bun, and I quickly and greedily took a big bite, to show him it wasn't going anywhere.

A grizzled man in a blue shirt and cap began shouting and waving, and the crowd began to ooze from the terminal through the open doors to the dock, handing him their tickets as they passed. The Kowloon-bound ferry was not full, as it was still early morning, and there was room for me to scamper around, looking out through portholes and sticking my tongue out at those who dared to glare at me.

"Come here, Ah Pao," said my father sternly. I shuffled back to where he was seated, a sullen look on my face. He took my hand and led me to the front of the boat. After a short word with the sailor who moodily stood watch there, he brought me forward into the bow. I watched in awe at the approaching cityline, leaning my face into the salt spray of the water, and holding my cowboy hat tight against my head with one hand. I could have stood there forever, but unfortunately the ride across the bay is a short one, and minutes after we'd left the Hong Kong dock we were told to prepare to land.

I smiled at my father as we returned to our seat. He smiled back, a tight, sudden smile that disappeared as quickly as it came.

Even though it was still early, I'd already decided this was the best day of my entire life.

The hubbub of Hong Kong's lower city was astounding, but it couldn't compare to the scene that greeted me upon stepping off the ferry in Kowloon. I'd never before seen so many people; so much living, breathing, moving flesh. Hanging onto my father's hand for dear life, I was jostled nearly off of my feet. Everyone had a purpose, headed for work after a long night's sleep or for home after a long night's play. What, I wondered, was ours?

We pushed our way down to Nathan Road, the main thoroughfare of Tsim Sha Tsui, Kowloon's commercial center, and then down a maze of side streets. The buildings were a uniform gray from the exhaust of motorcars, broken only by the shabby splendor of signs advertising food, music, and other, more cryptic pleasures. My head spun with curiosity, but my father was determined to move on, and I was dragged along in his wake.

Finally, one last turn brought us into a street lined with tenements whose windows were dark and shuttered. I felt a pang of regret: we'd reached our destination, wherever it was, which meant my dad would go about his business, and then bring me home—our adventure at an end.

"Here we are, Pao-pao," he said, with an odd catch in his voice. The sign before us proclaimed the building we were about to enter as the CHINA DRAMA ACADEMY, a name that told me nothing. My father swung the knocker on the outer door, and we waited silently on the stoop. Soon the door swung open, revealing the bald head of a husky adolescent—a boy perhaps eleven years of age, on the heavy side, but thick with muscle.

"What is it?" he said, wiping beads of perspiration from his brow. He stared at my father with suspicion, until he noticed me standing on the lower stoop, my fist wrapped in the hem of Dad's jacket.

"Oh, another one," snorted the boy. "Funny-looking kid, mister."

"Bring us to Master Yu," my father said, his voice bristling.

The boy shrugged, then turned and walked inside, motioning us to follow.

A DAY AT THE OPERA

ehind the door was a small courtyard, clean but sparsely decorated. Then came another door, from which issued the muffled sound of voices: numbers being chanted in unison by a high-pitched chorus.

Behind that door was an amazing sight: a large, open room in which twenty or so boys and girls, dressed in identical white and black outfits, filled the hall with a wild blur of motion. Some performed martial arts forms in tight, coordinated routines; others practiced somersaults and other acrobatic maneuvers; still others engaged in mock combat with swords, spears, and sticks.

For a hyperactive young boy brought up on stories of swashbuckling swordsmen and the warrior-monks of the Shaolin Temple, this was paradise. My father nodded his head in approval as an older man in a blue robe and black practice pants approached.

"You must be Mr. Chan," the man said, shaking my father's hand and bowing with graceful precision. "I am Yu Jim-yuen, the master of this academy."

"Your fame precedes you, Master Yu," my father responded, returning the bow. "I have long wanted to meet you."

"And this is?" said Master Yu. "A Western cowboy?"

"This is my son, Chan Kong-sang," Dad said, pushing me forward. Master Yu leaned down, putting his hands on his knees, and pushed up the brim of my hat to look at my face.

"Hello, Kong-sang," he said. "You seem like a healthy boy." And then to my father: "Is he fit? Any bad habits?"

"He's never been ill, and he's had no major injuries," my father said. "As for bad habits, I suppose that's why we're here."

Master Yu nodded silently.

I was paying very little attention to the discussion, just half listening while staring at the whirling bodies before me. Finally, the temptation was too much. "Dad!" I said, tugging on his jacket. "Can I go play too?"

My father looked at me with annoyance. "Can't you be still for just one moment?"

Master Yu gazed at me warmly, waving his arms in the direction of the others. "Go play, young man. I will bring your father to drink tea."

Taking my father's arm, he assured him I'd be all right, and patted my head as I ran past them toward a set of boys dueling with spears.

I spent the rest of the day with the other children—practicing kicks, swinging weapons, and trying to copy their elaborate poses and stances. Everyone was very kind to me, teaching me small things, and laughing without malice when I made mistakes. The older girls were particularly sweet, remarking on how cute I was in my little cowboy costume. I liked everyone on sight.

Almost everyone.

There was the teenager who'd met us at the door—the boy named Yuen Lung, whom everyone addressed as "Big Brother" (when they spoke to him at all). He moved with authority throughout the room, finding minute faults and dishing out verbal abuse to those stupid enough to make the same mistake twice.

Then, while showing me how to do an aerial backflip—a move that led me to clap my hands and shout with glee—one of the boys crashed into a pair of girls who were playing an elaborate clapping game nearby. The girls weren't hurt, but Yuen Lung's face still went red with rage. As the boy trembled, Yuen Lung raised his hand above his head, then looked in my direction and slowly lowered it to his side. His eyes wet with relief, the boy apologized repeatedly to the girls and to Big Brother, who grunted at him to be more careful in the future.

Yuen Lung stepped toward me, scowling. "Listen, cowboy," he said, his voice low and dangerous. "You may think this is all fun and games. But this is what we *eat, drink, and dream.* This is our *lives.*" Reaching back, he executed a perfect backflip, landing neatly on the balls of his feet.

"You just remember what I said. The next time we meet, you're gonna wish those little toy guns were real." He pointed his two index fingers at me, as if to go *bang bang,* and then turned and stalked away.

I wasn't stupid.

Yuen Lung, whatever his position here at the academy, was a force to be reckoned with. And somehow, though all I'd done was watch, I'd made an enemy.

A very bad enemy indeed.

I ate dinner with the students, sitting at the head of the table right next to the master, and talking breathlessly about all the things I'd tried and learned that day. The other children had taken to calling me "Western boy," because of my outfit, and some of the older kids passed around my hat, trying it on and laughing. After dinner, the students were dismissed to do chores, while I drank tea and ate cookies with Master Yu.

My prediction that this would be the best day of my entire life had come true. I'd never had so much fun—playing all day, eating as much as

I wanted, roughhousing with children my age. Not a hand had been raised to spank me, and the darkness and smell of the rubbish room seemed a million miles away from the open, well-lit practice hall. When my father finally came to pick me up and bring me home, I almost told him I didn't want to leave. As Dad and Master Yu exchanged farewells and some other pleasantries, I jumped around the empty hall, kicking at imaginary enemies.

Outside, in the academy courtyard, my father patted me on the head with unaccustomed affection.

"So, Ah Pao, did you enjoy yourself today?" he asked.

"Yes!" I shouted, the word echoing in the empty court. "I want to come back tomorrow. Can I, Dad?"

My father nodded silently to himself as we walked back through the growing evening crowds of Tsim Sha Tsui.

The next day, it was as if I'd never visited the school; never spent the day on our big adventure, or met the master and all of his friendly students. The day was wet and rainy, and the beautiful Peak view obscured by fog. Sulking and staring at the gray, I sat inside the laundry room as my mother ironed and hummed.

"Mom, why won't Dad take me back to the academy?" I asked, kicking a small metal tub.

My mother stopped her humming and set the iron on its holder.

"Mom?"

She turned to look at me. "Did you really have so much fun there, Pao-pao?"

I nodded, and then ran over to her and hugged her waist. "It was the best time," I said, "but not as good as being with you, Mom."

She hugged me back, and sighed.

"I'm sure your father will take you back again soon, Pao-pao." She disentangled herself from me and handed me a small pile of freshly ironed napkins. "Now help your mother fold. And be careful not to drop them, or I'll just have to put them back in the wash."

Mom was right. A week later, my dad took me to the academy again. And then again, a few days after that. And again. Each time I left, I found myself unwilling to leave. Each time, my father asked me, "So, did you enjoy yourself?" And each time I asked him when I could come back next.

Finally, one morning, I was shaken awake from a deep and heavy sleep. The light streaming in from the hallway meant that the sun was already over the horizon, and I realized with horror that I'd slept through dawn. Visions of garbage danced in my head, and my foggy brain tried to shape an excuse.

"I'm sorry, Dad . . . !"

Then I realized that the figure standing next to my bed wasn't tall, or angry. Or male.

"Mom?"

My mother sat down on the bunk next to me, smoothing out the cover with one hand, and tousling my hair with the other. "Did you sleep well, Pao-pao?"

"Where's Dad?"

"Your father is cooking breakfast. He . . ." She paused, folding her hands in her lap. "He thought you could use some extra rest."

Hearing this was like watching the sun go up in the west, or seeing cows and pigs soaring through the sky. It was . . . *unnatural.*

"Is Dad hurt?"

My mother blinked. "Your father is fine. I told you, he's in the kitchen."

"Did the ambassador get fired?"

"The ambassador is in the sitting room. Everything is absolutely fine, Pao-pao. Really." But her cheeks were wet, and I didn't believe her. I knew that something was wrong. And if it wasn't my father, or the ambassador . . .

I sat up and hugged my mother tight, my heart pounding. I was suddenly convinced she was sick, even dying. And here I was sleeping, when I could have been spending every moment with her. Taking care of her. Doing anything for her. Making her proud.

And then—

And then I saw the suitcase, sitting next to the bed. It was a small canvas bag that I recognized as my mother's. But I knew it wasn't packed for her. Because on top of the bag was a small ten-gallon cowboy hat.

I was going somewhere. And there was only one place I could possibly go: back to the academy. And this time, I wouldn't be going to play.

I'd be going to *stay.*

On the entire trip over, my mother, holding my cowboy hat in her lap, was silent. My father spent the time explaining to me that he had to go on a trip and might be away for a long time. To make sure my mother would not be too tired, I'd have to stay with people who could properly take care of a growing boy.

I was hardly listening. I was so excited I couldn't sit still: bouncing in my seat on the bus, dancing in place on line at the terminal, racing around the seats of the Star Ferry.

No more punishments!

No more chores, no more morning workouts!

No more school, forever!

THE BEGINNING
OF A BOY

Master Yu was waiting for us when we arrived. As soon as we walked through the door, he greeted my mother and father, put his arm around my shoulder, and ushered us into the hall. "Welcome, Kong-sang. We have enjoyed your visits, and we hope you will enjoy your stay here."

"Can I really stay, Dad?" I asked, still not believing my fortune.

"As long as you want, Ah Pao," he said.

On the long table where we all gathered during mealtimes was a scroll of paper. It was covered with writing that I couldn't read, so I ignored it. But my father immediately picked it up, holding it close to his face. My mother threaded her arm through his and looked over his shoulder.

"I believe it is all in order, Mr. and Mrs. Chan," said the master, drawing a chair for my father to sit. "All very standard. After you sign, I will have complete responsibility for the boy as long as he is here. I will feed, clothe, and shelter him at my own expense. I will provide for his care and protection, and I will give him the finest training in the world in an art that surpasses all others: the art of Chinese opera."

My father sat down. I wandered away to examine the rack of weapons.

"Perhaps he will even become a star," he added, smiling, as I drew a long tasseled sword, swinging it around my head.

"This agreement says that you have the right to keep any money he earns," my father said.

"We support the academy with performances," the master answered. "The students receive the benefit of our teaching, and in turn their skills allow our teaching to continue. This is traditional, and only proper."

My father picked up the pen as I tripped while running back to the table, dropping the sword with a clatter. The master's cheek twitched.

"It also says that you may discipline the boy . . ." my mother said, her voice shaking. "That you may 'discipline the boy, even to death.' "

"Yes, discipline is the soul of our art," said Master Yu. "It is said that 'discipline is at the root of manhood,' is it not so?"

Dad made a strangled sound at the back of his throat. Some of the other students had come into the room, and I was showing off my sword stances to one of the younger girls, making her laugh.

"Ah Pao, listen," he said, interrupting my demonstration.

"What, Dad?"

"How long do you want to stay here?" he asked. "You can stay five years, seven years. . . ."

"Forever!" I shouted.

My mother squeezed my father's arm so hard that her hands went white.

"The longest term is ten years," said the master, taking the pen and writing the number on the scroll. My father signed at the bottom. Then the master took his personal seal and made his mark over my father's name.

The deal was done. I didn't realize it at the time, but from that day on, and for the next decade of my life, I would be the property of the China Drama Academy and Master Yu Jim-yuen.

MY FIRST GOOD-BYE

S hortly after the document was signed, my parents called me away from the small group of other students with whom I'd been playing.

"Come with us to say good-bye, Pao-pao," my mother said. I didn't understand what she meant; couldn't we say good-bye right there? But the tone of her voice stopped me from complaining. I walked with her and my father out of the academy, waving good-bye to the students and my new master, and telling them I'd be back soon.

We returned to the house on the Peak, where my father busied himself with small matters while my mother disappeared into our bedroom.

I took the opportunity to say good-bye to the ambassador's wife and told her I'd be back to visit. She smiled and patted me on the head, and wished me good fortune, promising to give her children a hug for me.

Soon I heard my parents calling, and we left the house again for the lower city. My father was carrying a large bag full of clothes and personal belongings, and holding tightly on to my mother's shoulders.

"How long will you be away, Dad?" I asked him, as we took the winding bus ride down the Peak. He stared out the window of the bus, his face its usual solemn mask.

"Ah Pao, it is possible that I will not see you for a very long time," he said.

I was too young to really understand the passing of time; did he mean weeks? Months? Years?

My mother took my hands in hers. "Your father is going to work in Australia, across the ocean, so that someday we will be able to give you all the things you like."

That I understood. It seemed like a pretty fair exchange—my father going away in exchange for nice things.

We took the bus all the way down to the bay, and walked down the harbor past the ferry dock. I gawked at the sleek and enormous ships, the tall stacks of crated goods bound for a hundred countries, and the giant cranes being used to load and unload cargo.

"Ahoy, Chan!" shouted a gruff, strangely accented voice. My father waved at the approaching figure, a big, fat foreigner with a thick blond mustache.

"This is the man who is arranging for your father's travel," my mother whispered.

"Dad is riding one of those big boats?"

"Your father is going to take that boat over there."

The boat, rocking gently in the stiff breeze, was smaller than the giant cargo ships, but larger by far than the Star Ferry, the only boat I'd ever been on. I was suddenly overcome by envy.

"I want to go on a boat too!" I complained.

"Perhaps someday when you're older, Ah Pao," my mother said. "Now be good! You must draw a picture of your father in your head so you'll remember him until the next time you see him."

I squeezed my eyes shut and thought about my dad, tall, strong, and tough; shaking a knife at me in mock anger as I stole a scrap of food from his kitchen; slumped in exhaustion at the end of the day, his apron stained and his hands raw from scrubbing away the smells of a day's meals; silhouetted against the pink morning sky, his arms moving fluidly through a series of kung fu exercises. I thought about that day we first visited the academy, and the steaming-hot sweet buns we'd shared together.

When I opened my eyes, I was surprised to find that they were damp.

My father had finished his conversation with the foreigner and was giving my mother a rough embrace as he whispered into her ear. She nodded into his shoulder and whispered back. Then, releasing her, he came to me and squatted down on his knees.

"Kong-sang," he said, calling me by my given name, "you are a big boy now, big enough to take care of yourself. I know you will make us proud."

I nodded dumbly.

"I said that the next time I see you, you will have grown into a young man. I won't have the chance to give you a father's advice again, so I want you to promise me three things," he said. "First, you must never join a gang. Second, you must never take drugs. And third, you must never become a gambler."

Since I didn't know what any of these things were, the promise was an easy one to make.

"No matter what you become—no matter if life treats you well or poorly—you must keep your word on these three things," he said. "Then I will know that you are following the right path, and giving your family and your ancestors no reason to be ashamed."

And with that, he gave me one last quick hug and stood. The big foreigner called his name again, and my father turned and walked up the ship's gangplank. Two sailors cast off the boat's ropes as the gangplank was raised. The boat drifted away from the dock, toward my father's fresh start in a strange land. We waved at the ship as the water began to churn white behind it.

"Remember what I said, Ah Pao!" my father shouted, just before he slipped out of earshot. And then it was time for me and my mother to make our trip across the water, back to the academy and my own new life.

It was late by the time we arrived, and the lengthening shadows gave a creepy feel to the deserted backstreets. Through some trick of the light, the building that housed the academy suddenly looked forbidding, even frightening, more like a prison than a home.

I swallowed hard, telling myself that I was headed for fun and freedom, and that I really wouldn't miss my mom and dad *that* much.

The master welcomed us back and reassured my mother that all would be fine. She promised that she would visit me regularly and fussed over me, using the corner of her sleeve to wipe at a smear of dirt on my face. The other students giggled at the sight, bringing a hot flash of embarrassment to my cheeks.

"Don't worry about me, Mom!" I said impatiently. Finally, she let me go and was escorted to the door by Master.

She turned to look back at me, but I was already deep in conversation with the other kids.

I don't even remember the last thing she said to me before she left.

But as soon as Master returned from showing my mother out, it was as if something in the air had changed. The students quietly went back to their chores or private practice. The master took my hand and showed me around the academy, pointing out things I might have overlooked: the ancestral shrine, the kitchen, the large, outdoor shower area. We sat at the long table, and Master smoked cigarettes while asking me about my family and my old home on the Peak.

We talked for hours, until late in the night. Then Master, watching a yawn split my face, told me it was time to go to bed. He called out to the other students, who filed into the main hall carrying neatly folded blankets. Then, wishing me a good night, he patted me on the head and left the hall for his quarters elsewhere in the academy.

Getting up from the table, I watched as the kids, talking quietly amongst themselves, arranged their blankets around the edge of the practice room.

"We sleep on the ground?" I asked one of the boys I'd played with earlier in the day. He ignored me and flopped down on his stomach, pulling his old blanket around his body. I felt a thump of cloth against my back and turned around. It was my nemesis, Yuen Lung. He'd thrown a roll of fabric at me—a blanket as moth-eaten and worn as the others—and his face wore its customary scowl.

"Quit screwing around, new boy," he said. "Lights out in ten minutes, unless your ass is too dainty for the floor."

I lay down in a corner and spread the blanket out, bending my arm into a pillow for my head. Soon even Yuen Lung had readied himself for sleep, and the oldest of the students, a quiet young man named Yuen Ting, whose official title was "Biggest Brother," shouted, "Lights out!"

And the room went dark.

As hard as the wooden floor was, it beat the concrete of the rubbish room. I rolled onto my side and quickly fell asleep.

MY BROTHER, MY ENEMY

The next day, I opened my eyes to find that all of the other students had already awakened. Master and Biggest Brother stood at the front of the room, leading the boys and girls through a grueling set of warm-up exercises. Kicking aside my blanket, I stretched and wandered through the ranks of sweating students, whistling to myself and laughing at their expressions of exertion. Some of them shot dirty glances at me, but I didn't care; no one was telling me what to do, no one was yelling at me, and for the first time in my life, I was completely free to do whatever I wanted.

Breakfast had already been served, eaten, and cleared, so I wandered into the kitchen looking for something to munch on. It was empty, and all the food locked away in the pantry. That was too bad—I was dying of hunger.

Then I remembered that my mother had, on the walk over from the ferry terminal, bought me a bag of snacks and sweets. It was still sitting in the entry room, along with my small suitcase.

Rummaging quickly through the bag, I found some oranges and a handful of plum candy. I ran back to the practice hall and sat down in one corner, watching the students work while peeling an orange and stuffing segments into my mouth.

After an hour, the master called a short break, and the students broke into smaller groups to talk and catch their wind.

I had finished one of the oranges and set the other aside for later, and was sucking intently on a piece of the dried plum candy when a harsh voice broke my concentration.

"Hey, new boy, where'd you get that food?" It was Yuen Lung, his white shirt damp with perspiration and his face mean. Behind him was his constant sidekick, an equally tough older kid named Yuen Tai.

"My mom gave it to me," I said, my mouth full of plum.

"What'd you say?" said Yuen Lung, his eyes narrowing.

Yuen Tai stepped forward and stuck his hand in my face. "When you speak to an older student, you'd better call him Big Brother," he said. "*Say* it."

"My mom gave it to me, *Big Brother*," I repeated, gritting my teeth.

"Apologize to your Big Brother," Yuen Tai said.

"I'm sorry, Big Brother."

Yuen Lung's face lit up with a victorious smile. "Yuen Tai, what's the penalty for disrespecting your elders?"

Yuen Tai thought for a second. "Penalty is no more snacks, Yuen Lung."

Yuen Lung snatched away my second orange, while Yuen Tai pried open my hand to remove the remaining pieces of plum candy.

"Hey!" I said.

"You got a problem, new boy?" said Yuen Tai, his mouth full of candy.

The space between their two heads was suddenly filled by Master's stern and questioning face. "Is there a problem here?" he said, an edge in his voice.

"No, Master!" said Yuen Lung, shoving the orange into his pocket, where it bulged like a horrible tumor. Yuen Tai swallowed with difficulty, his eyes crossing, then rattled out a weak "No, Master" of his own.

I grinned to myself. You see, every piece of dried plum candy has a hard pit at its center. In his haste to get rid of the evidence, Yuen Tai had just swallowed four or five pits at once.

"Kong-sang?" said Master, his eyebrow quirked.

"Everything's fine, Master!" I chirped, folding my hands in my lap. Yuen Lung glared at me and mouthed a curse in my direction.

The two older boys went back to their practice, and I sat humming my mom's favorite song to myself, watching them happily until the call for lunch.

A HARD DISH TO SWALLOW

eals back on the Peak were simple: rice, some pickled vegetables, and a fried fish, or maybe some stewed meat. The food at the academy was about the same, only there was more of it—enough for a mob of young students and whatever teachers were working with Master that day. It wasn't as tasty as my Dad's food—he was probably one of the best cooks in Hong Kong at the time—but it was filling, and in my seat at Master's side, I got my pick of all the dishes before they were passed down the line. The seating order at mealtimes was always set according to seniority, that is, the boys and girls who'd been at the academy longest were at the end next to Master, the master's wife, and the teachers, with the youngest, smallest kids at the far end of the long table. I guess it was a matter of respect, but it meant that the little kids got almost nothing: by the time the food had been through the eager hands of a couple dozen young boys and girls, there were just scraps and sauce remaining.

Even though I was the newest student, I was treated like an honored guest; I ate even before Biggest Brother and the older boys like Yuen Lung and Yuen Tai. I assumed it was because Master had taken a liking to me, and why would I question the special honor? It meant more food for me.

After a few days of being treated like a prince, though, it dawned on me that the kids who used to be my friends were talking to me less and less. They didn't terrorize me the way Yuen Lung and Yuen Tai did, but they avoided me. In the morning, while all the other students were roused for their early workouts, I slept late. As they did painful stretching exercises and practiced kung fu and acrobatics until the edge of collapse, I played alone, imagining myself to be the great General Kwan Kung or the Monkey King or some other brave and ancient hero. Sometimes, I even joined in on the exercises, practicing handstands and stretches with the other kids—but only for a few minutes, before bursting out in laughter or becoming distracted.

Between my own snacking and the demands of Yuen Lung and the older boys, the bag of treats my mom had left for me disappeared quickly. I tried saving a few special things, like chocolates and cans of orange juice, as bribes to win the friendship of some of the smaller kids, but they curtly refused my gifts. Then they'd steal the treats out of my bag when I wasn't looking.

It didn't take me long to get the hint. Even though we slept together at night and sat together at mealtimes, my special status meant I was doomed to be alone. I guess I could have complained and asked to be treated the same way everyone else was, but that would have meant lots more work and lots less food, and frankly, I was happy just to be left to do as I pleased.

Little did I know how short this blissful period would last.

On the sixth day of my stay at the academy, I found myself in the kitchen examining the very last of my mom's treats—a bag of walnuts, still in their shells. I'd never had a walnut before, so I wasn't sure what they tasted like, and besides, getting the nutmeat out of the shell seemed as if it would be a real pain. This was why, out of all the nice things I'd had, the nuts remained—unstolen and uneaten.

Well, I'd missed breakfast again, and the needs of my stomach had finally overcome my basic laziness. I had no choice but to try to crack the nuts.

Master never left out anything that we could use to hurt ourselves (or one another); there wasn't a mallet or a knife or even a heavy pot in sight. Squeezing the nuts in my hands just left painful bruises on my palms, and I didn't want to risk my teeth on the rock-hard shells.

Out of frustration, I began hammering the nuts against the counter, until the bag ripped and the walnuts sprayed out and around the kitchen. Yelping, I began gathering up my last treasured snacks, only to realize that one of the nuts had rolled completely under the refrigerator and was now resting in the dusty crevice between the refrigerator and the wall.

I was a plump kid, but still small enough to reach behind the fridge, and I stuck one arm into the depths of the crack, stretching my hand as far as it would go into the dark, dirty space. After a few minutes of scrabbling, I felt a tightness around my waist. Someone had grabbed hold of my pants, and was pulling me back out into the light.

It was the master, and with him were Biggest Brother, Yuen Lung, and Yuen Tai, the last wearing an evil grin.

"See, Master?" said Yuen Tai. "I told you, he was playing around with the electric socket."

"No, I wasn't, I was just trying to reach my nuts!" I shouted.

Yuen Lung sniggered. "You shoulda kept your hands in your pockets, new boy."

Biggest Brother Yuen Ting watched the situation with a weary face, as if he'd seen this scene time and again. Master pushed me out of the kitchen and into the practice hall. I was terrified. I'd never seen kindly old Master looking the way he looked just then. His face was angry and cold, and I had a sudden flashback to my father's expression, just before he was about to punish me. Hard.

"Kong-sang, you are fond of snacks, are you?" Master asked. I nodded, then shook my head, not knowing which reaction would save me. Probably neither.

"I think it is time for some *jiajiang mien*," he said, gesturing to Yuen Ting.

Jiajiang mien is a spicy noodle dish, made with meat and served cold. The look on Yuen Ting's face as he passed suggested that he was not headed for the kitchen.

The other kids gathered in a wide circle around us, grinning as if they were aware of what was about to come next. Finally, Yuen Ting returned with a thin, supple rattan cane.

Master pushed me down to the ground and told me to lie flat on my belly. I closed my eyes and gritted my teeth. I felt my pants being roughly drawn down to my knees, as my belly and thighs collapsed on the polished wooden floor. Then a whistle and a crack, a sound that I registered in my brain just a flash before the pain raged from my buttocks up my spine.

I screamed.

The taut, bone-hard smack of the cane was more agonizing than my father's bare palm or even his wide leather belt—the worst I'd ever felt against my skin before. And each rip of the cane, each jolt of torment was followed by another, in steady, staccato rhythm, until my throat was hoarse and my buttocks almost numb.

Six strokes, delivered with all of my master's force.

Six raised and bleeding welts across my tender skin.

I began to cry, shouting for my mother and father to take me away. I wanted to go home—I wanted to go anywhere rather than stay in this place, which had gone from paradise to hell in one hot instant.

"Be quiet," thundered my master, perspiring from the workout of my beating. "Unless you want a second helping!"

I shut up. I saw out of the corners of my tear-filled eyes that Yuen Lung and Yuen Tai were laughing at me, mimicking the faces I'd made during my beating. I saw that Yuen Ting and the older girls had flat, expressionless faces, betraying neither glee nor sympathy. I saw smiles on most of the younger girls, but they were smiles that simply stated a fact: *We were there too. Now it's your turn. Welcome to the club.*

Master gestured a dismissal with his cane and walked out, allowing the rest of the kids to cut short their practice and escape to private things. Yuen Lung and Yuen Tai walked away together, discussing the best ways of cracking and eating my walnuts. Yuen Ting moved toward me as if to help me up, but then turned and silently left the room.

I lay alone on my belly for what seemed like hours.

Everything was over. I knew it now. The special treatment, the easy living, the freedom. The kindliness of the master had been a sham, and my loneliness was now complete. Even with my uncertain sense of time, I knew that I'd told my parents I wanted to stay here for a very long time, longer even than I'd even been alive.

But I didn't want to live anymore. Not if my days were going to be like this. Not with the fear of more pain, and even worse, this feeling of hollow aloneness in my heart.

Then I felt a hand on my back. One of the boys had returned, the one who'd many weeks ago shown me how to do a backflip and nearly bought himself a dish of *jiajiang mien* from Big Brother. He had a towel in his hand, dripping with cold water from the shower.

"It'll be easier if you put this on your butt," he said. "I *know*."

I managed a smile, and took the towel from his hand.

That night, I slept on my stomach, but I was no longer exiled in my own corner of the hall. The space between me and the other students was now filled with young bodies, marking me, at last, as part of the family.

The next morning, Master brought me in the front of the hall and officially introduced me to the other students.

"This is our newest student," Master said in a solemn voice. "He came to us as Chan Kong-sang, but now that he is part of our family, he must take a new name. Please welcome your brother, Yuen Lo."

The students came up as a group and surrounded me, some squeezing my shoulders, some patting me on the head and back, others taking my hands in theirs. They welcomed me. I was one of them.

And you know what?

When other new boys and girls came to the academy, glorying in their temporary specialness, I put a blank expression on my face, silently waiting for their first helping of spicy noodles. And when their day came, I grinned along with the rest.

Welcome to the club.

LEARNING
THE HARD WAY

Master Yu's personality seemed to have changed overnight. Before my initiation, he'd been my protector and my only friend, and we'd spent evenings drinking tea, eating cookies, and talking about my favorite subject: me. Afterward, I seemed to have turned invisible—I became just another problem, one whose solution was rigorous training, ear-shattering lectures, and the occasional beating.

I quickly learned to watch the other children carefully. Whenever they stood up, I stood up. If they sat down, I sat down. Whatever they said, I said, and whatever they did, I did. Not only did it make it less likely that Master would single me out for punishment, but it also helped to create a bond between us, me and my brothers and sisters. I made friends with many of the younger children, and even my worst enemies, Yuen Lung and Yuen Tai, stopped making me the constant target of their torments.

Things got better. Life was hard, but simple. I slowly grew used to the routine.

This was a typical day at the academy: At 5 A.M., Biggest Brother would wake us up—first with a shout, then a brisk shake of our shoulders if we didn't get up immediately. Then we'd fold and put away our blankets, and march outside to the stairway that ran up the side of the building, climbing to the roof. Making as little noise as possible to avoid disturbing the neighbors—who were all asleep—we'd run several laps around the rooftop, just to wake up.

After the run, we'd march back down to breakfast, the sweat still wet on our bodies. There was no time to stop for a bathroom break, because it was Master's theory that any need to use the toilet in the morning meant we hadn't been training hard enough. As he put it, all of the body's toxins should have been sweated out during the morning run . . . and so, the first time I made the mistake of asking to relieve myself, I was given ten extra laps to run. (Better to actually let loose in your pants—but heaven help you if Master found out.)

Breakfast itself was barely a meal, just a bowl of congee, which is a thin rice porridge. The idea was to fool the stomach into thinking it was full, but not to eat so much as to get in the way of practice, which lasted five or six straight hours with barely a chance to breathe: warm-up exercises, then footwork training, martial arts, and acrobatics, all performed in tight ranks in the academy hall, boys and girls together.

The most difficult instruction we had was in the aerial maneuvers that give Chinese opera its visual splendor: flips and somersaults, all learned and practiced without a net or harness. After watching the others do their backflips with ease and grace, I was eager to learn. Master, gratified at my enthusiasm, told Yuen Ting and Yuen Lung to teach me how.

Without warning, they grabbed me by the waist and flipped me over. All of a sudden, the room was whirling around and the floor was much too close to my head.

"The next time, your hands should be farther back," said Biggest Brother.

"You have to be stiffer in your neck and head," said Yuen Lung. And then they told me to try it on my own. That was the sum total of the teaching I had in this spectacular—and dangerous—maneuver.

After a series of tries on my own, under Master's watchful eye, I managed to land awkwardly on my feet, but not before some terrible and frightening falls. I was lucky, escaping with just bruises, head bumps, and the occasional twisted limb. Some kids weren't so fortunate. When a really bad injury happened, there was no doctor around to make sure that no permanent damage had occurred.

In fact, being hurt or sick was seen by Master as an attempt to get out of practice; in his eyes, if you could move, you could fly, so anything short of a crippling handicap was just a lame excuse—so to speak.

One day, one of the younger boys went to a corner and sat down during somersault practice, immediately drawing the attention of Master. Earlier that morning, he'd complained quietly to Biggest Brother about feeling dizzy. Biggest Brother had told him to take it easy, saying that he'd explain it all to Master.

But Master didn't want to hear any excuses. "Why are you sitting, boy?" he asked, his voice icy with contempt.

"Master, he told me he's not feeling well," said Yuen Ting, stepping between them. Master looked at Biggest Brother with surprise. Yuen Ting had never stood up to Master before. Then again, no one ever did.

Brushing Yuen Ting aside with a gesture, Master pulled the woozy student to his feet. "Do a dozen somersaults, and you'll feel better," he said.

A suggestion from Master was the same as a command, so the boy rubbed his head and attempted to flip himself through the air.

He managed two shaky somersaults, and then fell sideways, smashing his head against the corner of a table and landing on the floor, unconscious. All of us looked on in horror. Blood was oozing from a wound on his temple. He wasn't moving.

You'd think an injury like that might reasonably be expected to result in a quick call to the hospital. Instead, Master leaned down and checked the boy's pulse.

"Yuen Ting, bring my bag," he said, his voice firm.

Biggest Brother, his face pale, went into the hall to Master's room and returned with the small leather bag that was Master's all-purpose first-aid kit. From the bag came a handful of tobacco leaves, which Master pressed against the wound to stop the bleeding.

"Move him aside," he told Yuen Lung and Yuen Tai. The elder brothers quietly lifted the boy's prone body and set it near the wall, out of the way. Soon practice continued as usual.

Four hours later, the boy awoke, wincing at the pain in his skull.

"Master, he's awake," said Yuen Ting.

Master walked over to the boy and helped him to his feet. "You've been sleeping while the others were working hard," he said bluntly. "When lunch is over, you can show them what a well-rested person can do."

The boy nodded groggily and joined the rest of us for our noon meal, leaning on Biggest Brother's arm. I saw the expression on Yuen Ting's face. It was a grim look.

A look of hatred.

Lunch at the school was a more substantial meal than breakfast, consisting of soup, made from tofu and green vegetables, and then rice with fish. After eating, we were finally allowed to go to the bathroom. Then we moved on to the most essential—and painful—part of our training: flexibility exercises. Opera performers have to be able to do a complete leg split, horizontally on the ground, and vertically, holding one leg above the head. And so we practiced splits against the walls, against the floor, against everything. As soon as the exercises began, the room would be full of howling, because frankly, it hurt like hell.

The worst thing was that, if you couldn't split all the way, Master would send Biggest Brother over to push your body down until it felt like your joints were going to come apart. And if he couldn't do it alone, he would call other older students over, and they would hold your legs apart while he pushed you. It didn't matter how much or how hard you cried; eventually, you'd go down into a split.

It was a nightmare. This might sound terrible, but eventually you actually felt happy to see other kids crying, because it meant that someone else was being tortured, not you. Oh god, it was awful. And it would go on for hours, until walking, or sitting, or even standing was agony.

After we practiced splits, we would move on to handstands. An opera performer has to be as comfortable on his hands as on his feet, so the brief handstands that any adolescent child can manage were not enough for us. Master decreed that his students would have to be able to stay on their hands for at least half an hour at a time. After fifteen minutes, our arms would grow limp, our blood would rush to our heads, and our stomachs would begin to turn flip-flops. But we couldn't show any weakness at all. A limb that moved would receive a whack from the master's rattan cane, and woe to the student who allowed himself to fall over!

Still, Master could pay attention to only a single student at one time, and when he was occupied with adjusting his or her form—a blow at a time—one of the senior brothers would quietly turn his body to lean his legs against the wall. The rest of us would soon do the same . . . until Master turned around, of course, at which point he'd see an innocent row of dutiful young students, upside down and ramrod straight.

After practice, we'd be divided into groups—although, after doing splits for hours, we felt divided already. Some of us would be sent to do chores, like washing dishes, cleaning the hall, or tending to the ancestral shrine. The rest would go to singing or weapons instruction.

Then came dinner, which was just a larger version of lunch. We would always try to draw out dinner as long as possible, because what came afterward made all of the physical torment of the day look like a walk on the beach.

Once dishes had been cleared away, we'd file silently down the corridor into a large room with desks and chairs. At the front of the room was a chalkboard, usually covered with obscene words, stray graffiti, and unflattering drawings of the older brothers (or sometimes, if one of us was feeling really brave, of Master).

The first time I'd walked into the room, I'd felt betrayed. It was a classroom! I didn't mind training until I cried from exhaustion, or even being beaten when I deserved it—but *lessons*! That was more than I could stand.

Luckily, I wasn't alone in feeling that way. None of us at the academy were scholarly types, and putting fifty twitchy children in a single room with an unsuspecting tutor was a recipe for disaster. The lessons were mostly tedious stuff, like reading, writing, classics of literature, and Chinese history. The tutors were mostly old, retired schoolteachers or young, naive college graduates. Master was nowhere to be found, having left the academy to gamble or visit old friends. There is an old line about mice and cats, and what one does when the other's away—

And so, as soon as our poor tutor began his boring lecture in his dry teacher's voice, we'd do our best to drive him crazy. Books would be thrown on the floor. Faces would be made behind the teacher's back. The class would break into fits of laughter. Balls of crumpled paper would fly. Some of the younger boys would begin to wrestle, until the older ones had to dive in to break it up. The girls would talk loudly with each other, ignoring the chalkboard and whatever dull lesson had been scrawled on it (replacing our much more amusing pictures). If the tutor raised his voice, we'd just drown him out.

Of course, if Master came back early, he'd find us sitting quietly and politely in our seats, because the classroom had a window that overlooked the courtyard, and all of us had sharp eyes and ears.

It wasn't easy to find teachers who could stand this kind of treatment, considering the stingy pay Master gave them. If you walked into a classroom full of disobedient students, didn't make much money, and they treated you like dirt, you'd quit too, wouldn't you? During my time at the academy, we burned out eleven different teachers, none of whom lasted more than a year. About the only thing we ended up learning was how to say "Good afternoon, Teacher!" Because that was how far class would get before things dissolved into chaos.

Sometimes, when we were on trips outside of the academy, we'd run into schoolboys and schoolgirls in their uniforms, good little boys and girls who laughed at us ragged-looking kids—all the boys with shaved heads and all the girls with short hair and no pretty dresses. And even though they teased us, we didn't envy them at all. We never even thought about what it would be like to be in a regular school, sitting in class and doing lessons all day. Those kids had nothing in common with us. Our life was all about surviving. Each of us knew that, if the master hadn't hit us that day, then that day was a very good one, and we were very lucky. And that was all that mattered.

If Master was in a good mood, after our lessons was another training session, though less rigorous and more fun than the morning and afternoon sessions. This is when we'd learn interesting things, like kung fu, face painting, and the proper way to use props and opera costumes. All in all, between our morning and afternoon and evening sessions, we'd practice more than twelve hours a day. Our art was a complex one, involving many different skills. And we were expected to be experts in all of them before we set a single foot on the stage.

Training would go on until bedtime, which was midnight. All of us students from the six-year-old newcomers to the Biggest Brothers and Sisters, had the same schedule: 5 A.M. to 12 A.M., five hours of sleep, and then another day of training—day after day, seven days a week. Free time was rare, and a cause for celebration; opportunities to go out, away from the academy, were even rarer. So, until we grew old and skilled enough to perform, the gray walls of the China Drama Academy were nearly all the world we knew.

About the only contact I had with the outside world was through my mother, who came to visit me at the academy every single week. At first I loved these visits, because being with Mom was what I missed most when I first came to the academy. Lying on the floor and staring at the cracked, white ceiling of the practice hall, I would remember all the nights she'd sung me to sleep, and all of the nice things she'd cooked for me. And I would remember how it felt to lie in my lower bunk, knowing that my mom was in the bed above me—that she and Dad would protect me from any kind of harm.

But strangely enough, after I had been at the academy for several months, my attitude began to change. I'd learned how to survive at the school, and my carefree days on the Peak seemed farther and farther away. When my mom visited, she brought me candy and snacks, and I eagerly took them and shared them with my friends. But her visits were also times when she showered all the affection on me that she saved up during the days she was away. I was a growing boy, and her hugs and kisses humiliated me in front of the other students. Some of them had visitors, too; Big Brother Yuen Lung's grandfather came and saw him once in a while, but their meetings were short and simple: his grandfather would ask him if he was healthy, and he'd say yes, and they'd talk for a while about the family and about the academy, and then his grandfather would leave, after thanking Master for his diligent training.

Not my mom. In addition to cuddling me like I was still a little child, she'd always baby me in another way that I couldn't stand. Along with her sacks of treats, she'd also bring large plastic bags full of boiling water. Asking Master for a large metal basin, she'd pour the bags in and give me a hot bath, scrubbing me down and washing my hair. I was the cleanest kid at school, but also the most embarrassed. After her visits, my clothes damp and my head wrapped in a towel, I'd be cornered by my older brothers, each with something stupid to say.

"Hey, mama's boy, how was your bath?" Yuen Lung would sneer. Not to be outdone, Yuen Tai would jump in: "She remember to change your diapers?" And then another brother: "Maybe she wipes your ass after you crap, too, huh?"

And I'd just have to grit my teeth and walk away, because if there was one unbreakable rule at the academy—well, there were a lot of them, but this was the one we were taught *never* to forget—it was that you couldn't hit an older brother. Even if he hit you first. Because if he hit you, you probably deserved it, but if you hit him, that was as terrible an act as hitting Master himself. And hitting Master was unthinkable. It was like hitting God.

One day, when my mother arrived, bathwater in hand, I grabbed the bags from her and dropped them on the floor. "No bath today, Mom!" I said. "I don't need one. And I *especially* don't need you to wash me. I'm big enough to wash myself."

My mother looked at me with silent shock. I was always a rude little boy, and I'd always talked back to my father, with the expected results, but

I'd never said anything impolite to her. She didn't say anything; she just nodded, quietly, and sat down to open the sack of snacks instead. As she was untying the knots that kept the plastic bag closed, I noticed that her hands were raw and red, chafed almost to the point of bleeding. And then I remembered the long walk from the house on the Peak to the bus stop, and the even longer ride down the mountain road, and the lines at the ferry dock, and the crowded, twisting streets from Kowloon terminal to the school.

Mom had boiled the water for the bath in the ambassador's kitchen, and carried it for over an hour to bring it here to me. She did this once a week, every week. And I was telling her that all of her caring and exertion and pain was for nothing.

I pulled her hands away from the bag and hugged her tight. "I'm sorry, Mom," I said. "I . . . I guess I didn't realize how dirty I was. I really could use a bath."

And I smiled up at her. She really was the greatest mother in the world. And she smiled back.

When she left that day, the older boys were ready to taunt me as usual.

"How was the bath today, honey?" said Yuen Lung, pulling his round face into a mockery of maternal affection.

I looked at him and wrinkled my nose.

"It was great, Big Brother," I said, scrubbing the towel across my wet scalp. "You know, maybe you guys should consider taking one yourselves. 'Cause *something* really stinks around here."

And as their jaws dropped to the floor, I walked away humming one of my mother's songs, towel in one hand, her bag of treats in the other.

THE NEW ORDER

That was one of the few times in my life at the academy that I ever got the best of Yuen Lung and his cronies. For a few days, I rode a wave of admiration from the younger kids, because I'd actually dared to mouth off to Big Brother Lung—and survived.

I didn't know at the time just how big a mistake I'd made.

You see, the system we lived under at the school was simple and straightforward. Master believed in just three things: discipline, hard work, and order. Discipline came quickly and painfully, measured in strokes of the cane. Hard work was the rule of the day—a few minutes of stolen rest often meant an hour of extra practice for the unlucky students caught slacking off. And order: order was imposed by a strict line of command that placed Master at the top (never to be disobeyed or disrespected); then his wife, Madame; followed by the instructors who taught singing, boxing, and weapons skills; and then us students at the bottom.

Even among the students there was an order. Each of us was ranked by seniority, with the Biggest Brother (the one who had been at the school the longest) at the top, and the Littlest (the newest student) at the very bottom of the entire heap.

The order was *never* to be challenged. If a brother who was more senior told you to do something, you did it. If you told a more junior brother to do something, he did it. And if Master gave a command, *everybody* jumped. The order was enforced by the fact that anyone who disobeyed it was beaten soundly, either by the master's cane or, among students, by the simpler (but not any less painful!) means of a hard-swung fist.

Seniority didn't just mean power; it also paid off in a more direct fashion, in the only currency that meant anything at the academy: food. As I mentioned before, seating at mealtimes was arranged from top rank to bottom, and all dishes were passed down the table, from Master to Madame to the instructors to Biggest Brother, and finally, after dozens of other hands had touched it, to Littlest Brother, by which time almost nothing would be left.

After I became an "official" member of the school, I found myself moved from my privileged place right next to Master, all the way down to the very end of the table. As Littlest Brother I'd stare in horror as dishes of meat or fish worked their way along the row, getting smaller and smaller, until just a bone or some scraps of fat were handed to me, very cold and not at all filling.

These were grim times indeed for a boy who loved to eat. Especially with Yuen Lung up near the head of the table, just a few seats away from Master. As second-biggest brother, he was in a good position to grab a healthy portion of each dish long before it came down to us young kids, and he was as big a glutton as they came. You could tell just by looking at him. Even though we worked like dogs all day, he was a pretty heavy boy, and he kept his chunky build up by eating twice as much as any other student—even Biggest Brother Yuen Ting.

Out of all the older students, I liked Yuen Ting the best. Well, you couldn't really *like* any of the big brothers, since their main goal in life was to abuse us exactly the way *they'd* been abused by their big brothers before them. But Yuen Lung and Yuen Tai took an unholy pleasure in administering beatings and applying punishments. Yuen Ting seemed to do it only out of a sense of duty. When he was given Master's cane and told to supervise us while Master was away, he showed us no mercy—but he never used his position to take advantage of us, the way Yuen Lung did.

And we didn't know it yet, but things were about to get worse. A lot worse.

It was just a few weeks after the incident of the somersault injury, the one that should have sent our brother to the hospital. (He was lucky; he didn't have a concussion, just a bad bruise, but for days afterward he turned white and shaky as soon as Master announced it was time for acrobatics practice.) Ever since that day, Yuen Ting had been in a strange mood. He'd never been one to joke or pal around with the other older kids, and we younger kids weren't worth noticing, much less befriending. But Yuen Ting had gone from being quiet and withdrawn to being a complete loner—shaking off any attempts at kindness, even telling me to go away when I offered him first pick out of my mom's magic bag of goodies.

"What a weirdo," snarled Yuen Lung, just out of Yuen Ting's earshot. "You try to talk to the guy, and he acts like you don't even exist. Rude is what I call it."

Yuen Tai, his mouth full of almond cookie (which he grabbed away from me without even asking, as usual), nodded in agreement, ignoring the crumbs falling from his chin.

"Stupid, too, getting in Master's way during training," continued Yuen Lung. "You fall, you get back up again. You're hurt, you just gotta try twice as hard to do it *right*. Those're the rules. Biggest Brother's job is to *enforce* the rules. If he don't like it, he should get the hell outta here. This ain't no place for weaklings or sweethearts. . . . Hey, gimme those cookies, dammit."

Their conversation dissolved into an argument about how much of my loot each of them deserved. But, sitting and carefully guarding the rest of my snacks, I saw Yuen Ting quietly slip out of the room. He'd heard the conversation.

If I were him, I thought to myself, I'd knock Big Brother's block off. *Hey, Yuen Lung, what's the penalty for disrespecting your elders? Boom!*

But it looked like Yuen Ting was just going to eat it. Ignore the whole thing.

Maybe he *was* too soft to be the biggest brother.

"We want more cookies, twerp," said Yuen Lung. Evidently they'd settled their argument by deciding that I should just cough up more stuff to even out their piles. I groaned and reached back into the bag.

When midnight rolled around, everything seemed normal. I was tired and achy, having made a mistake on a difficult acrobatic maneuver that not only led to a cracked jaw but a demonstration of Master's cane technique on my butt. I pushed one of the younger boys who was crowding my space, and he rolled over, grumbling.

"Lights out," shouted Yuen Ting, turning off the overhead electric bulb. I'd feel better in the morning, after a good five hours' rest. I hoped.

But I couldn't sleep. I don't know whether it was because of the pain in my jaw or the bruises on my rear, but regardless of how I turned, I couldn't get comfortable.

And then I heard noise—not just the rumbling of Yuen Lung's thunderous snores, or the usual shifting of bodies. I opened my eyes and got used to the darkness. Someone was moving around the room.

It was Yuen Ting. Carrying a bag over one shoulder.

"Hey!" I whispered, sitting upright.

He turned and saw my silhouette in the dim, reflected light of the moon. We stood staring at one another for a few moments, each waiting for the other to speak.

Then Yuen Ting put one finger over his mouth, asking me to remain silent. And with that, he carefully opened the door into the hallway and left.

I was stunned.

Biggest Brother was running away.

I lay awake most of the rest of the night, wondering what new surprises morning would bring. The queasy feeling in my stomach suggested an answer: *nothing good.*

My chin was trembling, but I refused to cry as the rod came down again on my palm. *Whack!*

"I will ask you again, Yuen Lo: do you know what happened to Yuen Ting?" The master's face was ugly with fury, twisted up in a way we'd never seen before.

I shook my head, afraid to open my mouth for fear of screaming.
Whack!

"Still no words?" Master said, disgusted. "Get back in line."

As Littlest Brother, I had the misfortune of being first in line for Master's interrogation session regarding Yuen Ting's disappearance. I knew exactly what had happened to Biggest Brother, but I wasn't about to talk—and besides, I didn't know where he'd gone, so what was the point? Ratting on Yuen Ting wouldn't have helped anyone. We all knew in our hearts that he wasn't coming back.

I took my position against the wall and rubbed my abused hand, watching as the next-littlest brother took his licks. The entire session lasted most of the morning, giving us a welcome break from practice (except for the fact that we'd all gotten beaten, of course).

Finally, the master reached Yuen Lung, who looked almost as angry as Master did. You could tell what he was thinking by looking at his face: *Damn that Yuen Ting! It was all his fault, ditching and getting us in trouble. The coward.*

"Hold out your hand, Yuen Lung," said Master. Big Brother extended his palm, his face blank.

Master raised the rod, and then put it gently into Yuen Lung's hand. "There was once a student here named Yuen Ting, who was your Big Brother. He failed to live up to his responsibilities, and so he is no longer a part of our school, and no longer a part of our family. We will not speak his name again within these walls."

Master turned to the rest of us as Yuen Lung looked down in shock at the rod in his hand.

"This is your new Biggest Brother, Yuen Lung," said Master. "I hope he will not disappoint us." And with that, he told Yuen Lung to lead us through practice for the rest of the day. There would be no breakfast, as the time for breakfast had long since passed. And, because we had wasted so much training time in the fruitless questioning session, there would be no lunch as well.

All of us younger kids wanted to scream. This was hell. And as long as Yuen Lung was in charge, there would be hell to pay.

"Okay!" shouted Yuen Lung, slapping the rod against his beefy thigh. "You heard Master! Stretching exercises . . . begin!"

THE GREAT DICTATOR

That was the first day of the worst days of my life. Yuen Lung used his authority in ways big and little, and all of them were designed to make things as rotten as possible for the rest of us.

As I mentioned, Yuen Ting hadn't been an easy taskmaster, but he was usually fair. Yuen Lung, on the other hand, was a tyrant. He was one of the school's best fighters, a sure hand with weapons, and surprisingly graceful in acrobatics. In short, he demanded perfection from himself and no less from the rest of us—even those of us who'd been at the school less than a year.

He found flaws with everything. If it wasn't in our execution, it was in our style. If it wasn't in our style, it was in our energy. If it wasn't in our energy, it was in our attitude. Sometimes he just didn't like the way we looked. And every mistake we made was greeted with a taste of Biggest Brother's iron fist . . . unless he had Master's stick, in which case he heartlessly beat us with the full force of his thick arms.

Outside of practice, Yuen Lung was even worse. None of us little kids were safe when Yuen Lung was near; he would demand his tribute as Biggest Brother, and thrashed any junior who dared to deny him. If he liked your clothes, he'd just say, "Nice T-shirt," and the next day he'd be wearing your T-shirt. If he saw you eating something, he'd say, "How's that taste?" and he'd walk off with it in his hands. There was no help for it. Everybody gave him whatever he wanted. Because if you didn't, you knew that the next day he'd be leading practice again, rod in hand, and that he would remember.

Yuen Lung was a bully and a thug, and I have to say that through most of our time together at the academy, I hated him. But looking back, I've realized that Yuen Lung wasn't crueler than the rest of us by nature. This was the way he was expected to behave according to the system under which we lived and learned. It was like being in military school: seniors had rights, juniors didn't. Living through abuse at the hands of big brothers bound us younger kids together. And surviving our master's punishments helped turn all of us students into a team.

As harsh as it may have seemed, it was a system that had worked for decades, even centuries, producing the very finest acrobats, singers, and fighters that the world has ever seen.

The kind of training we received just doesn't exist anymore. There are still opera schools, but they don't allow you to punish students physically; that kind of discipline is now against the law. And to tell the truth, younger generations of performers aren't as good as we were, and the ones who went before us. The schools are still good, and the students still learn, but many of them are just doing it because their parents want them to, or because they want someday to star in movies. *We* did the training even if we didn't want to. Because there was always the stick. Unless we wanted to follow Yuen Ting—and what a humiliation that was! what a waste of years of study!—we didn't have a choice. There was never a choice.

So I guess you could say the system worked. But even the constant threat of beatings couldn't completely crush the will to rebel. Especially not in a boy like me—someone driven by a love for independence and a hatred of authority. Even back on the Peak, I'd always hated it when older kids pushed younger ones around; it turned my stomach. And I couldn't stand it at the academy either.

It wasn't a problem when I was the littlest brother, because when I was at the bottom of the food chain, I could take care of myself. But time passed, we grew older, and our family eventually had to expand.

And though I didn't know it at the time, the arrival of our newest brother was a momentous occasion; one that would eventually change the path of my life—and the life of my nemesis, Biggest Brother Yuen Lung.

FRESH BLOOD

One day, as we went through the rigors of our afternoon workout, the creaking of the hallway door announced a visitor.

Yuen Lung, who had been assigned to train us while Master was away, slapped the floor with his cane and snapped at us to ignore the distraction. But the arrival turned out to be Master himself, who nodded benevolently at the sight of his sweating students and called for tea to be brought to his guests.

The visitors were a young couple with a small boy, who was clearly somewhat frightened by his new surroundings. "And this is our grand practice hall," said Master importantly, "and these are our students!"

The couple sat down quietly, and the boy, who looked even younger than I was when I'd arrived at the school, quickly ran to his mother's lap.

We knew what was happening, and it brought hastily hidden smiles to our faces. Fresh meat was on its way. This was good news, especially for me; there was now a new low man on the totem pole.

But we didn't have much time to think about the consequences, because Biggest Brother was eager to show off his teaching skills in front of Master and his visitors. He barked a set of new orders, and we jumped back into action.

After tea was served, the master brought out the papers and his seal, and the teaching contract was signed. Master congratulated the parents, assuring them that their son would receive the very best care and training.

We'd all heard it before.

The couple hugged their son, bid him good-bye, and left the academy.

Putting his arm around the boy, Master introduced him to his new brothers and sisters. "Everyone welcome the latest addition to our family!" he said, flashing his nicotine-stained teeth in a wide smile.

We dutifully bowed to the new boy, and Master took the cane from Biggest Brother, who went to his customary position at the head of the practice formation.

The new boy spent much of the morning session in tears, demanding to know when his parents would return. I saw Yuen Lung and Yuen Tai exchange knowing glances, guessing that this small and fussy boy was likely to be easy prey.

It was all too much. Feeling sorry for the newcomer, I went over to the new boy and introduced myself.

"Don't worry, kid," I said. "We all went through this. You'll be all right."

Pleased at the attention, the boy dried his eyes, took my hand, and followed me to the lunch area. The master motioned for the boy to sit next to him at the head of the table, which brought a smile to his face. You could tell the new boy was thinking that things were looking up.

After lunch, we went back to training, beginning our somersault and acrobatics practice. Sitting by himself against the wall, the new kid watched our antics with awe. I looked in his direction and gestured with a shake of my head: *C'mon over and give it a try.*

The new kid shyly covered his face, but the temptation proved to be too much: after a few more minutes, he timidly walked over and tugged on my shirt. As Yuen Lung executed a complex set of tumbles, I explained to him how a somersault worked.

"Let me try," he said. "I can do it!"

"It's tricky. . . ." I said, remembering my clumsy first attempt. I unconsciously rubbed my head, remembering the bump I'd received upon smashing into the hard practice room floor.

The new kid took a deep breath, ran forward a few quick steps, and performed an almost perfect somersault. The master looked on with pride and surprise; the other kids watched with envy. And Yuen Lung stood there stunned. As far as he was concerned, the new kid should have spent the day crying and sobbing for his parents—not showing off in front of his elders. The attention he was getting didn't make them happy at all. For the rest of the day, the kid proved again and again that he was a natural, a born acrobat.

"All of you should learn from this boy's example!" shouted the master, in a display of fine humor. "One day under my training, and already he could almost perform on the stage!" And with that, he canceled the rest of practice and led the boy away, calling for tea and cookies.

Yuen Lung grabbed onto Yuen Tai's arm as we filed happily out of the practice room, heading for the courtyard to spend the rest of the afternoon at play.

"That kid showed us up," Biggest Brother growled.

Yuen Tai nodded. "Can't have that."

They walked off together, plotting their revenge.

And I decided that it wasn't going to happen.

That evening, Master sang the new boy's praise with the arrival of each dish at dinner.

"Look at him, such a small boy," he said to Madame. "But I can tell already he's going to be a big star!"

The new boy laughed and took another piece of fish. Yuen Lung and Yuen Tai exchanged conspiratorial glares. They'd wipe that smile off his face.

When dinner was over, Master and Madame left the academy for the evening, visiting friends elsewhere in Kowloon. We were between tutors at the time, so there was no evening lesson, and Master didn't even tell Yuen Lung to put us through a nighttime drill.

Yuen Lung had other plans. He and Yuen Tai followed as the new kid brought his small bag into the storage room where we kept our personal belongings. Like a trained hit team, the pair drifted in behind him, taking care not to draw attention from the other kids. Yuen Tai secured the doorway. Yuen Lung quietly grabbed the boy from behind.

The new kid yelped and was silenced by Biggest Brother's broad hand.

"Shaddup, baby," he said. "It's only us, your big brothers. Nothing to be scared about, unless you disrespect us, right, Yuen Tai?"

"Right, Big Brother," snickered Yuen Tai. "Can't have that."

The new boy began to cry, and Biggest Brother gave him a rough shake. "It's all about respect, baby," he said. "You want to show us you respect us, you got to pay the 'tribute.' "

"Wh-what tribute?" said the kid, muffled by Yuen Lung's hand.

"Well, whaddya have?" said Yuen Lung.

"Nothing . . ." said the new boy.

"Everybody's got *something*," said Yuen Tai.

Despite their attempts to be unobtrusive, I'd seen the big brothers slip away, and I knew what they intended to do. As a result, just as Yuen Lung raised his fist to administer the traditional penalty for disrespecting elders, I found myself ducking under the arm that Yuen Tai had stretched out to block the hallway door and stepping into the tiny storage room.

"What do you want, Big Nose?" said Yuen Lung. "This doesn't concern you." Biggest Brother had lately taken to calling me Big Nose. I had to admit that the insult fit, not just because I do have a rather big nose, but also because I had a tendency to stick it where it didn't necessarily belong.

"Leave him alone, Big Brothers," I said. "Master's gonna be back soon, and you know that the new kid's off limits." *Until he's gotten his first serving of* jiajiang mien, I added to myself silently.

As much as he hated it, Yuen Lung knew I was right. He left the new boy and pushed him away with a sullen glower. Yuen Tai wasn't about to give up that easily.

"Who the hell do you think you are, *Little* Brother?" he shouted. "You think this is any of your business? Get out of here, before I kick your ass."

"Don't you mean 'kiss my ass'?" I retorted.

Without warning, Yuen Tai swung out and slapped me across the face, bringing a sudden sting of tears into my eyes. I couldn't hit him back.

That was against the rules. But nothing was going to stop me from using my mouth.

"Screw you, asshole," I said.

Not believing his ears, Yuen Tai slapped me again. "What did you say?"

"Screw you!" Another slap.

"Screw you!" Yet another slap. Now blood was trickling down my chin.

He kept on hitting me. I kept on repeating it. My face began to swell with bruises. And I never lifted a hand against Second Biggest Brother.

"Screw you. Screw you. Screw you."

Finally, Yuen Lung, who'd decided not to get involved in the situation, heard Master coming in the hallway. He ran out, with the new kid on his heels, shouting Master's name. By the time Master arrived at the storage room, blood was pouring from my mouth and nose, my jaw was swollen like a chipmunk's, and I was mumbling "Screw you" dazedly beneath my breath.

"Stop!" shouted Master, breaking Yuen Tai from his trance. If Master hadn't intervened, he might have gone on hitting me forever. And I'd have just kept on cursing him out, until my lower face collapsed off my skull.

"What the hell is going on here?" Master said angrily, looking at my damaged face.

I looked at Yuen Tai, who seemed suddenly frightened. "We were having a disagreement," I said.

Master looked at Yuen Tai, who was unmarked, and then at me, my clothes spotted with blood and my face a bruised disaster. "A disagreement," he repeated. He turned around and walked out the door. "If I see that any of you have a swollen nose or bruised face again, I will kill you," he said, as he headed back toward his quarters. "How can anyone perform with a damaged face?"

Yuen Lung and Yuen Tai left the room, knowing that they'd escaped a sound beating by the skin of their teeth. And the new kid looked up at me with starry-eyed admiration.

"You know, I was lying," he said.

"Lying?" I mumbled.

"When I said I don't have nothing," he said, digging into his bag. He pulled out a handful of candy bars and gave me one of them. I tore one of them open, and then winced as I tried to open my jaw wide enough to bite it.

"I think I'll just save this for later," I said.

"That's okay," said the new boy. "There's more where that came from. I just—I just wanted to thank you, Big Brother."

That was the first time anyone had ever called me that. I smiled and led the new kid out of the room, feeling good despite the aching of my face.

The funny thing is, the whole time I never even knew the kid's name. And I didn't find out, either, until a few weeks later, when he received his traditional first dish of *jiajiang mien*. And then it didn't matter, because he had a fresh name to replace it.

From that point on, we knew him as Yuen Biao, our newest Littlest Brother.

I feel like everything I've said so far has made life at the academy sound like torture and Master Yu sound like a monster. Well, it certainly felt like that was true at the time. There wasn't a day I was there when I didn't think of taking Yuen Ting's way out: escape.

But I had nowhere to run. My mother couldn't have taken care of me on her own, and anyway, if I'd gone back to the mansion on the Peak, I wouldn't have had anything to do. I was too young to work, and I wasn't suited for school. The academy was the only place where my abilities could be developed into something worthwhile, the only place where I had a future.

And look where I am now. I'm the son of a cook and a housekeeper. I grew up fighting for food and eating scraps. I never had toys, or nice clothes, or even a room I could call my own. Yet today I'm one of the most famous people in Asia, maybe even the world, with more money than my parents ever dreamed of, traveling everywhere, meeting famous people, *making movies.*

Every time I think about the ten years I spent in Master's hell, I just think about how Master lived the last decade of his life in an Alzheimer's haze, barely able to recognize his own family. He spent his last two years in a coma, hooked up to machines that kept his heart pumping and his lungs breathing. When he died at the age of ninety-five, it could only have been a blessing.

You might think I was happy he was gone, that I was relieved finally to be free of the man responsible for a decade of suffering. You couldn't be more wrong. As far as I'm concerned, Charles Chan was the father of Chan Kong-sang, but Yu Jim-yuen was the father of Jackie Chan.

CENTER STAGE

While we were at the academy, we didn't think much about the outside world. Between lessons and chores and practice—and our few stolen moments of personal freedom—all of our time and energy was expended, and it was rare that we thought about more than when our next square meal would be coming, or how to avoid the watchful eye (and cane) of Master.

But there was a reason why we were training so hard, and it wasn't just to impress our instructors. Even if we didn't think about it often, we knew in our hearts that we would eventually be players in one of the world's most demanding and exciting theatrical genres, one that combines gymnastics, stage combat, mime, acting, and singing. And to fully prepare us for our time before the floodlights, we eventually needed to see the goal of our efforts for ourselves—an opera performance in all of its glory.

As usual, we had no warning when the fateful day arrived. One day Master just told us during our morning training session that there would be no afternoon practice; instead, we would be taking a trip.

A trip! This was big news. We buzzed excitedly in small groups, wondering where we might be going.

"I hope we're going somewhere fun," said Yuen Biao, always the optimist.

Yuen Tai barked out a laugh. "Yeah, right, we're going to an amusement park. We'll go on all of the rides and eat until we're sick, and then Master will give us foot massages and tuck us into bed . . . *moron!*"

"Leave him alone, Big Brother," I said. "You mean *you* don't know where we're going?"

Second Biggest Brother let out a snort. "Just because I'm smarter than the rest of you dummies doesn't mean I know everything."

Then Yuen Lung came over and told us to get ready to leave. "Chat time is over, babies; we're getting out of here. And no wandering around, 'cause if you get lost, we ain't gonna waste time looking for you."

We quickly got in line, oldest first, youngest last, and set off after Master on the short walk to the bus stop. It was great to be out in the big, real world again, and despite the admonitions of Biggest Brother to keep

quiet and stay in file, we couldn't help talking and laughing among ourselves from sheer joy at leaving the stifling confines of the academy.

We made it to the stop just in time to catch the big double-decker bus
as it pulled up to the curb. The driver stared at us in shock as we boarded
his vehicle, dozens of small boys and girls in identical outfits. Master
didn't even yell at us when we raced up the narrow spiral staircase that
led to the bus's upper deck.

"Yaaaaaaahooooo!" shouted Yuen Kwai, a rowdy boy about my age
who was one of my best friends, when he wasn't being a giant pain in the
ass. He'd pulled open one of the bus's sliding windows and jammed his
body and arms through it, waving at passing pedestrians and hawking
loogies at the ones who gave him dirty looks. Even the girls, usually models of innocence compared to us boys, were pushing and tugging at one
another, competing for seats near the windows.

"Where do you think Master's taking us?" whispered Yuen Biao, seated
quietly next to me. I'd elbowed us over to a window seat and was enjoying
the feel of the wind whipping across my face.

I shrugged. "Why don't you go ask him?"

Yuen Biao looked at me with horror. "No!"

I laughed and kept watching the view from the window. In the far distance, I saw the Peak. It had been many months since I'd left the ambassador's mansion. I wondered how the ambassador's wife was, and her
little daughter. And then it struck me that I could barely remember their
faces or the sound of their voices. My life had truly changed forever. I'd
never be able to go back to those days. I couldn't ever go home again, because the academy was my home now, and my opera brothers and sisters,
more than anyone else, were my family.

Suddenly, the bus stopped, and a familiar bellow from below signaled
that it was time for us to disembark. And as we stepped off the bus, all of
us found ourselves staring around us in disbelief.

Yuen Tai's mouth hung slack and open, as if he'd been struck dumb.

I thumped Yuen Kwai on the shoulder, and he grabbed me by the
waist and lifted me over his head, grinning like a madman.

Yuen Biao screamed at the top of his lungs, and then quirked an eye at
Big Brother Yuen Tai. "Does this mean we get foot massages too?" he
said, the picture of innocence.

Before us was a wild vision of crowds and noise and smells and motion,
of hawkers selling food and toys and, in the distance, the sound of laughter as games of skill and chance were played.

It was the Lai Yuen Amusement Park.

We'd died and gone to heaven.

"Stop gawking," grunted Biggest Brother, herding us younger boys after Master.

Obviously, the purpose of our visit wasn't to play the games or to ride the rides.

Crestfallen, we followed Master to a large and garishly decorated building surrounded by a crowd of men and women clutching slips of paper in their hands. It was a theater, and from its dark interior came the sounds of instruments being tested and tuned.

The man at the gate waved us quickly past the line of ticket holders, greeting Master with familiarity.

"So these are your students, Master Yu!" said the ticket seller. "They look quite promising."

Master shrugged and offered him a smile. "We shall see, " he said. "In time."

Inside, the room was dark and somewhat smoky. Yuen Biao stumbled over someone's foot and bumped into Yuen Kwai's back. Yuen Kwai pushed him roughly away. One of the younger girls let out a whimper at finding herself trapped behind a small group of strange men. Biggest Sister retrieved her and brought her back to our group.

"Don't make noise, and don't move about," warned Master, signaling with his hand that any misbehavior would be met with severe punishment upon returning home.

As the rest of the room bustled with people settling onto their wooden benches, a clacking noise drew attention to the front of the hall, where a set of tall yellow curtains hid a nondescript wooden stage. The curtains parted, and music began: wailing, keening strings that followed the clipped rhythm of drums and other percussion instruments. Suddenly, with a whirl of fabric and flashing metal, the stage was filled with performers, acting out the opening of a grand battle.

We'd practiced these moves for months, we'd learned to paint our faces and modulate our voices, but this was the first time we'd seen these skills in action.

It's all worth it, I thought, looking at the rapt faces of the other audience members. I realized that, more than anything else, I wanted that to be *me* up there on that stage; I wanted to hear a crowd clapping and cheering and screaming for *me.*

The performance left all of us, even the big brothers and sisters, in a state of excitement. We'd seen our future, so close, so loud, so *real* for the very first time. It was like what Biggest Brother had told me, my first day at the academy. This was what we ate, drank, and dreamed. This was what we lived for. And it had finally arrived.

As we buzzed and whispered outside the theater, Master told us that he had business with the theater owner, and that we should take the same bus back to the academy on our own.

As usual, he placed Biggest Brother in charge. Cuffing Yuen Kwai on the back of the head—Yuen Kwai had strayed a bit too close to a stand selling fried sweet bread—he waved at us importantly and marched us toward the amusement park exit.

As we filed out of the theater, taking one last longing look at the attractions around us, Yuen Biao tugged anxiously on my sleeve.

"Big Brother, I can't find my return ticket," he whispered, his voice urgent.

I stared at him in horror. "Just get on the bus," I whispered back. "Don't worry."

But I was worrying. What could we do? None of us had any money . . . except maybe for Biggest Brother, who was already gesturing impatiently at us stragglers to board the return bus.

"What the hell is taking you guys so long?" he muttered as we hustled inside, Yuen Biao first, me close behind. Irritated at the delay, the driver pulled away from the curb as we were dropping our tickets into the box. His eyes watering, Yuen Biao cleared his throat and stammered, "Big Brother, I can't find my ticket. Can—can you give me money for the fare?"

Yuen Lung scowled, and then let a slow smile spread across his face. "So, baby, you got 'nothing' again, huh?" he said, raising his eyebrows. "Screw you. I'm not giving you any of my money. You can walk back."

Then Biggest Brother spat out something unprintable about Yuen Biao's mother.

I'd had enough.

"Take that back about Yuen Biao's mother," I said.

Surprised, Yuen Lung pushed me away. "What the hell is it to you?"

"If you said it to him, you said it to me," I answered. "Him and me, we're brothers."

The driver pulled over to the curb. "Listen, you little brats, you don't have a fare, get off the damn bus."

I handed Yuen Biao my return ticket and flipped Yuen Lung the finger, then jumped off the bus. Biggest Brother growled and leaped after me, murder in his eyes.

The bus had stopped near a movie theater, and even in the early evening, there were crowds. I weaved and whirled among the moviegoers, keeping an arm's length away from my furious big brother. I may not have been the best acrobat or the best fighter or the best singer in the school, but I was one of the quickest, having long since lost my baby fat. Heavy, husky Yuen Lung had no chance of catching me in a flat-out footrace. Once I was past the movie mob, I gunned my engine and ran like the wind.

And all the way back to the academy, I taunted Big Brother, leaping and dancing out of reach.

When we got back, of course, there was nowhere left to run and nowhere to hide. Big Brother was puffing like a locomotive, but he wasn't too tired to give me the thrashing of my life.

But the bruises were worth it: without raising a fist, I'd gotten my revenge on the tyrant, Yuen Lung.

MY SECOND GOOD-BYE

The next few years were relatively peaceful ones at the academy. We kept learning and continued to hone our skills. Once in a while, we went back to the theater at Lai Yuen Amusement Park, watching in rapture as veteran players made age-old stories come to life. We grew stronger and taller, advancing rapidly toward adolescence. Other kids joined our school, both boys and girls, and after they took their licks, we accepted them as one of us.

Master continued to rule us with an iron hand and an iron cane. Yuen Lung and Yuen Tai rode us with no more mercy than before, but we were old enough to take it, and once in a while, even dish it out.

My mother continued to visit me regularly, and even if I still blushed bright red when she pulled out her sponge and bags of hot water, I never once complained.

But I hadn't seen my father for years. I received regular news about him from Mom, and occasionally she even brought his voice, captured on audio cassettes. The tapes came in brown packages signed in his neat but simple hand; each tape was an hour-long lecture about ways I could improve myself, mistakes I should avoid, and threats regarding what would happen to me if I screwed up. There was always a handful of wrinkled bills tucked in with the tape, and after a while, I started throwing away the tapes and just keeping the money.

It's not that I didn't think about my father; I did wonder what it was like down under in Australia, in a land of foreigners, full of strange creatures, like koala bears and kangaroos. We talked about it sometimes, late at night.

"D'you think you'll ever get to go visit your dad, Big Nose?" That was Yuen Kwai. He'd picked up the annoying habit of using Biggest Brother's stupid nickname for me. The first time he said it, I'd slugged him, which only resulted in his refusing ever to call me anything else. I'd gotten used to it.

"Dunno," I said, rolling over onto my side.

"They have all sorts of animals down there," he said. "Natives, too, I heard. They run around half-naked."

That was an intriguing thought.

"Girls, too?" I asked.

"That's what I heard," he said.

I wasn't quite old enough to be interested in girls, but I was curious. The whole prospect—weird beasts, naked natives, and all—made me wish I could talk to my dad, even see him.

"You guys shut your mouths or I'm going to come over there and shut 'em with my fist," grumped Yuen Lung from the far side of the room.

We shut up.

A few weeks later, Master asked me to stay and speak with him after dinner. I quickly ran through the day to see if there was anything he might have reason to smack me for, and nothing came to mind. Nothing he possibly could have found out about, anyway. I walked to the head of the table fairly confident that I wasn't about to get a whipping. Still, I wondered to myself what it was he wanted to tell me. It was hardly ever a good thing to be noticed by Master.

"Yuen Lo, I have received a message from your mother," he said, puffing on his after-dinner cigarette. "She will be visiting the academy tomorrow, so be ready."

That was hardly news. It wasn't her usual visiting day, but it wasn't something Master would particularly care about, either. There had to be something else.

"Master?" I said, with a questioning look.

"Oh, yes," he said, rousing himself from distraction. "She will be bringing your father."

My *father*!

Was he back for good? Were they going to take me out of the academy? Would he take me to live with the animals and natives of Australia?

Or had he found out I was throwing away his tape recordings, and come here to deliver his lectures in person?

I gulped as Master waved me impatiently away. I hated the school, the training, the beatings, and even some of the other students—but I'd worked so hard, and hadn't even had the chance to perform! I wasn't ready to leave. I wasn't going to give up my future on the stage.

"What's wrong, Big Brother?" It was Yuen Biao, noticing my black expression.

"Nothing," I said.

"It's not nothing," he countered.

I sighed and filled him in.

"So you think he might be taking you away?" said Yuen Biao.

I nodded.

"I wish *my* parents would come and take me away," he said somberly.

I looked at him. He wasn't the Littlest Brother anymore, but he was still one of the youngest kids at the school. And he really missed his parents; they hardly ever visited, although they showered him with presents and hugs whenever they did.

When I first realized that my life with Master wasn't going to be the easy ride I'd hoped for, I hated my dad. I resented how he'd tempted me with visits and then trapped me here for good, and I wondered how he could abandon his only son to the wolves.

I understood better as I got older. There was no way Dad could have supported me and Mom if we'd all stayed at the Peak, and he couldn't have afforded to bring us all with him to Australia. The school was what was best for me at the time.

But now—it was a puzzling, mixed-up situation. I didn't know what to think or feel anymore. I understood my father, but I resented him. I dreamed of escape, but I wanted to stay. What would I say when I saw him again? What should I expect from this unexpected reunion, and what would become of me?

All night long I turned these questions over in my head, coming no closer to finding answers. In the morning, I was given leave to prepare for my father's arrival, scrubbing myself clean and putting on my best outfit—no longer my cowboy suit, which I'd long since outgrown, but a pair of faded blue pants and a fresh white T-shirt.

Washed and groomed, I sat at the long, wooden table in the practice hall, waiting with Master for the knock that would announce my parents.

The wait was awful. I could hear Yuen Lung screaming at the other students in the background, and wished I was practicing with them rather than sitting anxiously on the hard wooden bench, afraid even to shift my posture.

There was a soft thumping on the door. Master patted me on the back and led me to the entranceway. I opened the door, and for the first time in years saw the man who'd brought me into the world.

Australia had not changed my father much. He was still the same tall, stern man of my memories, with a few more lines on his face, and a bit more color to his skin. He seemed as awkward in my presence as I was in his, and we stood there staring at one another until Master beckoned my parents in off the stoop. He and my mother stepped inside, and Mom immediately put her arm around me.

We walked to the long table and sat down, as Master signaled for tea. Father sat on one side of me, and Mom on the other, with Master at the head of the table.

"You've grown, Ah Pao," he said, his voice gruff. "Maybe you've even outgrown your name." He was right; now a skinny adolescent, I no longer deserved the baby name "Cannonball." I was more like a rifle: lean, compact, and hard.

Master looked into my face and nodded in my father's direction. His expression carried a suggestion: I hadn't seen my father for such a long time. Shouldn't I embrace him?

I swallowed and turned to Dad, folding my arms around him in an unfamiliar gesture of affection. My father responded clumsily in kind. He'd never been one for demonstrations of his feelings—the softer ones, anyway—and clearly felt uncomfortable at this display. But Master seemed pleased, and my mother positively beamed at the sight.

My father cleared his throat, as if to change the subject. The tea arrived, giving us something to do with our mouths other than talk. It was a relief.

Mom was the first of us to break the silence. "Kong-sang, how are you doing in your studies?" It was the first time she'd ever called me by my given name, and it sounded strange from her lips. Bemused, I nodded, my expression blank.

"He is doing well," said Master, saving me from having to respond. "He is not our best acrobat, or our best singer, or our best fighter—"

So much for my savior!

"—but he is sufficiently accomplished in all things, and nearly ready to advance to performance. You should be proud of your son."

Master's words were like treasure. I'd never heard him directly praise any of us, so hearing him tell my parents that I had been worth all of his effort brought a smile to my face. And the more I thought of it, the more I had to agree with him. All of my brothers and sisters had something in which they excelled—my brother Yuen Wah had good form, little Yuen Biao was a tremendous acrobat, and Biggest Brother was one of the most powerful fighters. I wasn't the best at anything, but I was *good enough* at everything. I had no special talent—but that was a blessing in disguise. Because if I had been the best singer, then the teachers would have made me concentrate on singing. If I had been the best actor, then they might have made me specialize in acting. Instead, I got a chance to learn everything and do everything well.

My father looked at me with surprise, as if he'd never expected me to succeed.

"Oh, Kong-sang, we *are* so very proud of you!" said my mother, squeezing me.

I was pretty proud of myself! Because the master had said something else that I'd nearly missed; he'd suggested that I was nearly ready to perform, to show off my skills in public. And that meant that my dream of the crowd, the audience cheering in the dark, was going to come true. Sometime soon. Unless . . .

Unless my parents took me away. My stomach flip-flopped, and the smile faded from my face. The dream, once so close, now gone forever.

I stared at the soft cloth slippers on my feet, suddenly wishing that the day had never begun at all. "May I be excused?" I asked in a subdued voice. Master, deep in conversation with my parents, waved me away, and I slipped from the wooden bench to return to my brothers and sisters. They were taking a breather, their faces red with exertion. Yuen Lung was leaning against the wall, the master's cane at rest against his shoulder.

"So, Big Nose, how are Mommy and Daddy?" he said.

I ignored the sarcastic tone in his voice. "They're fine," I said.

"Are you going away, Big Brother?" piped Yuen Biao, sitting with legs outspread on the practice floor.

"Dunno," I said. "No one's said anything."

Yuen Lung laughed. "Nice knowing you, Big Nose. Don't let the door hit you on the ass when you leave."

I clenched my fists. "I ain't going anywhere." *Not yet*, I thought to myself.

"Yah, just admit it, you're a washout," he said. "Just like 'Big Brother' Yuen Ting."

Get angry enough, and reason and training go right out the window. Every cell in my body screamed that I *couldn't* pick a fight with Big Brother, that doing so would be against hundreds of years of tradition. If I so much as raised a hand in anger in his direction, any chance I had at a career in the opera was history.

Then I remembered that it was probably history anyway. So who cared?

"Listen, Yuen Lung," I said, my throat constricting in anger. "I'm not gonna let you push me into doing something stupid right now. You're still my big brother. But I swear to you, the first time I run into you outside of these walls, I'm going to kick your ass."

Yuen Lung pushed himself forward, slamming the rod hard against the wall. "You little—!" he shouted. "Ya better bring an army, shrimp, 'cause you're gonna need one."

"Don't think so," I said, with more courage than I felt.

"Yeah, I think so," said Yuen Lung, his grin suggesting he was looking forward to the opportunity. The rest of the kids gathered in a semicircle around us, horrified and eager at the same time. No one had ever committed the crime of challenging a big brother. Which is also to say, no one had ever had the *guts* to challenge a big brother. Until now. And so . . . the students wanted blood.

Feeling sick, I suspected they'd get it—only it was going to be mine.

"Students!" said Master, his eyes flicking suspiciously back and forth between Biggest Brother and me. We quickly dropped our hostile expressions and fell in line with the other kids. "I wish to announce a special surprise. Mr. and Mrs. Chan have brought food for a celebration feast. Today, instead of afternoon practice, we will have a going-away party!"

The assembled students screamed their approval. Even Biggest

Brother, after throwing me a final rude gesture, relaxed his scowl and cheered—food being the ultimate peacemaker at the academy.

Only I stayed quiet.

"Hey, Big Nose, send me a picture of a koala," said Yuen Kwai as he ran past me. "Or better yet—a naked native girl!"

It was all going the way I'd feared.

My opera life was over.

"Big Brother?"

Yuen Biao poked his head into the storage room, to find me sitting in my good pants on the dusty floor, my chin on my knees. I lifted a hand in greeting.

"What's wrong?"

Yuen Biao came in and sat down next to me.

"Have you ever had a dream, Little Brother?" I said.

He cocked his head, thinking. "Sure," he said. "I dream all the time. Mostly I have nightmares, though."

"No, I mean like something you really, really want."

Yuen Biao stared at the floor. "I really, really want to go home," he said. "Back to my parents. Like you—you're so lucky. . . ."

"I don't feel so lucky," I said.

Little Brother looked at me in shock. "You mean, you really want to stay here? Why?"

"'Cause if I go, I won't be able to do opera. Going onstage. The lights, the audience . . . you know. Being a star."

With a strange laugh, Yuen Biao buried his face in his hands. "You think we're really going to be stars?" he said, in a voice that sounded much too cynical coming from such a young mouth. "All we got to look forward to is more *practice* and more *hurting* and more screaming from Master, and maybe someday we'll get to perform, but there are dozens, maybe *hundreds* of kids just like us out there. And *they* all want to be stars, too. What makes *us* so special?"

I put my arm around Yuen Biao, who was sobbing gently. "Hey, Little Brother, don't cry," I said, trying to sound comforting. Even if I felt like joining him. "You know what makes us special? We're the *best*, that's what."

Yuen Biao looked up and smiled, wiping his eyes.

"And I don't care what happens. If my parents drag me away, I'll jump off the plane. I'll come back here, find you, and we'll go become stars together."

"I saw some kids doing backflips in the street last time we went to the park," Yuen Biao said. "People were giving them money."

"We're better than them," I asserted. "We could get rich!"

"No more Master," he said.

"No more Biggest Brother," I responded.

"I guess this is what you'd call a dream, huh, Big Brother?" said Yuen Biao.

I laughed. "Nah, a dream is when you eat until you're *sick*. And that's what we're gonna do right now." Grabbing Yuen Biao's hand, I pulled him out of the storage room and down the corridor, toward the sound of clicking chopsticks and clattering dishes that signified a party under way.

THE LITTLE PRINCE

When I went to sit at my usual place in the middle of the long wooden bench, I was led by my father to the head of the table, where I sat next to Master facing my parents. It was the first time I'd been honored this way since my "honeymoon" years before.

The table, usually bare, had been covered with a rich red cloth. The simple dishes of stir-fried vegetables and steamed fish we were used to were nowhere to be seen; you could almost hear the wooden planks groan as they supported platters of roasted duck, huge steaming tureens of tofu-and-watercress soup, pork knuckles braised in soy, and thick yellow noodles in brown sauce. Master had opened a round jug of plum wine and was drinking small cups of it in honor of my mother and my father. In a rare gesture of magnanimity, he even poured tiny amounts in glasses for the big brothers and me, and led us in a toast.

"To our special guests, Mr. and Mrs. Chan, who have so graciously provided this feast," said Master, raising his cup. We drank from our glasses, swallowing the thin brown fluid. Yuen Tai coughed as the deceptively sweet wine burned its way down his throat, and Biggest Brother broke out into hearty laughter as he slapped his choking friend on the back.

Master ignored the faux pas. "And now, we have a special announcement about our brother Yuen Lo," he said, returning to his seat as my father rose from his.

"Master Yu," he said haltingly. "Good students of the China Drama Academy, I thank you for taking care of my son."

He put his hand on my mother's shoulder.

"I have come back to Hong Kong to do something I wish I had been able to do years ago. . . ."

I tensed in my seat. This was it.

"I am bringing my wife Lee-lee to Australia."

Master nodded. The students looked at one another in confusion. And I—I found myself unable to breathe. My mother!

Mom was going to leave. I would be alone, truly alone, for the first time. And as much as I'd been embarrassed at the teasing of the other boys when Mom had visited, I couldn't imagine what life would be like without her.

I thought back to my earliest memories, of Mom ironing as I played in the washtub. Of being cradled in her arms as she waved away mosquitoes and sang me to sleep. Of her smile, and soft hands, and gentle voice. I pushed away my plate, barely hearing my father as he continued to talk.

Yuen Lung and the other elder students looked at one another. What did this have to do with the academy?

But my father wasn't finished.

"And so, Master Yu, I want to ask a special favor of you," he said. "Since neither I nor my wife will be here in Hong Kong, I would like you to consider adopting our boy as your godson."

I gave a start and looked up. So did the other students. Adoption!

Master looked at my parents and then at me. "Though he is not the best behaved of my students, I think there is potential in this boy," he said. "I will agree to adopt him."

Yuen Lung and Yuen Tai gritted their teeth. *Me*, the master's godson! This was too much! But there was nothing they could do. Master had made his decision.

My heart was pounding, and my head seemed filled with noise. What could this mean? I began dinner prepared to pack my bags; now, I found myself being given a position of unprecedented honor.

But one thing was certain.

I was here to stay.

We finished dinner in shocked silence. As the dishes were being cleared and the other students drifted away in groups, discussing the weird new state of events, Master took a small red box out of his pocket.

"Yuen Lo, come over here," he said, opening the box. Inside was a glittering gold necklace. I bent my head, and he fastened it around my neck. "From this day on, you are like a son to me," he said solemnly. My parents looked on with unrestrained pride.

I guess I should have been happy. After all, I would have my chance to make it on the stage, to win the applause I knew was mine. And I would do it not as a no-name player, a ragged unknown boy, but as Master's godson—the "prince" of the school. It was a position any of my big brothers would have given their left arms to receive.

But I was beginning to remember the challenge I'd thrown down to Yuen Lung, when I was certain I was on my way out. If he had it in for me before, this would be the straw that would break the camel's back—and possibly my neck.

I looked at Master. I couldn't think of a single thing to say.

"Thanks," I mumbled.

I was doomed.

EVERYTHING HAS
ITS PRICE

S o there was a black cloud over my head as I set off with my parents for the airport. I knew this would be the last time we'd all be to-gether for many years, but the swift turnarounds of the past few hours had left me—usually known for having a big mouth to go along with my big nose—completely speechless. Dad must have been doing well in Australia, because instead of the bus, we took a taxicab, the three of us squeezing into the backseat.

My mom wanted to tell me how much she would miss me. I wanted to reassure her that I'd be okay, that I'd make her proud. My dad wanted to say something, anything that would seem appropriate, given the situa-tion, but I guess he was as tongue-tied as I was.

Finally, he broke the silence. "Will you be all right alone in Hong Kong?" he asked.

I nodded again.

And then Mom, overcome with emotion, lurched forward and told the cabdriver to stop. With a jerk, he pulled the car over, turning to shout at my mother for scaring him half to death and nearly causing an accident—but she'd already thrown the door open and pushed her way outside. Neither Dad nor I had any idea what she was doing, and after a moment's hesitation, we both made a move to go after her.

Then we saw her weaving back through the crowd, in her light wool coat and cotton dress, her hands weighted down with a red plastic bag of fruit. She struggled to pull it into the cab after her, and then almost shyly presented it to me. I looked at the bag, and at my mother, and it was like a dam broke inside me. I let the bag slip to the floor of the cab and hugged her, squeezing her with all of the force of my thin young arms. I felt a soft pressure on my shoulder, and I knew it was my dad, adding his own restrained display of emotion to the tableau.

The car pulled into the airport, with the three of us still in that pose. Dad paid the driver and sent him off after retrieving Mom's baggage from the trunk. And then there was an endless wait on line, and papers exchanged and passports stamped, and then the parade down the long white corridor to the exit gate. Mom's bags were heavy; after all, they con-tained everything she owned. I struggled with two of them, while my father carried the others, refusing to let my mother trouble herself even with the lightest of her possessions.

"This is it, Kong-sang," my father said, as we reached the queue of strangers bound for Australia. Though some of the passengers were foreigners, many were Chinese: men, women, and even little boys and girls boarding the plane, headed for vacations or new lives in that unusual, unfamiliar place. Mom embraced me one last time, and told me that she would always be thinking of me, to take care of myself and not worry her. Dad patted my head, and then pressed some money into my hand, telling me to use it to buy admittance to the airport viewing platform, where I'd be able to watch their plane take off. He probably suspected I'd just use it to buy candy, but not this time.

I watched as the back of my father's head disappeared through the gate, and saw my mother briefly turn her face and smile, her eyes full of tears. And then I ran like hell down the corridor to make it to the viewing platform, caroming off tourists and knocking businessmen aside in my rush. The man at the turnstile looked at me like I was a dangerous lunatic; still, he took the cash I handed to him, and simply watched as I pounded my way up the spiral staircase.

I was feeling very strange. Like there was a wall of stone in my heart, blocking something significant. I didn't know why, but getting to the platform in time to see my parents' plane take off was suddenly the most important thing in the world.

Breathless and rumpled, I made it to the top of the tower just in time to see my mother and father's plane taxi down the runway. I was alone on the platform, and the thick double-paned glass cut off the sound of the engines and the screech of rubber tires. In utter silence, the plane picked up speed, lifting its nose, and pulled away from the ground, fighting against gravity.

Then, with a roar, it turned and elevated, and disappeared into the clouds.

It was only then I realized that tears were running in uncontrollable streams down my cheeks. In that screaming silver bird were the last ties I had to my blood and my memories, my innocence and my childhood. There was an entire world in that plane. A world I no longer belonged in, and that I'd never see again.

And what did I have instead?

I fingered the gold chain around my neck, lifted the heavy bag of fruit over my shoulder, and headed back down the stairs, back to the only place I could now call home and the only people in Hong Kong that I could call my family.

When I got to the school, Master squeezed my shoulders roughly and welcomed me back. Then he lifted the gold chain from around my neck.

"With you running around so much, you might lose this," he said. "I will keep it in a safe place for you."

And he did. So safe that I never saw it again.

I didn't see my mother for many years after that. Not until I'd reached adulthood, and by then she was older, a little grayer and more fragile than in her prime, as I'd known her. We kept in touch, through the tapes that she and Dad continued to send, and occasionally through letters. My mother had no education and couldn't read or write. So every time she sent me a letter, I knew it wasn't in her hand. But if anything, that made it even more special to me, because to get that letter written, she'd had to spend her free time cooking or cleaning for other people, doing special favors for people who were better educated than she was. They would write her words, and they would read what I sent back, explaining the characters and describing the scenes I related. I thought of her crying as I told her of the exhausting practices and the struggles I had to gain the skills I needed to succeed. I never told her about the beatings, the discipline I received from Master and from the big brothers, but I knew she knew. And when I read her words, or listened to her voice on tape, sitting in the storage room behind the back staircase that led to Master's quarters, I'd cry too, letting tears run down my face just as I had when I saw her and Dad fly away that day at the airport.

It was always the same. "I miss you," she would say. "But you're a big boy now. Listen to Master. Be good. Make sure you keep clean, and eat well." But the heart in those words shone through, building a bridge that crossed an ocean, a bridge of shared tears.

As I grew older, and more unwilling to lose myself in my emotions, I started to set the taped messages aside, promising I'd listen to them later. The tapes gathered dust and piled up in the storage room. I never found the time. And one day, I realized they were gone. To this day, I don't know what happened to them. There's a piece of my history with my parents that will always be missing. All my fault, and something I'll always regret.

When I arrived back at the school, I realized that I was stepping across the threshold as a different person from when I left. My master's declaration of my adoption couldn't help but change things somehow. Or would it? Maybe it was just a gesture to comfort my mother before she left. Maybe everything would go back to the way it was before. Like normal— if it could ever have been called normal.

As usual, I was wrong. It was dinnertime when I arrived, and the long table was lined with expectant faces awaiting the evening meal. We'd eaten so much at our lunch feast that you'd think we wouldn't be hungry again so soon, but food was so precious at the academy that we'd eat like goldfish, until we died of overstuffing, if we had the opportunity. There were plenty of lean times to make up for the very few chances we had to act like pigs.

All eyes were on me as I walked toward the table, headed for my customary place.

"Yuen Lo," said Master. "Where are you going?"

I stopped in midpace. "To sit down and eat, Master."

"You are now my godson," he said. "From now on, your place is here."

I walked like a zombie to the seat next to Master, as Yuen Lung shifted his weight over and made room.

"Pass Yuen Lo the fish, Yuen Lung," said Master, returning to his meal. Biggest Brother looked like he wanted to dump the dish over my head. If we'd been in a cartoon, there would have been steam shooting out of his ears. But with Master a few feet away, he didn't dare make a move to hurt me as I knew he wanted to—a kick under the table, a stray elbow jab, a chopstick in my eyeball.

This, of course, only made him angrier. It was remarkably fun to see him so frustrated, sitting there like a big fat rice cooker building up steam. As I took the head of the fish—the best part—and started to shovel food into my mouth, I decided that I could get used to this godson thing. I couldn't have gotten deeper under his skin if I'd slapped him across the face.

We were still without a new tutor, so Master declared that, following dinner, we'd have a special practice to make up for what we'd missed during the day. As I stretched in preparation for the workout, Yuen Lung went to take his position at the front of the hall. I felt his foot come down on my toes with crushing weight as he crossed before me. I stifled a yelp.

"So, shall we bow to you now, Your Highness?" he whispered at me under his breath. "Guess you're now the 'Prince.' That's my tribute. Plenty more where that came from."

Not good.

And then training began.

"Today we will focus on forms and positions," said Master. We groaned to ourselves. This was one of the most difficult aspects of Chinese opera: the striking of poses that had to be held with absolute stillness, often for minutes at a time. Sometimes, during practice, if Master thought that we were slacking off, he'd call out "Don't move!"—and, regardless of the position in which we found ourselves, we would have to freeze until he gave us the signal to continue. An unlucky student who moved a limb would instantly pay the price of Master's displeasure, as the cane came out and slapped the errant arm or leg. Stumbling out of position would demand even worse punishment: kneeling at the head of the class, pants down, as

Master deliberately and harshly applied the rod to the wretched student's backside. And, of course, the rest of us would have to maintain our frozen positions.

We stood quietly in our rows, wary of what the practice would bring.

"Yuen Lung, lead the students in basic forms," Master said, crossing his arms, his eagle eyes ready to spy the tiniest of errors.

"Okay, let's go!" yelled Biggest Brother. "On my count: one, two, three, four!" Punch, sway, turn, punch, kick . . .

"Stop!" shouted Master.

We froze in place, our legs high in the air. Master walked slowly around us, watching for signs of movement. Seconds, then minutes went by, and our brows began to sweat, knees to feel weak. Somehow, everyone managed to stay upright on one leg.

"All right!" he said, finally, "Everyone can move—except Yuen Lo."

The other students collapsed in relief, dropping their legs and panting. I gritted my teeth and remained immobile, my heart pounding and my muscles stiffening. Master stood expressionless before me, ignoring the increasingly desperate look on my face. And then he motioned Yuen Lung over.

"Bring me the teapot, Yuen Lung," he said. Biggest Brother nodded and headed for the kitchen, moving with unusual slowness. By the time he returned, I could feel my stomach beginning to buckle, and my left leg, the one on which I was balancing, was a mass of pain.

Master poured himself a cup of tea, and sipped it, relaxing as his face was framed by steam.

I wanted to scream.

"Now that you are my godson, you have to set an example for the others," he said, finishing the tea and pouring himself a second cup. "When your brothers and sisters train, you will train twice as hard. Everything they learn, you will learn twice as well. You will make me proud, because that is what I expect from my own children."

He then leaned over and carefully balanced the cup of tea on my leg.

"If you spill any tea, you will be punished," said Master. "And godson—when you are punished, you will receive twice as many blows."

Standing to the side with the other students, Yuen Lung suddenly looked like it had turned into the happiest day of his life.

The teacup fell, splashing hot liquid as it shattered.

Master looked at me, shaking his head in disappointment, and making a familiar gesture with his stick.

At least kneeling on the floor gave me a chance to rest my legs.

Things only got worse from there. During handstand practice, Yuen Kwai was caught taking a covert rest, and was hit twice with Master's stick—once for each leg that was leaning against the wall.

Then Master came over to me as I displayed my perfectly erect upside-down form . . . and hit me *four* times.

"Since you are my godson, his failure is your failure, and his punishment is your punishment," said Master. "It is up to you to set a better example."

Yuen Lung couldn't help but let out a sudden guffaw at my plight, and Master came over and gave him a quick slap with the rod.

And then *I* got two more slaps.

"Do you see, Yuen Lo?" said Master. "From now on, every time there is punishment, you will be punished . . . only twice as much. I am trying to teach you the merits of responsibility. You must share your brothers' and sisters' joys, and also share their pain. Now, everyone, take a rest."

I knew better by this time than to think that Master's words applied to me. *Legs straight,* I thought to myself. *Arms steady. No wobbling. Legs straight, arms steady . . .*

UP IN SMOKE

After the most excruciating practice of my life finally came to an end, I was completely aware of the fact that my princehood was going to make me miserable. At this rate, would I even survive to graduation? For the first time, I thought seriously about gathering my things and quietly slipping away into the night, as Yuen Ting, the first Biggest Brother, had done years ago. Yuen Biao's suggestion of becoming a street acrobat didn't sound like a bad idea.

I slumped down against the wall of practice hall, exhausted. After the workout, Master had left the school to go meet friends, giving us a rare evening to ourselves. It was hours yet until lights out, so I headed for the storage room to catch some quick shut-eye.

Dazed and stumbling, I almost didn't recognize the rough hand that grabbed my shoulder as I made my way down the corridor.

"What is it?" I mumbled, listlessly turning around. It was Yuen Lung. Oh no, my clouded brain thought. Not now.

But Biggest Brother didn't look like he wanted to fight. Not this time, anyway.

"It's Yuen Biao," he said. "He's sick. You'd better come over."

Out in the courtyard, a crowd of students were crouched around Little Brother, who had his hands clenched tightly to his stomach.

"What's wrong, Yuen Biao?" I said, shaking the sleep out of my head.

"My stomach hurts," he said tearfully.

"Ah, you probably just ate too much," said Yuen Tai. "I saw you cramming cookies in your face at lunch."

Yuen Lung gave Second Biggest Brother a punch on the shoulder. "Shut up, moron," he said. "Master and Madame won't be back until late. If the kid croaks, we're gonna be neck deep in crap."

Yuen Tai gulped. "Uh, maybe should we give them a call."

Biggest Brother rolled his eyes. "Yeah, anyone know where they are? Besides, *I* ain't gonna be the one to interrupt Master on his night out."

I helped Yuen Biao sit up. "What's good for a stomachache?" I asked.

The other students muttered to one another.

"Ice cream?" said Yuen Kwai. Yuen Lung slapped him in the head.

Then Yuen Wah spoke up. He was a thin kid whose mastery of martial arts form had us all in awe. When we did "freeze" practice, he'd still be as motionless as a statue long after the rest of us collapsed. He could stand on his hands indefinitely. In fact, once when Master told us to take a break, he kept on going, head to the ground, until someone realized that he'd actually *fallen asleep* upside down.

It was all almost inhuman, and it lent a kind of supernatural air of authority to his words. He didn't speak a lot, but when he did, we listened. Even Biggest Brother. "I heard that smoking cigarettes was a good way to cure an upset stomach," he said. Other kids quickly chimed in that they'd heard that, too.

The problem was that the only cigarettes to be found anywhere at the academy were owned by Master and Madame. And so, to save Yuen Biao's life, someone would have to sneak into their room and steal some smokes!

A discussion began as to who would be the best candidate for the job. Yuen Lung and Yuen Tai refused, on the grounds that such a matter was best handled by juniors. The younger students responded that it was the duty of the elders to take care of them, so *they* shouldn't be doing it, either.

Meanwhile, Yuen Biao moaned.

"I got it," said Yuen Lung, finally. "Prince Big Nose'll do it."

"What?" I sputtered. "Why me?"

"He's *your* best friend," said Biggest Brother. "Besides, figure it this way: if anyone else is caught doing it, you're gonna get punished too, right? So why get two people screwed when you can take the heat on your own?"

I had to admit, the logic was inescapable. After some more halfhearted attempts to pass the buck, I threw up my hands and went back inside.

Master and Madame's quarters were in the same building as the school, down the corridor from our complex. My heart was pounding as I crept down the hallway. Opening the door, I went into their bedroom and saw several packs of smokes scattered on Madame's bedside table. One of them was open and half full. I grabbed it like a lifeline, pulled out a few cigarettes, and headed back toward the corridor.

Then I had a revelation: when they got back, Madame would surely realize that cigarettes were missing, and the jig would be up. But what if I took an entire pack? She'd probably just think she'd dropped it on the floor. She probably wouldn't even notice it was gone at all. Feeling clever, I put the pilfered cigarettes back and slid one of the plastic-wrapped packs off the tabletop into my palm. Holding it concealed in my hand, I tiptoed back out of the room, feeling stupid; it's not like there was anyone to witness my crime, so why was I sneaking around like—like a thief?

Even so, I walked down the hall looking over my shoulder, as if at any moment Master was going to jump out of the shadows and whip me silly. When I finally made it downstairs and out to the courtyard, I felt like a conquering hero. I'd gone into the lion's den and smuggled smokes out from under his nose.

Well, not really. But I'd certainly done something that even big-shot Biggest Brother was too chicken to do.

"Damn, he did it," said Yuen Lung, seeing me walk forward, the pack held high above my head like a trophy. "Didn't think you had it in you, Big Nose."

It was backhanded praise, but from Biggest Brother it was like honey from a rock. He took the pack from my hand and pulled off the plastic wrapper, tossing it to the ground. Soon, all of us were sitting in a circle in the courtyard puffing on cigarettes, Yuen Biao's troubles mostly forgotten in our eagerness to try out this new vice.

"How's your belly, baby?" said Yuen Lung to Yuen Biao, his lit cigarette dangling from his lower lip. He was the only one of us who managed to make it look kind of cool. As for the rest of us, one of the younger sisters accidentally burned herself and threw her cigarette away, screaming. Yuen Kwai was rolling on the ground coughing and hacking. Yuen Tai couldn't keep his lit, and settled for holding it in the corner of his mouth, hoping that the other big brothers didn't notice he was faking.

To me, the whole experience was like inhaling car exhaust, but I wasn't going to be the only one to say so. Meanwhile, Biggest Sister, comforting the girl who got burned, told me that smoking was a filthy habit.

"Ah, we shouldn't be wasting good smokes on girls anyway," I responded, disgusted that she didn't appreciate the glory of my victory. She picked up Little Sister and stalked off to put some soy sauce on the injury. They were soon followed by Yuen Biao, whose face had slowly turned green as he sucked on his smoke. It wasn't long before he bolted from our circle and ran indoors, headed for the kitchen sink.

He came back a few minutes later, wiping his mouth on his sleeve. "I think I feel better," he said. We broke down in laughter, and he puffed out his cheeks, pouting. "Stop it, guys, I told you I was sick!"

We were all feeling a little queasy by this time, so after declaring that the cigarettes were the smoothest ones we'd ever tasted (not to mention the only ones), we crumpled up the empty pack and carefully picked up stray butts and other evidence of the big smoke-out. "Ahh, nothing like a good smoke before bed," said Yuen Tai.

Yuen Kwai and I looked at each other. "Whatever you say, Big Brother," said Yuen Kwai, stifling a chuckle.

"Lights out in ten minutes," shouted Biggest Brother. And we prepared to settle in for the night.

It was 3 A.M. when we were woken by a pounding on the door to the practice hall.

"Dammit, Big Nose, we're *screwed*," muttered Yuen Lung, kicking his blanket away. "I thought you said he wasn't gonna figure out we took 'em."

I was in a state of panic. How did Master know? Did we leave something incriminating lying around in the courtyard? My earlier paranoia seemed justified. It was like magic. Master had eyes everywhere.

The door opened and Master walked in, his face blank. "Stand up and form a line, hands out, palms up," he said. We quickly arranged ourselves in order of seniority, Yuen Lung at the head and the littlest brother at the end. Using the tip of his rattan cane, Master flipped over each of our blankets in turn, searching for the missing cigarettes—not knowing, maybe, that all of them had long since been smoked.

He then turned back to us and studied the line, examining our faces, each in turn. There was a half-empty pack of cigarettes in his hand.

"I thought you said you put the loose ones back," whispered Yuen Kwai out of the corner of his mouth, as Master turned his attention to the littlest kids.

"I did!" I whispered back. Didn't I?

Master gazed at the head of the line. "Some of Madame's cigarettes have been stolen," he barked. "There is a thief here. Who is it?"

No one spoke.

Master went to Yuen Lung and looked at him full in the face, tapping his cane against one palm.

And then Yuen Lung, in an act of nicotine-fueled courage, asked Master a question. "Master, how do you know they were stolen? Is it possible they just got lost?"

Master shook the half-full pack and thrust them into Yuen Lung's face. "This is not the way Madame keeps her cigarettes," he said, his voice icy.

I looked out of the corner of my eye at Master's hand and flinched. Several sticks jutted out of the pack. But instead of the familiar tan filters of Madame's fancy American cigarettes, white stubs showed. In my rush to leave the scene of the crime, I'd put the cigarettes back in the pack *upside down*.

"Now, I will repeat myself. Since you seem so interested in how I take care of my property, perhaps you know what happened to it. Yuen Lung, who stole my cigarettes?"

"I don't know," he responded. Master quickly struck him three times with the cane.

He then went to Yuen Tai, who answered the same. He, too, received three blows.

Next in line was Biggest Sister, who looked furious at being included in this disaster. She was usually the sweetest of girls, always protecting the younger kids and taking care of us when we'd suffered particularly hard beatings. Not this time.

Master turned to her assuming she, like the others, was not going to talk. But as he lifted his stick, she pulled her hands away. "I know who did it, Master," she said. "It was Yuen Lo." Her finger pointed directly at me, halfway down the line. Master's gaze followed the accusing digit, and his brow creased in fury.

Girls! I thought to myself, clenching my fists. *Can't trust them worth a damn.*

Master walked slowly over to me and grabbed me by the shirt. The others watched as he pulled me across the hall and over to the long wooden dinner table.

"Yuen Lo, which hand did you steal with?" he asked.

I thought quickly. If I was going to lose a hand, it might as well be one I don't use as often. "The . . . the left, Master," I responded.

"Put your left hand on the table," he said.

I complied, trying not to shake. Master raised the cane and hit me hard, five times. Because the back of my hand was against the hard wooden surface of the table, each blow felt like a hammer, bruising my knuckles while simultaneously raising thick red welts on my palm. Somehow, I managed not to scream, or even wince.

When the beating was over, I released my breath and rubbed my throbbing hand. I wouldn't even be able to make a fist for days. But I'd gotten off easy. Five blows wasn't even twice what Yuen Lung and Yuen Tai had received.

Master stopped me before I could turn and walk away. "Yuen Lo, which hand did you smoke with?" he said.

I closed my eyes and whispered, "My right." Swallowing, I put my other hand down on the table and took another five blows on that palm.

Master turned and left the hall. The first day of my princehood was over.

Biggest Sister turned out to be right after all.

Smoking really *was* bad for your health.

THE CHOSEN ONES

I guess I deserved what I got. I forgave Biggest Sister later, when she helped me tie strips of cloth soaked in ice water around my hands. But it was a long time before Master let any of us forget the crime. It seemed like he'd figured out that we'd all shared in the ill-gotten gain of my thievery, and so he ran us ragged, extending our practices by hours, pushing us to the very limit of our endurance.

And then, finally, a few months later, he made an announcement over dinner that served partly to explain why he was driving us so hard.

"Students, I have trained you for many years, and your skills have become nearly acceptable," he said. The words were as close to words of praise as Master could come. "But you are not training in order to please me," he said.

We looked at one another in silence. That was news to us.

"No, you are working for a much greater goal, and a much more demanding group of critics," he continued. "The audience! Because when you make a mistake before me, you may suffer punishment, but when you make an error before them, you damage your reputation, and the reputation of the school and its master. This is not something that will heal as easily as a bruise. And that is why you have been working so hard these past few weeks. Because when you step on the stage, even for the first time, you must be perfect. And that time is coming soon."

The dream. Applause, the cheering of the crowd, fame and glory. It was about to come true!

Master told us the date of our first public performance, which would take place at the theater at Lai Yuen Amusement Park—familiar ground. He explained that each of us would play important roles during the show—some of us behind the scenes, working the curtains and shifting props, others assisting with makeup and costumes, and still others in the chorus that would play crowd scenes and fill the ranks during battles.

But a select few—the best and most skilled of us—would be placed in positions of special honor. They would be the school's stars, performing each opera's heartbreakingly difficult leading roles.

These chosen ones would stand at that grand altar of communion between player and audience: center stage. For the brief space of an opera turn, they would command the attention of a mob of rapt worshipers, becoming princes and emperors and heroes—and gods. Upon hearing Master's words, each of us knew in our hearts that this, and only this, was what we wanted, that any other place in the repertory would be second-best, and thus, nothing at all.

We practiced with extra determination that evening, knowing that Master would be announcing his selections in the morning. Each of us tried to catch his eye, although it was unlikely that a single night's work would alter an opinion formed after years of observation. Afterward, we prepared for bed, cursing ourselves for mistakes we remembered from months gone by, or congratulating ourselves for recollected moments when we'd brought a tiny smile to our master's face.

"Lights out!" shouted Yuen Lung on schedule, and we settled into our blankets. But none of us could sleep.

"Hey, Big Nose," whispered Yuen Kwai. "Who do you think got it?"

I knew what my guesses were: Biggest Brother, of course, because he was the school's best fighter, and because he was Biggest Brother. Yuen Tai would probably be selected as well. Yuen Wah, certainly. But I didn't want to say anything for fear of being overheard. Clustered together as we were for warmth, a private conversation was impossible. "I dunno," I said.

"I bet you got it," he said. "You're the prince, right? How could he *not* pick you?"

I thought for a moment. Was Yuen Kwai right? I *was* Master's godson. But ever since the cigarette incident, he'd barely spoken to me and treated me with no particular favor. "He'll probably not pick me just to spite me," I said.

I felt a sudden sharp pain in my ankle as something heavy hit me. It was Yuen Lung's foot. "Hell!" he said. "How many times do I have to tell you to shut up when other people are trying to sleep?"

"Sorry, Big Brother."

"Sorry, Big Brother."

We pulled our blankets over our heads and tried to doze off. It took a very long time.

The morning sun seemed especially bright the next day, filling the practice hall with light. We stood in our rows, hands at our sides, listening to Master with undivided attention.

"I will now announce the students who have been selected for our performance troupe, which will be known as the Seven Little Fortunes," he said.

So there would be seven lucky students. Seven chances to be a star.

"Each of you, as you are called, please come to the front of the room. Yuen Lung!" he said, looking at Biggest Brother. Yuen Lung stepped forward, swaggering like there'd never been any doubt.

"Yuen Tai!" Again, no surprise.

"Yuen Wah! Yuen Wu!" Our school's reigning king of martial arts stances joined Yuen Lung in line, followed by another older boy who was one of the academy's best singers.

"Yuen Kwai!" Yuen Kwai gave a jump and looked up. Grinning like an idiot, he walked up to join the line. *Just two more,* I thought. *Two more shots.*

"Yuen Biao!" As disciplined as we were trying to act, the sound of Yuen Biao's name triggered an involuntary buzz of whispering. Little Brother was one of the youngest of our student body; for him to be selected as one of the stars of the school was outrageous. But, we had to admit, he was a natural acrobat, capable of twisting his small body into positions we could only dream of, as comfortable in the air or upside down as we were upright and on our feet.

There was just one position left, and dozens of qualified candidates. I was sure I'd lost. I was destined for a future of lurking in the wings, or carrying spears. I was going to be a nobody. And all of my father's ambitions for me to become a great man, all of my spotlight dreams, were for nothing.

"Quiet!" shouted Master, silencing the muttering. "There is still one more member of our troupe to be named." And we all leaned forward, our mouths slightly open, anticipating the call.

"Yuen Lo, step forward."

My mouth dropped open. Me! He'd picked me!

I bolted from my position and ran forward. Out of sheer ecstasy, I did a forward handspring on my way to the front of the room. Master looked surprised at my impromptu stunt, but smiled benignly.

The seven of us stood proudly by Master, our backs straight, our faces fixed in wide smiles.

"Fortunes, bow to your brothers and sisters," said Master. We bent at the waist and dipped our bodies low. "Students, welcome the Seven Little Fortunes of the China Drama Academy."

And, as disappointed as they were, our siblings broke out into cheers. They were proud of us. They were happy for us.

It was our first moment of applause, but certainly not our last.

SMALL FORTUNES

In the small world in which we traveled, we Fortunes were stars. Not only were we the academy's elite, acknowledged by all as the best and the brightest, but we also bore the responsibility of keeping the school alive, because it was our performances that generated the academy's only revenue. And so, being selected for the troupe was an unquestionable honor, a status that carried no negative stigma—unlike being the master's godson and the prince of the school.

Over the years, the ranks of the Seven Little Fortunes constantly changed. Students came and students left, and Master filled the absences according to his whims. Soon after we were chosen, Master quickly selected seven students as alternates, who would fill in for our roles when we were sick or when we formed a traveling company. (Unspoken, but understood, was the fact that if any of us well and truly screwed up, there were always seven eager bodies right behind us, waiting for their own turn in the spotlight.)

Upon our being named to the Fortunes, a new phase in our training began. All of our practice and working out was just the raw material of our art—a basic foundation. We had learned very little about opera itself and had never been given parts to play or roles to inhabit. But even as we sweated out our exercises, Master and the other instructors had been observing us carefully, noting subtleties in style and form, evaluating our body types, and imagining the result that puberty might have on our voices. A husky student like Yuen Lung was destined to portray kings and warriors, like the great General Kwan Kung. My moderate build and agile reflexes made me a natural for roles like Sun Wu Kong, the Monkey King. And a thin, delicate boy like Yuen Biao might be doomed to play female roles, which historically had always been filled by men. Times had changed; though there were still many more boys than girls at the academy, the days when women were considered a curse and banned from the stage were gone, and Master had accepted progress with relatively good grace. However, boys still had to be girls when necessary, since the Fortunes were chosen for our talents rather than our gender. With his bulk, Biggest Brother would have made a ridiculous—or rather, terrifying—girl, so he dodged the bullet. And my voice, though considered one of the better ones at the school, was luckily of the wrong range for female songs. We mercilessly teased Yuen Biao and others who were stuck with feminine parts, telling them how pretty and sexy they were until they cried or threw fists.

The truth was, though, that the chance to play any starring role—even in woman's clothing—was a thrill that exceeded anything we'd experienced to date. But there were other fringe benefits to being a Fortune. On days when we had pleased Master with a particularly outstanding rehearsal, he would take us out for a meal of dim sum. For those of you who don't know Chinese food, dim sum, which means "a little bit of heart," is a wonderful way of eating. Instead of ordering food from menus, you sit at your table watching as silver carts roll by, loaded with small dishes, dumplings, cakes, sweet buns, and bowls of mixed delicacies. If you see something you like you simply point, and it's placed on your table—no mess, no fuss, no waiting. It's a glutton's paradise: immediate gratification of your appetite, without even having to move from your seat. The food comes to you, you pick it, you eat it. It's that simple.

And compared to the bland stuff served at the academy, anything different was as good as a feast. Of course, anything we did with Master, even dim sum, had its own set of disciplines and rituals. The first time Master treated us, we sat enthralled at the sight of the rolling food, eager to grab anything that came within range. But when Yuen Kwai reached out his hand to point to a tasty-looking dish of dumplings, Master drew his chopsticks like a sword and rapped him lightly on the knuckles. "I will order for you," he said.

Yuen Kwai winced and sat back, subdued.

Master waved a waiter over and told him to bring seven bowls of roast pork over rice. The waiter nodded and glided off to the kitchen. Meanwhile, Master began selecting his own meal from the splendid array of dim sum specialties that paraded by us, a look-but-don't-touch vision.

We knew better than to complain, and roast pork with rice was better than nothing at all—a lot better, because as far as I'm concerned, Chinese roast pork is one of the great culinary treasures of the world. Marinated in barbecue sauce and five special spices and roasted in long strips, it comes out of the oven moist and flavorful, with a deliciously sweet red glaze. We never got it at the academy, where meat was as rare as a day without practice.

So when we got our heaping bowls of steamed rice, crisscrossed with slices of pork, lightly crisp on the edges and so tender inside, our mouths watered. We took our chopsticks and lightly set the pieces of pork aside, preferring to eat the rice, rich as it was with inherited fla-vor, before consuming the delicacy. Then, a slice at a time, we ate the pork, savoring each chew as if it were the most precious of gourmet foods.

As usual, there was never enough. And through the remainder of lunch, we were expected to sit quietly, drinking tea and watching Mas-ter eat his fill. My belly was outraged that I had stopped putting food into it, and I stared glumly at my empty bowl, wishing for a miracle. Then I realized that a miracle wasn't necessary: after all, I was in a restaurant. And even if Master wouldn't let me order any of the treats that continued to circle us so temptingly, he couldn't possibly object to my getting another bowl of rice. At the school, the prepared dishes were gone by the time they reached the littlest of our brothers and sis-ters, but rice was the one thing that never stopped flowing. It wasn't uncommon for us to make a meal out of just steamed white rice and soy sauce.

And so I did something that seemed very normal at the time. I raised my hand and signaled a waiter, pointing to my empty rice bowl. The other students looked at me like I was crazy, but Master said nothing as the waiter came and padded a large, fluffy scoop of rice into my bowl. I mixed the rice up carefully, to soak up any last bits of roast pork gravy, and ate it quickly and happily. Yuen Lung and the others looked on with envy, but none of them had the guts to ask for their bowls to be filled, too. As a result, I was the only one to go home to the academy with my hunger satisfied and my stomach full.

"You little pig," said Yuen Lung, as we prepared for afternoon prac-tice. "I can't believe you ate two bowls."

"Ah, you just wish you'd had the balls to ask for seconds yourself," I said.

"Screw off," Biggest Brother said, throwing a punch in my direction. I weaved past him, laughing. Things could have gotten uglier, but Master had arrived at the practice hall, and we hastily separated, running to our assigned positions.

The workout that day was grueling. Master ran us through every rou-tine in our repertoire, throwing in sudden "freezes" or calling for us to practice at double time, then triple time. There were no breaks, and every group of moves we completed led immediately to a new and more difficult set of commands. Finally, Master waved his cane, signaling the end of the workout.

"Damn, that was crazy," said Yuen Kwai, breathing heavily. Yuen Biao slumped to the floor cross-legged, too tired even to talk. I, meanwhile, had built up a raging appetite, despite my double portion at lunch. Din-ner awaited; there was no time for rest or idle conversation.

Then Master tapped me briskly on the shoulder with his rod. "Yuen Lo, you continue practicing," he said. "After all, you ate more at lunch, and so now you should be stronger than the others. Everyone else, join me at the dinner table."

I gasped. The other Fortunes smacked me on the back as they passed. "Food's gonna taste great after all that sweating," shouted Yuen Tai.

"More for the rest of us," said Yuen Kwai.

They were heartless.

"Yuen Lo, I would like to see some high kicks. Begin," said Master as he took his seat at the head of the table.

And then he turned to the cook, who was laying plates of food down and arranging chopsticks, and said, "Please make sure there is plenty of rice."

Heartless!

If there's one thing you can say about Master's brand of discipline, it's that at least you were rarely tempted to make the same mistake twice. But it wasn't as easy to learn from example. If it was difficult enough for me to resist temptation when so much food was around, for Yuen Biao, the dim sum outings were like extended torture. He would watch the carts pass with the eyes of a drowning man catching sight of land, or a dying desert survivor spotting an oasis. In particular he was tormented by the trays of pastries and other sweets, so close and yet so far.

One day it all became too much: as a cart loaded with sponge cake passed, he involuntarily yelled out an order. The waiter placed the cake on the table and moved on, as all of us, even Master, looked at Yuen Biao in shock. Realizing the enormity of what he had done, he burst into uncontrollable tears and wouldn't stop even when we returned to the academy, despite the fact that the cake sat at the table uneaten. For a change, Master didn't even have the heart to punish him.

As Yuen Biao sniffled, sitting by himself in the corner, Yuen Kwai shrugged without sympathy. "He should have at least eaten the cake," he said. I punched him in the shoulder and went to comfort Little Brother.

But as I mentioned before, the best thing about being part of the Fortunes was simply getting the opportunity to perform—to revel in the joy of the spotlight and drink in the appreciation of the audience.

Because my voice was fairly good, after a few performances in which I took supporting roles, I soon began training for my first lead part: a star turn in an opera performed only on special occasions, such as weddings or birthdays. It was a showcase role, and one that I learned with relish, since when I performed it, all of the other stars in the troupe were forced to act as my subordinates. Even Biggest Brother and Yuen Tai were just soldiers in my army, while Yuen Wah played the squire who held my horse.

Because this opera was performed so rarely, it was a while before I had the chance to do it live. When the day finally came, Master told me that I shouldn't feel nervous, that I was very well prepared for my debut, and that the audience was sure to be appreciative. I didn't need him to tell me that. My entire body was charged with excitement; the lines blazed in my head like letters of fire, and my voice sounded strong and loud as I warmed up backstage. I was so deep in character that I took to gesturing importantly at my servants, demanding my robes and my headpiece and admonishing Yuen Kwai for not finishing his makeup earlier. Yuen Lung, adjusting his armor, looked like he was considering clobbering me with his spear, but the backstage of an opera is crowded and busy, and the curtain was about to rise. There wasn't time or room to beat me properly; that would have to wait until after the show.

And then Master stage-whispered the order to be silent. My big turn, my premiere as the king of the theater, was about to begin. Holding the hem of my robe to my hip, I marched out of the wings, my other arm before me in a martial stance, and walked out before the lights.

I sang, and the audience roared. I ordered my armies to charge, and all the big sisters and brothers rolled from the wings in response, obeying without question. When I shouted "Halt!" they stood in formation, shouting "Yes, sir!" in unison. And when I reviewed my troops, they bowed down before me, me, the king of the theater. Whatever I did, people clapped and cheered. I was a hit!

And then I looked offstage, and saw Master standing stiffly in the wings, his cane in hand, an expression of mute disapproval on his face. *What did I do wrong?* I thought to myself. Suddenly, I didn't want to leave the stage—not just because I was enjoying myself so much, but because I knew that Master had found fault with me, and as soon as the curtain went down, I would pay for whatever error I'd made. But I couldn't delay the inevitable, and after I'd sung my last note, and the armies at my command rode off into the sunset, the curtain came down.

The king of the theater was gone. Long live the once and future king, my master.

"Come here, Yuen Lo," he said, his voice icy.

"You're gonna get it now, Big Nose," said Yuen Lung, poking me with the butt of his spear as he passed. I winced and walked over to Master.

"Hands out, palms up," he said. And then he hit me, five sharp blows.

"Master, what did I do wrong?" I said plaintively, reviewing my performance in my mind.

"Nothing," he said. "You were very good. But I want you always to re-member this: no matter how well you perform, you must never become too proud. There are others on the stage with you, and you are as depen-dent on their abilities as you are on your own."

And with that, he left me standing, still in costume, to direct the breakdown of the set and the storage of our props.

MY UNLUCKY STARS

Besides the occasions on which we were hired to perform off-site, usually in odd locations and with makeshift stages, we put on most of our shows at the stage where we'd had our first taste of the opera, the theater at Lai Yuen Amusement Park. After a few months of performing, we had gained enough of a following that we would occasionally be recognized in public—pointed to on the street, or even approached by fans. This would always put Master in a terrific mood, and didn't hurt our egos either, though after the incident after my debut, all of us were careful not to show our pride too much.

But it is Chinese tradition that every period of good fortune is always followed by an equal and opposite stretch of bad. Our months of seemingly effortless perfection lulled us into a false sense of confidence. Chinese opera is so complex that there are literally thousands of things that can go wrong. Well, several months into our show business careers, it seemed like all of them began going wrong at once.

I remember when the bad luck started. I'm not the most superstitious guy in the world, but I have to say, I began to believe in spirits—and their temperamental natures—after our miserable run began.

And of course, it all turned out to be my fault.

One of the chores we did at the school was the tending of the ancestor shrine. The shrine, which contained tablets and statues dedicated to relatives of Master Yu, as well as opera performers long past, was in a position of honor at the far end of the practice hall. Before each performance, Master would have us bow and shake incense before the shrine, appealing to the ancestral ghosts to look favorably upon our efforts and to give us luck and skill and easily impressed audiences.

Taking care of the shrine was an honorable duty, but a painstaking one. There were dozens of small icons to dust, and old incense to dispose of, and offerings to place in properly respectful position. Everything had to be arranged just so, or there would literally be hell to pay. Because I'd been adopted by Master, he soon decided that it should be my special responsibility to care for the shrine; as he reminded me, these were my ancestors too, even more so than the rest of my brothers and sisters.

I knew I should have felt fortunate, but the truth was, I thought that the entire job was a pain in the ass. The tablets and statues and incense

pots were sacred items, and it was essential that they be treated with appropriate reverence. But after sitting for a week or so in the practice hall,
they were inevitably covered with dust, and to clean them properly meant
getting on your knees, leaning down, and brushing them off gently with a
feather duster.

As the rest of the students were ordered to go clean up the courtyard—
it was a nice sunny day, so outdoor duty was almost a pleasure—I was left
on my own in the hall, duster in hand, and facing a task that would take
hours to complete.

I sighed, and evaluated the job at hand. My attitude toward the objects
in the shrine was a practical one. Sure, they were sacred and everything,
but they were also dirty, and they needed to be made clean. There was a
quicker way of getting this done, and I wouldn't have to break my back or
bruise my knees to do it, either.

I headed for the kitchen and got a damp rag, and then carefully removed all of the icons from the shrine and stacked them in a pile on the
floor. Whistling while I worked, I gave each statue a good scrubbing
down, spit-shining them to a polished gleam. And then I heard footsteps
behind me. It was our new tutor, arriving early at the school to discuss
our progress with Master.

"What are you doing?" he shrieked, seeing me sitting cross-legged on
the floor, wiping an ancestral tablet like it was an old pot or pan. "Put
those down at once!"

I nearly dropped the tablet, then set it down next to me and
scrambled to my feet. "I didn't mean it!" I said, looking wildly around
for signs of spiritual disapproval. For some reason, the shock in his
voice had triggered a flood of guilt in my conscience. "I'm sorry! I'm
sorry!"

The teacher began lecturing me on the need for respect, while looking nervously out of one eye at the scattered statues and tablets. I
dropped to my knees and began putting the icons back in place.

"Teacher, please don't tell Master," I said to the tutor in a frightened
voice. It was bad enough to have heaven and hell angry at me; I didn't
want the powers of Earth on my back, too.

The tutor agreed, wanting to get away from the shrine as soon as possible. Once the icons were back in place, I made a deep and heartfelt bow
to the shrine. *Accept my apologies and forgive me for treating you with such disrespect,* I pleaded silently. *And please don't let Master find out, or I could be
joining you up there a lot sooner than you'd like.*

Teacher made good on his word and didn't tell Master, but the ways of
the spirit world are mysterious and subtle; the ancestors found other
means of expressing their displeasure.

Ironically, in our next performance, I was assigned to play one of a set of five ghosts—a small but crowd-pleasing supporting role. Makeup alone wasn't enough to express properly the ghastliness of the undead, so each of us had to wear a wooden mask that completely covered our faces. The problem was, the masks were really made for adult performers, not young prodigies like us. They fit loosely on our heads, no matter how tightly we tried to tie them, and the tiny eyeholes were set a little too widely apart for us to see properly. When the performance was already under way, and our cue was about to come, I was still fiddling with my mask, trying to get it to stay in place.

"Sheesh, Big Nose, what's your problem? Stop screwing with your face and get over here!" said Yuen Lung, standing with the other four ghosts at the entrance to the stage. The music that signaled our supernatural arrival began, and I scrambled to my place in line, willing the mask to hold.

No such luck. As we walked out into the lights, our arms extended, I realized that the mask was slipping down—completely blocking my vision. I couldn't adjust the mask while onstage, so I whispered a brief prayer to whatever stage gods there might be that I'd be able to perform the scene blind. And for the first few steps in our routine, everything seemed to be going okay, until a move in which all of us ghosts were supposed to turn around and jump forward in unison.

The leap seemed to take longer than expected, and I nearly fell over as my feet hit the ground. I heard muffled gasps around me, and I realized in horror that I'd jumped entirely off the stage, almost into the laps of the front row of the audience.

Adjusting my mask with one hand, I quickly scrambled back up, hoping against hope that Master had not noticed.

On our way offstage, the other ghosts refused even to look in my direction, and even after the performance they wouldn't talk to me. I understood the reasons: not only had I messed up a perfectly good scene, but I'd broken our string of performances without errors. I'd snapped the good-luck chain. No one wanted to get too close to me, because my aura of misfortune might rub off, infecting the entire troupe. Even Yuen Biao seemed scared to get too close to me, though he whispered a word or two of sympathy from several arms' lengths away.

Besides, standing between me and Master's eventual explosion of rage was probably unhealthy. Each night, after our performance, Master would tell us to sit on the edge of the stage as he discussed the evening's show with any of his friends who had attended. This was a nerve-racking time for us, since any offhanded mention of a flaw in the program would result in Master pushing back his chair, ordering the sinner into his presence, and instantly delivering retribution with his cane, with the number and severity of the strokes proportional to the degree of the crime.

Falling off the stage was about as big a mistake as one could make, so I sat alone on the end of the line of students, my heart in my throat, waiting for the moment when Master would throw back his chair and call out my name.

Surprisingly, it never came. Master's friends had nothing but compliments to offer about our show, and so, after bidding them farewell, Master contentedly told us to line up and march back to the bus station.

No one would sit next to me on the bus, so I was left to puzzle out what had happened on my own. I'd never escaped punishment for a mistake before. It seemed like a stroke of good luck, but I knew better. A feeling of dread came over me as we took the long ride home.

Something awful was about to hit. And I was right there, at ground zero.

By the time we set off for the amusement park the next afternoon, I was a mass of anxiety. Would the bus drive off the road, or explode? Maybe I'd be struck down by a falling set, or take a mistimed leap onto someone's outstretched spear. There seemed to be a shadow over everything I did. The spirits were toying with me now, but their ultimate revenge was sure to come sometime soon.

Well, that day's opera featured me in only a very small role—a one-line cameo, in which I would enter, shout a command to the troops, and then exit grandly offstage. Maybe I'd dodge the bullet again.

Once I got backstage, just to make sure that my performance would be perfect, I prepared everything in advance. There would be no mistakes tonight, if I could possibly help it.

My part was small, but my costume was complex: an ancient and splendid set of robes, embroidered with dragons. Once I'd put them on, they were difficult to take off. So, a good hour before the show began, I went and relieved myself, and began the arduous process of getting into character. I carefully shook out the robes, counted the pieces, and checked for stains and funny smells. I stretched myself out and examined my ears and teeth. And I painted my face carefully, making sure there were no stray streaks or unusual splotches.

Satisfied that everything was in order, I got into my robes and headdress. The only thing I didn't put on was the elaborate beard that completed the costume, because it was so hot and itchy.

Finally ready, I sat stiffly in a chair, waiting for the show to begin. Just one line. What could go wrong?

And then there was a tap on my shoulder. I shook my head, realizing that I'd fallen asleep. I hadn't gotten to bed until late the night before, worrying about the state of my soul. The heat and pressing weight of the heavy robes must have put me out like a light. I looked up, and saw Yuen Tai, fully dressed for his entrance, his eyes wide with panic in his painted face. "The curtain is open, dammit!" he whispered through gritted teeth. "Get out there!"

I struggled upright and calmed my nerves, and then strode regally onto the stage. "Go!" I shouted in a deep, warlike voice. "Kill them!" And I spun on my heel to make my exit, stroking my beard for effect.

My beard? There was nothing there! I'd forgotten the beard backstage!

Sweating profusely beneath my robes, I lifted the hem and hustled off into the wings.

This time I'll be pounded for sure, I thought. It was almost a relief.

But once again, after the performance, Master failed to pull me out of line.

Worse luck yet! I'd escaped two beatings in a row. It was clear that disaster was looming, somewhere right around the corner.

"Students, today we will premiere a new opera: one that you have practiced often, but never had a chance to perform in public," said Master, his voice booming through the practice hall. "Yuen Lo—"

I froze at the sound of my name.

"—this will be your chance to impress us all!" he finished, smiling in my direction.

Oh no! We were going to be performing an opera about the God of Justice, the judge whose wisdom was so great that his decisions were sought out by god, devil, and man alike.

It was a wonderful opera.

And it starred *me.*

Justice was indeed at hand, and there was no doubt in my mind that the spirits had been waiting for this moment of maximum irony to strike.

Well, I resolved, I'd show them! Just because they were dead didn't mean they could push me around. I'd somehow manage to escape their vengeance, even if it killed me.

All the way over to the theater, I recited my lines to myself and reviewed the preparations I'd have to make. The outfit worn by the God of Justice was even more complicated than the one I'd had to put on the day before. In addition to the heavy robes and thick face paint, the costume included four pennants attached to my back on stiff rods. These pennants made it almost impossible to sit down once the costume was put on. It was a blessing in disguise; there'd be no sleeping on the job this time.

As I struggled into my outfit, Yuen Lung grabbed me and swung me around. "Listen, asshole," he growled. "You'd better not screw up tonight. I don't know how you got to be so lucky, the last two days. But if you make another mistake, I won't wait for Master to give you your medicine. I'll doctor your ass myself."

I couldn't deal with his threats at that moment, and so I impatiently waved him away with one hand as I applied makeup to myself. When I was finished with my paint and my costume, I put my hands on my hips and looked at myself in the full-length backstage mirror. I looked fearsome, my pennants streaming behind me, my face perfectly painted, and my thick black beard lending my face an appropriately impressive demeanor. The final touch was my tablet of office, a carved slab of wood carried in one hand that indicated my status as a high-level scholar.

I was convinced. Tonight would be perfect; I would avoid my fate after all. And with that, I carefully removed my beard and placed it back in the properties box, setting the tablet down near the stage entrance, where I wouldn't misplace it.

I had two major scenes in the opera, the first of which was a long song of fifteen minutes, followed by a half-hour break in which other stuff was happening onstage, and then a climactic final scene in which, with my tablet of office, I, as God of Justice, would render a wise decision to end the conflict. I had had trouble with the first song in the past, so I used the time before the play began to review the lines in my mind.

"Yuen Lo, curtain's up. It's your cue," whispered Yuen Biao, shaking me from my reverie. Prepared and refusing to rush, I walked toward the stage door, remembering to retrieve my beard from the prop box first. As I entered the wings, I pulled the thick clump of hair around my face, adjusting it so as not to block my mouth, and hooking the earpieces behind my ears.

The spotlight came on, and I raised my hands and began to sing. But the front-row audience looked puzzled. What was wrong?

Beginning to perspire, I surreptitiously reached for the front of my costume, and suffered a minor heart attack. It was the beard! Somehow, while sitting in the prop box, it had gotten tangled with a second beard, with the result that the combined length of facial hair stretched almost to my knees.

Worse yet, the part I'd actually placed over my face wasn't the carefully cleaned and groomed one I'd chosen before the performance; it was an old and unclean one, carrying the horrible stink of dried saliva. Every note I sang brought more of the stench into my lungs, and I had to use all of my self-control not to gag onstage.

When the scene ended, I marched offstage and nearly collapsed. I tried untangling the beards, but they were knotted tight, and the other fake beards were all being used. I would have to finish the show wearing an absurd length of facial hair.

Yuen Lung and Yuen Tai gaped at my long-bearded face as they marched onstage in their soldier outfits. "Oh, man," I heard Yuen Tai whisper to Biggest Brother. "He's done."

Onstage, the battle commenced. Unable to sit down because of my pennants, I leaned against the prop shelves to catch my breath and attempt to calm my tattered nerves. Somewhere in the distance, I imagined I could hear the vengeful laughter of ancestor ghosts.

But I had little time to ponder the perversity of the spirit world; the battle was finished, and it was once again my cue. All eyes would soon be on me, the God of Justice, as I brought peace to the bloody field of war.

What else could possibly go wrong? I sighed to myself.

I picked up my wooden tablet and adjusted my ridiculous beard, and then walked as solemnly and magnificently onto the stage as I was able. As soon as I reached the lights, I began to make my pronouncement, raising one arm dramatically in the air.

And then I dropped my tablet.

It fell to the stage with a heavy wooden thunk. The noise seemed to echo around the theater. For a performer, there is no more horrible sound than absolute silence. It generally means something has gone terribly wrong. Embarrassingly wrong.

But that wasn't the end of the matter. I leaned over with as much grace as I could muster to pick up the fallen tablet, only to hear a sudden explosion of laughter.

What was going on? My mistake was tragic, but not particularly funny. Peering upward at the crowd, I caught a glimpse of something waving out of the corner of my eye. It was hanging down over my shoulder, and its size and color made it clear that it wasn't part of my costume.

I stifled a scream. Somehow, while I'd been leaning against the prop shelves, one of my pennants had hooked a pair of jeans, which was now flapping idiotically behind my back.

There was no avoiding it now. Tonight, I knew I would get the beating of my life. And undead justice would finally be served.

I thought I'd seen Master angry before, but I hadn't seen anything yet. As soon as I bolted offstage, I nearly ran into him, his body coiled like a giant spring, and his face so red that he looked like he was wearing opera makeup. He'd not been so humiliated in many years, and as a result, he'd never been so infuriated.

He didn't bother sitting us on the stage or talking to his friends. There was no need. This was simply the most catastrophic performance any lover of Chinese opera had ever seen, and the audience had cleared out of the theater long before Master emerged from the wings.

Once I was back in my street clothes, the other students gave me a wide, wide berth. I couldn't have been less popular if I were radioactive and stank of piss. Yuen Lung and Yuen Tai could barely restrain their laughter.

"Everyone on the bus!" Master shouted, waving his cane wildly around him. The ride back was utterly silent, though the gleeful grins of the big brothers made it clear that they couldn't wait to see what would happen next. When we got back to the school, Master grabbed me by the ear, threw open the academy doors, and walked directly to the ancestor shrine, shaking with fury.

I didn't struggle. I'd decided to face my doom like a man.

"Ghosts of my ancestors!" shouted Master. "Do you see this pile of dog excrement here before you? This absurd mockery of an opera performer?"

I winced as he twisted my ear between his thumb and forefinger.

"This useless trash is my godson!" he roared. "I present him to you, to do with what you will."

Jerking me down, he made me stumble to my knees.

"Recount your sins," he said, waving to the shrine.

I swallowed. "The tablet," I said. "And my beard . . . and the pants . . ."

The students behind me burst out in laughter.

Master looked toward the shrine, which somehow seemed unsatisfied. "Is that all?" he thundered.

There was no helping it. You couldn't lie in front of the ancestors.

"Well . . . yesterday, I forgot my beard completely," I admitted. "And the day before that, I fell off the stage."

Master raised his eyebrows. "Oh, you did, did you?" he said. "I missed that."

I squirmed. So much for honesty.

Master motioned me forward. "Bow down before your ancestors."

I let my body drop into a prone position before the shrine. Master yanked down my pants. "Begin apologizing!" he said, lifting his cane.

I started offering up pleas for forgiveness. "I'm sorry." *Whack!* "I'm sorry!" *Whack!* "I'm sorry . . . !"

After twenty strokes, Master turned away, bowed to the shrine, and left the hall.

"Get to bed," he shouted out behind him, and turned off the lights. "Tomorrow we practice without meals, since it is obvious you have all become too satisfied with your skills."

We groaned. But the tide of bad luck had been broken—across my butt—and the fearful wall that had stood between me and my brothers and sisters was now gone. Once again I was one of many. And finally getting what was coming to me took a load of worry off of my mind.

As I shifted on the floor, attempting to find a sleeping position that didn't cause me pain, I sent a short mental message in the direction of the ancestor shrine: *Now, we're even. Right?*

As sleep closed my eyes, I thought I could see the statues gleam.

A MIDNIGHT RAID

My years at the China Drama Academy went by with surprising speed. I went from boy to teenager, barely noticing as I added birthdays, inches, and pounds. Though I'd gotten bigger and taller, I hadn't changed much in personality. I was a mischief-loving boy, and I became a spirited and rowdy adolescent, always popular among the younger boys and still the nemesis of the older ones.

And life at the academy, formerly just a series of long, dull days spent in practice and short nights spent in exhausted sleep, had gotten much more exciting since we'd begun performing. It seemed like a day didn't go by when we didn't have some sort of adventure, with me generally right in the middle.

Not that our life had become too complicated. The joys we had continued to be small ones—bits of spare time spent playing marbles or other games, until we were interrupted by one of the instructors; surreptitious catnaps taken during lessons, with one eye open in case Master suddenly made his presence known; and, of course, food, always food.

As we grew up, we were increasingly given our independence. Often, we'd be sent to perform at the amusement park on our own, while Master taught the younger students at the academy. When we got this kind of freedom, we took advantage of it to indulge ourselves in the best way we knew how: by filling our stomachs. The snacks that were denied to us when Master was around were ours for the buying when he was away, and before our shows, we'd gorge ourselves on the best delights the amusement park had to offer.

The problem was that, after our long and strenuous performances, we'd always be hungry again. Even if we still had any money, all of the glorious food stalls were usually closed before we'd finished changing and cleaning our faces. So we walked through the deserted park discouraged, with nothing to look forward to but a long bus trip and then the hard practice room floor, since the kitchen cabinets were always locked tight against our prying fingers.

"Damn, I'm starved," moaned Yuen Kwai. "I can't believe the stores are closed! I'm dying for a bean bun." Yuen Tai chimed in his own food wish, lotus seed cake, followed by Yuen Biao's plaintive expression of lust for sponge cake, and Yuen Wah's rhetorical inquiry regarding roast pork buns.

"God, will you guys cut it out?" groaned Yuen Lung. "All this food talk is killing me. I'm *never* gonna make it to breakfast."

Yuen Kwai suggested something that Yuen Lung *could* eat, which led Biggest Brother to roar with indignation and chase him around the empty park. The chase didn't last long; both pursuer and prey were too weak with hunger.

I eyed the shuttered stalls, my stomach grumbling as loudly as those of my brothers. The stalls were ramshackle contraptions; just clapboard walls, chicken-wire windows, and an open roof—when it was wet, the vendors would provide scant temporary cover against the rain by draping plastic sheets across the tops of the walls.

We'd worked hard that day, and our performance had brought plenty of people into the park. We deserved better than bed without supper. And since there didn't seem to be anyone around . . .

Without a word, I ran over to the nearest stall, a baked goods vendor, and peered through its chicken-wire window. "Hey, Yuen Kwai—give me a boost," I shouted, leaping up and grabbing the upper edge of the wall by the fingertips.

"What the hell do you guys think you're doing?" said Yuen Lung nervously.

His eyes scanning the horizon for cops, Yuen Kwai moved over to my hanging legs and grunted as he pushed me up and over the stall wall. I landed lightly on the inside of the stall, and began searching around for anything that might be considered edible.

Despite their fear of being caught, the call of the belly was more than the other Fortunes could resist, and soon their faces were pressed up against the wire, watching me search.

The owner of the stall had done a good job of cleaning it out; everything of any resale value had been locked up or taken home.

"Look over there," said Yuen Lung, pointing through the screen at an alcove set into the back of the structure. It was a rubbish storage area. Considering where I spent a good part of my childhood, I probably should have recognized it immediately.

Well, no harm in checking. I poked my head into the storage bin and found a small brown paper sack. "Yahoo!" I shouted, hoisting the bag up over my head. It was full of bread crusts, too hard and stale to be sold, but not more than a day or so old.

To us, this was like finding buried treasure. Throwing the sack over the wall, I leaped up onto a counter, scrambled my way back to the top of the stall, and leaped down into the waiting arms of my brothers.

"What are we gonna do with this bread?" asked Yuen Tai. "I mean, it's as hard as a rock."

"Hey, food is food," said Yuen Kwai, hiding the bag under his shirt. "You give me something edible, I'll find a way to eat it."

All the way back to the academy we whispered different ideas on how to eat the bread.

"Maybe we could toast it," said Yuen Biao.

"Yeah, right, you already could break your teeth on this stuff, and you want to toast it?" snorted Yuen Tai. "We're trying to make food, not *pottery*."

"I think we should just toss it," said Yuen Wah. "Who knows how old it is?"

"Aw, it can't be *that* old; they throw trash out every day at that place," said Yuen Lung, thinking with his stomach. "Hey, I just thought of a great way to cook this stuff."

Back at the academy, we crept through the hallway on tiptoe and sneaked our way into the darkened kitchen. There, Biggest Brother began boiling a pot of water, into which he poured a double handful of sugar. After a short time, the water began to boil, thickening to a syrupy consistency. Then he threw in the bread crusts, which absorbed the sugar water and puffed up into a kind of sweet bread pudding.

I gathered some bowls and set them out next to the stove, inhaling the sweet aroma of the boiling bread. Soon Yuen Lung pronounced his dish done. The finished delicacy was ladled into bowls, and we greedily consumed the results of our nighttime scavenging.

"Hey, this ain't half bad," said Yuen Kwai.

Yuen Biao smiled and held out his empty bowl. "More!"

After a strenuous day, the soft, delicate pudding was soothing, and more important, filling. And the adventure of breaking into a locked stall to harvest the bread crusts gave the dish a special zing. I still remember that meal as being one of the best I've ever had.

We each had several helpings, laughing to ourselves and imagining we were conquering warriors, raiding helpless villages for our food. Today it was bread crusts; tomorrow, the world.

And then the kitchen lights came on. It was Master, awake, and as usual, enraged.

"What are you eating?" he said.

"Bread and sugar water, sir," said Yuen Biao, nearly dropping his bowl.

"And where did you get the bread?"

All of us fell silent.

"We didn't steal it, we found it!" I said defensively. "It was going to be thrown out anyway."

Master tapped his cane against one foot. "Whether it was going to be thrown out or not doesn't matter. Do you think I want people to believe I don't feed you? That you have to go through garbage bins to eat?" he shouted. "How much shame do you want me to feel?"

That night, each of us received five hard strokes of the cane, except for me; I got ten because I was the "prince."

But you know what? The next night, and for many nights after, we returned to the scene of the crime. Only, from then on, we made sure we didn't get caught.

TAKEN FOR A RIDE

Of course, we didn't always have to steal leftovers to fill our stomachs. Sometimes our performances ended early, giving us the chance to wander through the park, spending our bus money on the wide array of goodies available. Of course, this meant that we would have to walk six miles back to the academy—but for the treat of a sweet bean bun or sugar rice cake, it was worth it.

One day, one of our more friendly instructors, a hearty middle-aged man who taught us martial arts, told us a secret: his son worked as a driver at the bus company. If we ever found ourselves in need of a ride, we could say that our father was "Tsui Luk, employee number 1033," and the ticket vendor would let us on the bus for free as a family member.

We looked at one another in glee. All the snacks we wanted, and we'd never have to walk again!

The following afternoon we gorged, confident that we would ride home in luxury, courtesy of the bus company.

"You sure this is going to work, Biggest Brother?" I asked, a little dubious.

"Of course, dumbass," he said. "Teacher wouldn't screw us over. You just make sure you remember what to say." And when the bus arrived, Yuen Lung stepped smartly into the stairwell, nodded his close-cropped head at the ticket taker, and told him that his father was Tsui Luk, employee number 1033.

The vendor looked up and down at Biggest Brother, appraising him. Finally he nodded back and sent him into the interior of the bus.

It worked. Our hearts leapt in our chests. Free fares, anywhere we wanted, anytime we chose!

Then it was Yuen Tai's turn. "My father is Tsui Luk, employee number 1033." He, too, was allowed in.

But the ticket taker was beginning to get suspicious. By the time Yuen Biao, last in line, stammered his "father's" name and number and boarded, it was clear that something was wrong. No driver as young as Tsui Luk could have so many kids, all boys, and all with their heads shaved clean!

Cursing his own gullibility, the ticket taker stomped toward the back of the bus, shouting for us, the bald-headed kids, to come down and pay our fares. Of course, we'd long since eaten our fares, not to mention any other spare pocket change we happened to be carrying.

"Hey, you can't do that! We'll tell our father on you!" shouted Yuen Lung in desperation.

"Driver!" the ticket taker barked. "There are illegal riders on this bus! Take us to the police station!"

Yuen Biao began to whimper. The police station! Though none of us were afraid of cops, we didn't dare to imagine what Master would do when he found out we were in police custody. Jail—even execution— would probably be merciful by comparison.

"Let us off the bus," pleaded Biggest Brother. "We were just playing around."

By then, the ticker taker was too incensed to listen, and told the driver to go faster. I looked at Yuen Kwai and he nodded back. Charging toward the front of the bus, we pushed the ticket taker over, and then ran up the stairs to the second level of the double-decker bus, followed close behind by the other five Fortunes.

"Why the hell did we come up here?" shouted Yuen Lung. "We're trapped!"

Yuen Tai pulled open a window.

"Are you crazy?" shouted Yuen Wah. "We'll all be killed!"

"One way or another," said Yuen Tai, as the enraged ticket taker burst out of the stairwell. He stuck his legs out of the window, holding on to the metal frame, and then let go, falling eight feet into the roadside shrubbery. "Outta the way," shouted Yuen Lung, who followed his junior, grunting as he passed his heavy body through the narrow opening. Yuen Wu and Yuen Kwai followed in quick succession, and then, whispering a quick prayer to himself, Yuen Wah.

While I held back the ticket taker, who was screaming obscenities and nearly foaming at the mouth, Yuen Biao froze by the window, staring terrified at the scenery rushing past.

"Go!" I shouted.

"I'm scared!" screamed Yuen Biao.

I gave the ticket taker a shove that nearly sent him falling back down the stairs, picked up Yuen Biao and threw him out the window, then leaped after him, headfirst.

Forget everything I've done since then; that first "stunt" was the most terrifying thing I've ever done. The bushes we'd been passing just moments before had dwindled into scrub, and I saw the ground rushing at me at a painful speed. I had time for just one thought before I hit the ground: *Why did I jump out the window headfirst?*

The only thing that saved me and Yuen Biao from broken necks was the rigorousness of Master's training. We'd done somersaults and acrobatic rolls so many times that we could—and, in the case of Yuen Wah, *did*—do them in our sleep. Out of sheer reflex, we tucked our bodies properly and cushioned our falls to the hard, unyielding ground.

We could still hear the ticket taker's screams as the bus disappeared into the distance. We'd gotten off lucky; besides a couple of scrapes and minor bruises, less than we'd get in an ordinary day of practice, none of us were hurt.

But we were nowhere near a bus station and didn't have money for fares even if we had been. And, since the police station was in the opposite direction of the school, the walk we faced had expanded from six miles to seven.

"Whose stupid idea was *this?*" yelled Yuen Lung, stomping down the road in the general direction of the school. The rest of us just marched on after him, wisely keeping silent.

THE BIG BRAWL

After so many months of working and performing together, we Fortunes built a special kind of bond. Even Yuen Lung and I learned to depend on each other—we had to, after all, on the stage—although we still argued more than we agreed, and I still went out of my way to irritate him, just as he went out of his way to push me down.

But the relationships that existed among us, and between us and the other students at the academy, were far from simple.

Imagine a family with thirty siblings, ranging in age from toddlers to teenagers. When we were out in the real world, nothing could separate us from one another; it was all for one and one for all, like we were the Thirty Musketeers. But when we were alone at the school, all bets were off. Under Master's intense pressure to perform and compete, we formed ties that one day could be stronger than steel, and the next a half-forgotten memory. For instance, one day I might vow that another student was my blood brother, my friend forever. The next day we'd fight and swear never to talk to one another again. And then the day after that, we'd find a reason to renew our vows of eternal brotherhood.

The only thing you could depend on at the school was that no one could be depended on, except yourself. Even Yuen Biao, whom I always protected and took care of, occasionally strayed to other "best friends"—if they treated him to food.

I mentioned to you that Yuen Kwai was one of my best friends at the school. He was not only a fellow Fortune, he was also nearly my size, my age, and my match when it came to making trouble. We often competed for roles, for food, and for attention. Sometimes we'd mix it up, but we'd always find a way to cool down before things got too serious.

Until the day that Yuen Biao's parents made a rare visit to the academy. Along with a sack of edible treats, they brought a new amusement into our midst: a stack of comic books. As Yuen Biao gleefully flipped through the stack, we all gathered around, staring with curiosity and envy at the brightly colored pages. They depicted martial artists and swordsmen testing their superhuman might against devious monsters and madmen. In short, they were the stuff that boys' dreams are made of, and Yuen Biao was instantly the most popular student at school.

At the time, however, Yuen Biao's newest blood brother was none other than Yuen Kwai, who announced that he would read every single one before anyone else would be allowed to touch them. No performance was scheduled for that evening, so we had a few hours of free time before lessons began. Ignoring our pleas and protests, Yuen Kwai and Yuen Biao spread the comics out on the training room floor and began reading.

Yuen Biao was my blood brother too, so I figured Yuen Kwai's stupid decree didn't apply to me. Making myself comfortable on the ground next to them, I picked up a comic and began to pore voraciously over its lurid visions of heroic fantasy. Then Yuen Kwai looked up from the book he was reading and noticed my intrusion into his turf.

"Hey, you can't read that until we're done," he said sharply. "These are Yuen Biao's and mine."

"You're not reading it," I said, absorbed in the book.

"Doesn't matter, it ain't yours," said Yuen Kwai. Reaching over, he grabbed the comic out of my hands. Irritated, I slapped at Yuen Kwai's fist, and the book tumbled to the ground.

Sensing tension in the air, the other students drifted into a sloppy ring around us. Meanwhile, Yuen Biao quickly gathered the rest of his treasured books and fled for less dangerous ground.

Yuen Kwai, his eyes flashing, bent down to pick up the fallen comic. "Asshole!" he said. "Who you trying to mess with?"

Mad enough to spit, I kicked out one of my feet and snapped the comic away. It slid away along the polished wooden floor.

Head down, Yuen Kwai stood still for a moment, as the crowd around us murmured nervously. With a howl, he launched himself at me, blood in his eyes.

Now, I was the fastest kid in school. When I had room to move, no one—*no one*—could touch me. In fact, the only people in school who were ever able to beat me up were Yuen Lung and Yuen Tai, and that was just because I couldn't hit them back.

Yuen Kwai, just a bit bigger than me but quite a lot slower, was no challenge at all. As he charged, I stepped aside, ducked a wild swing, balled my fist, and punched him hard in the face.

The room went silent. Then Yuen Kwai screamed bloody murder and grabbed his nose. In my overconfidence, I'd forgotten the cardinal rule of fighting in the school: it officially wasn't allowed, but if it ever happened—and everyone knew it happened—you were *never* supposed to hit a fellow student in the face.

Our faces were an important part of our livelihood. Even when Master administered a beating, it was always on the hands or buttocks. Body injuries could be hidden, but a blackened eye, swollen lip, or broken nose would defeat all efforts at disguise with makeup, and might put a performer out of commission for days. And to be unable to perform was something that neither Master nor the students wanted. It was the worst punishment imaginable.

Yuen Kwai ran to the mirror and examined his face. His nose was bleeding. "If my nose swells up, you're really going to get it," he snarled.

Yuen Biao, who'd run up to me upon hearing Yuen Kwai scream, was horrified. "Big Brother, you didn't have to hit him in the face!" he said.

Realizing that I'd made a big mistake, I dug my toe into the ground and wondered what to do next. Meanwhile, Yuen Kwai's nose was blooming like a rose. It was indeed swelling, becoming grotesquely huge. Bigger even than mine.

I couldn't resist. "Now who you gonna call Big Nose?" I taunted.

With a speed that I hadn't realized he had, Yuen Kwai swung out and caught me with a punch to the jaw, then threw me to the ground. Soon we were pummeling each other like bar brawlers, while the other students cheered us on.

As if on cue, it was at that very moment that Master walked into the hall to call us to evening lessons. He was incredulous. Of all the many ways that we'd managed to screw up over the years, he'd never seen anything like this scene before: two of his best students openly beating each other to a pulp, while the others laughed and made guesses as to who would be the winner.

"STOP!" he shouted.

Instantly, Yuen Kwai and I froze, my arm around his head in a hammerlock, his knee about to smash into my groin.

Master walked into the ring of students, looking from one to the next with a chilly expression on his face. "So, you like fighting, do you?"

No one dared to answer.

"All right, then," he said, pushing at us with his toe. "Get up and fight."

We pulled ourselves up, looking at him without comprehension.

"I said *fight!*" yelled Master.

Yuen Kwai punched me weakly on the shoulder.

Master slapped him with his cane. "You can do better than that!"

Yuen Kwai hit me harder. Much harder. Then Master waved his cane toward me, and I punched Yuen Kwai back. Directed by Master, the two of us kept hitting and kicking one another, our blows landing solidly without defense, long after we were too tired to fight, and long after the reason for the fight had been forgotten. Our faces became bloody and swollen. Our fists and feet felt like lead. Our bodies ached everywhere. Still Master urged us on, until finally we collapsed on each other's shoulders and begged for mercy.

"You should have asked for mercy from each other before all of this happened," he said. "Keep going."

And so the fight, if you could call it that, continued for hours, sodden blow after sodden blow. By the time we were allowed to stop, we had no strength left for anything but sleep—and even that was difficult, as sore as we were. In fact, we were too beaten up to practice the next day, and our injuries kept us from performing for weeks. During that time, Master coolly substituted two alternates into our places in the Seven Little Fortunes. When we'd healed sufficiently to get back to work, he made us beg him for our roles back.

After that experience, Yuen Kwai and I never hit each other again.

At least not in a way that left any evidence.

THE SECRET

The Great Comic Book Battle had an unexpected side effect—one whose importance I didn't realize until much later.

See, the fight was the first time that Yuen Kwai and I were really put out of commission. Neither of us had ever suffered a real illness before, and so we chafed under the restriction we suddenly faced: no working out, no running around, lie in bed, don't talk, don't make trouble. The only nice thing about being grounded by our injuries was that Biggest Sister and two of the other girls took it upon themselves to take care of me, putting ice on my bruises, giving me their extra food, and otherwise pampering me in a way I hadn't experienced since my mother left for Australia. Yuen Kwai got similar treatment. Suddenly, we found ourselves thinking weird new thoughts.

"Hey, Yuen Kwai, d'you ever think about how boys and girls are different?" I asked.

Yuen Kwai sat up and shifted a pillow behind him, breathing sharply as he stretched a muscle that still hurt. We'd been put temporarily in a side room meant for guests while we recovered. There were even real beds in it, and it was right next to the big sisters' room, the private area of the older girls. For some reason, Madame demanded that Master put sisters over a certain age in a room by themselves.

"Sure, Big Nose," he said, after some thought. "Number one: boys hit harder. Number two: boys eat faster. Number three: girls apologize and boys don't. And number four: girls share snacks without fighting."

"That's not what I mean, you idiot," I said. "I mean, have you ever seen what a girl looks like, you know, without clothes?"

"You mean naked?"

"What *else* does without clothes mean?"

"Of course I have," he said, trying to sound cool and world-weary. "All the time."

"Yeah, right!" I said, wounded. "If you know so much, how are they different from us then?"

Yuen Kwai turned red. "They don't have 'little boys,' " he said.

"What?" I said.

"Penis. No penises," he said.

I laughed. "How do they pee then?"

Yuen Kwai threw a pillow at my head, "Ahh, shut the hell up, I don't know!" he said.

Since we had nothing better to do, we decided that we'd find out for sure. It would take a little effort, but the answer to the Great Big Secret of Girls was close at hand.

You might think we were naive, not knowing anything about men and women and sexual things. After all, back then, most kids had a pretty good idea of how their bodies worked by the age of twelve. But we didn't go to school. We didn't have much time to play around. And who was going to explain to us, anyway? Master? Madame? If we'd even asked them an innocent question, we'd probably have been whipped within an inch of our lives.

So that pretty much left it up to us to figure things out for ourselves. And that was harder than you might imagine. For us, boys and girls were pretty much the same. That is, we knew that girls and boys *acted* differently—but until age thirteen or so, all of us were in the same boat, training together, getting punished together, even sleeping in the same room, side by side. About the only thing we didn't do was go to the bathroom and shower together.

In most of our social activities, we naturally divided ourselves into brothers and sisters, but we boys basically thought of the girls sort of as weaker versions of ourselves. They cried too much—more than Yuen Biao, even—frankly, they weren't really very interesting.

But now I was determined to get to the bottom of this whole boy-girl thing. After the other students got back from the day's performance, Yuen Kwai and I grabbed together some of our fellow junior brothers and outlined our plan. We didn't let Yuen Lung or the other older students know, mostly because we realized they'd tease us mercilessly for being so socially retarded.

The plan went like this: the girls' shower was outside, on a balcony across the hall. It was a somewhat badly constructed facility, and it regularly leaked, leaving large and very deep puddles in the area. Though Master had forbidden boys to hang around the open entranceway to the shower, I'd noticed that the puddles, when viewed from the proper angle, gave a pretty precise view of what was going on inside.

The older sisters usually took their showers last, after the younger girls had finished their washing up. Skipping our own showers, we quietly made our way to the edge of the balcony, to a place where the light from the shower turned the dark pools of liquid into mirrors.

"No noise," I whispered to Yuen Biao and the other little kids. The water was running in the shower. In just a moment, whoever was inside would step into the spray, putting her girl stuff on display. There was a flash of pink, and we all held our breath—and then released it. The girl was facing the wrong way!

"Aw, c'mon, turn *around*," said Yuen Kwai, jockeying for better position in case she did. I pushed him back into place, but not before he got a quick glimpse of the bather's face.

"Oh, my god, that's *Madame*!" he whispered to us in terror. The littlest brother let out a squeal and bolted, followed quickly by Yuen Biao and our other curious companions, and then, almost as an afterthought, by me and Yuen Kwai.

Unfortunately, Madame heard the noise of us attempting to make ourselves scarce. And screamed.

Just as we reached the doorway, Master burst outside, nearly running us down.

The next day, Yuen Kwai and I went back to practice. Not because our bruises were completely healed, but because it hurt so much to sit down.

After the failure of our little exploration of the gender gap, it was a long time before we dared experiment with the opposite sex again. Although we were surrounded by girls our age, the shared hardships of life at the academy encouraged us to see our different-sex peers as siblings, not as potential mates or sexual partners. And we rarely if ever had any contact with boys and girls from outside the academy. Besides, when all was said and done, we simply didn't have the time or energy to indulge in more than curiosity.

And so, after the burst of excitement that came with the onset of adolescence and the beginning of our performing careers, our teenage years went by in relatively constant fashion, one day rolling into the next. There were meals to be eaten, skills to be practiced, and operas to be performed. Occasionally, the cycle would be broken by some excitement, usually ending in punishment. But even the punishment became routine. And actually, as time went on, and both we students and Master got older, beatings became less frequent—probably because delivering physical discipline to thirty-odd wayward boys and girls was almost a full-time profession in its own right.

Of course, every so often, new students came and others went. But the faces and names were mostly forgettable, and none were close enough friends for me really to miss them. As for me and the other Fortunes, leaving school was something we'd pretty much put out of our minds.

Until Biggest Brother had the accident.

THE TRAGIC FALL

It should probably be clear by now that injuries were not particularly rare at the school. And, as I mentioned before, when they did happen, no one—least of all Master—gave them too much concern. So when Yuen Lung hurt his ankle, Master merely told him to get up and move to the side, away from the training area, as usual.

It was a silly accident, a freak mislanding on a simple handspring. Someone as big and strong as Yuen Lung should have just laughed at it and gone on, and usually when such things happened, he did.

This time he just sat on the floor, his face pale. "Master, I can't," he said, his voice straining. "It . . . it hurts too much."

Master stiffened. "Help him up," he ordered to Yuen Tai and Yuen Kwai.

The two complied, wincing in involuntary sympathy as Biggest Brother sucked in a breath of agony upon being pulled to his feet. They brought him into an unoccupied corner and then resumed their positions in practice.

But several hours later, we noticed Yuen Lung had not moved. Yuen Tai went over to him, concerned, and then called out to Master.

"Biggest Brother is out cold!" he said. Yuen Lung's ankle had swollen to monstrous size, with the edges of his soft-soled training shoe cutting deeply into his flesh.

Recruiting several of us to help him, Yuen Tai moved Yuen Lung onto a cot in the small side room, as Master—for the first time since I'd been at the school—called for a physician.

The doctor came quickly, and his diagnosis was simple: Biggest Brother had broken his ankle. Though it would eventually heal, he'd have to be in the hospital for weeks, and forbidden to walk, much less work out, for months. Master frowned, but the doctor raised a finger.

"He absolutely can't perform for at least two months," said the physician. "If he strains this ankle too much before it's healed, he'll be partly lame for life."

There was no helping it. Master called for a car, and he and Madame took Biggest Brother to the hospital.

"I guess I'm Biggest Brother for now," said Yuen Tai. "Okay, back to practice." But Yuen Tai's heart wasn't in it; he was worried about the boy who'd been his closest friend since he'd arrived at school.

I didn't much like Yuen Lung. In fact, usually I hated him. But this time—well, I understood what was probably going through his head.

The only thing he and I had in common was that we both loved what we did. We loved performing. We loved martial arts. We loved the control we had over our bodies, the ability to jump and roll and dive and balance in ways that shocked and awed normal people. If I'd been told that I had to stop performing for two months, I would probably have gone insane.

He would have hated to hear it, but . . . I felt sorry for Biggest Brother. Sorry and sad.

For the next two weeks, Yuen Lung sulked. He was trapped in bed in the hospital, without anything to do besides look at the ceiling. Like the rest of us, he couldn't read very well, and his room—a dingy multibed ward—didn't have a TV. He was bored. And restless. He couldn't practice and he couldn't even go to the bathroom without help.

Every day, a different group of students was assigned to go visit him; each one was met with a scowl and a nasty tongue-lashing. "I don't want your pity," he'd say, throwing whatever was close by.

The nurses learned to take away his bedpan immediately after it had been used.

When it was finally my turn to pay him a visit, I brought with me a bag of snacks that his grandfather had sent to him.

"Hope you're feeling better, Biggest Brother," I said, trying to keep things light.

He looked at me with an expression of bitter anger.

"I bet you think you're great now," he said. "Big Brother can't walk, Big Brother can't perform. But the prince still lords over everyone."

I set down the bag, looking at Yuen Lung in silence. This was the worst thing that could happen to one of us, so used to days of endless, exhausting activity.

"I'm really sorry, Biggest Brother," I said finally, having nothing else to say.

Yuen Lung reached out for the bag and made a pushing gesture with his hand. "Get the hell out of here."

I turned and left the room.

After a few weeks in the hospital, Biggest Brother was deemed well enough to be taken back to the academy. As soon as he returned, he limped over to the main hall, where he sat in a corner and watched us practice.

Occasionally, when Master left on errands or to meet friends, Yuen Lung would still be given the responsibility of leading us in drills, but without the ability to punish us, the aura of authority and fear that Biggest Brother was once able to project was gone.

Biggest Brother's grandfather continued to send treats for his ailing grandson, and Yuen Lung, mad at the world, refused to share them with anyone. This high-calorie diet of snacks, combined with his complete lack of activity, soon led to him ballooning in size. He was always a stocky lad, but now he was out-and-out fat.

Despite Master's disapproval, Yuen Lung would not stop his frustration-driven consumption. The result was tragic. Even after Biggest Brother's ankle had healed enough for him to return to active duty, Master forbade him to take part in performances.

"You are too fat!" said Master. "How can I put you onstage with the others? You'd better lose that weight!"

And Yuen Lung, shamed by his banishment from the Fortunes, said nothing. But Master's decision ate at him—and this, in turn, only led him to eat more.

Finally, there was just one decision that Biggest Brother could ultimately make. His pride, which was always proportionate in size with his girth, couldn't take going from Big Brother to bit player and backstage hand. Despite his weight gain, his martial arts hadn't diminished, and he was remarkably graceful for a fat guy. He'd already done some work as a movie stuntman—something that we younger kids were looking forward to—and he knew that he'd find a demand for his exemplary fighting skills. He had nothing left to gain from staying at the academy, and everything to lose.

We Fortunes and some of the older students gathered around him as he packed his small bag of personal belongings to leave. Coming to the decision seemed to have lifted the cloud from Yuen Lung's brow; he was nearly back to his old self, joking and snapping at his fellow big brothers, and even making predictions as to the brightness of his future.

"The movies, that's the deal," he said, thumping his thigh. "The age of the opera is over. Look at the crowds you've been getting recently"—already he thought of us, his schoolmates, as "you"—"barely half the theater, and all old guys, too. What happens when they kick the bucket, eh, chums? Got to go where the excitement is, that's where I'll make my fortune."

Now, all of us had done work in movies—not as stuntmen, but as extras and kiddie props. We'd even had some of our opera scenes put on camera, though we'd never seen the results. We tried to reconcile what Yuen Lung was saying with the reality we'd experienced: shoddy sets, minuscule budgets, and lots of bellowing fat men shouting at us to get into position. True, we'd gotten the chance to work with real movies stars like Li Li-hua. And while we were filming movies, we didn't have to do any practice; in fact, most of each shooting day was spent just sitting around. Which wasn't a bad deal. All in all, though, the film industry hardly seemed like a world of glamour.

Then again, what did we know? We were small potatoes; we'd never done stuff as important as stunt work. And we certainly hadn't been *movie stars.*

"Listen, kiddies," said Yuen Lung, lifting his bag onto his shoulder. "When you decide to get out of here, look me up. *I'll* get you into the business, and not the small stuff that Master has you working, either."

He clapped a glum Yuen Tai on the shoulder.

"After all, what's a Big Brother for?" he said.

And with that, he was out the door, and gone.

GROWING UP

One thing Yuen Lung had said was clearly true: the audiences for Chinese opera were dwindling, and though Master said nothing, the school was clearly suffering. Increasingly, Master lent us out as film extras and—as martial arts films became more popular—as stuntmen, because, powered by the resources of the Shaw Brothers movie empire, kung fu cinema was turning into an international phenomenon.

An unintended effect of all of this loaning was that we started to see a whole lot more of the real world than we'd known growing up at the academy. Hanging out with stuntmen, we were thrust into an adult world—one considerably more adult than most, in fact, full of drinking and gambling and fast living. Stuntmen, who risked their lives daily for just a few dollars a scene, were philosophical people. If you might die tomorrow, why not live as much as you can today? Get everything you can out of life, because it's much too short, and never as sweet as you'd like it to be.

Our exposure to these tough, incredible individuals changed us dramatically. It made us realize that we could have lives outside of Master's shadow, and that we should take control of those lives as soon as we could. Besides, we were starting to meet girls. And learning a lot about the difference between "sisters" and girls. *Real* girls.

One day, Yuen Tai, who was now Biggest Brother at the school, called a meeting of the older boys.

"The fact is, *we're* the ones making the money," he said, leaning back against the wall of our meeting spot, a deserted alley behind the academy. Several of the other seniors nodded their heads, but some also looked troubled.

"I think Master's in trouble," said Yuen Biao. "I mean, I've never seen him like this."

"Maybe he's sick. He hasn't hit anyone in *days*," said Yuen Kwai, who then burst out laughing at the absurdity of his statement.

But it was true. Master had grown a lot softer in his discipline recently—almost as if he were losing his heart for it.

"Well, *we're* still the ones who are sticking out our necks," said Yuen Tai. "I think we should be getting a bigger share of our earnings. Not everything, but, you know, more."

"Yeah, we got expenses," said another older brother, looking self-righteous.

I was torn. On the one hand, the HK$5 we got out of every HK$75 we earned was almost insulting; for a younger child, it was a handful of candies, but for an older boy, it was a joke.

On the other hand, it was clear that the school was not what it used to be; no new kids were coming in, and the number of students at the academy was gradually dwindling as the older ones left, one by one.

And though we hated to admit it, it was obvious that Master himself was getting older.

After some further discussion, we came up with a plan: Biggest Brother would ask Master for a meeting, and explain our request. But each of us other brothers, in turn, would speak a sentence, too. This way, as a group, we could say what no single one of us dared. So we practiced our lines and gathered our courage, and then we knocked on the door to Master's room.

Master answered, his face emotionless. "Hello, boys. Come in."

We filed into his room, suddenly unsure of ourselves. Then, Yuen Tai finally screwed up the courage to speak.

"Master, we—we've been talking...." he said, his voice choking. "It's about our wages ... now that we're older, we don't have enough money—"

Master turned away, hiding his face from us. "I understand."

The room was silent for several minutes, as we felt the sickening burden of our request sink onto our shoulders. All of us had forgotten the lines we were supposed to say.

Then Master turned back toward us. "You're grown men now," he said. "You've grown wings. You can fly." There were tears in his eyes.

As of that day, he told us, we would get HK$35 out of the HK$75 we earned for each film.

Grateful, we thanked him and shuffled out of the room. The door closed behind us.

"Thirty-five dollars!" crowed Yuen Tai. "That's almost half! That was a lot easier than I thought."

The others began talking about what they'd do with their newfound riches. But something was troubling me.

I don't know why, but as soon as Master had closed his bedroom door, it felt like a chapter of our lives, and perhaps history, had ended.

MY THIRD GOOD-BYE

My feeling proved to be correct. The era of opera was over. Yuen Lung had pointed out the trend, but with the collapse of Master's authority, I had felt the passing. Opera had transformed from the core of Chinese popular culture into a quaint traditional art, enjoyed only by connoisseurs and old men and women. There was not room for schools like Master Yu's in modern Hong Kong. The training methods the China Drama Academy used were increasingly seen as archaic, even barbaric. And in the fast-paced, future-forward lifestyle that the new Hong Kong was inventing for itself, real numbers-and-words education was becoming a necessary trait for survival.

Our generation of students was the last to be raised within the opera, the last to have nothing but our martial arts and our performance skills between us and the streets. I can't say that I regret the end of that era. I look at young people today and I see what they are able to do today, and I think to myself, if I'd been born twenty years later, that might be me. As it is, I know how to use a camera, how to direct and edit a scene. But as for 3-D animation, digital effects—all the things that make up a Hollywood blockbuster—well, a boy who barely learned his math will grow up into a man who doesn't know how to use computers.

The only way I know how to do it is the way I learned it: for real, with my life and my reputation on the line. I console myself by thinking, one of these days I might learn how to use computer graphics.

But Hollywood directors will never learn how to drop one hundred feet to a concrete floor—and survive.

As students left one by one and the academy faded away, there was no putting off the inevitable. The old performing gigs that Master had been able to rely on—the weddings, the festivals, even the Lai Yuen Amusement Park—were disappearing one by one. Other schools were closing, and professional opera troupes were disbanding; the trained and talented men and women who found themselves cut loose from their art had nowhere else to go but the movies. Me and the remaining older brothers had been working for several years at Shaw Brothers and other studios as junior stuntmen. But the dumping of so many experienced

I'm wearing my favorite American cowboy outfit, with my parents in Hong Kong.

Growing up
on the grounds
of the French
Ambassador's
mansion on
Victoria Peak.

I'm fourth from the right, posing with the rest of the Seven Little Fortunes.

I'm in the second row, far left, with three other members of the Seven Little Fortunes: (from left) Yuen Biao, Yuen Mun, and Yuen Bo, and two unidentified female fans.

Here I am (second row, center) smiling for the camera during my Chinese opera school days.

With four of
my fellow bald-
headed Chinese
opera school
classmates:
(from left) Me,
Yuen Wah, Yuen
Mun, Yuen Tai,
and Yuen Mo.

Dragon in drag!
A young Jackie dons a dress.

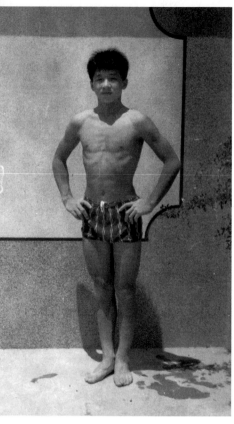

Ready to take the plunge!

Posing with my Big Brother,
actor/director Samo Hung.

I'm with an identically attired Yuen Kwai. Known also as Corey Yuen, he would later become a famous action director.

A cool pose.

Theater owner and philanthropist Sir Tang Siu Kin presenting to me a momento after *Fearless Hyena* broke all-time box office records in Hong Kong.

Here's an early "glamour" magazine shot of me. I look like I should be disco dancing instead of kung fu fighting.

Some of my favorite scenes from one of my first big hits: *Drunken Master*.

With *The Young Master,* my first film for Golden Harvest, I took the things we'd
worked on in *Snake in Eagle's Shadow* and *Drunken Master* to their limit.
After that, it was time for something new: a journey to the West. . . .

My first two attempts at
making it in America were
disasters. I may be smiling
in this photo—taken at a
publicity event for *Battle
Creek Brawl*—but I was
screaming on the inside.

Years later, *The Protector,*
my second try at the big time
Stateside, was no better. It
did give me inspiration for
my greatest action successes,
though—*Police Story* and
its sequels.

Checking out a shot—the "Bun Pyramid Fight" sequence—on the set of *Dragon Lord* with Willie.

Ready for success! This photo was taken around the time of my first attempt to break into the American movie market.

Another shot from *Dragon Lord.*

opera performers into the film industry meant that there was suddenly much more competition for every job. The work had once been steady. Now Master found himself scrambling to keep us employed. And despite all our promise and ability, none of us had yet managed to rise to prominence. It seemed as if the Fortunes, stars in our small and shrinking world, were doomed to fade away completely in the much larger and faster world of the cinema.

As much as I owed Master, I decided that I had to leave the school. I knew I could do better than the miserable jobs that he was getting us. I knew my destiny was to be more than just a crowd extra or an anonymous stunt performer. And if I didn't leave right away, I realized I'd lose any chance of breaking out of the pack—there were so many of us now, all fighting for the same increasingly elusive opportunities.

I didn't waste any words in telling Master. I knew he wouldn't respect anything but the straight and honest truth. Most of my fellow Fortunes, the ones I'd grown up with, had already gone. I'd stuck around out of loyalty to Master, and because I didn't want to abandon Yuen Biao. But he was big now, too. And Master had to face the facts as much as any of the rest of us.

Master took the news of my decision with weary acceptance. He pulled a cigarette from a worn and rumpled pack, lit it, and drew a long drag. "Would you like a cigarette, Yuen Lo?"

I shifted uncomfortably on my feet, shaking my head.

"I remember when you enjoyed my cigarettes very much, very much. . . ." he said, his voice drifting off. "Well, once the mind is set, the body must follow. I wish you well."

I'd spent a decade with this man, this distant and domineering figure, and never received more kindness than a dry smile or a pat on the head. I was telling him I was leaving, perhaps never to see him again, and he was acting like I was only going out for a walk in the courtyard.

I felt no pain, and had no tears at our parting. But still, this stiff ending, this hollow good-bye—it somehow left me feeling a deep and unquenchable sense of loss. I didn't want to stay around any longer. I hoisted my bag onto my shoulder.

"Good-bye, Master," I said, turning to go.

Master stood in the doorway, watching me depart.

"Good-bye, son," he said.

And then the door closed, with only a faint blue curl of cigarette smoke to indicate that Master had ever been there.

THE OLD MASTER

I did see Master Yu again. By that time, our roles had changed: he was aged and feeble; I was a man in the prime of my youth and career. He had moved to the United States with his family. He lived in Los Angeles, and taught martial arts and classical opera at the community center. In Hong Kong, he left behind a daughter, Yu So-chau, who became one of the great actresses of the early Cantonese cinema—famous enough that it was once said that there was no one over the age of twenty-five who didn't know her name, and few who hadn't seen her image on the silver screen.

In 1988, on the occasion of his birthday, he came back to Hong Kong, and all of his students threw him a party. At the party, he was in high spirits, still as active and sharp as he'd been when he'd terrorized us as children.

After he returned to America, however, we didn't hear from him for years. His Alzheimer's disease came on suddenly and he degenerated rapidly.

And on September 8, 1997, old age and the ravages of time finally took him from our world.

But about that party in 1988: gathered together as we all were, it was amazing to see how many of us were in the film world—and how many of us were thriving at the top. These days, if you look carefully, you will find a "Yuen" nearly everywhere in Hong Kong cinema.

And so it could be said that Master Yu wasn't just my godfather, but one of the godfathers of the Cantonese movie industry.

Not a bad legacy, wouldn't you say?

BREAKING IN

And so for the first time in my life, I found myself alone—and free. I was seventeen years old, in the prime of my youth. I was determined to make a life for myself, and a name, and maybe even fame, in the wild, beautiful city of Hong Kong.

But first I had to deal with some loose ends.

You see, when I was thinking of leaving the school, I'd called my parents, to tell them that my ten-year contract with Master was ending soon. My father immediately told me I should join him and my mother down under.

Well, I'd lived under the eyes of adults all my life, and I wasn't going to pass up the chance to finally kick up some dust.

"Kong-sang, you will like it here," said my father, his gruff voice broken by the static of a bad international connection. "I'm sure we will be able to find you a job, and of course you can stay with us until a flat is available."

"I can't hear you, Dad," I said, even though I could hear him quite well.

"Kong-sang?" he shouted. I held the phone away from my ear and winced.

"Dad, I'm not going."

"The line is bad; I thought I heard you say you are not coming."

"I'm not."

"You certainly are," he said, his voice taking on a familiar edge. "Your contract is up, there is no more opera company for you to join, and you are old enough to begin earning a living for yourself. There are many jobs here in Australia, much opportunity."

"I'm working already, Dad," I retorted. "I'm doing movies. I'm a stuntman."

"How much do you think you can make doing movies?" he said.

I realized that I had absolutely no idea. All of my movie fees went directly to Master, and the amount he gave us as our spending money was barely enough for snacks. Could I live on a stuntman's pay? Maybe I *was* crazy.

"There is no way you can survive," said my father, breaking into my thoughts.

Nothing makes me more determined to succeed than someone telling me something's impossible.

"Of course I can, Dad!" I said. "In fact—"

I gulped, because I suddenly knew exactly what would force my father to let me to stay, if that was what I really wanted. And it was. *Right?*

"In fact, the reason I have to stay in Hong Kong is that I've signed a contract with a movie studio. I'll be working for them all the time now. A *contract*," I said.

There was silence on the other end of the line. I mentioned before that my father is from Shandong. Well, the people of Shandong are known for two things: they always face death without fear, and they always live up to their word. A contract, even a verbal agreement, is unbreakable, no matter how unfair it is, or how terrible the price of keeping it. That's why my father had kept me in the school, even though he could have afforded to bring me to Australia years earlier. No matter what happened to me, even if I'd been crippled or worse, I was committed to stay there by the contract he'd signed with Master—and if I'd run away and somehow managed to join them in Australia, well, he might have killed me himself. No son of Shandong could live with such humiliation, and no Shandong father could bear to have such a cowardly son.

So if I'd signed a contract, I was untouchable. I was bound to fulfill its terms.

"How long is the contract for, Kong-sang?" said my father, after a long pause.

I told him the first number that came to mind. "Two years, Dad."

"And where will you live for these two years?"

"I—uh . . ."

He had me there. I couldn't stay at the school, and with most of its students leaving or already gone, the school wouldn't be around much longer anyway. We'd often overheard Master discussing the possibility of leaving Hong Kong, to start over in a place so culturally backward it had barely even been exposed to Chinese opera: Los Angeles, in the United States.

"Kong-sang, it would be shameful for you to dishonor an agreement that you have already made," he said. "But it would be even more shameful for a son of mine to be living on the streets."

I knew it. He was going to demand that I give up Hong Kong and my last chance at freedom.

"I suppose," he continued, "that I have no choice but to buy you an apartment."

"But Dad, if I go to Australia—what?" I reevaluated what he'd just said through the static. "I'm sorry, the line is bad. . . . I thought I just heard you say you were going to buy me an apartment."

"I did," he said.

"You aren't!"

"I certainly am," he said, and I swear I could hear him smiling. "You may consider it a graduation gift."

So on the day when I finally walked out the door of the academy, I had somewhere to go: my own apartment. It was very small, and not in very good shape, but it was mine, and it was home. My *first* home. I'd spent my entire life in other people's houses, and while I lived under their roof I had to obey their rules. But in my tiny seventeenth-floor flat on Xing Pu Jiang, I was the king, and I could stay up as long as I wanted, and sleep as late as I chose.

That apartment cost my father HK$40,000—a huge amount for him to spend at the time. It's the nicest thing he's ever done for me, and something I can never forget.

In fact, I still own the place. I've thought about selling it, but my father told me that the *feng shui* of the place must be very good, since I've had so much luck since then. Maybe he's right, maybe he isn't. I'm not a very sentimental or superstitious person, so even though I never went through with a deal, I had a real estate agent come and look at the flat. She said that if I sold it, I could get more than *HK$3 million.* Which should tell you something about how much Hong Kong has changed over the past three decades.

(It's gotten a lot more expensive, for one thing.)

A CITY VIEW

That first night in my new place was very strange.

I had no furniture, so I lay down on the floor—but I was used to that. The thing I wasn't ready for was the feeling of being alone in the dark. Without the muffled noises of other bodies, the snoring of Biggest Brother, and the creak of the old wooden floor as it moved under our shifting weight, the night seemed terribly empty.

I couldn't sleep. I got up and walked across the room to the window that faced out into the street. The glass was faded with old dust, but I could still see the lights of the city beneath me: blinking neon and the occasional flare of automobile headlights.

I pushed at the window, grunting as I struggled against the layers of rust and old paint that stuck it to its frame. When I finally got it loose, the night came alive with noise. Even as high in the air as I was, I could hear the sounds of Kowloon after dark.

Hong Kong had always been crowded; now it was a permanent mob. It had always been fast, but now it swarmed with constant motion. There was action in the streets, the kind of action young men were told to stay away from if they wanted to grow up into old men—women, drink, drugs, fighting, and gambling, always gambling.

This was the early '70s, when Hong Kong was just beginning to turn into a real economic power, one of Asia's "Little Dragons." The postwar wave of refugees had fueled the growth of the island's industry with their labor, first pouring out their sweat in tiny basement workshops, and then in big factories, making garments and toys and plastics.

Some people had become very rich. But even those who hadn't—from shop owners to businessmen to the hawkers in the streets—believed that, with enough determination and hard work, they could, too.

The city I was named after was growing up, and so was I. We would grow big enough to take on the world together. There wasn't a doubt in my heart.

That night, there in the air above the streets of Kowloon, I made a vow. I was Chan Kong-sang, man of Shandong, son of Hong Kong. I would survive. I would succeed. And all of them—my ancestors, my city, my father—I would someday make them proud.

And with that thought in my mind, I shut the window, curled back up on the floor of my new home, and slept.

So there I was, a teenage dreamer with an empty apartment and no job. As one of the last older kids to leave the school, I'd lost track of many of my brothers who'd "graduated" before me. The word would get out that I was around, and eventually we would connect; the Hong Kong movie world was still small enough that everyone knew everyone. Until then, though, I didn't have much to do but wait. I spent my first few days of freedom building furniture—tables, chairs, shelves—out of stray wood I'd begged from the building manager.

The manager was a kind old gentleman, and he would sometimes ask me down to his apartment for tea, where he would tell me stories about his youth and lecture me in grandfatherly tones.

"Hong Kong is a bad place for a young man now, Kong-sang," he would warn me. "You must try hard to stay away from troublesome people."

To him, "troublesome people" meant everyone from street punks to flower girls to tenants who were slow paying their rent. I suppose if I followed his advice, I'd just stay in my apartment all night, talking to the untroublesome cockroaches.

That wasn't my style.

Besides, I had a reason to go out now—a better one than I'd ever had in my life.

Her name was Oh Chang.

WOMEN, AND OTHER MYSTERIOUS THINGS

O h Chang had come into my life just as I was thinking of leaving the school. In fact, if it hadn't been for her, I might have stayed—stayed until it faded completely away, as it did just months after I set out on my own.

She was my first girlfriend, my first love, and my sweetest memory of those early days on my own.

I mentioned before that it took a while for me to get interested in girls. Well, not just me; all of us boys at the academy were slow to learn that the soft, nice-smelling people known as women were not the same as us—and that that was a *good* thing.

Of course, our sexual curiosity didn't have much of an outlet while we were at school; as I said before, our sisters were our *sisters*, and it just wasn't possible to think of them as girls, really.

But once we became old enough to start working outside of the academy on a regular basis, everything changed. This was Kowloon, after all, and during our travels to the studios where we did stunt work we'd get an eyeful of a totally different kind of woman. They were sleek and groomed, with long, carefully styled hair. They wore lush outfits of embroidered silk, and they had painted faces—but definitely not of the opera variety.

"Willya look at that!" said Yuen Tai as we strolled down the street one night. Yuen Kwai and I were straggling behind him, tired and frustrated from a long day as extras on a martial arts film. Despite all of our training, our inferior junior-stuntman status meant that we were forced into the very worst jobs on the set. We'd do practice stunts that never made it onto film, fetch and carry for the stunt coordinator, and, most humiliating of all, we'd be called upon to play dead bodies, lying on our bellies for hours at a time. By the time we headed back to school, we'd be covered with dust and sweat.

Yuen Tai had stopped walking and was staring in admiration. She was the tallest woman we'd ever seen, as tall as any foreigner, but with jet-black hair falling in soft waves around her exposed shoulders. Her body—well, the girls we'd spent our lives with had their shapes disguised by loose-fitting practice outfits, so Madame was the only female available for comparison . . . and there was *no* comparison.

As we caught up to Yuen Tai, the woman shifted her weight from one long leg to another, causing her body to strain against her painted-on dress.

"Hey, pretty lady," he drawled, putting on his best attempt at cool. The woman slid her eyes over to us, taking in our ragged, dirty outfits and our still-gawky adolescent bodies. Without a sound, she turned on one heel and swayed into the neon-lit entranceway of a nearby club.

"What?" shouted Yuen Tai plaintively. Yuen Kwai and I held each other upright as we nearly collapsed in laughter.

"Guess you ain't her type, Big Brother," I said.

"That kind of girl, she's *anyone*'s type," said Yuen Kwai. "You know, a 'chicken.' "

"What the hell's a 'chicken'?" I said, puzzled.

"A chicken's a woman who does it for money, little boy," he snorted. "Don't think you can afford that kind of dish."

Yuen Tai kicked at the curb and then resumed walking, his face sullen. "Ah, screw you guys," he said. "All this talk about chicken's making me hungry. Let's go home."

And the whole way back to the school we hooted and made clucking noises in his direction, until he threatened to smack some respect into us if we didn't shut up.

Well, as badly as it turned out, Yuen Tai's close encounter with the goddess kept him from sleeping easy that night. Even after he'd called lights out, he kept muttering to himself, nursing his battered ego and cursing the whims of women.

"She was fine, wasn't she, though?" whispered Yuen Kwai to me. "Man, if we weren't stuck in this place, we'd meet women like that all the time, wouldn't we?"

"Yeah, I guess," I said, pulling my covers over my head.

"I mean, if we had money and nice clothes, we could really be big men," he said, yanking my blanket down. "We're almost movie stars, right?"

"I guess it could be fun," I mumbled. "Kissing and stuff."

"Kissing?" Yuen Kwai chortled, grabbing at his crotch. "Yeah, she could kiss this right here, brother!"

Yuen Tai broke off his agonizing long enough to deliver a swift kick to Yuen Kwai's leg. "Why don't you go to sleep, asshole," he said. "Closest you're gonna get to a woman is in your dreams anyway."

"Look who's talking, Big Brother," said Yuen Kwai. *"Here, chickie chickie . . ."*

There was a muffled sound of struggling as Biggest Brother threw his blanket over Yuen Kwai's head and began punching him in the stomach. The rest of us turned onto our sides and slid away from the wrestling pair.

I didn't want to admit to Yuen Kwai that I had no idea what I'd do with a woman like that even if I did meet one. Yuen Tai and Yuen Kwai always played at being big men, groaning and making dirty remarks when they saw fast women in hot outfits. But when I closed my eyes, I envisioned girls like my little friend on the Peak, the ambassador's daughter: sweet, quiet women who liked talking and laughing and listening to my stories. Women who were soft and gentle, like my mother and our big sisters, always caring for me when I got hurt. Women whom I could protect from harm, like the brave swordsmen of my childhood storybooks.

Call me old-fashioned, or a closet romantic, or socially backward, but kids these days, all they think about is sex. I didn't think about that at all.

Well, not often. But what I mostly dreamed about was finding someone who would understand me and care about me and stay with me, the way no one else in my life ever had.

It really didn't seem like *that* much to ask.

The next day, I was chosen by Master to represent the academy at a special exhibition, in which I would demonstrate our school's skills to visiting foreigners. Although all of Chinese opera has the same roots, the country is so big and is made up of so many different kinds of people that it has evolved into different forms—Beijing opera, which is the most traditional form, and which our Master taught; Cantonese opera, which is the form practiced in much of the South; and so on.

Even though it was a big responsibility, I didn't take it too seriously; after all, the foreigners were probably too stupid to know the difference between good and bad opera anyway. So the trip was like a little vacation for me—a chance to slack off, avoid practice, and maybe even spend some of my precious pocket money, if I saw something that looked appetizing.

The bus trip to the hall where the exhibition was being held was long and boring, and I spent the time dozing, and thinking—just a little bit— about girls. I'd just about decided that they weren't worth the trouble when the bus arrived at my destination, and I was forced to scramble to make it out the door before the driver pulled away from the curb.

"Stay awake on the bus, ya stupid kid," the driver shouted as I stumbled onto the pavement. Turning my head to retort, I felt my body thump into something solid and soft, something that let out a gentle squeal as it toppled over. Babbling apologies, I attempted to untangle myself from my unintended victim, and realized that she was a girl, and about my age, and very beautiful.

Not beautiful like the chicken woman. She had soft black hair, pulled back against her head in a simple ponytail; she was wearing a clean but plain cotton outfit, and her body—what I could feel of it, accidentally— was slender and petite. Her eyes were huge and as clear as mirrors, and the expression I saw within them was not frightened, but shyly amused.

"I'm sorry!" I shouted too loudly, as I rolled instantly away. She pushed herself up on her arms and brushed at her clothes.

"That's all right, I'm fine," she said, smiling. "You must be in a hurry. . . ."

I helped her to her feet, my face blushing red. "No, no hurry," I mumbled. "I mean, I'm not going anywhere special."

It was odd. I usually didn't have any trouble talking to anyone, but in front of this strange, wonderful girl, my tongue felt thick, like a lead weight in my mouth. "I'm sorry."

"You said that already," she said, looking at the ground. There were two spots of red on her pale cheeks. "I have to go now. You should walk more carefully, or you could hurt yourself. Or somebody else!"

And she waved, and walked quickly away.

I could only stand there with my mouth open, feeling like I'd never felt before. Like I'd swallowed a gallon of warm, syrupy stuff, as sweet as milk—a kind of pleasant pain that came up from my belly and into my throat. And I was frozen, even though I knew that she was walking away, and if I didn't see her again, I would die.

Somehow I got my muscles going again and threw all other thoughts out of my head—the foreigners and their ignorant curiosity about Chinese opera could go hang, if it meant that I'd be able to catch up with that girl. It would be worth any number of beatings by Master. Even a day without food. A week. A year!

So I chased her, running around the corner, and saw her meeting up with a small group of other girls dressed like her, entering—

Entering the very hall I was due to appear at myself.

I looked down at my wrinkled, dusty clothes, once clean and neatly pressed. If she was going to be in the audience, I would put on the performance of a lifetime, of all my lifetimes. My heart beat strongly in my chest. I walked proudly into the performance hall.

The man in charge of the exhibition was standing at the doorway, dressed in a traditional outfit, and looking anxious. Spotting me, a slightly dirty-looking young boy, he made a move to shoo me away, but I quickly raised my hand.

"I'm here from Master Yu Jim-yuen's China Drama Academy. My name's Yuen Lo—I'm performing today."

He stared at me up and down. "What happened to you?"

I shrugged. "I had an accident."

He grabbed me by the shoulders and hustled me down a side corridor. The foreigners, he told me in a harsh whisper, were already seated and waiting. I was to go on second, and the entire show had been waiting on me to begin. How could I make Master Yu lose face this way, arriving late and in a mess?

I didn't care; my thoughts were focused on that girl, and meeting her again.

Backstage, I saw a number of small groups of young people, stretching out, talking quietly, or arranging their costumes. My own exhibition was going to be mostly acrobatics and forms, so I had no makeup or special outfit to prepare; some of the other groups were going to perform short scenes in full dress, and they stood out in their finery. I stared intently at the other boys and girls, searching to see if the girl was among them. Boys who noticed me staring looked back in challenge; girls looked away shyly, or blushed prettily, but not so prettily as the girl I'd run into outside. She wasn't there. Could I have made a mistake?

And then I heard applause coming from the stage area, and realized that the show had begun. Stepping softly to the edge of the heavy cloth backdrop, I pulled a fold of it aside and peered out at the stage and audience. A group of girls were posed, frozen in a silent pattern, as the orchestra offstage began to play. They turned in time with the music, and began their scene. And from the side, I caught a flash of the lead performer's face.

It was her!

She was one of us—an opera actor—and from the way the Chinese in the audience responded to her, she was a star. Her every move was graceful as she gestured and swept across the stage, beginning a lilting song of love and challenge. I recognized her opera style as coming from the Chieu Chow province—but she could have been singing a pop song and made it sound elegant.

When her song ended and the troupe stood still and quiet on the stage again, I realized that I was barely breathing. I had seen my sisters perform before, but they had always seemed like little girls wearing the clothes and makeup of adults. This girl, who'd looked to be about my age when I'd knocked her down outside, seemed every inch a woman—a *princess*—even with nothing on her face but some powder and her perfect smile.

"Ayah!" someone whispered in my ear. "What are you looking at? It's your turn!"

I jumped back. I'd nearly forgotten! I wasn't here to enjoy, but to perform—and I hoped, I somehow knew, that the girl would be watching me as I'd watched her.

The organizer of the exhibition was finishing his introduction of my school, my master, and the style of opera that I was going to represent. As the audience began its polite applause, I felt a strange sense of power welling up inside me. I was invincible, untouchable. I was the prince of my school, the king of the stage. I would show all of them, especially that girl, what a student of Master Yu Jim-yuen could do.

And to the rolling sound of the drum, I somersaulted onto the stage, flipping up into a perfect handstand, before dropping in mock clumsiness into a drunkard's pose. As an old man, an imaginary wine jug under one arm, I fought invisible enemies, then transformed with a backflip and a shift of my features into Sun Wu Kong, the Monkey King, my body as agile and wild as any ape. I was a general, a scholar, a warrior mad for vengeance. Without a word, without costume or weapon, I became every character I'd ever portrayed on that tiny stage at the Lai Yuen Amusement Park, all in perfect time with the music, with form so ideal that even Master might have nodded and smiled. The music hit its climax, the orchestra began to play its final bar, and with a last swagger of defiance against the world, I performed three quick somersaults in succession and disappeared into the wings.

The hall roared with applause. I pitied the performers who would have to follow me; it was their bad luck that I'd been put so early in the program. No one would remember anything but me that day, especially the foreigners, who had dared to look bored throughout my girl's wonderful singing.

I was already thinking of her as *my* girl! Even though I didn't even know her name. I caught my breath and walked around the corner and into the backstage area. A girl with a ponytail was standing at the edge of the backdrop, peeking through it at the stage.

"Hi," I said softly, tapping her on the shoulder. It was the girl—my girl—and she turned pink when she saw it was me. "Did you see me?"

She nodded. "You were very good," she said, smiling again and giving a little shake of her hair.

"Not as good as you," I said, and meant it.

The organizer, who was helping the next group adjust their costumes, threw a nasty glare in our direction. There was a performance going on out there; making noise backstage was rude and, worse, bad luck.

Holding one finger to my lips, I took the girl's wrist and pulled her after me toward the corridor that led to the front of the hall. Once we got there, I let her go, hoping she wouldn't run. She simply looked at me, with that half-amused, half-shy expression that had charmed me when we'd first met.

"I'm sorry I ran you over before," I said, losing my tongue again.

"I'm sorry I was in your way," she said, smiling. We were silent again, looking at each other.

"Where are you from?" I asked her, hoping for an address, or at least a general area where I could look for her again. She told me that her school was in Kowloon, not far from ours, but that she lived with her parents; her training hadn't been as harsh and isolated as ours. I told her that our academy was in Kowloon too, and was about to ask if I might possibly be able to see her again, when the door to the corridor swung open and a group of laughing young women ran out. It was the girl's company, and they stared and whispered at us as they emerged into the hallway.

"Come on, Madame told us to go back to the school right after the performance!" said one of the older girls in the group, tugging at my new friend's sleeve. "Don't waste your time talking to that boy. We have to catch the bus!"

"He isn't much to look at anyway," whispered another, and I felt my face flushing red. The group, pulling my girl along, gossiped their way down the corridor.

And suddenly, I realized that I *still* didn't know her name!

"Hey!" I said, running after the group, down the hall and out the door. The girls were at the bus stop, and a double-decker was just opening its folding doors to let them in and take them away. "Wait! My name is Yuen Lo! What's yours?"

The other girls pushed my girl into the bus, making faces at me. I was crushed. I was losing her. Maybe forever.

Then I heard her clear voice over the sound of the bus motor. "My name is Oh Chang!" she said, poking her head out of an open window.

"Can I see you again?" I shouted.

She smiled and nodded, and was pulled back inside by her friends.

Oh Chang! Her name was as lovely as she was. I said it to myself again and again as the bus rolled off into the distance.

Then I slapped my forehead in disgust. That was *my* bus, too! And who knew when the next one would come along?

I cursed my own stupidity and set off on the long walk back to the academy, frustrated and alone.

HEART-STRUCK

That was how it began—my first love.

I didn't tell any of the other guys what had happened, in part because it made for a lousy story, but mostly because I was scared that if I did I'd jinx it and she'd disappear like a ghost, never to be found again. And I didn't want to face a bunch of questions that I couldn't answer—like what her last name was, or when I'd see her again.

The next day, Master told me to report to the movie studio where most of the other older students were working, just in case they needed an extra body. I nearly ran out the door, knowing that this was my chance. I took the long bus ride back to the performance hall where I'd met her the day before, and found the organizer who'd brought us all together. Wearing my best innocent expression, I told him that my master wanted to express his compliments to Oh Chang's teacher, and asked him the address to her school. It was so simple! The organizer was glad to assist a man of my master's stature, and even gave me directions on how to get there. On the bus ride back to Kowloon, I planned out everything I'd say to her and thought about where I'd take my dream girl on our first date.

And that's when I started to get nervous. I'd never gone on a date before and had no idea what most people did on their evenings out. What would Oh Chang enjoy? Would she like to go drink tea? Or see a film?

I really didn't know anything about her!

Preoccupied, I nearly missed my stop and once again had to run out of the bus in a panic. I half hoped that somehow fate would intervene, and I'd bump into her on the sidewalk, just like the day before, but life is never that simple.

Her school was just a few blocks from the bus stop, and it was very impressive compared to ours—newer and cleaner, at least from the outside, with a shiny metal gate that had been freshly painted. The girls who learned opera here probably had never slept on a wooden floor in their lives.

My stomach felt hollow. Her friends didn't think much of me. What if she saw me and told me to go away, or worse, laughed at me until I was forced to leave in shame? I turned away from the gate, telling myself that there was still time to go to the studio.

But as I began to walk back toward the bus, I heard a voice in my head that sounded as stern and disapproving as my father. Was that all I was good for—lying on the ground and playing dead? And then the voice became a chorus: my father, my master, all of Shandong, shouting together that I was a weak excuse for a man, afraid to stand up to the laughter of small girls, too afraid even to reach out for the most important thing in my life.

I didn't care if she laughed at me! There was more shame in running away than in trying and failing. And, my heart beating as strongly as any of my brave ancestors', I walked back to the gate and swung it open, and stepped into the courtyard beyond.

The stones paving the courtyard were even and neatly kept, without any weeds or cracks in sight. The door was as bright as the gate had been, with the characters that made up the name of the school neatly carved into the sill above it and painted in gold. I straightened my clothes and knocked—once, twice—and waited, my mind a complete blank.

The door opened, revealing the face of an old woman with deep lines around her eyes. "Yes?" she asked. "What can I do for you?"

"I'm sorry, Madame, but I have a message for one of your students." I stiffened my back and tried to look official.

The woman blinked. "I'm not a teacher here; I'm the housekeeper," she said. "Madame is out on appointment; which student do you need to see?"

I swallowed. "The girl's name is Oh Chang."

The gray head looked at me with faint suspicion. "Miss Oh Chang is rehearsing right now."

"The message is a short one," I said, fighting back a wave of nausea.

"If you give it to me, I can pass it on," she said.

"Ma'am, I was told to give it to her in person," I said. My resolve was about to crumble; I wanted to run away. Let the voices in my head argue with this old bag if they thought it was so important.

The housekeeper sighed, and motioned with her hand. "Wait right here; I'll find her," she said. "But you really will have to be quick."

Success! I'd gotten past the first test—like Monkey from the old stories, tricking the guardian at the gate to heaven. After a few moments, the door opened again, and I faced her—Oh Chang—again, her mouth and eyes as round as Os in surprise at my unexpected appearance.

She had apparently been in the middle of a full dress rehearsal, because her delicate features were powdered white, with streaks of rose above her eyes. Her hair was pulled back with sparkling combs, and the plain outfit of yesterday's exhibition had been replaced with a flowing gown with long sleeves, cut from a richly embroidered fabric.

"Hello," I managed to choke out. "You look different. . . ."

Even as I said the words, I cursed myself as a fool. All of the things I imagined saying had sprung out of my head when I'd finally found myself facing her again. If I was lucky, maybe she wouldn't call the police.

"I'm sorry," she said, covering her cheeks with her hands. "I was rehearsing—we have a tour coming up, a trip to Thailand, and we have a lot of new things to practice."

"Don't be sorry; you look wonderful," I said. What was I saying?!

She laughed in her shy way. "Did you really have a message for me?" she asked. "The housekeeper will be coming back soon. . . ."

"The message is," I said, and stopped. I summoned up all of the determination I could, hearing the distant encouragement of the voices. "The message is that you have an appointment later."

"And who is that appointment with?"

"With me," I said cockily.

She laughed again, in spite of herself. "What time is this appointment?"

"What time are you free?"

Oh Chang leaned against the door, furrowing her brow. "I go home at ten o'clock," she said. "But usually I just go straight to sleep."

"Sneak out," I said. "I'll wait for you."

"You don't even know where to wait!" she said.

"I will if you tell me," I responded, flashing my best smile.

And she did.

And then she closed the door, after giving me one last smile and wave.

Monkey had entered the gates of heaven, and the voices in my head were cheering victory.

I spent the rest of the afternoon walking around Kowloon, just waiting until night. I managed to kill time walking in slow circles around the neighborhood, watching the crowd and eating snacks. I thought about going to the studio, but they wouldn't take me on for a half day, and besides, I wanted everything to be perfect for my big date that night—no dirt, no sweat, no bruises or sprains. And then, as I ate my third sweet bean bun, a stray thought began nagging at me. As far as Master knew, I was at the studio all day, doing the same boring stuff my brothers were doing. But tomorrow morning, he'd line us up after breakfast as usual and ask us for the pay we received the day before.

With horror, I imagined the scene in my head. "Where is your money, Yuen Lo?" he'd ask, as I stood there empty-handed. "Did you lose it? Or spend it foolishly?"

What excuses could I have? He'd give me seventy-five smacks with his cane, one for every dollar I was missing—and even though he'd gotten grayer and stiffer, he hadn't lost any of his strength.

There was no help for it. I walked to the bank where my father had opened an account for me, and asked the teller to withdraw HK$75.

I'd give Master the money, and he'd never know the difference. But, I thought to myself, girls were turning out to be an expensive habit.

At exactly ten o'clock, I found myself standing outside of the gate to Oh Chang's house, on a very nice block in one of the wealthier parts of Kowloon. The lights were out, and the windows shuttered closed. For a split second, I thought that I'd been tricked, that she was upstairs in her bed dreaming about what an idiot I was. And then the gate swung open, and her lovely face peeked out into the street.

"Hello," I said, putting one hand on the gate in what I hoped was an appropriately casual pose.

"You came," she said, smiling. "I wasn't sure you'd be here."

"Where else would I be?" I said, smiling back. "Come on."

She stepped out into the street, and I thought I'd never seen anything so pretty in my life as Oh Chang at that moment, wearing a simple cotton dress, her hair down and falling around her shoulders, lit only by the pale glow of the moon.

We walked side by side down the street in silence. Then Oh Chang asked me about my school, and it was like a dam had broken open inside me. I told her about the aches and pains of practice, and knew she was listening, and that she understood. I told her about Master's hard discipline, the beatings and punishments, and she sighed in sympathy. I told her jokes and riddles and funny stories about my adventures with my brothers, and she laughed, and I felt like I could watch her laughing like that forever.

We walked and walked, until finally we found ourselves on the edge of Kowloon Park. Sitting there on a wooden bench, the moon high in the sky and a light breeze rustling the leaves of the trees around us, I somehow found the courage to take her hand, and she didn't pull away. I still remember how small and warm her hand was, how soft and graceful it was, so different from my rough, callused fists. It was like our hands were from two different worlds: hers were the hands of the wealthy, soft and delicate, and mine were practical, purposeful. They were tools—or weapons.

We sat there together for hours. Talking a little bit. Mostly just looking at the moon and each other. Then she said, "Yuen Lo, I have to go. It's almost midnight," and the spell was broken. I didn't argue; it was already much more than I could have hoped for, a poor, ragged guy like me and a rich, pretty girl like her. I pulled her up off the seat and we began the walk back to her home.

"It was nice to see you," she said, as we approached her block. I nodded, squeezing her hand.

We stood in front of her gate, the night at its darkest hour, and I wondered if I should kiss her. Somehow, it didn't seem right—like if I did, it would break some secret, unspoken rule, and she'd disappear forever—

and so I just watched in silence as she waved good-bye and crossed into her courtyard.

And then she peeked her head out again, knowing I hadn't yet turned to leave. "Will you come visit me again, Yuen Lo?" she asked, her cheeks pink and her eyes looking modestly away.

She liked me! I broke out in a wide grin, my heart leaping. "How could you keep me away?" I said, and before she could answer, I blew her a kiss and ran into the night, hearing her giggles trail off behind me in the warm, humid air.

From that point on, I went to visit her nearly every day of the week, ditching work, inventing excuses, and drawing dollar after dollar from my dwindling bank account to give to Master. Every day I saw her cost me U.S.$10, which was a big amount—you could eat for a week on that—but what did I care? That money was buying me love.

Of course, I had to tell my brothers that I had a girlfriend, so that they would cover for me if Master got suspicious. After all, *they* knew I wasn't going to the studio to work. But, if I wanted to waste my money that way, who were they to criticize? The only bad part was hearing the awful jokes they'd make about Oh Chang and what we were probably doing, out in the park alone every night. It wasn't like that, but they'd never understand. I let them have their fun . . . and resolved never to let them meet her, if I could possibly help it.

Then, about six months after I started seeing her, Master told me he was sending me on another exhibition. This one wouldn't take place in Hong Kong at all—it would be in Southeast Asia, in Singapore, thousands of miles away. I broke the news to Oh Chang, expecting her to be sad, but she just laughed.

"Don't be silly; it's only a few weeks," she said. "Besides, don't you remember? I'll be on tour in Thailand at the same time—we'll be practically next door to each other."

So, after half a year of being together, we would be apart for the very first time. I made her promise not to forget me, and she made me promise the same. I knew in my heart that promises like that weren't necessary for me; it didn't matter how long or how far away she was, she would always be in my dreams.

HEARTSICK

On the trip to Singapore, I felt lonely for the first time in a long while. Living in the crowded school, I was hardly ever on my own, so going on trips by myself was actually sort of a luxury. Now that I had Oh Chang, and now that we were apart, every moment felt empty. There was always something missing.

And so there I was, far away from my home, counting down the days. The hosts of the exhibition had put me up in a house, a much nicer place than the school, with a real bed and even an indoor bathroom. Other than at meals, they pretty much ignored me, and left me to wander the city on my own. I worked out during the daytime, hoping that good honest sweat would help me forget about Oh Chang, just for a little while; at night I explored the City of Lions.

I thought I could make it through the two weeks away without going crazy, and I almost did. The night right before I left Singapore, I went walking by myself as usual, staring at buildings and people, listening to the shouts of street hawkers selling unusual treats in an unfamiliar tongue. It was my last chance to see the city, and so I walked farther than I'd gone in all the nights before, until I found myself in a deserted street, miles away from my host home. In my eagerness to get away from my own thoughts, I'd forgotten about the time. It would take me hours to get back, and I'd be lucky to make it before dawn.

That's when the rain began—not a gentle spray, but a sudden, tearing downpour that quickly built into a full-scale monsoon. Sheets of water fell from the sky, and the wind whipped at cloth canopies and brightly painted signs. I ran through the storm, my head down, instantly soaked, knowing that I'd never make it back on foot. Then I saw an old, rusting bicycle, abandoned on a street corner by its owner, and straddled it in the half-shelter of a doorway. The wind would make riding difficult, but I'd get back faster than walking. I pushed it out into the street and began to pump with all my might, headfirst into the gale, standing on the pedals and leaning forward on downhill strokes.

I wanted to be with Oh Chang forever. I'd give away ten years of my life if I could spend what was left with her. I'd give up anything. In my frenzied brain, it seemed to me that somehow, if I rode out this storm, if I made it home in one piece, my wish would come true. I pedaled harder, like I was racing against my own bad luck. And then in the white brightness of a lightning flash, I saw a figure in a balcony above my head, and somehow I knew it was her, that I'd won the race, that she was mine forever. I threw the old bicycle aside, splashed through the dirty water of the street, and leaped up to grab the side of the balcony, clambering up and over despite the slickness of the wet ironwork.

It was a woman's wet blouse, left twisting and forgotten on a drying pole, that I'd mistaken for her—for my Oh Chang. I laughed to myself; it was a sign of how stupid I was. How could she be here, in Singapore? Why would she be standing out in the rain? She was hundreds of miles away, being showered with praise and the attention of rich admirers.

Stupid me! She was sweet and beautiful, she lived in a nice house, and she was one of the most famous actresses in the Chieu Chow opera circle. And me, I was a poor dumb stuntman, a big-nosed, ugly kid with no future.

Huddling under the pitiful shelter of the balcony canopy, I put my head down on my knees and dropped off to sleep. The wetness on my cheeks could have been rain, or something else.

I apologize: I didn't intend to go so far off course, but Oh Chang was probably the most wonderful thing to happen to me up to that point, and just thinking about her still makes me a little happy and a little sad. Many years later, Oh Chang retired from singing in the Beijing Opera and opened a small boutique in Hong Kong. Every so often, I would send one of my assistants over to check on the store, to make sure things were going okay, and to buy expensive items of clothing, which we would later donate to charity. I didn't want her to know that I was keeping an eye on her—she would never have let me support her like that, even as a friend, so everything had to be done in complete secrecy.

Recently, she decided to move from Hong Kong, and announced to her customers that she was closing the store. I gave all of my female staff members money and told them to go over to the boutique, and they ended up buying everything that Oh Chang had! Oh Chang was happy that she had so many loyal customers—and my staff members were happy to get some nice things for free.

You know, she never got married, and didn't even have a boyfriend.

It makes me wonder sometimes.

But I've said it before: history is history, the past is the past, and that's where it belongs, in our happy memories. I'm sure she'd agree with me. That's the kind of person she is.

HEARTBROKEN

Once I'd settled into my new apartment, my furniture built—it wasn't very pretty, but it suited my needs—my life in the real world could really begin. Without Master on my back all day and my brothers and sisters at my side all night, I had twenty-four hours each day to play with. After waking up in the morning at the luxurious hour of eight o'clock, I'd go buy some buns and eat them on the bus to the movie studio, where I'd stand around with the other junior stuntmen, waiting to be called out for work. Some of them were my brothers, and we'd sit around on the set in the shade, telling jokes, bragging, and watching the actors and senior stuntmen. Usually we weren't impressed with what we saw. Even today, making movies can be a pretty tedious job—if you're at the bottom of the food chain. Most of it is waiting around while other people argue and shout, trying to doze and look alert at the same time. It's a tough skill to master, but we had plenty of practice while we were at the school, and it served us well.

You never wanted to look like you were too bored, because then someone would grab you and make you carry things around, even if you weren't working that day. Then again, you didn't want to look like you were too interested, because we were young, and even back then, you had to act like you didn't give a damn about anything if you wanted to be cool.

Hong Kong's biggest studio at the time was owned by the Shaw Brothers, Run Run and Runme Shaw—two of Hong Kong's first tycoons. It was called Movie Town, and it was huge, over forty acres in size, with hundreds of buildings ranging in size from prop sheds to giant soundstages and dormitories for actors who were working on contract for Shaw Brothers. It even had a mock-up of an entire Ch'ing dynasty village, which served as the set for most of the Shaws' movies—since most of the films they were making at the time were period martial arts epics and swordsman films. That's why stuntmen (even "stunt boys" like us) were in such big demand: we were the unknown grunts who made all of the slashing, smashing, diving, jumping, punching, kicking, flying magic possible.

The studio wouldn't risk its big names doing things that might hurt them, not because they cared what happened to them (most contract actors got just a HK$200-a-month stipend and HK$700 per film), but because an injury might stop or slow down production—and Shaw Brothers churned out dozens and dozens of movies a year.

We, on the other hand, worked cheap, and we did everything, no matter how dirty or dangerous, and if they didn't need us on a given day, they just ignored us. At least they gave us lunch, though the food was even worse than the meals at school, if you can imagine that—just rice and vegetables or soup dumped out of big pots.

I mentioned before that most of the time, junior boys like me did the very worst jobs: we played corpses, or were extras in crowd scenes, wearing the oldest, smelliest costumes and standing in the back. But no matter how rotten the jobs were, they put us right in the middle of the action. We watched the seniors, and learned, and thought to ourselves how much better we'd be when *we* finally joined their ranks.

The day wouldn't be over until late at night. When a movie has to be finished in less than a month, you aren't stopped by a silly thing like the sun going down. Even though it didn't match the look of daylight, they'd bring out huge electric lamps and keep us shooting, knowing that we'd cost the same—one day's pay—whether they wrapped at suppertime or at midnight.

Usually I managed to leave the studio in time to get back to Kowloon by ten o'clock (Movie Town was in Clear Water Bay, on the Hong Kong side). By that time I'd be starving, so I'd grab some noodles or rice from a roadside vendor and eat it on the way to Oh Chang's house. It's funny: my father's a cook, one of the best I've ever seen, but in all the time I lived on my own in Kowloon, I never made a real meal for myself. It was always the same street food, cheap, quick, and hot, day after day—but back then, that was what I loved. I'm still a simple eater today. I'll take a rice bowl with some roast pork over a fancy gourmet meal anytime.

And then, like clockwork, Oh Chang would peek her head out from the gateway to her house, and wave, and walk with me on the long, slow walk to Kowloon Park, to our bench, our moon, and our two hours together. Each day I'd carefully remember all of the strange things that happened on the set—a director got so angry at an actor that he fell out of his chair! One of the senior stuntmen fell off a roof the wrong way and landed in a horse cart, and the cart broke and wheels rolled everywhere!—just so I'd have something new and interesting to tell her. Hoping that I'd be funny enough that she'd want to see me the next night, because I didn't know what I'd do if I showed up and saw the gate closed and locked . . .

It was a few months after we'd returned from our trips to Southeast Asia when my worst fears finally came true.

I was a little late getting to Oh Chang's, delayed because the director had gotten into a screaming match with the stunt coordinator over how a certain scene should be choreographed. I was just window dressing in the shot—a bystander in the crowd watching the fight—but the stupid director wouldn't let any of us leave until he got his way, even though he knew that the coordinator should have say over all stunt sequences. That was stupid: you never wanted to alienate a good stunt coordinator, and the whole thing had made the coordinator lose face before his stuntmen. The director would be lucky if the rest of his film had a single battle worth watching. If I were the coordinator, I'd have walked off the set on the spot.

But as a junior nobody, I couldn't walk away—not if I wanted to come back the next day. So I ran, breathless and sweaty, all the way from the bus stop, not even pausing to eat.

She was still there! My heart jumped up, since I'd half expected her to have gone inside and back to sleep. And then I noticed that her expression wasn't the sweet and happy one I was used to, and that I loved so much. Her face was pale, and her eyes red. What had happened?

"Oh Chang, what's wrong?" I said, swallowing hard.

She shook her head.

"I'm sorry I'm late, Oh Chang; it was the director—" She turned away from me, and the story I was ready to tell her, about the stupid director and his fight with the stunt coordinator, faded away unspoken. I was crushed. I knew in my heart that something was wrong, and that it didn't have anything to do with my being late.

"Yuen Lo ..." she said softly, a catch in her voice. "I can't see you anymore."

And then she walked inside and closed the gate behind her.

I stared at the gate, a metal wall cutting me off from my happiness, and then began to run.

I wanted to scream, and if I screamed, I wanted to be as far away as possible.

I spent that night slumped in a corner in my apartment, just staring at the walls, the lights out and the shutters closed. In the pitch black of my room, I could almost imagine that I was surrounded by people, by my brothers and sisters, sound asleep and as quiet as the grave. It was better than realizing that I was alone.

I called her the next day, begging the building manager to use his phone.

The phone rang for what seemed like hours, before a stern male voice answered.

"Hello?" it said, without an ounce of kindness.

"Hello, sir," I said, finding my tongue after a moment's hesitation. "I'm—I'm looking for Oh Chang."

The voice was silent. "Oh Chang is not home," it said, and the line went dead.

I stood there with the receiver in my hand, horrified and shaken. Obviously, her father—the voice couldn't have been anyone else's—knew she was dating me. And just as clearly, he didn't approve.

I had to talk to her. I had to find out what she thought for herself—about me, about us, about any kind of future we might have together.

It was then that the building manager's granddaughter came calling to visit, a bright young girl who was very kind to her elderly grandfather. It didn't take much convincing to get her to make a phone call for me; she could tell I was hurting, and her romantic schoolgirl's heart had mercy on me.

She dialed the number and spoke in her soft girl's voice, and all of a sudden, Oh Chang was home and available to talk. With a wink, the girl handed me the phone.

"Good luck," she whispered, and ran to join her grandfather outside.

I put the receiver to my ear.

"Who's this?" I heard, and the voice was sad, sweet, and familiar.

"Oh Chang, it's me, Yuen Lo," I said.

She said nothing.

"You have to tell me what's going on," I pleaded. "How can you just walk away? How can you end things this way?"

The line stayed silent.

"Oh Chang . . ." I said. "At least—see me one more time. Tonight. One last time."

I could hear her holding back a sob. "Okay," she whispered. "Tonight."

And without saying good-bye, she hung up the phone.

The rest of the day passed in agony. I attempted to fix one of my handmade pieces of furniture, a chair whose legs were uneven, and ended up smashing it to pieces instead, releasing the anger that I'd bottled up inside. Not at Oh Chang, whom I could never hate even if she spat in my face. Not even at her father, who was just doing his duty as a Chinese dad, protecting his girl from bad decisions.

I was angry at the world, which made rich people and poor ones, and kept them apart. I was angry, maybe, at myself, for being who I was.

I had never really wanted to be rich before, or even famous; suddenly, I wanted to be both. I could imagine the conversation in my head, Oh Chang in tears, caught sneaking back into the house after midnight by her father. He accuses her of being a loose woman, of acting like a "flower girl"; she denies it, telling him that it was just one boy she ran out to see, and that we did nothing but talk, sit together, and hold hands. He asks, his voice harsh and his face wooden, the name and background of this boy, the boy who has stolen away his daughter. She tells him who I am, what I do, how hard I work, how promising I am. *A junior stuntman!* he shouts. Just a ragged boy trying to learn a dangerous trade. How could he provide for a family? How could he compare to the wealthy young admirers who came to Oh Chang's performances, left bouquets of flowers and rich gifts at her doorstep, and constantly, always, asked for her hand?

The answers to these questions were obvious, but still I had to hear them from her lips. And so, at the usual time, I waited in the usual place. The sky was gray and overcast, and the moon—our moon—was hidden behind an ugly yellow haze. At ten o'clock, the gate opened, and she stepped out onto the street, looking at me with eyes reddened from crying. Without speaking, she stepped forward and put her thin arms around me, squeezing me tight, wetting my cheek and shoulder with her tears.

I held her a moment, then pulled away, taking her hand and walking with her to the park, to our bench and our view of the sky.

"Why?" I asked her, knowing what she would say.

"My father," she said, and my suspicions were confirmed. And then: "I have . . . I have a letter for you." And she pulled a folded piece of delicate paper from under her coat, still warm from her body and smelling faintly of her sweet perfume.

I took it from her and opened it up. The characters, neatly drawn in her feminine hand, were like so much chicken scratch to me; my reading ability—reading was not seen as an important skill at our school—allowed me to understand street signs and restaurant menus, but not the words of an educated girl's good-bye letter. And I, I who hadn't cried since my first month at the opera academy, who had stood up to beatings and backbreaking workouts and the abuse of boys twice my size without shedding a tear, I began to howl, my body shaking with the force of my crying.

This is the last way I wanted her to see me, but there was nothing I could do. To be given this letter and know that it, like her, was closed to me, was the final blow.

"Yuen Lo . . ." she said, her voice breaking. "I'm sorry."

I swiped my face with my shirtsleeve, willing myself to stop crying. To breathe and relax. "I understand, Oh Chang," I said. I turned my face to stone. "We are from two different worlds, and I don't belong in yours any more than you could survive in mine."

I helped her up and began walking back toward her house. She trailed me, as if reluctant to leave, but I had to get away, as soon as possible, before my will broke down and I begged her to stay with me.

Pulling her close, I bit down on my lower lip, finding the strength to push her away. "Good-bye," I said.

She nodded, tears streaming down her face. "Good-bye," she said. "Will I ever see you again?"

Stuffing my hands in my pockets, I turned away and began to walk. "No," I said, my voice flat. "Not like this."

Not the way I am today, I thought to myself, as I turned the corner and began to run. When you see me again—if you see me again—it will not be as Yuen Lo, the poor stunt boy.

I hated Yuen Lo. I had nothing but contempt for him—lazy, good-for-nothing, loser Yuen Lo. He would have to die, I realized. For me to be what I wanted to be, I would have to kill Yuen Lo.

And become someone else.

A DIRTY JOB

In my short career in the movies, I'd already met a lot of famous actors and directors. I was never very impressed; they were pretty, or handsome, or (in the case of the directors) loud and domineering. But none of them could do what I could do: fight, and fly, and fall, and get up and do it again—even if I was broken or hurt. I couldn't really understand what made them so great.

But the senior stuntmen were something else. They were a wild and rugged bunch, living one minute at a time because they knew that every day they spent in their profession could be their last. They smoked, drank, and gambled, spending every penny of each evening's pay by the time the sun rose the next day. Words didn't mean anything to them; if you wanted to make a statement, you did it with your body—jumping higher, tumbling faster, falling farther. With Oh Chang out of my life, I began to hang out with the senior guys after shooting wrapped. Every night, we'd brush off the dust of the day's work and find ways of laughing at the injuries that we or our brothers had suffered—"we get paid in scars and bruises," one older stuntman told me, only half joking. Of course, every small injury was just a reminder that the next one around the corner could be the big one that might cripple or kill; and so we drank, and we smoked, and we played, partly to celebrate surviving one more day, partly to forget that when the sun rose again we'd be facing the same giant risks for the same small rewards.

The senior stuntmen had a phrase that described their philosophy, as well as the men who were fearless and crazy enough to follow it: *lung fu mo shi*. It literally meant "dragon tiger"—power on top of power, strength on top of strength, bravery on top of bravery. If you were *lung fu mo shi*, you laughed at life, before swallowing it whole. One way of being *lung fu mo shi* was to do an amazing stunt, earning shouts and applause from the sidelines. An even better way was to try an amazing stunt, fail, and get up smiling, ready to try it again. *"Wah! Lung fu mo shi!"* they'd shout, and you'd know that your drinks would be paid for all night.

For us, especially us junior guys, to be *lung fu mo shi* was the highest compliment we could imagine. And so I threw myself into my work, putting every last bit of energy into proving that I had the spirit of dragons and tigers—impressing stunt coordinators with my willingness to do anything, no matter how boring or how crazy. I'd get to the studio early, and leave with the very last group. I'd volunteer to test difficult stunts for free, to prove that they could be done—and sometimes they could, sometimes they couldn't. I never let anyone see me scream or cry, waiting until I got back home to release all of my pent-up pain. My neighbors would pound on the walls in annoyance as I howled in my apartment alone early in the morning; they never bothered me in person, because they probably thought I was a dangerous lunatic.

One day, we were working on a scene in which the hero of the film was to tumble over a balcony railing backward, spin in midair, and land on his feet, alert and ready to fight. The actor playing the hero was, of course, sitting in the shade, flirting with one of the supporting actresses and drinking tea. It was our job to take the fall.

Most falls of this type were done with the assistance of a thin steel wire, attached to a cloth harness that went underneath the stuntman's clothing. The wire would be run through a pulley tied to a solid anchor—in this case, the railing of the balcony—then fastened to a stout rope, which two or three stuntmen not in the scene would hold on to, their feet planted firmly. This would prevent disaster in case the fall went wrong, allowing them to yank on the wire and stop an out-of-control plummet to the ground.

Today, we were working with a director whom we stuntmen universally considered an idiot. He was a no-talent hack—which didn't make him any worse than a lot of the directors working at the time; the problem was that he was a no-talent hack with pretensions toward art.

We'd learned pretty quickly that that was a combination that could get stuntmen killed.

"No wires," shouted the director, his puffy, bearded face turning red. The stunt coordinator, a lean, hollow-cheeked man in his mid-forties, crossed his arms in quiet defiance. My fellow juniors and I thought the coordinator was just about the coolest guy in the world, partly because he never treated us like kids, and partly because he'd stood up time and time again to directors with unrealistic expectations. The night after one epic argument, he treated us to drinks all night at our usual bar.

"Even if I wanted to direct, they would never let me, because I have made too many enemies," he confided to us. "But I will give you a word of advice, in case any of you should find yourself in the big chair. If you want the respect of your stunt people, and that is the only way you will make good movies, never ask them to do a stunt that you can't or won't do yourself. If you learn nothing else from me, remember this rule." And then he shouted, *"Kam pai,"* which means, "Empty cup," and so of course, we did.

I still follow that rule today.

I know that some people call me a crazy director, saying I demand the impossible—but I know they're wrong, because every risk I ask my stunt-men to take is one that I've taken before. Somehow, it didn't kill me, and so they understand that—with the luck that stuntmen depend on to survive—it won't kill them.

The director we were working with that day was so fat he could barely walk, much less do stunts. He had no idea how dangerous a fifteen-foot fall could be, even for a trained professional.

"Do you realize that one of my men could be killed doing this stunt?" asked our coordinator, showing remarkable restraint.

"That's what they're paid for," retorted the director. "If you use wires in this scene, the fall will look like a puppet dropping to the ground. Unacceptable!"

The director even refused to lay out a padded mat or a stack of cardboard boxes to cushion the fall, wanting to shoot the scene from a wide angle in a single cut.

"Ridiculous," said our coordinator. "You want this stunt done that way, you do it yourself. None of my men will volunteer to take that kind of risk."

Throughout this dialogue, I was considering the setup for the stunt. The main problem with the fall was that it took place backward. You couldn't see where you would land, or figure out how far you were from the ground. But it was all a matter of timing—counting out the moments in your head before twisting your body to avoid a messy impact.

I could do this stunt, I decided. I could, and I would.

"Excuse me," I blurted. "I'd like to try the fall."

The stunt coordinator looked at me with a stony expression, then pulled me aside.

"Are you trying to make me look foolish?" he said angrily.

"No," I said, sticking out my chin. "You're right. The director is an idiot. You don't want to risk any of your experienced people on this stunt, because you need them. But I'm nobody, and if I don't do something like this, I'll always be nobody. If I fail, then the director knows you were right. If I succeed, I'll say that it was because you told me exactly what to do—and he'll know better than to challenge you again."

The stunt coordinator looked at me with narrowed eyes. "Yuen Lo," he said, "you're a clever boy. Don't make the mistake of trying to be too clever for your own good."

Then he turned back to the director and threw up his hands. "All right," he said. "There's actually someone stupid enough to try this stunt your way. I've just done my best to tell him how to do it without killing himself. Maybe if he's lucky, he'll just be crippled for life."

And then he walked up to the director until his face was just inches away, close enough to feel the heat of his breath. "And you," he said, his voice flat and dangerous. "You cross me up again, and all of us walk off this set. I don't give a damn about your reputation, your big ideas, or your ego. We risk our lives because we are stuntmen, and that is what we do. Not because you piss in our direction."

The director turned purple, and then pale. Not a single stuntman moved or made a noise. Finally, he nodded, and waved his flabby hand at the cameraman.

I felt the coordinator's touch on my shoulder. "Good luck," he said. "Keep your body loose, be ready to roll as soon as you hit the ground. And whatever you do, don't land on your head or back. I don't mind taking you to the hospital, but I don't want to take you to the cemetery."

And then I was pulling on my costume, while a makeup girl dabbed rouge on my cheeks and streaks of fake blood across my brow. I climbed the stairs to the balcony and looked down at the crowd below. Every eye was on me, and the camera was ready to roll. But at that moment, the only eyes I cared about were the eyes of my fellow stuntmen, watching me do something foolish and fantastic.

Lung fu mo shi, I thought. It was time to prove myself. The actor playing the villain who would knock me over the railing joined me, staring at me and shaking his head in disbelief. I shrugged and smiled at him, then raised my hand to show I was ready.

"Action!" shouted the director.

"Rolling!" answered the cameraman.

And then, as the fake kick from the villain nearly brushed my nose, I vaulted backward over the railing, counted quickly in my head, and arched my back, twisting my body smoothly through the air. I saw a flash of ground as my head came up and I got my legs underneath me, just in time to catch the ground with my feet. I stumbled a bit, giving a small stutter step as I pulled myself upright.

Success! The director cut the camera and actually pulled himself up and out of his chair. The stunt coordinator trotted over to where I was standing, as my brothers shouted my name. He slapped me on the back, grinning broadly. "You'll be a stuntman yet," he said.

Maybe it was cocky, but cocky was what being a stuntman was all about. "I almost lost my footing on the landing," I said. "Let me try it again—I'll get it perfect this time."

He laughed, squeezing my arms until they ached. "Try it again?" he bellowed. "Did you hear that, men? Once is not enough for the boy. *Lung fu mo shi!*"

And my stunt brothers echoed the phrase: *"Lung fu mo shi!"*

That night, the stuntmen gave me a new nickname: Double Boy. "Once ain't enough for Double! Better try again!" they laughed.

"He wants to work twice as hard, he has to drink twice as much, right?" said the stunt coordinator. "One more round, Double. *Kam pai!*"

That night, for the first time since I left the school, and the first time since I'd lost Oh Chang, I felt like I'd found a place where I belonged. I was with family.

I was home.

THE STUNTMAN

O nce I'd proven myself, I started getting real jobs and making real money, and I was accepted as a full stuntman by my stunt brothers. Not that there was anything official about my new high-class status. Even though we acted like a team, there was no real organization, not the way there was at school. We weren't permanently hired at any studio. As long as work was available somewhere, that's where we'd plant our feet. There was no system of ranking—except that if you were good, everyone knew it, and treated you with the respect you deserved, whatever your age or background.

We were brothers, but we were brothers of convenience—close as blood so long as we were all working on a shoot, ready to fight until we dropped for one another's honor when the occasional bar brawl happened. If you were a stuntman, only another stuntman could really understand you, and so we were companions on the set and off.

But the names and faces changed from week to week and month to month. As production slowed at Shaw's, the stuntmen who weren't getting work drifted off to try their luck at Cathay. When nothing was happening at Cathay, we'd see a tide of fresh faces in the crowd that squatted and leaned in the shade of the set at Movie Town, hoping to be picked up for a day's work at a day's pay. But stranger or friend, if you were a stuntman, you were family . . . so long as shooting ran.

It was an exciting, ever-changing life, our stuntman's world. It made us old, or maybe even dead, before our time . . . but it also kept us from growing up, because if you weren't a kid at heart, you couldn't deal with that kind of pace and pressure. And so if we were kind of wild, it was understandable.

After all, we had to bite off as much of the world as possible, as long as we were still in it.

HIGH RISK

Out of the many bad habits—like drinking, smoking, fighting, and cursing—that I picked up while I was a young stuntman, one thing stood out as the worst.

Every day, I risked my life for a fistful of dollars.

And almost every night, I risked my pay—all the money my dangerous job had earned me, and more—on games of chance. One evening, it might be mah-jongg. Another night, it might be betting on billiards. HK$100 a ball, HK$1000 a game. And still other nights, my stuntman friends and I might find our ways to the smoky, back-alley rooms where the craziest game of all was played: *pai gow*—the game of "heavenly dominoes."

When my father had left me at the airport that day so many years ago, he'd given me three words of caution: Don't do drugs. Don't join a Triad gang. And don't gamble.

I guess two out of three isn't so bad.

Now, when my dad told me not to gamble, I know he didn't mean it; that is to say, he knew that I'd make bets or play cards, just for fun, just to be with the guys. Everyone did that.

Pai gow was different.

In *pai gow*, there are no limits.

When you play mah-jongg, okay, even if you lose all night, you might lose HK$20,000. Play—and lose—for three straight days, you might lose HK$2 million.

A losing night in *pai gow* could mean you owed HK$10 million. Even HK$100 million. And the people you'd owe the money to usually wouldn't be the type who'd let you pay them by installment. *Pai gow* destroys families, breaks marriages, and ruins lives. My father knew this and avoided the game like the plague.

But in our world, if you showed fear, you showed weakness. To be *lung fu mo shi*, we couldn't afford *not* to take risks.

It's easy to get into a *pai gow* game. It's very, very hard to get out.

Let me explain the rules. The game uses a set of thirty-two dominoes, made of ivory or plastic. The dealer gives you and your fellow players four dominoes each. These have to be arranged into two hands of two dominoes—a front hand and a back hand. One of the players acts as banker, putting a certain amount of money that he's willing to risk on the table, and taking "action" (accepting bets) from the other players up to that amount. The banker compares his hands to those of the other players; to win the game, you have to beat your opponent both front and back. (Winning on only one or the other is considered a draw, although the banker wins exact ties.)

What makes the game really scary is that even people who aren't actually playing can put "action" on the table. And if you recklessly shout out, "Cover all!" meaning you'll take as much action as people can give, you can end up facing a table worth hundreds of thousands of dollars.

When I was banker, I took action from everyone. Sometimes I won. Sometimes I lost. But every game I played, I put more money on the table than I earned in a month. And when I came out ahead, I'd put it down again. And again. And again.

Soon I had another nickname, to go along with Double: Yeh Fu Pai. Which was short for *Yao li yeh fu pai, shei geng shei lai*—meaning "You gamble with everyone you meet."

There were nights when I had to be dragged away from the tables by my friends, kicking and screaming. There were days when I woke up in the morning, broke, hungry, and hungover, vowing that I would never gamble again. Nothing mattered, and nothing helped. As soon as someone flashed a wad of cash or suggested a "friendly" round of mah-jongg, I'd be counting my change and wondering if I could borrow enough to *get back in the game.*

At that time, when the stunt business was at its peak, I was making around HK$3,000 a month—plenty for a young, single guy to live on. Determined to stay away from gambling and save some money (not to mention my soul), one night I left my friends early and headed home alone. I'd gone to the bank that day to take out money to pay back my building manager, who'd helped me through a period of bad losses with a no-questions-asked loan.

But as soon as I stepped off of the Star Ferry and set foot in Kowloon, I felt the same old sizzle in the air: fast games. High risk. Big money. As hard as I tried to walk toward my apartment, I felt myself being drawn in the direction of an old familiar alley, where I knew I'd find the hottest action in town.

It's still early, I said to myself. *I might as well stand around and watch. I don't have to bet.*

Two hours later, my sleeves were rolled up, and the HK$3000 I had in my pocket was stacked in front of me, telling the packed room that I had the action, and that I was willing to take them on.

"Just three thousand dollars?" shouted one drunk player, tossing his bankroll on the table. His stake was nearly HK$10,000. Soon other players and bystanders threw their money down too, as if to tell me that a young kid like me had no business in a room full of *real* players. Twenty thousand dollars. Thirty thousand dollars. Fifty thousand dollars.

Soon I faced a table heavy with cash—almost $120,000 in Hong Kong money. More money than I'd ever seen in my life. More money than I thought I could ever earn in my career.

But I've never been able to turn down a challenge. Even though a voice inside my head was screaming at me, telling me to walk away—or run—I found myself saying the two words no one expected to hear.

"Cover all."

One hundred twenty thousand dollars! Three times what my entire apartment was worth! And I was telling the crowd that I'd take them on, all of them, and that I could afford to lose.

The dealer looked at me with a hard glare, and then passed out the dominoes. I guess God, or my ancestors, or luck—whatever you happen to believe in—was on my side that night. I kept my face straight as I looked at my four pieces, and realized that I had a perfect front hand, *gee joon,* the "supreme combination," and an almost perfect back hand.

I was unbeatable. Which meant I would soon be rich beyond my wildest dreams.

The dealer turned over my tiles and sucked in his breath. The other players howled. But as I started to rake in the stack of cash, I felt a thick hand on my shoulder. I turned to see the ugly face of the club's "enforcer," probably the biggest Chinese guy I'd ever seen in my life.

"Show me the money," he grunted, his voice low and dangerous.

I shrugged, and pointed to my winnings.

"Not that," he said. "You said, 'Cover all,' right? So you'd better have enough money in your pockets to make the bet, kid."

My eyes nearly popped out of my head. "But I won!"

The enforcer leaned into me, squeezing my shoulder in his fist. "You don't want to be telling me that you made a bet without being able to cover, do you?"

A few minutes later, I found myself being thrown out into the alley, rubbing my sore shoulder and picking up stray bills that had come loose from my $3000 wad.

If I were a better person, after that night, I would have learned my lesson and stopped gambling forever. I can't say that's true—but at least I never did anything that stupid again.

In my movies I beat up people twice my size, and fight entire crowds at once.

I don't think I'd enjoy seeing if I could do the same in real life.

HELLO, BIG BROTHER

In a lot of ways, these were the good times for me, maybe even the best times. I worked hard, but I got to keep (and spend) what I earned.

I tried not to think about Oh Chang.

Somehow I got by.

Once in a while, I'd see my brothers, people I knew from school, but despite the bond we'd had, once we were on the outside, we had different lives to lead. A lot of them were stuntmen, too. None of them were doing better than I was, although we heard stories now and then about our older brothers—Yuen Wah, who'd become one of the most sought-after stunt doubles, simply because he could see a fighting style once and copy it almost perfectly; Biggest Brother Yuen Lung, who'd fulfilled his vow to become a big man, succeeding as a stuntman despite his bulk.

As for Yuen Biao, after the school finally shut its doors, he'd decided to try his luck abroad, moving to Los Angeles with Master and his family.

I didn't know it then, but I should have taken his decision as an omen and a warning.

The good times weren't going to last forever. In fact, they were just about over.

The closing of the opera schools meant that a flood of raw, young, death-defying talent was coming onto the scene, and even though the movie business was doing as well as ever, a deadly struggle for jobs was just about to begin.

The real world was showing its teeth. Work became scarce, and for us freelance stuntmen, money got tight.

I began to get worried when I started showing up for one of the dozens of stunt jobs available at the usual studios, and saw hundreds of guys as young—or younger—than me, all squatting in the shade, all waiting for the call. I was a hard worker; I'd do double shifts if they were available. But more and more, they weren't.

Often, after half a day of useless waiting, I'd leave the studio and head back home, knowing that even the most senior guys were just hoping for the chance to play a corpse or fill out a crowd scene. How could I compete?

And so I slept and ate as much as I wanted, and found ways to waste time. I didn't have the money to gamble anymore, and no one else did, either, so borrowing money was out of the question. Sometimes I even thought about making the call I'd never intended to make, admitting to Mom and Dad across an international line that I had no future in this business, and that I would join them down under, if they'd only send me a ticket.

Once in a while, I hung around outside of Oh Chang's school, half hoping I'd bump into her accidentally. I never did.

Since I couldn't make them anymore, when I had nothing else to do, I watched movies—scraping together the cash to see anything that landed at the local theaters, from Hollywood films to the latest Hong Kong releases. Do you know what my favorite film was? *The Sound of Music*, with Julie Andrews. As the slow months passed, I saw it seven times.

Then, one evening, I went down to the old bar where my stuntmen used to hang out—most of them were working late, if they were working at all, so the place was almost empty.

I bought a beer and grabbed a cue from the warped and dusty rack, setting up the balls for a solo game of billiards.

Click. Clack. My luck at pool was no better than my luck at finding jobs.

And then I heard the sound of a familiar voice.

"Well, if it isn't the prince," the voice said with a sly and hearty laugh. The sudden recognition broke my concentration again, and I blew my shot.

I turned around, to see none other than Yuen Lung. My Biggest Brother. I nearly dropped the cue.

Yuen Lung tweaked the stick out of my hand, bent his heavy frame over the table, and coolly sank a ball.

"How've you been, Little Brother?" he asked.

I shrugged, trying to make it seem like meeting him was nothing. "Not bad. Busy."

He looked at me pointedly. "You don't *look* too busy." He sank another ball and called for a beer.

What could I say?

"Listen, don't you remember what I told you when I left the school?" he said. "If you needed work, you should have let me know. After all, what's a Big Brother for?"

I gulped. I hadn't known what to expect from Yuen Lung—gloating, maybe, or sarcasm—but certainly not a genuine offer of help. I wanted to believe that the nemesis who'd helped make a decade of my life a living hell had suddenly turned into a nice guy. I couldn't help but be suspicious.

"Why would you help me out?"

Yuen Lung scowled and shot another ball. "Hey, I'm trying to do you a favor, okay?" Clack-clunk. "Don't give me any shit. It's *heng dai*."

Heng dai is a Cantonese phrase that describes the relationship that is traditionally supposed to exist between older students and younger ones. As my senior, Yuen Lung deserved my respect and obedience. As his junior, I could expect his support and assistance—when he wasn't running roughshod over me, anyway.

Begrudgingly, I apologized for being ungrateful.

"That's okay," he said, smirking. "You got plenty of time to learn how to behave toward your betters. Here's the deal: I'm in good with this stunt coordinator—I've saved his ass plenty of times; he owes me. So I get work whenever I want. And anyone I send to him gets work, see? You just mention my name, and you're in."

Even though I knew that Biggest Brother relished being the big man, handing out favors to nobodies like me, I was grateful. I was at the end of my rope, almost out of cash, and just about ready to abandon my Hong Kong dreams.

"Thanks, Yuen Lung," I said, properly humble.

Biggest Brother rolled his eyes. "Don't call me that," he said. "I'm a real stuntman now, not some schoolkid. The guys gave me a nickname; Samo, that's my name now."

I laughed into my beer, and even Biggest Brother—Samo—looked a little sheepish. See, Samo is the name of a fat little cartoon character who was really popular back then. ("Samo" comes from the fact that this character had just three hairs, sticking out of the top of his head—*sam mo*, "three hairs.") So Mr. Big Man's stunt nickname was as if a U.S. actor were to call himself, say, Snoopy. Or Garfield.

But it made sense, in a way. Biggest Brother had left the school because of his weight; it was something that embarrassed him, something he hated. The only way he could survive, with his ego, was to lose the fat, or turn it around—make it something he was proud of, something he joked about.

I guess it was easier to change his name than to diet.

Somehow, hearing his new name broke the ice between us. We didn't talk about the past or share any old memories. We were starting over. And the two of us drank, and laughed, and played pool late into the night. Sometime after midnight, we fell asleep at the bar—a tradition we'd keep up many loud, late nights in the future, At dawn, we were woken up by the owner—just in time to head out to Movie Town, to make the day's casting call.

Samo and I spent many evenings together this way in the months that followed. I grew to understand things about him that I'd never seen when we were together at the school. He was brash, and rude, and a rough customer—his temper would go from jolly to mean in the blink of an eye, and he wasn't afraid to use his fighting skills to back up his mouth. "You want to take me on, bring an army," he'd brag, pointing to the half-moon scar on his upper lip. He'd gotten that in a brawl over a girl at a nightclub. The beating he received from the girl's boyfriend— who slashed Samo with a broken bottle, the coward—disfigured him for life. But in return, Samo had knocked the boyfriend unconscious, and left two of the guy's friends bleeding in the gutter.

"And I woulda gone back for the girl, too, if it wasn't for this little cut," he boasted.

With his tough-guy example to follow, the other stuntmen and I who hung out in his circle often found ourselves in bad scrapes. One time, drunk and rowdy, we stole a motorcycle and took turns taking joyrides until we were noticed by cops; the luckless kid who was on the bike at the time ended up getting taken down to the lockup, but we raised the bail for him between us, and managed to "convince" the owner of the motor- cycle not to press charges. After all, we'd only borrowed the bike.

We even gave him money for gas.

But what I hadn't realized before, when we were younger, was that un- der all of Samo's gruffness and bluster was a surprisingly sensitive heart. Usually the sensitivity was directed inward; no one was more aware of Samo's flaws than he was. Sometimes, though, his feelings showed through his big body. He was good to his friends and generous. But he expected in return a total gratitude and loyalty that most of the young people in his circle were willing to give.

It was harder for me. I don't like kissing anyone's ass, and Samo's was a particularly big one to have to kiss. To him, he'd always be Biggest Brother, and I'd be "the kid."

Sooner or later, I had to be my own man.

I had to stand alone.

About a month after our reunion, we had another surprise member of our family join us—Yuen Biao, who had returned from America having failed miserably at breaking into Hollywood.

"No luck with the foreign devils, huh, Yuen Biao?" I said, as we cele- brated his return the usual way, drinking and shooting pool.

"You don't get it, Yuen Lo," he said, pushing up the thick black spectacles he'd had to wear ever since he hit adolescence. "When we go over there, *we're* the foreign devils. I can do this," and he hopped off his stool and flipped backward onto his hands, walking upside down with easy grace, before softly dropping back to his feet. "But my hair is like this, and my eyes are like this, and my tongue is like this. There's no place for a Chinese man in the American movies."

"Ah, stupid, they just haven't seen me yet," yelled Samo, beating on his chest. "Just you wait, America, I'll be your big hero!"

"Big is right," I snorted. "I don't know if America has screens big enough to fit you and your ego, Brother."

More than ten years after we first met, and Samo still wasn't fast enough to catch me when I had a running start.

After Yuen Biao returned, we had many evenings like that one. We'd drink and joke through the night, fall asleep on one another's shoulders in the small hours of the morning, and then slap ourselves awake at sunrise, ready for another day of risking life and limb.

Sometimes, on days when work was slow, the three of us would even ditch the studio and go to the park, where we'd eat, nap, and kick around a soccer ball, enjoying as teenagers the childhood we'd missed while we were at the school. As we lay on the grass in the sun, someone would usually bring up the subject of movies, setting off talk about the actors we knew (talentless), the directors we'd worked for (stupid and overbearing), and the things we'd do if we were in charge (turn the Hong Kong film industry upside down—and get rich in the process, of course).

"Okay, you wanna know the problem with the movies?" asked Samo one afternoon, as we lay on our backs looking up at a blue sky flecked with little white clouds.

Yuen Biao snorted and rolled over on his side. "If we said no, would it stop you from telling us?"

Samo ignored him. "The movies stink because the action ain't real," he said. "You got actors pretending to be martial artists who couldn't punch their way through a loaf of bread. You got people flying around on wires, jumping twenty feet into the air, and knocking people over houses with one punch. Who wants to see that crap? A fight oughta be a fight, is what I say."

I pushed myself up onto my elbows. "Heroes are supposed to be like that. Better than regular people."

"I said it's crap. A hero should be a real guy, not some fake pretty boy," retorted Samo.

"Yeah, a hero should be ugly, like you," mocked Yuen Biao. "That'd be something to see. *The Amazing Adventures of Fat Guy.*"

"Ah, look who's talking, four-eyes." Samo leaned over and thumped Yuen Biao in the stomach, and the two began wrestling, half seriously.

Watching the clouds drift across the sky, I decided that Samo had a point. After a while, all the martial arts movies were the same—the heroes were invincible and handsome, the bad guys evil and hideous, and the fights weren't like real fights at all. They were more like dancing: staged and gimmicky.

"I bet any of us could do a better job than the guys making movies now," I said. "*I* could, anyway."

"That's even better: *Fat Guy Meets Super Nose*," piped Yuen Biao, gasping as Samo sat on his chest.

Soon all three of us were rolling around, punching and kicking. But when we finished our play-brawl, we made a promise that if any of us ever got the chance to make a movie, we'd find our brothers—and make it together.

Back then, we thought we were joking. After all, we were just stuntmen—the bottom of the movie barrel.

We didn't know what the future would bring. And the idea that someday we could be stars—well, that was crazy.

FIRST STRIKE

The months continued to pass, and we somehow managed to survive and thrive. With the help of Samo, Yuen Biao got his foot in the door as a junior stuntman and began developing a good reputation. Samo himself moved up from senior stuntman to stunt coordinator, signing on with an upstart studio called Golden Harvest.

As for me, I'd risen to the top of the stunt profession, becoming the highest of high-class stuntmen—someone the coordinators asked for by name when a hard or dangerous scene needed to be shot.

Then, one day, I got a call that I thought would change my life.

"Is this Yuen Lo?" said the voice on the phone. It was a voice I knew well—sweet, feminine, and kind, a voice out of my youth.

"Biggest Sister!" I shouted, drawing a stare from the building manager, who had let me use his telephone. I hadn't talked to her since she'd left the school, years before. It turned out that she, too, had gone into the film business, working as an assistant for a big-time producer.

"I've heard so many good things about you, Yuen Lo," she said. "You've made a real name for yourself."

I guess I couldn't help bragging about myself after a comment like that, so I told Biggest Sister about how I'd risen like a rocket through the ranks of stuntmen. "I can jump higher, kick faster, and hit harder than anyone," I told her. "And I'm not afraid of anything. I just wish I had a chance to show what I can really do."

There was a chuckle from the other end of the line. "Maybe I can help you get that chance, Little Brother," she said. "A producer just contacted our office looking for a good fighter for a new picture he's doing; I don't think it'll pay much, but it's better than taking punches while someone else gets the glory. . . ."

I almost dropped the phone. Me, a martial arts star? All of us had talked about it, even dreamed about it secretly—but we also dreamed about growing wings and learning how to fly, and that wasn't likely to happen either.

"I'll do it," I said.

"Like I said, I'm not sure how much they'll pay you—"

"I don't care if I have to pay them," I said.

She laughed at that, and promised to recommend me for the film. And I got the role!

I'd like to think it was because of my skill or reputation, but the truth is, Biggest Sister got me the part; even after all these years, she was still looking out for me.

As I said before, sometimes I think I've been pretty lucky in my life.

Then again, sometimes I think life stinks. As soon as I got on the set, I knew something was wrong. The film was a cheap kung fu story called *The Little Tiger of Canton.* I was supposed to be the Little Tiger, I guess, but with the budget they were using, I'm not sure if they could have afforded a kitten, much less a tiger. The whole thing was even less professional than the cheap "seven-day" movies we used to act in while we were still kids at the school. (We called them "seven-day" films because that's how long they took to shoot!)

The whole experience was so embarrassing that, when they asked me what name I wanted to put on the credits, I told them to call me Chan Yuen Lung—Biggest Brother's school name. I figured *he* wasn't using it anymore, so what did it matter?

While I was working on *Little Tiger,* my respect for directors sank to a new low. There wasn't much of a script, and even less direction. Usually, I was just told to stand in front of the camera and do whatever seemed to make sense—which was nothing, as far as I was concerned. The other actors talked constantly about quitting; the crew complained about the rotten conditions, the long hours, and the outdated and broken equipment. Of course, no one was getting paid.

It shouldn't be a surprise that the whole thing ended up falling apart. One night, the director and producer quietly disappeared, taking with them any hope that the film would be finished. Or that we'd get our wages. So weeks of work were just wasted, and my hopes of becoming a big-screen idol were smashed for the first time.

I was depressed and angry after that failure, but I knew there was always stunt work to be done. And even if that wouldn't make me famous, it would keep me well fed.

If there was one thing that growing up in the school drummed into me, it's that nothing is quite as important as a full belly.

ENTER THE DRAGON

I didn't know it at the time, but while I was going through my first disastrous experience as a martial arts actor, something important was happening in the world of Hong Kong cinema.

It really started back in 1970, when Raymond Chow, a top executive with Shaw Brothers, got tired of the studio's penny-pinching ways and decided to go off on his own. The company he founded, Golden Harvest, got off the ground by distributing works by independent producers, but Chow knew that it would take something really big to make the film world take notice.

Then, in 1971, something really big arrived. That October, the stunt community buzzed with the news about a new guy Chow had hired—and for the biggest money anyone had ever heard of, despite the fact that he'd never starred in a movie, here or in the West.

He was a U.S.-born Chinese whose supporting role in a popular American TV series had made him a cult figure, both there and in Hong Kong. The word was that he talked big. The word was also that he could back up everything he said.

His name was Bruce Lee—Lee Siu Lung, or "Little Dragon" Lee, in Cantonese.

In the few years he lived, he hit Hong Kong's film industry like an earthquake.

Just a few months after his being signed to Golden Harvest, the studio released his first movie—a picture called *The Big Boss*. The film showed a different kind of hero and a harder, faster, and more exciting kind of martial arts fighting—as quick and lethal as a cobra strike, pared down to the bare essentials.

Unlike the stiff, stilted combat of the swordsman movies that had made the Shaw Brothers rich, it looked rough, nasty—and painfully believable. And Lee's hero wasn't a stoic, noble soul, living his life in search of honorable revenge. He was a street brawler, a juvenile delinquent, sent away from home because of his love of fighting.

In short, he was a real guy.

When my brothers and I went to see the film, we found ourselves in a huge crowd of people who'd waited hours to get tickets. We wouldn't have gotten in at all, if it wasn't for our sneakiness and acrobatic abilities (the former led us to an open back window to the theater; the latter enabled us to vault up and into the packed house without causing a disruption, though no one would have noticed anyway).

Despite the fact that we hadn't paid to get in, we were prepared to hate the film. We really wanted to. After all, this overseas Chinese guy had come in out of nowhere, was making hundreds of times our salaries, and had Hong Kong eating out of the palm of his hand.

We wanted to, but we couldn't.

The film was everything the movies we were making weren't. And even though *The Big Boss* may not seem very impressive today, for us then, it was a revelation.

"Just what I said," shouted Samo on the way out of the theater, pumping his fist in the air. "Real fighting. Real hero. I like it."

"Ah, he ain't nothing," I said. "If you think it's so real, how come when he fights a whole crowd of people, they only attack him one at a time?"

"Yeah, that doesn't happen in real life," chimed in Yuen Biao. We all had bruises to prove it.

Samo shook his head and waved us away. "You guys don't know what you're talking about. I bet this is the beginning of something big, and if I'm wrong, I'll eat my shoes."

"Probably do it anyway when you get hungry enough," I muttered.

And then, as usual, the chase was on.

As it turns out, however, Samo was right. *The Big Boss* was a big hit—a blockbuster not just in Hong Kong, but throughout Asia. Its success turned the man called Dragon into Hong Kong's hottest star, and Golden Harvest from an upstart into a contender.

In the process, it turned the Hong Kong movie industry upside down. You see, the Shaw Brothers had always been the undisputed kings of Hong Kong cinema. They were almost like a monopoly. They had the biggest actors, the top directors, and the most money to throw around—not that they ever spent more than they had to.

But by losing Bruce Lee to Golden Harvest, the giant had stumbled, and now the industry realized that Shaw could be beaten. Everyone knew that Lee had gone to Shaw Brothers first and been offered a standard minimum contract—barely enough to live on, and certainly not worth moving to Hong Kong.

Lee would pay Shaw back for that insult millions of times—once for every box office dollar he put in Golden Harvest's bank account.

And meanwhile, every independent producer, studio executive, and wannabe movie mogul in Hong Kong was scouring the sidewalks for martial artists who looked, talked, acted, or fought like the Dragon—hunting for the next Bruce Lee.

It made for very exciting times for us stuntmen. Exciting, and just a little bit frustrating. When we gathered in the evenings to drink and talk, the conversation always ended up turning the same way: what did Lee have that we didn't? What was the secret of his success?

Is it any wonder that all of us wanted to see this man, this phenomenon, for ourselves?

It wasn't long before I got my chance.

As usual, it all started with a call from Big Brother.

"Hey, Big Nose," said Samo, "have I got an offer for you!"

Samo was calling from the offices of Golden Harvest, where he was now a resident stunt coordinator.

I listened with growing excitement as Samo told me about a new film project being developed at Golden Harvest. Set during the Japanese occupation of China, *Fist of Fury* was a story of rivalry and revenge between two competing martial arts schools, one Chinese, one Japanese. There were dozens of stunt parts available.

"And you can have one," said Samo, "if you want one."

Before I could even say yes, Samo added, almost as an afterthought: "Oh, yeah—the star of the movie is Bruce Lee."

I shouted a curse over the phone, and Samo laughed in response.

"I guess that means yes, huh? Well, show up at Golden Harvest at the crack of dawn tomorrow. If you're late, you're out of luck, so don't screw up. And don't forget you owe me a big one."

I knew that Samo would lord it over me the whole time I was on the set—he never missed an opportunity to make me kiss his butt when we worked together—but if there was ever a time when it was worth it, it was now.

I'd watch, and listen, and learn.

And if I got the chance, I'd show the Little Dragon what a Shandong boy can do.

When I walked onto the set the next morning, I realized that just about every stuntman with any kind of reputation had been hired onto the project. A shout of hello got my attention, and I saw Yuen Biao, standing off to one side with his hands in his pockets. Next to him was a lanky young man whom I soon recognized as my Big Brother Yuen Wah. It turned out that Yuen Wah had been cast as Bruce's own stunt double—partly due to his impressive skills, and partly due to the fact that his body type matched Lee's lean, whip-quick physique.

The resemblance in their build was even more obvious when Lee burst onto the set, shaking his head in barely disguised fury. What Yuen Wah couldn't match was Bruce's intense personal magnetism: even when he was just walking, the Dragon seemed to crackle with electricity.

The reason for his anger was soon apparent. Hot on Bruce's heels was the heavy, bespectacled figure of the film's director, the famous filmmaker Lo Wei.

Lo had made a number of successful movies, including Bruce's debut, *The Big Boss,* and often bragged of being Hong Kong's first millionaire director. Stuntmen who'd worked with him had a slightly different opinion of his skills; for all of his boasting, he was best known for falling asleep in his chair on the set. Even worse, Lo was a hard-core gambler who favored horse racing; while scenes were being shot, he'd turn on the radio to listen to the post-to-post coverage from the Happy Valley Racetrack, utterly unconcerned about the action going on around him. In fact, if someone dared to interrupt the post-to-post coverage, he'd unleash his famous temper, shouting the wretched individual off the set so he could follow his ponies in peace.

It was clear that Bruce had nothing but contempt for the man who called himself "the Dragon's mentor."

"The quote was out of context," harrumphed Lo at Lee's back.

"It's in the paper, isn't it?" said Bruce, a lethal edge in his voice.

"I never said I taught you how to fight," said Lo, waving his hands in an attempt to reassure his star. "I only said I showed you how to fight for *the cameras.* The skill, the talent, that's yours, Bruce. At most I, ah, gave you a little polish—"

The rest of us were watching this scene with discomfort, unsure of whether to get involved. It seemed pretty likely that something nasty was about to happen, but after all, we were just stunt players. What right did we have to get involved in a confrontation between the movie's director and its star?

If there was even going to be a movie, that is. The black, enraged look on Lee's face suggested that Lo's days might be numbered.

Just as it seemed like the situation was about to explode, a petite hand reached out to touch Bruce's shoulder. It was Liu Lianghua, the director's wife. "Please, Siu Lung," she said. "Don't take what my husband says so seriously. There is no insult in his words. Everyone knows that you are the master, and we are all just students!"

Bruce put down his fists and allowed his shoulders to untense. Lo casually took a sideways step that put his bulk behind the slim body of his wife.

"All right, Madame Lo," Lee said finally. "Out of respect for you, I'll forget that this happened. But if your husband ever talks to reporters about me again, I'll give *him* a lesson on how to fight." And Lee walked off to the side of the set, shaking his head.

The most important people in my life surrounding me.
(Clockwise from left: Willie, Dad, me, Mom.)

I toured Europe to recuperate from the head injury I
sustained during the filming of *Armor of God*. Here I am posing in
France alongside Willie (far left) and my father.

Yes, that's me, dressed
as a Chinese opera heroine,
standing with Willie.

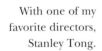

With one of my
favorite directors,
Stanley Tong.

At a social
function in the
excellent company
of (far left) Samo
Hung, actress
Sibelle Hu, and
Golden Harvest
head Raymond
Chow.

Here's one of the great loves of my life—I'm talking about auto racing, not my friend (and frequent costar) Maggie Cheung! This was shot at the Macau Rally, where my racing team was competing.

Leonard Ho and me on location, shooting *Who Am I?* in South Africa. It was our last movie together before he passed away.

The lovely and talented Michelle Yeoh, the only woman who's ever tried to top me, kick for kick and stunt for stunt. She almost did it, too—take a look at *Supercop*, where Michelle does a motorcycle jump up a ramp and onto a moving train!

Veteran director Lau Kar-leung and I had some creative differences on the set of *Drunken Master II*, but don't worry—we're just kidding around here.

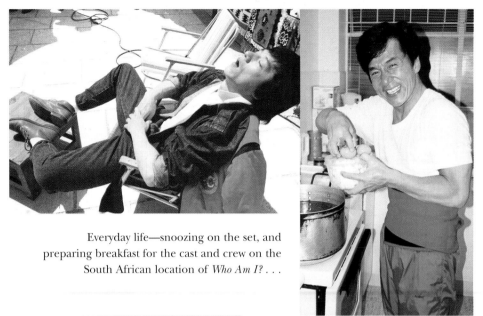

Everyday life—snoozing on the set, and preparing breakfast for the cast and crew on the South African location of *Who Am I?* . . .

. . . and very special days. I received the MBE (Member of the British Empire) from Queen Elizabeth II . . . and immortalized my handprints (and nose!) in cement in front of the famous Mann's Chinese Theater in Hollywood.

Looking tough with Sly Stallone and Whoopi Goldberg, my costars for a cameo scene in *Burn Hollywood Burn: An Alan Smithee Film.* I only did the movie to work with Sly, one of my best Hollywood pals.

Stanley, Michelle, Samuel L. Jackson, and me.

Steven Seagal

Michael Keaton

With Quentin Tarantino (who presented me with the MTV Lifetime Achievement Award), Mira Sorvino, and Michelle.

Giving Oliver Stone some directing tips.

Killer director (and old pal) John Woo, Willie, and Stanley Tong.

Sly and Bruce Willis—good friends and business colleagues (we're all partners in the restaurant chain Planet Hollywood).

On the set of *Rush Hour*—hanging on to
another chance at Hollywood success . . .

Lo blanched. "Was that a threat?" he shouted, waving anxiously at the rest of us. "Did he threaten me? All of you are witnesses!"

We stuntmen had watched with distaste as Lo hid behind his wife's skirts, and we had nothing to say to him now. As Lo stared at us, his face betraying a mix of fear and annoyance, we turned away and went back to our idle conversation.

"Okay, people, we have a movie to make!" bawled Samo as he walked onto the set, the cameraman a few steps behind him. "Quit jawing and look lively!"

When Samo and the cameraman arrived, we suddenly jumped to our feet and fell into a loose line, our faces alert and our bodies at attention.

I think our attitude toward our new director was pretty clear, don't you?

People always ask me about Bruce Lee. And why not? He was the biggest star Hong Kong cinema ever had at the time, an icon when he was alive and a legend after he died. He brought the martial arts movie to the attention of the world—and without him, I don't think that anyone would ever have heard of Jackie Chan.

I learned a lot from watching him, both in *Fist of Fury* and later, in *Enter the Dragon*. People have said enough about him to fill a thousand very thick books, and it still doesn't do him justice. He had enormous charisma—a physical presence you couldn't ignore. If he was in the room with you, it was impossible to ignore him, and difficult to pay attention to anyone else. He was an amazing martial artist, every bit as good as people have said. I don't think I could have beaten him in a fight, and I wouldn't have been dumb enough to try. (Believe it or not, Samo did! One day, he ran into Bruce in a hallway at Golden Harvest, and they got to talking about kung fu, and right then and there, they had a little match. Samo says it was even, but there were no witnesses, so who can confirm or deny?)

But the thing that was most obvious about Bruce when you met him was that he was a driven man, obsessed with perfecting himself, determined to achieve his goals. On the set, he worked like he was ten men, choreographing fights, instructing us individually in what he expected of us, and even looking through the camera to make sure that what ended up on screen was exactly what he imagined in his brain. Lo Wei might have been the director of the movie, but Bruce Lee was in charge, and everyone on the set knew it. Lo was perfectly content to let him take over. It meant less work for him. And besides, after the ugly incident at the beginning of the production, Lo wasn't about to get into a fight with his very dangerous, very temperamental star.

Still, if you ask me what I learned from the time I spent with Bruce, I would say I learned two things—both of which have been very important to me.

The first is that great success comes only with great ambition. As a child, I never had any interest in going into the movies. As a teen, more than anything else, I wanted the freedom to play and eat and sleep and live as I chose. I would have been very happy to be a stuntman for the rest of my life—or, if I ever thought about the future at all, maybe a stunt coordinator.

But in Bruce, I met someone who wanted to change the world, someone whose idea of success was to be admired and loved and remembered by millions. And in a career of less than a decade, in the space of just five films, he achieved his goals.

I guess maybe that's when I first realized that the horizon of what was possible was bigger and grander than I'd imagined. After all, if Bruce could do it, why couldn't I?

Because—and this was the second lesson I learned from being with Bruce—the Dragon was not a fairy tale, not a god. He was a *man*. He was someone you had to admire, but not someone you needed to worship. When we were on the set, he was always surrounded by people trying to get close to him, all of whom were telling him, "Bruce Lee, you're the best, you're the greatest."

I was in awe of him as much as anyone else, but I could never bring myself to join that crowd. I'd stand a hundred feet behind his followers, watching at a distance and feeling a little sick that even stuntmen with decades of experience were kissing his feet. After all, we'd all felt his punches and kicks by that time, and they were strong and skillful—but I knew people who were just as strong, or stronger, and just as skillful, or even more so.

It didn't matter. Bruce was Bruce, and for that reason alone, he was the best.

Bruce didn't demand that kind of treatment. He was smart enough to know how empty all of the praise was, how dependent it was on his staying at the top, and making money for the studio and all of its flunkies.

Later, after I had risen to success myself, I grew to understand the position Bruce was in. When you're a "superstar," whatever that means, there will always be people who treat you like you're no longer a human being. In remembering him, I don't make that mistake. To me, he is not and was not Bruce Lee, the mighty Dragon. He was and will always be Bruce Lee, a great teacher, a kind person, and a good man.

And you know what?

I hope that's how I'll be remembered myself.

THE DRAGON'S FIST

My role in *Fist of Fury* was almost invisible. I was one of many stuntmen on the film, and I barely got on camera. But if you look very carefully, you'll see me in one early scene in which I'm sparring with another student. The film's story is about how a Japanese martial arts school puts Bruce's kung fu school to a challenge—one that ends up killing Bruce's master. Treated with contempt by the Japanese school (they tell him that the Chinese are the "sick men of Asia"), Bruce takes his revenge, first on the rival school's students, then on its master, the evil Mr. Suzuki.

Even if my role wasn't one that might be obvious to people in the audience, I still had the chance to make my mark. We were filming the big final fight, and Bruce was patiently walking through the scene for us stuntmen.

"I give a punch here, and Suzuki moves here," he said, in his firm but reedy voice. "And then *pow!* another punch, and then *pya!* a big kick—" He gestured through the air, tracing an arc that sent the villainous Suzuki through a paper shoji door, then ran around to the other side of the door. "And *bang!*" he finished, pointing at a spot some twenty feet away.

We looked at each other. Obviously, no one could shoot a person twenty feet through the air with a single kick—a blow of that force would crush someone's chest anyway—so the stunt would be done with the help of wires. This meant that the lucky stuntman would strap a harness around his body, which would be attached to a steel wire that would yank him suddenly backward, just as the kick was landing. The problem was, the wire couldn't be used to hold the stuntman up in the air; the stunt had to look like a real fall, not like flying!

So the stuntman would have to push back with his legs, precisely upon impact, and then allow himself to go limp as the wire jerked him through the air. He would then have to hit the ground and absorb all the momentum from the twenty-foot drop.

No one had ever taken a fall of that height before. And the concrete where the stuntman would have to land didn't look very soft.

"Okay, who will do the stunt?" Lee said, his hands on his hips.

The set was silent, as the stuntmen around me calculated the likelihood that they would come through the stunt alive and relatively un-damaged. I'm not that patient, or maybe I'm just more foolhardy than the rest of my stunt brothers. Pushing forward to the front of the group, I nodded at Bruce, letting him know that I'd do the fall—if only to get the cameras rolling. Standing around was getting boring.

As I was strapped into the harness, I considered my options. This stunt wasn't like the backward tumble I'd done earlier. The wire would pull me back very suddenly, and I'd have no control at all over how fast or in what direction I'd be moving. By the time I was falling free, I wouldn't have time to shift my body—and besides, the idea wasn't to land safely on my feet, but to hit the ground *hard*.

Preferably without getting killed.

As we took our marks and the cameraman signaled that we were ready to shoot, Bruce checked to make sure my harness wasn't showing, and took the opportunity to whisper in my ear: "Good luck, boy."

Then he shouted for the camera to roll—this would ordinarily be the director's call, but Lo was listening to the radio, content to be a by-stander. And I braced myself, as the thud of Bruce's foot against my lightly padded chest triggered the stuntmen behind me to pull with all of their might. The harness tightened against my torso, and all the air came out of my lungs as I launched myself backward. There was the ripping of paper and the splintering of wooden slats as I went through the door. And then—

Falling, falling, falling.

Something, maybe radar, told me that I was about to hit the ground. I let my muscles loosen and rolled slightly, making sure I didn't land on my spine, my neck, or any of my limbs.

It was like being hit by a car! The pain slammed through my body, and I almost screamed. But screaming would mean that I'd have to do the take again, and I had no intention of doing that. So I clenched my jaw and ignored the red fog that was filling my head.

I guess I must have gone unconscious for just a little while, because when I opened my eyes again, there was a rolled-up piece of cloth under my head, and Bruce and Samo and Lo Wei were standing around me, with expressions of varying concern on their faces.

"Very good," said Bruce, letting loose one of his grins. "That's a print."

Samo just snorted, but I knew he was impressed.

And Lo, who'd actually moved from his usual position, slumped back in his director's chair, reached out his hand to help me sit up. "Not bad, kid," he said. "Not bad."

It was nice to get encouragement from three people who loomed so large in my life back then—my Biggest Brother, the millionaire director, and the greatest Chinese star in the world.

What I didn't know then was that someone else was watching, too—standing on the sidelines, not bothering to introduce himself. He was an executive with the Cathay Organization—the other film-industry giant of the Shaw Brothers era. With the rise of Golden Harvest and other independent companies, Cathay had chosen to shut down its film production arm and concentrate on distribution. As a result, Cathay executives often visited Golden Harvest to see what goods might be available.

This particular executive was well known as a shrewd operator and a kindhearted man. Born in Malaysia, he came to Hong Kong to find his fortune—and found it in the movies, quickly becoming a member of the colony's "fast crowd," the toast of cinema society.

He had an eye for films and rising talent, and I guess something about me—the ugly, big-nosed boy with a reckless disregard for his own safety—intrigued him. Later, he'd remember me at just the right time, and we'd begin a friendship that would rock the foundations of the Hong Kong film industry—and shape the rest of both of our lives.

His name was Willie Chan. And if I'm a superstar today, you can give the thanks to him.

I feel like I should add a little bit more about Bruce Lee, the man.

I can't say I was close to him; not too many people were, because he was such a big star, and after all, we were nobodies. But that was the best thing about him. Even though we didn't know him, he was very good to us. The little people. He didn't care about impressing the big bosses, but he took care of us.

I remember a few years later, when I worked as a stuntman on *Enter the Dragon*—the film that brought him back to the United States in glory. (Someone told me that Bruce specifically asked for me to work on the stunt team, although I guess I'll never know for sure whether that was true.)

Anyway, there's a scene at the end of the movie where he's infiltrating the underground compound of Mr. Han, the traitorous evil son of the Shaolin Temple. The compound is a maze of dark hallways, filled with Han's henchmen, and Bruce must fight his way through every one to get to Han's hideout.

It's a scene that anyone who's seen the movie will remember: Bruce, surrounded by over twenty attackers, pulls out his nunchakus, the deadly, whirling stick-and-chain weapons that he made famous around the world.

Each of the thugs tries to knock Bruce down. Each of them falls, one by one. Once again, Bruce is victorious against incredible odds.

I came in to take my punishment at the very end. In rehearsal, I was told that he would hit me lightly, I'd fall down like I was unconscious, and then he'd pose briefly for the cameras before running away.

Well, that's how it was *supposed* to happen!

Once the cameras were rolling, the adrenaline of the moment must have taken over: I ran in to attack him, he spun around, and pow! *POW!* Bruce's stick hit me right in the face!

As he was posing, I was lying on the ground, trying not to make any sounds and trying not to reach for my aching head. You wouldn't believe how much it hurt.

I can feel it even as I'm thinking about it now, decades later.

But Bruce knew the mistake he'd made. As soon as the cameras were off, he threw away his weapon, ran over to me, and said, "I'm sorry, I'm sorry!" and picked me up. And the whole rest of the day, between scenes, he would just look over at me and say, "I'm sorry," because my face was all swollen, like a chipmunk's. . . .

Of all the things Bruce did, and all the things he represented, I admire him most for his kindness that day.

But what about Bruce's movies, you might ask? What about his legacy?

Well, when I look at his movies now, I say to myself, they were masterpieces. They set the standard that everyone else wanted to follow. They're just evidence of what he could have done someday—if he hadn't died so young.

He had the talent and personality to make movies that would have been classics for all of history.

His life ended before he had the chance.

I look at films by Buster Keaton and Harold Lloyd, Charlie Chaplin, Gene Kelly, Fred Astaire, and I say *wow*. These are classics, and they are great even today. Bruce's movies are like seeds that never had the chance to sprout.

I've had a much longer career, and I've made movies that I think I can be really proud of. I don't know whether they will be seen as classics after I'm gone; I guess history will answer that question.

Even today, however, people try to compare us, me and Bruce, and make it seem as if we were competitors.

Nothing could be more ridiculous. There were things he could do that I couldn't do; there are things I can do that he couldn't do.

But you know, I never wanted to be the next Bruce Lee.

I just wanted to be the first Jackie Chan.

TO BE NUMBER ONE

One thing that came out of my experience on *Fist of Fury* was a realization that I was sick of kissing people's asses.

I'm sorry to say it so harshly, but it was true. As a stuntman, even as a high-class stuntman, I was at the mercy of everyone: the director, the producer, and especially the stunt coordinators.

When it came to action sequences, the stunt coordinators were completely in control. Even the directors bowed down to them, although as more and more stunt coordinators have turned into directors, this is less true today.

That's why we stuntmen had a special nickname for stunt coordinators: *she tao,* or "the head of the snake." On a dangerous and complicated action shoot, the coordinators might supervise over two hundred people. This gave the *she tao* a lot of power *on* the set—because he choreographed and directed action sequences—and *off,* because he was responsible for choosing and hiring all of the people under him.

Unfortunately, this meant that stunt coordinators were surrounded by people who flattered them, bought them drinks, and treated them like big men. Successful ass-kissers got lots of regular work—if you can call that working: favored suck-ups were given soft, easy stunts that any baby could do.

The rest of us did the high jumps and hard falls.

No matter how good you were, though, you still faced a lot of competition. And if you weren't willing to grovel in front of the coordinators, there was only one other way to insure you'd be called out.

You see, we were paid a set rate for each day of work, about US$15. The producer usually gave the *she tao* a budget for the film, broken down by stunts, with each stunt taking a day to shoot. But after we'd finished a scene, instead of wrapping production and paying us, the coordinator would usually bark out orders to set up for a second scene—knowing that, if he finished two stunts in a day, he could put one day's fees for all of the stuntmen in his own pocket.

It meant we were doing double the amount of work for the same pay. There were no rules or unions protecting us, so we had no one to complain to about this treatment. But even if there had been, we wouldn't

176 • I AM JACKIE CHAN

have argued. It was like a tradition. They took away your money one day, but they'd call you back the next.

It kept you on the list.

All of us were angry about this injustice. We were sweating, hurting, and risking our lives for half of what we were due. Of course, there was nothing that I or any of the other stuntmen could do about it, any more than I could find it in myself to hit my elder brothers when they tyrannized me and my fellow younger brothers. This was just the way the system worked. Instead, I decided that I'd find a way to become a *she tao* myself—the youngest one in the history of Hong Kong cinema. And when I put my mind to it, I feel like I can do just about anything.

I was in a somewhat embarrassing position when I finally faced my opportunity—leaning over and rubbing my back like an old man. I'd just taken a hard, painful fall on a film Samo was coordinating for Golden Harvest, and he was yelling at me to do the stunt again, saying I'd shown my face to the cameras.

"Stop wasting time, Big Nose; the sun's going down," he shouted.

It didn't matter how many years we were out of the school. Samo still treated me like a little brother, and I think he always will. I considered telling him to screw off, but decided it wasn't worth the effort or the trouble. Straightening up with a wince, I shook the dust off my body and checked my neck to make sure it was still doing its job, keeping my head attached to my shoulders.

That's when I noticed the stranger standing off on the sidelines of the set. I knew most of the people who hung around the Golden Harvest studio, as well as the freelance stuntmen who went from set to set looking for work, and I couldn't place his face among them. What would a stranger be doing hanging around the set so late in the day?

Thinking about it was another thing that wasn't worth the trouble or effort. I shrugged and headed back toward Samo, who was huffing at me with his arms crossed and his face crunched up like he was about to explode.

One more time up the wall.

One more time down to the ground.

"Okay, good enough, it's a wrap," shouted Samo, heaving himself up out of his chair and motioning to his flunkies.

It hadn't hurt as much the second time around, but I was so exhausted that I just lay on the ground for a while, my eyes closed. Eventually someone would tell me to get up, I figured. Until then, I'd just rest for a little while.

"Excuse me?" said a voice.

Go away, I thought to myself. *Let me die in peace.* But I opened my eyes anyway.

It was the stranger, looking skittishly around at the laborers who were breaking down the set.

"What do you want?" I said, boosting myself up to my elbows.

"I really shouldn't be here," he said.

"Who are you?"

The stranger squatted down next to me. "I'm Bao Hok-lai," he said. "Director."

I shook his hand. "I've never heard of you."

"Nobody has," he said, with a wry grin. "I'm with a small production company called Da Di; we're about to start a picture, and we're looking for a stunt coordinator."

"Oh," I said. I got up and began brushing the dust from my pants. "Well, he's over that way."

Bao got up, looking puzzled. "Not that guy," he said. "I was thinking of you."

I looked at him, my eyes narrowed. "What?"

"Heard around that you're pretty good," he said by way of explanation. "We'd like to give you a shot at stunt coordinating, if you're interested in a contract."

A contract! For a freelance stunt guy like me, getting a contract—as a stunt coordinator, yet—was the big time. I probably should have spent more time thinking about it, but at the time I wasn't about to question my luck. "Where do I sign?" I blurted. *And Samo could just go to hell.*

Bao was a bit surprised that I was so quick to say yes, I guess, so he told me just to show up at their office the next morning to work out the details. "Welcome aboard," he said, as he ducked off the set.

"Well, it'll be nice working for you," I called after him, "considering you went out of your way to pick me over guys with more experience."

He turned and shrugged sheepishly. "To tell you the truth, we couldn't afford them anyway," he said, and then left.

Like I said, I probably should have thought about it longer.

The offices of Da Di (which translates as "Big Earth") weren't particularly big, but they were . . . dirty. My hopes were still high, though—even if the biggest studios controlled the top stars, there were still some good films being made by small independent companies. Bao introduced me to the head of production, who complimented my work, even though he hadn't personally seen any of the films I'd done. Then we took our turns signing the contract, and shook hands.

"The first picture we want you to work on is *She Wang Yao* ["Four Kings, One Queen," but it was called *The Heroine* in English]," said Bao. "The budget—"

"The budget is not a problem," said the production head. "Money isn't what makes good movies; talent is. And we know you have the talent."

"We can't afford—" said Bao.

"We can't afford not to do our best!" the production head interrupted. "We have a lot of faith in you, lad! The old saying is, 'Youth will rule the world,' correct? The shoot starts tomorrow! Good luck!"

And then he folded the contract, got his coat, and walked out of the office.

I looked at Bao, and Bao looked back at me.

"Can I at least hire some assistants, or do I have to do everything myself?" I said glumly.

Bao winced, and then nodded. "Hire whomever you need," he said. "We'll work it out somehow."

My expression brightened, and I shook his hand again before leaving.

Tomorrow was the beginning of my new career. I would be in charge, a real *she tao*, and I knew exactly whom I wanted at my side.

"I don't know about this," Yuen Kwai said to me, watching as the cameraman argued with the producer about the state of his equipment.

Yuen Biao, leaning against a nearby wall, shrugged and nodded in our direction. "Hey, it's better than fighting for jobs with that herd of stuntmen over at Golden Harvest," he said. "Seems like every day there are more people wanting work. Money is money, I guess."

I gave a halfhearted smile at my brothers. "Let's not talk about money right now," I said. "Think of this as the beginning of an adventure."

Yuen Kwai spat at the ground. "If I want an adventure, I'll go to Africa," he said. "I thought you said this was a high-class operation."

I punched him in the shoulder. "High-class is about people, not about budgets. You think you're high-class enough to be an assistant stunt coordinator? You prove it, brother."

He rolled his eyes and sighed.

We watched as the cameraman kicked the shoddy wooden skeleton of the set and almost knocked the flimsy facade to the ground.

"High-class all the way," he said. "I always wanted to live the glamorous life."

"You want me to punch you again?" I said, gritting my teeth.

To be perfectly honest, the movie was terrible. I'm not trying to insult Bao by saying so; most of the movies we made back then were bad, and some of them were very bad. But all that mattered to me was the action, and for that, Yuen Biao and Yuen Kwai and I did our best.

And I loved it.

I found myself enjoying the chance to make decisions and give orders, not because I liked to be the boss, but because I finally had the chance to shape the world around me. I even got a chance to act in the film, playing the second male lead—not that I'm proud of my performance. I guess I had a lot to learn about acting. Still, I'd always thought that being free meant no one telling me what to do; now I realized that it meant having the ability to control, to create, to make things happen.

Unfortunately, one thing I couldn't do was force people to watch the film, which made just HK$70,000 at the box office—a disaster.

Bao was crushed. Da Di's head of production tried to put a more positive spin on the situation. "Don't worry, boy. It's not the end of the world. Or of Big Earth!" he chuckled. "We'll get 'em on the next one."

The next one was a movie called *Police Woman*, and it was better than *The Heroine*. Not much better, but we'd all learned a few lessons, and I think we put them to good use. We waited for the box office results with anticipation, hoping that it would at least break even, maybe make enough money to pay our back salaries, which were beginning to pile up.

It didn't. *Police Woman* was another flop.

The movie wasn't good, but that wasn't the only reason why it failed so badly.

Something awful had occurred in the meantime.

Bruce Lee, the man who had transformed the Hong Kong film industry, who'd brought martial arts films to the world, had died. And somehow, the industry had died with him. People weren't watching action films anymore; they were turning to melodramas, to romances, to comedies—anything that didn't have the ghost of Bruce hovering over them. Desperate producers were trying to resurrect him in absurd and insulting ways, releasing cheap knockoff films starring fake stand-ins—actors calling themselves Bruce Lai, Bruce Leung, Bruce Lam. No one was fooled. And very few people wanted to watch.

The day the bookkeeper announced the numbers, the head of production looked pale, and Bao looked like he was ready to cry. I didn't know what to say, so I kept my mouth shut. It looked like something terrible was about to happen.

Sometimes I hate being right. At the end of that miserable day, the production head and some of the other principals of Da Di called me in to a meeting they were having. Bao had already left, without saying anything to anyone.

"Hello, come in, Yuen Lung," said the production head (I was still using Biggest Brother's name at the time). "I have something to tell you, and I know it will make you upset. I'm devastated, myself."

He looked uncomfortably at the other principals, who made a point of looking elsewhere around the room.

"What is it?" I said, having a funny feeling I knew what was coming. I'd been through this before, on that stupid movie *Little Tiger of Canton,* and I suspected the tiger was about to bite me in the ass again.

"We've decided to shut down the company," he said. "We don't have any more money, and we can't even pay back wages. I'm sorry."

He put his head into his hands. "I'm sorry."

I stared at the men, who all suddenly looked very old and tired. I nodded, turned on my heel, and left the building.

"What's up, Big Brother?" It was Yuen Biao, catching up to me as I walked out onto the street. "What's going on?"

"Nothing," I said. "Nothing's going on anymore. It's over. They can't pay us, they're not making any more movies, and we're out on the street."

Yuen Biao looked shocked, and his shoulders bent down. He hadn't been in the business as long as I had; at the age of just nineteen, I was a veteran. I had a little money in the bank. I could afford not to be paid for a while. But Yuen Biao was struggling, and I could see that this loss was hitting him hard.

I patted him on the shoulder. "Don't worry!" I said. "It's not all terrible. You just call Samo tomorrow; I'm sure he can get you work. And besides—they gave us some going-away money. Tonight, let's not feel sad over the end of this job. Let's celebrate the beginning of our new lives, whatever they may bring!"

He brightened, and was soon laughing again. Together, we went back to my apartment. I retrieved my stash of savings—about HK$800 total—while Yuen Biao went to call Yuen Kwai about the bad (and good) news.

After he joined us, we headed for the seamier side of Tsim Sha Tsui, spending our "bonus" on a wild night drinking and gambling. By the time the two of them left for their apartments, I had just ten Hong Kong dollars remaining, and an incredible headache.

I slept all of the next day and woke up in the evening, just in time to spend my last ten dollars on dinner at a nearby restaurant.

I'd finally hit bottom. I had no job, no money, no girlfriend, nothing but the clothes on my back and the furniture I'd made with my own hands.

There was just one thing I could do.

"Dad?" I said, to the voice on the other side of the transcontinental connection. "I'm coming home."

DOWN AND OUT

I lived on money I borrowed from the building manager for the next few days, until my parents could send me my ticket to Australia. I didn't tell my friends and brothers I was going; I didn't want them to worry or to try to convince me to stay. It was a hard enough decision as it was.

The entire time I was in the air, I reminded myself that the movies weren't everything, and that there were plenty of careers for a young boy with ambition. I could be a policeman. I could be a chef. Maybe I could build furniture, I thought with a bitter laugh. I didn't need Hong Kong, and Hong Kong certainly didn't need me.

But when the plane touched down in Australia, reality struck me a painful blow. I wandered with my bag through the airport, looking for my parents, completely puzzled by the instructions they'd given me. None of the landmarks that they'd told me about were visible. There were too many people, and none of them spoke Chinese. When I approached people with my scrap of paper, which I'd gotten the building manager's granddaughter to inscribe carefully with the embassy address and phone number, people looked at my shoulder-length black hair, my Asian features, and my poor clothing, and they ran away.

I was alone, without even my parents, in a country full of foreigners. Or, I corrected myself, in a country where I was a foreigner, and always would be.

Finally, I found an airline attendant who could speak a little Chinese, and was told that I wasn't just lost—I was in the wrong city! The plane had landed in Sydney, the main city of Australia; my parents lived in Canberra, a short plane hop away, but far enough so that my handwritten address was incomprehensible and useless.

With her help, I got on the right plane and arrived in my parents' city hours later than I was expected.

The Canberra airfield I stepped out onto was dusty and brown, and the sky and landscape were completely alien. I walked around the airport looking for my parents. There weren't as many people there as at the Sydney terminal, and I couldn't imagine that I'd have any problems finding them—if they'd waited for me.

But after half an hour of walking, I saw no one I recognized. I sat down on a bench, dropped my bag next to me, and put my head into my hands. As bad as it had been to fail in Hong Kong, this was worse by far. Who could understand me here? How would I find transportation to the embassy?

And then I felt a hand on my shoulder.

I looked up into the face of my mother, into her teary eyes and smile.

"Mom!" I shouted. And embraced her with all of my strength.

Just behind her was my father, still tall, but a little stooped in his shoulders. The biggest difference: his hair was completely white.

The years had passed, and I hadn't seen either of them for so long, and they'd changed—gotten older, tanned by the hot Aussie sun. And I'd changed: I'd grown so much, and my hair was long and unkempt. We'd probably walked by each other in the hallways, not recognizing one another, until my mother took the chance that this thin, miserable-looking young man was her son.

"Welcome home, Kong-sang," said my father, squeezing my shoulder. And my mother kept on holding me.

But the words sounded strange.

Was this my home, a place I'd never been?

Or had I *left* my home—the only home I'd ever really known?

Part of the reason my father was so happy I'd decided to come back was that, at age nineteen, I was almost too old to become a legal resident of Australia through my family connections. Always a practical man, my dad knew that Hong Kong, the place that had sheltered him from the Japanese army, would not be safe forever—that uncertainty would be coming, a few decades later, when the island was returned to China. He was Chinese in his heart and soul, but he had seen how the Communists treated his countrymen, and he wanted me to have a safe place to run to if things went bad in the year 1997.

But when I finally got my Australian passport, signifying that I had a right to enter and stay in this strange new land, I felt more foreign than ever. I lay on my bed, looking at my picture, at the sullen, ugly face that stared back at me. My face in the photo was unhappy, and it reflected how I felt. The booklet gave me the freedom to come here whenever I wanted, but it also gave me the freedom to leave. And after months of living like a parasite on my parents, struggling with the language, the culture, and the food, that's what I wanted to do, more than anything else.

I found my dad resting in our common space—there was more room for us here in the embassy than there ever had been in our house on Victoria Peak. His eyes were closed, but I knew that he was awake and that he had heard me enter.

"Dad," I said, softly.

"Hello, Kong-sang," he said. Now that I was grown—taller than him, and as skinny as a rail—he never called me Ah Pao anymore. The name wasn't completely gone, however; the English-speaking embassy staff had taken to calling me Paul, after hearing from my mother that her nickname for me was Pao-pao. "Did you want to talk to me?"

I nodded. My passport was clenched in my right hand. "I spoke to someone in Hong Kong," I told him. "They want me back. There's—I have a new contract waiting for me."

My dad looked at me in silence. He knew I was lying. I don't think I've ever been able to fool him in my entire life. But he also knew I was miserable here, and I was old enough to make mistakes of my own, while still being young enough to survive them.

"I suppose there is no help for it," he sighed. "A contract is a contract."

I held out my hand to him, and he squeezed it. He looked at my hand, which still showed scars from my many years of falling on cue.

"But son—never forget," he said softly. "You will always have a place here with us."

A NEW BEGINNING

It almost killed me, but I bit my tongue and made the call anyway.

Back in Hong Kong, after six months of inaction, whatever reputation I'd been able to build had crumbled away. Just like my apartment, which the building manager was kind enough to check in on every so often, to make sure nothing had been stolen; as nice as he was, he was too old and busy to clean it for me, so when I returned, the place was a terrible mess, full of spiders and dust. I started out my second life in Hong Kong with a day of sweeping and fixing things that had mysteriously broken.

And then, like I said, I made the call.

My life is full of uncomfortable phone calls.

"Yeah, who is it?" said the rough, familiar voice.

"It's me," I said. "Yuen Lo."

Samo barked out a laugh. "Yuen Lo. The exiled prince. What brings you back to our little island? Or are you still down under with all the other beasts?"

I swallowed hard, trying to keep my pride from bursting out of my chest. This was even more difficult than I'd thought. "Big Brother, I'm back, and I need a job." *And I'm willing to kiss your ass for one,* I said to myself silently. *That's how desperate I am.*

"Well, well, well, you need Biggest Brother to bail you out again, huh," he said. "As usual, you're a lucky bastard, and I'm a nice guy. In about a month, I'll need an assistant. Guess you'll do as well as anyone—that Yuen Kwai has a mouth on him, and Yuen Biao was always useless."

Assistant! After I'd gone all the way to the top, a *she tao* myself. And to have to bow down to Big Brother day in and day out, just like my school days. Plus, the job was a month away; what would I do until then? My pockets were as empty as my belly, and I still had to pay back the building manager.

"Samo, I need work now," I said. "I'm out of cash."

He grunted. "Yeah, and don't ask me for any loans; I'm strapped too. Okay, there's a film starting up here now that could probably use someone. I'll put in a good word for you."

"Thanks, Big Brother," I said, genuinely grateful. "I'll take it."

"That's another you owe me."

"I know. I know," I said, my gratitude straining. "Who's the director?"

"Never heard of him," said Big Brother. "He's some new guy—name's Woo."

I'd never heard of him, either.

I bet most of you have, though. Because today, John Woo is one of the most famous filmmakers ever to come out of Hong Kong—and now, one of the top directors in Hollywood. It's funny how paths cross, and lives turn. John and I still talk once in a while, when we're in Hollywood together. Both of us started at the bottom. Neither of us can believe where we are now.

Like I said, it's funny.

But back then, on *Hand of Death*, well, we were still young and starting out. I enjoyed the film, and I enjoyed working with John. Though I'd originally expected just to do stunts, I ended up playing a supporting role in the film, and John even taught me a few things about what directing was all about. I'd never wanted to direct before, partly because most of the directors I'd worked with were incompetent.

John was different: he knew what he was doing, even as a first-time filmmaker, and he had a vision. He didn't fall asleep when action sequences were being filmed. He cared about every move, every stunt, every fight, as if he were performing them himself. He was kind and treated us well. If I ever did get the chance to direct, I realized, this was the kind of director I wanted to be.

But that would come later. Much later.

At that time, all I had to look forward to after the movie wrapped was months of hard work under Samo's thumb.

Welcome back, I said to myself. *I hope you're happy.*

Actually, as it turns out, I *was* happy. Stunt work was still what I was best at, after all, and once I'd spent some time with Samo, I even got used to his shouting and his put-downs again. I'd lived with him most of my life, and we knew each other better than anybody. Working with him was like being a part of a machine, because he knew exactly what I was capable of, and I knew exactly what he was looking for. I probably could have been content that way if nothing changed for the rest of my life. But the world isn't like that.

Change is the only thing we can rely on in life.

And so I should have probably expected that, just when I was getting settled back into a pattern, just when I was feeling secure again, everything would turn upside down.

"What do you mean, there's no work?" I said, as Samo flinched. It was rare that he reacted that way, so I knew he wasn't just blowing smoke.

"The studio isn't doing so well right now," he said. "Ever since Bruce died, well, it hurt Golden Harvest more than anyone else. They just canceled a lot of projects, you know. The trend is moving away from action— it's all comedies now."

I groaned. He was right. The slate had gotten thinner lately; more and more of the films Golden Harvest was releasing were coming from outside, cheap pickups of independent productions. Even though I'd been working pretty regularly, assisting Samo and doing the odd stunt job, the opportunities had gotten fewer and fewer. I was finding it hard to stay afloat. My confidence had been shaken after the disaster with *Little Tiger*, and it went down even further when Da Di went out of business. I'd always thought of myself as lucky, but maybe the truth was that I was bad luck—for everyone else.

"What are you trying to tell me, Samo?" I said, hoping he wouldn't say what I knew he'd have to say.

"I'm telling you we got problems," he said. "Look, you gotta believe me, I'm giving you every gig I can find, and I know it isn't enough. There ain't much more I can do. Tell you the truth, I'm worried about my own job now. . . ."

I leaned back in my chair. We were sitting in an office at Golden Harvest, looking up at a wall of pictures and memorabilia of past movies. Past glories.

"What am I going to do?" I said.

"What are *any* of us going to do?" he retorted. "If this keeps up, we'll all be sleeping in the gutter. Hell, it's probably getting crowded down there already; it ain't as if we haven't kicked out half the stuntmen who hang around here already. Listen, Little Brother—"

He looked at me, and his expression was serious. This wasn't Samo and Yuen Lo stuff, our usual rivalry and bickering. This was Big Brother and Little Brother—*heng dai.* "You want to hear my advice? I think you should go back to your parents. You've got your nice little Australian passport; you can go anytime you want. You get out now, and you'll save yourself a lot of heartache. The rest of us don't have that option. If the industry goes down, we're going down with it."

I slumped down farther in my seat. He stood up and patted me on the shoulder, which was about as affectionate as he'd ever gotten with me. "Things have got to change sometime," he said. "When they change, you can always come back. And with any luck, I'll still be here. I'll always be your Big Brother."

And he turned away and walked out of the room, a cloud of gloom following him as he went.

Samo had given me good advice, but it was a painful mouthful to swallow. I'd told my dad I was here on a contract. I'd been here less than a year—I couldn't tell him the contract was complete. And I couldn't face him with an admission of my failure. After all I'd been through, I would rather have gone to work sweeping garbage than return to Australia with my head down.

But I didn't have any other skills, and I barely had enough money to eat for a week. I regretted ever coming back—if I'd stayed, I might have died of boredom, but at least I wouldn't have died of shame. Or starvation.

The walk back to my apartment was like torture; it seemed like the city was mocking me, with its signs of life and bustle, the money changing hands and businesses growing before my eyes. Hong Kong was expanding very fast at that time, turning into one of the world's economic capitals. The irony left a bitter taste in my mouth.

Once back at my flat, I collapsed onto my bedroll. Desperation had drained the energy from my body. I didn't move even when I heard a gentle tapping sound.

Someone was knocking at my door.

I couldn't remember the last time I'd had visitors; it didn't sound like the building manager, or his granddaughter, and certainly not one of my stuntman friends. I considered whether there was anyone to whom I still owed money, and decided to take the chance of answering the knock anyway.

Nothing could have prepared me for what I'd see.

Or rather, whom.

"Oh Chang . . ." I said, choking.

She was older, a little taller, more beautiful than ever, if that was possible. Dressed nicely, and wearing her hair and her makeup in the style of a young woman, not a girl.

"Yuen Lo," she said.

I wanted to tell her I'd missed her, that I'd never thought I'd see her again, and that I'd still do anything to be with her.

Instead I just stepped aside so she could enter the apartment.

"You have a nice place," she said.

I looked at the rough, handmade furniture. The cracked pane in the window. My old bedroll on the floor. "It's not much," I said.

"But it's yours. That's nice," she said.

Pulling my only chair out, I motioned for her to sit down. All the things I wanted to say were jumbled in my head. The only thing that I could get out was the word "How . . . ?"

Somehow, she understood. "I—I went to your studio looking for you. I met a friend of yours. . . . He said you went home."

I slumped down cross-legged on my bed. "I got out early today," I said.

She stood up, slowly walked over to where I was sitting, and then sat down on the bed next to me. Close enough that I could feel her warmth.

"Yuen Lo, he told me about—about your problem," she said softly. "I know how hard this must be for you. And I want you to know that—that I believe in you." And she put her hand over mine.

I heard the sympathy—no, the pity—in her voice, and I couldn't stand it. I pulled my hand away. "Believe in me?" I shouted. "Believe in nothing! Everything your father said is true! I'm just a poor stunt boy with no future, no job, and no right to be with someone as good as you."

She looked shocked, and then sad. "Yuen Lo, please don't say that! You're wonderful, and you're talented, so very talented. You'll succeed someday; it's just—the time isn't right yet. . . ."

"When will the time ever be right?" I said. "Oh Chang, what are you doing here? You should be on a stage in the spotlight, or out walking with someone rich and handsome, or at home, in your big house, with your parents. I'm leaving this stupid island, anyway. I don't need your pity. I don't need your kindness. I don't need *anything*."

She looked at me with those lovely eyes, misted with tears. "Are you sure you don't need anything?"

And she opened her purse, pulled out a package wrapped in tissue paper, and put it down on the bed.

We both stared at it for a while, without speaking. Then, trembling slightly, I reached for the package and unwrapped it. It was a stack of crisp, new bills, totaling HK$20,000. Half of what my entire apartment cost.

I carefully wrapped it back up and then tossed it back down.

"I can't take this," I said.

A sudden fire lit up her eyes, and she spoke with a passion that I hadn't ever heard before. "Yuen Lo, I know you don't have any money. Even if you want to go back to your parents, how will you buy a ticket? Are you going to ask them to pay for you? Is that what you want?"

Suddenly, tears ran down my cheeks. My parents, who'd worked so hard all their lives, and who were still working even though they were old—I couldn't take the humiliation of begging them for money, and I couldn't go back to them with failure written all over my face! Oh Chang understood my heart, even without having to be told. I knew at that moment that we could never be together, but that we'd always share something special. I reached out for her, and we embraced tightly, and—for just a moment—we kissed. . . .

The moment passed, and she put the package back into my hands, pressing it lightly into my palms. "You can pay me back when you become rich and famous," she said. "Because I know you will someday. I think it's a good investment." And she smiled, and the room brightened.

Seized by emotion, I reached under my bedroll and pulled out my passport. "Oh Chang," I said. "Go home and pack your bags. Come with me to Australia. My parents would love you, and I . . . I—"

Still smiling, she shook her head. "Yuen Lo, I can't. My parents would miss me. But I'll see you again, someday, won't I?"

I nodded.

"And until then, remember me."

And she got up, walked to the door, and left, after blowing me another kiss good-bye.

Her scent hung in the air, sweet like the smell of a peach. Yes, I would remember her.

Always.

DOWN AND OUT AGAIN

I told my father I was rich. I told him I'd worked so hard in the months that had gone by that I'd saved a bundle of cash. Enough to go back to Australia in style, so I could support him and my mother in their old age.

He didn't call me a liar. Pride was as important to him as it was to me.

Before I left, I went to a jewelry shop nearby, an expensive place that I'd stared at from the outside in the past. The owner looked at me with suspicious eyes, but treated me politely once I flashed my roll of cash. Even loaded down as I was with the money Oh Chang had lent me, the prices were steep. I chose a Rolex watch for my father, which cost over HK$3,000, and a gem-studded ladies' watch for my mother.

After my purchases, I barely had enough to buy my ticket, pay back some debts—I didn't expect ever to come back—and give a gift to the building manager.

"It's to pay you for watching my place," I said, knowing he wouldn't take the money otherwise. "Buy something for your granddaughter."

And then I said good-bye to him, to my apartment, and to the city of Hong Kong forever.

My mother was very happy to see me and congratulated me on my success. The watch almost made her cry—it was the nicest thing she owned, and the first thing I'd ever given her. My father wasn't as pleased with his gift. I know he was wondering where I'd gotten the money—knowing that I couldn't have earned it in such a short time.

"Son," he said quietly. "You remember what I told you at the airport when we left?"

I nodded. "Don't worry, Dad," I said. "It wasn't like that." I explained that my contract was for work on three films, which I'd been able to complete very quickly, so I'd gotten a bonus from the studio as compensation. "And then I decided that there are enough stuntmen in Hong Kong—I should be with my parents."

He glared at me from under his bushy eyebrows. "Oh, you've suddenly turned into such a good son, eh?" he said.

My cheeks turned a little red. "Listen, Dad, if you don't want the watch, I'll take it back."

"No, it's a very nice watch," he said. "But I'm not so stupid that I don't know what time it is, Kong-sang. Remember that."

He clapped me on the back and walked away, polishing the face of his new Rolex.

For a while, life at the embassy was just as it had been the last time I'd come to Canberra. I had nothing to do. I still couldn't speak much English. I sat around my room, and when I got bored, I went to the kitchen where my father worked and watched him cook. I guess I'd been an annoyance when I was a little kid, following my mom or dad around; now I was an embarrassment.

After my father almost dropped a pile of dishes running into me as I leaned glumly against a counter, he set the dishes down and grabbed me by the arm.

"Son," he said, controlling himself. "I'm sixty years old. I can still cook, so I cook for a living. You're twenty years old. Will you still be able to fight when you're sixty?"

Then he hustled me out the swinging door.

I got the picture. That day, I had my mother enroll me in a basic English class and began to do my best to learn some useful skills.

The class was taught at the government school, and it was full of Arabs, Chinese, and Indians, people from all over the world who'd emigrated to Australia. The teacher was a tiny middle-aged woman who came up to my chin, and I was one of the shorter students.

"Look, class, we have a new student," she chirped, making me stand in front of my assembled schoolmates. They were all adults, and most of them were older than me. None of them looked as if they had any idea what she was saying. "Young man, what's your name?"

I understood that much, so I told her. "My name is Chan Kong-sang," I said, in broken English.

"I'm sorry, dear?" she said.

"Kong-sang."

She blinked. "Hong Kong?"

"Yes," I said, thinking she was asking where I was from.

"Your name is Hong Kong? How unusual."

I shook my head. "No, my name is Kong-sang. I am from Hong Kong." I'd exhausted my supply of English words.

"Oh, okay," she said. "Well, we'll just call you Steven, then."

I shook my head again. If they were going to call me by an English name, it might as well be the one that the embassy staff used. "Paul," I said.

"Pow?"

I pointed at myself. "I am Paul."

Finally understanding, she smiled, and introduced me to the class as her new student, Paul Chan.

It was obvious that there wasn't going to be a lot of learning going on in this class.

I did work hard, or I tried to, anyway. But I couldn't even get past the ABCs. Trying to listen to the teacher made my head ache, and the bright outside view from the window seemed to call out to me. After so many years of physical activity, sitting in the classroom day after day was pure torture. I was wasting my time.

"Dad, I'm quitting the class," I told my father, after one particularly frustrating session. "School isn't for me. If I don't do something that lets me *move*, I'm going to explode."

Any last dreams my father might have had of my becoming a scholar evaporated. The next day, he introduced me to a friend of his named Jack, a big, hearty Australian man with rough hands and a deep voice.

"Jack is a construction worker," my father told me. "He said there are jobs available at the site where he's working. You won't need to talk to anybody, and you can move around as much as you want."

It didn't sound like such a good deal to me—moving bricks around in the hot sun. But what choices did I have? I would rather have been beaten every day than go back to class. The next morning, Jack showed up to take me to work.

"You look like a strong kid, hey, Kong-sang?" he said, grinning in the pale early light. "You can do a lot of work, hey?"

I nodded. I didn't know what he was talking about anyway. Then we got to the construction site, already swarming with workers.

"Hi, Jack!" shouted one, obviously a friend. "Who's the Chinese kid?"

Jack looked at me, and then looked back at his friend. It didn't take much for him to realize that Kong-sang was not a name Australian construction workers would get an easy grip on. "Aw, hell, his name's Jack, too," he said.

"That's cute, Jacko," said another. "How we going to tell you two apart?"

The workers broke out into laughter.

"Simple," he said. "I'm Big Jack, right? He's Little Jack. Now that's enough out of you lot, get back to work."

Over the months, "Little Jack" became "Jackie." I decided I liked the name, and began correcting the embassy staff whenever they called me "Paul."

And that's how Jackie Chan was born.

CHAN TO CHAN

The backbreaking work at the construction site took up my days, and kept me from thinking too much about my failures while the sun was up. Nighttimes, though, were still long and painful. I thought of what I'd left behind in Hong Kong, and I thought of Oh Chang and her kindness. I thought about the promise that my life had once held. Even after my hours of hard labor, it was difficult to sleep. Rather than lie awake, turning in bed, I took a second job, working as a kitchen assistant in a local Chinese restaurant. I didn't know how to cook, despite my dad's talent, but I knew how to chop vegetables, and restaurants always needed a strong back around. My life turned into a never-ending whirl of work, exhausted sleep, and more work. I stopped thinking about my troubles. I stopped thinking at all.

My father was happy that I was at least staying out of trouble. My mother, on the other hand, knew that something was wrong.

After I'd spent several months at this breakneck schedule, Mom confronted me, late at night, as I walked in from my second job.

"Jackie,"—even Mom had taken to calling me by my adopted name now—"it is nice to have you here with us. We're happy, but I think you aren't happy."

I sat down in a chair and lay my head back on the headrest. "I'm happy," I said, without much conviction.

She came over and put her hand on my shoulder. "Jackie, I am your mother. I know you better than you know yourself, and even if your father is willing to look the other way when you lie to him, I cannot. I know this is not what you should be doing with your life."

"What can I do?" I shouted, sudden feelings of bitterness welling up in my heart. "I spent my entire life learning a useless profession. I've got nothing left."

My mother hugged me and reassured me that I had much more than I thought. I had the love and faith of my parents, I had my health, and I had my youth. "Remember, Jackie, you came to us in the Year of the Horse," she said. "You were born to be a great man, and you will go on to do great things. But you can't do them here. This is not where you belong."

And then, with her mother's heart, she told me to go. Knowing that it would hurt to lose me again, she still pushed me away.

Because to her, as always, my happiness was more important than hers. That's a mother's love.

I decided then that I would have to go back to Hong Kong, to somehow succeed—if only to make my mom's faith in me come true.

But how? My brothers were mostly struggling to find their own way in the industry, after Bruce Lee's death; and though my reputation as a stuntman was still one of the best in the industry, going back to the grind of stunt work was no reason to take the long trip back—even if there *were* jobs available.

It was at this point that someone who would become one of the most important people in my life entered the picture: my manager and very best friend, Willie Chan.

As I mentioned before, Willie, who was working then as the assistant general manager of the Cathay Organization, used to come around to my old studio all the time. Because Willie was in charge of scouting films for his company to distribute, he was a regular fixture around the place. In fact, Golden Harvest had bought Cathay's old studios, so the connection between the two companies was very strong.

Of course, I didn't really know him then. As a stuntman, I never spoke to anybody important. And Willie was a big man—in addition to working for Cathay, he'd produced a hit movie of his own called *Love is a Four-Letter Word*, and he always hung out with the top stars in Hong Kong.

The first time I really met him was at a big celebrity wedding: Charlie Chin, who was a very popular actor from Taiwan, married his girlfriend, an actress named Sing Wong Fang, and to make sure the fans didn't cause any trouble, they wanted a bunch of us stuntmen to serve as bodyguards. I volunteered, and tried to be as helpful as possible. I remember Willie complimenting me on how well I handled the situation, and he gave me his business card, though he probably didn't think I'd ever call him.

It's funny, because later, I ended up starring in some movies with Charlie, along with my brothers Samo and Yuen Biao. By that time, I'd gotten to be very successful, and I don't know if he ever knew that I'd been doing crowd control at his wedding.

Anyway, when I got to Australia, I wrote some letters to people back in Hong Kong, just to let them know that I'd moved. One of them was Willie, mostly because I still had his card. I never thought he'd read the letter, but actually, when I brought it up to him one day recently, he pulled open his desk drawer in his office and showed me that he'd kept it—after all of these years.

I was very touched.

Willie sometimes says it was because of the letter that he decided to contact me. Other times, he says it was because he was impressed with my behavior at Charlie's wedding; still other times, he says that he'd seen me doing some of my stunts and thought I was talented, although young and not yet a very good actor. I really don't care why he did. Whatever the reason, his call saved me from spending the rest of my life in Australia, cutting vegetables and laying bricks, and for that, I'll be grateful to him for the rest of my life.

At that time Willie had just left Cathay to work as general manager at a new production company, formed by the millionaire director Lo Wei.

Lo had made quite a few hit films, and—of course—he had directed Bruce Lee in *The Big Boss* and *Fist of Fury*. After Bruce's tragic death, the martial arts film industry had suffered greatly, and it wasn't just us stuntmen who ended up out on the streets. Luckily for Lo, he had enough of a reputation to land on his feet, going into business on his own.

His first big project was going to be a remake of *Fist of Fury*, his most successful film ever, starring most of the original cast. The problem was that the original was successful for one reason, and one reason only—Bruce Lee—and no other action star was big enough at the time to step into Siu Lung's shoes. No one could convince Lo that that was true, of course; with his ego, he probably thought that any half-decent fighter could be successfully plugged into the lead role. Lo was the millionaire director, after all.

As he was fond of bragging, he didn't ride on stars. He *created* them.

The first step toward the resurrection of my career was actually a telegram that came while I was out on my day job. I arrived home, sweaty and tired as usual, to find a white envelope on my bed, along with a note from my mother saying that it had come for me that morning. I opened the envelope and read, through eyes blurry with exhaustion, that Willie Chan wanted me to give him a call about a job. The originating address of the telegram was Lo Wei Productions, Ltd.

What could he possibly want from me? I thought to myself. Somehow, my hazy brain processed the fact that whatever he wanted from me was better than what I was doing now. So, after changing out of my perspiration-drenched clothes, I went to find someone who would let me use a telephone.

The phone rang eight or nine times before someone picked it up. "Hello?"

"Hello, this is Jackie Chan . . . is Willie there?"

There was a pause. "This is Willie. Who is this?"

I'd forgotten that no one in Hong Kong knew me as Jackie! "I mean, um, this is Chan Kong-sang. Chan Yuen Lo."

"Yuen Lo?" The voice sounded even more puzzled.

"Yuen Lung!" I said, in desperation. I'd been using Biggest Brother's old name on the productions I'd done before leaving Hong Kong. By this time, even I was confused about what my name was! "You sent me a telegram."

"Oh! Yes. Yuen *Lung*," said Willie. "Forgive me. Yes, I wanted to know if you were available to work on a film."

I didn't want to seem too eager. "Well, I'm retired right now," I said. "What's the film?"

"You're somewhat young to be retired, aren't you?" said Willie. "The film is called *New Fist of Fury*. Lo will be directing it."

New Fist of Fury. As reluctant as I was to stand in Bruce's shadow, working on a remake of Bruce's blockbuster hit sounded like a terrific opportunity. I tried to keep the enthusiasm out of my voice.

"Well, what do you need? There are plenty of out-of-work stuntmen around," I said. "Doesn't seem like you need to call across an ocean to find someone qualified."

"Actually," said Willie, "we're looking for someone to play the lead."

The lead? Replace Bruce?

Me?

"Oh," I said. "Ah—I see."

"Can you do it?"

"Well, of course," I said, my voice breaking slightly. "If the money is right."

"Mmm," said Willie. "That could be a problem. We can only pay you three thousand Hong Kong dollars a month."

"What? *Three thousand dollars?*"

I've never been very good at math, but even so, figuring out how little this was was simple. Between my two rotten jobs, I was making about U.S.$1000 a month. Three thousand Hong Kong dollars was about *four hundred* U.S. dollars.

"I know it's not very much, but this is our first production," said Willie. "And besides, we'll be taking a risk using you—an unknown actor."

I gulped. So much for trying to sound cool. "I guess I'll take it," I said.

"Good! You'll have to come to Hong Kong immediately. Shooting starts in two weeks."

"Uh—"

"Yes?"

"Can you at least send me a plane ticket?"

Willie laughed. "I suppose we can do *that*. See you soon . . . Jackie."

I hung up the phone feeling dizzy. I was back in business . . . but at a discount price. I wasn't even sure if I could survive on HK$3000 a month. And what if the project failed, like Da Di and *Little Tiger*?

Then again, what if I wasted the rest of my life peeling vegetables here in Australia?

I'm an optimistic person by nature. I decided that I'd figure out what to do about money when it became a problem. Until then, I had at least one thing to look forward to: quitting my lousy restaurant job.

I grinned, and left the embassy for my last day on the night shift. I'd enjoy the chance finally to tell my boss what he could do with his stupid vegetables.

BACK IN BUSINESS

Saying good-bye to my parents again was hard. My mom cried, even though she knew it was what I wanted. My father gave me an ultimatum: two years. If in two years I hadn't succeeded, I'd come back—and this time, I'd stay for good.

Two years wasn't a very long time to prove that I could succeed, but it was plenty of time to prove I was a failure. Reluctantly, I agreed.

Anyway, if I couldn't make my fortune in two years, I didn't deserve to make it at all.

I arrived at Kai Tak Airport with my head held up and my spirits high. I'd spent a lot of time in airports over the past few years, coming and going. This was the first time I was landing on Hong Kong soil—my home turf—with a bold and bright new future ahead of me.

I had a job, even if it didn't pay much, and a chance at the big time. And I was going to be the lead in a movie directed by one of the top names in the business. Willie even said that they'd send a car out to the airport to pick me up. I'd never experienced that kind of luxury before.

Leaving the gate with my duffel bag over my shoulder, I looked for the driver from Lo Wei Productions.

"Jackie! Over here!"

Turning my head, I was surprised to see Willie himself, standing on the other side of the security rope. He was smoking a cigarette, despite the annoyed stares of the airport personnel, and dressed in one of his trademark flamboyant outfits—a fantastic silk shirt printed in a jarring rainbow of colors, a three-button white jacket with lapels wide enough to land an airplane on, and bell-bottom polyester slacks.

Well, it was the '70s.

Of course, twenty-five years later, Willie still dresses the same way, so I guess that's not really an excuse.

Willie blew a plume of smoke and smiled at me a little sheepishly. "I told you we were a small operation," he said. "Besides, I wanted to welcome you personally! We have very big plans for you."

A little dazed, I followed Willie to his car, a small but serviceable coupe with a shocking purple paint job.

"How was your flight?" said Willie, as I put my bag into the trunk.

"It wasn't so bad," I said, examining my new friend out of the corner of my eye. His wardrobe was wild, and he was a real showbiz type, but unlike most of the people I'd dealt with in my years in the film industry, he seemed kind and open and honest.

Maybe a bit *too* open and honest.

"*New Fist of Fury* will be very big. Enormous," said Willie. "Bruce is a legend, of course, but it's time for a new generation to take charge. 'Youth will rule the world,' eh? And we have a good deal of faith in you. When I suggested to Lo that you'd be perfect for the role, I said to him, 'Lo, okay, so he's not what you'd call *good*-looking, but he can really throw a punch.' "

He narrowed his eyes and scanned my face. "Hmm . . . I hope we can do something with that nose in makeup. Anyway, with Bruce gone, the industry's in the toilet, and everyone's running around like chickens, looking for a new star to pin their hopes on. And that, my young friend, is *you*."

All I heard was the word "star." A *star*! My mother was right all along; I was destined for greatness. Someday, the world would put my name up there right next to Bruce's, or—did I dare imagine it?—maybe even slightly above Bruce's. Yes, *definitely* above Bruce's! I felt my old confidence returning and settled back into the passenger seat of the car. It was going to be a very good year.

And then the car jolted forward, nearly sending me through the windshield.

"Er, excuse me," said Willie. "The motor's a little bit balky. Watch your head."

Stardom could wait.

Putting on my seat belt and gripping the armrest tightly, I concentrated on surviving the drive to the studio.

LO'S WAY

Lo Wei Productions, Ltd. had hardly existed three weeks, but, I was assured, it had phenomenal potential. This, despite the fact that, other than Lo Wei as marquee director and producer, the full-time staff consisted of Willie—who was hired as general manager just a week before I arrived—and a few administrative personnel. Everyone else in the company's small Kowloon offices was a contract worker, hired on a project-by-project basis or signed to a short-term deal.

Including me: Lo Wei's first star-in-training.

As we ascended the stairs to the office, Willie's showbiz instincts seemed to struggle with his basic sense of honesty.

On the one hand, as general manager, he felt obliged to pump up the company's prospects as much as possible. "The sky's the limit, my dear Jackie," he said, gesturing toward the ceiling, from which bits of cracked plaster occasionally dropped. "Hong Kong today, tomorrow the world. We'll be taking *New Fist of Fury* to Cannes—that's in France, you know—and looking for international distribution."

My eyes went round as his words sank in, and I almost tripped and fell backward down the stairwell.

"Ah . . . be careful, Jackie, I believe that step is a bit loose."

On the other hand, Willie punctuated his glorious predictions with wry apologies about the company's minuscule budget. "We aren't quite working in top-of-the-line facilities, I'm afraid," he said. "Of course, that will all change once we've gotten some product out on the market-place. Truly, Jackie, it's all about *potential.* Just remember that one word—potential—and we'll all be fine. Ah, here we are."

Willie struggled with the landing door, which was tacked with a hastily painted paper sign indicating that it led to the offices of Lo Wei Produc-tions, Ltd. I reached around Willie, who was cursing under his breath, and yanked on the doorknob. Luckily, rather than coming off in our hands, it pulled open, revealing an open space that might have been a converted storage loft, and probably was.

A few tables with beat-up phones were scattered around the front of the room. A middle-aged receptionist sat at one of them, reading a wrin-kled newspaper. The walls were decorated with posters from movies made during Lo's golden days. Some of them I recognized; none of them, I noted, featured Bruce. Lo and Bruce had parted ways in a very hostile manner. The papers, always hungry for good gossip, printed rumors that Bruce had threatened to kill Lo with a knife, although, when asked, Bruce responded that he'd hardly have needed a weapon to take care of his nemesis. "If I wanted to kill Lo, I could do it with two fingers," the superstar snorted.

Remembering the argument the two of them had had on the set of *Fist of Fury*, I had no doubt that the breakup was nasty indeed. Bruce's temper was infamous. Almost as legendary as Lo's ego.

Still, I was a bit starstruck at the idea of working with a filmmaker who had played such an important role in Hong Kong's cinematic history.

"Here we are," said Willie. "Your new home. I'll introduce you to the other staff later; they're at lunch right now, I suppose. Follow me, dear boy; I'll take you to meet Lo Wei."

We walked to the far end of the room, where a folding screen blocked off a sort of open-air office. A thick fog of smoke from behind the screen turned the sunlight streaming through the dirty windows a hazy shade of blue. Two voices were engaged in a discussion—one in a bellowing, masculine tone, the other in a gentle and feminine one.

Willie pulled a folded handkerchief from his breast pocket, gently dabbed at his nose and mouth, and then took a deep breath and composed himself.

"Excuse me," he shouted. "I'm back from the airport with Jackie." There was a break in the conversation.

"So what are you waiting for?" the male voice shouted back. "Bring him in."

In the small space behind the screen sat a large, fat man with thick black spectacles and an equally thick cigar. His face was red and damp, and his elbows were resting in a clutter of paper scattered across a heavy metal desk. I immediately recognized him as Lo Wei—a bit grayer, a little older, but still as imposing a figure as ever. Next to him, sitting in a rickety swivel chair, was a young and attractive woman, whom Willie introduced to me as Hsu Li-hsia—Lo's new wife.

I was surprised to hear that Lo had divorced Liu Lianghua, the former actress who had worked as production manager on many of Lo's films; Ms. Liu had been a shrewd woman and a good mediator between the temperamental director and his actors. Of course, it was certainly common for big men like Lo to marry many times, and to have girlfriends and mistresses. In fact, one of the most powerful women in Hong Kong film, Mona Fong, had started out as Run Run Shaw's mistress, before being appointed to a position near the top of the Shaw Brothers studio.

Ms. Liu, a former actress, had been a tough customer who always stood up for what she believed with passionate intensity. She often would say that she wasn't afraid of anyone, and she wasn't—not even Bruce Lee. Raymond Chow, the head of Golden Harvest, had actually sent her to America as his representative in negotiating Bruce's contract with the studio. (Raymond laughs that, in her meeting with the future superstar, she'd outlined the studio's offer, guaranteed him that it was the best he'd find anywhere, and told him that the offer was nonnegotiable—all while waving her finger in his face! Luckily for Golden Harvest, Bruce found her determination charming rather than infuriating, and the deal was made.)

The new Madame Lo, Ms. Hsu, was cut from a different cloth entirely. She seemed quiet and almost delicate, and she had a beautiful smile, which she graced me with as I walked into the office area.

Lo, on the other hand, didn't even spare me a wave hello. Instead, he looked me up and down like a farmer examining a possible prize cow. Stepping to one side, Willie waved at the noxious cigar fumes in the air with his handkerchief, and then shrugged and gave in, lighting up a cigarette.

"He seems fit," said Lo, finally. "Can he talk?"

Willie nodded in my direction.

"I can talk," I blurted out. "I was trained in Chinese opera—singing, fighting, acrobatics. I'm the best stuntman in Hong Kong, and I can be the best actor, too—if I get the chance."

Lo shrugged his heavy shoulders and leaned back in his chair, puffing on his cigar. "There are a dozen unemployed stuntmen in the alley behind this building who trained in the opera," he said. "Let me tell you, kid, the opera is dead. This is the *movies*."

Lo shifted his weight forward and leaned on his desk. "The camera doesn't care how well trained you are, how hard you can take a fall, or how many somersaults you can do," he grunted. "It'll love you, or it'll hate you, and sometimes you won't even know why. If the camera loves you, why, you can be a superstar. And if it hates you, you're *nothing*, you got that?"

Lo tamped his cigar out in a ceramic ashtray already littered with butts. "Now, I didn't become Hong Kong's biggest director by making mistakes, kid. If Willie says you're the real deal, I'm willing to give you a chance. But you listen to me: I'm the director. It's my set. It's my movie. You forget that, and you'll be out there in the alley with the rest of the deadbeats."

I nodded, and Willie patted me on the shoulder. Lo turned his attention back to his conversation with his wife. Apparently dismissed, the two of us filed back out of the office.

"You'll do fine, Jackie," Willie said. "Don't worry about Lo; his bark is worse than his bite, as they say. And I do believe we'll make you a star, my boy. I do believe it."

INVENTING THE DRAGON

The process of turning me into a star began the very next day. I met Willie for lunch—his treat, to welcome me back to Hong Kong—and was told a little bit more about the company's plans.

"First we do *New Fist of Fury*," he said. "We're calling it a remake, but it's not a remake, really. All of the original stars will be playing their roles from the first film, but it will be a completely new story. More of a sequel, in fact."

I nodded, wolfing down my food. It's always hard for me to concentrate on business when there's a meal in front of me.

"Of course, before anything else, we'll have to sign you to a contract. Standard operating procedure, you know," he said. "All by the book."

"Could I have another bowl of rice?"

Willie smiled benevolently. "Anything you want, dear boy." He gestured with one finger and a waiter quickly brought a steaming, fresh bowl of white rice to the table.

I decided I could get used to this kind of star treatment.

After lunch, we went back to Lo Wei's offices, and I proudly signed my first-ever acting contract. The agreement was pretty much the same as most contracts back in those days. I agreed to act exclusively for Lo for eight years, receiving U.S.$400 per month, and an additional U.S.$400 at the completion of each movie. I'd have to work on whatever projects Lo wanted me to work on. I'd have to play whatever roles Lo wanted me to play. And Lo would have the power to veto any major decision in my life—according to the contract, I couldn't even get married without his approval. ("Why would women pay money to watch a married hero?" said Willie philosophically. "Besides, marriage is a distraction! You're young; your career should come first.")

It sounds pretty harsh, and I guess it was. You have to remember, though, this was back in 1976, and it was Hong Kong, not Hollywood. Here in America, the stars are very powerful; they have agents and managers, and they have control over every aspect of their professional lives. Hong Kong has never really given up the studio system. Actors still work under contract, and they still don't have the kind of clout you'd expect. Even the very biggest stars often work on two or three films back to back, shuttling from production to production, and sacrificing sleep—and their personal lives—in the process.

Hong Kong stars are workers, doing a difficult and often tiresome job. The rewards can be great, but we don't have the illusion that what we do is glamorous. That stuff is made up by the tabloids and magazines.

After I signed the contract, Lo introduced me to the other members of the company's skeleton staff. Everyone seemed very nice, but the person I felt most at home with was Madame Lo, who reminded me of my big sisters back at the academy. She was in her early thirties, ten years older than me (and quite a bit younger than her husband), but she treated me very much like a son.

In fact, a few years later, she had to have an operation that left her unable to have children. When Willie and I went to visit her at the hospital, she was heartbroken and crying. "Don't worry," I told her then. "*I'll* be your son."

And from that point on, I always called her "Mother," and it always made her smile.

I never really understood her relationship with Lo. She was his second wife, and they'd been together for a few years; they would stay together until Lo's death in 1996. From her appearance, you wouldn't think she was tough enough to stand up to Lo's constant shouting and screaming, but of all the important people in Lo's life, she stayed with him, even when Bruce and Raymond Chow—and later, Willie and I—all left him behind.

I suppose he was good to her. Underneath all of the bluster, he had a softer side, which he rarely showed to the rest of us. Then again, Ms. Hsu would bring out the best in anybody.

Lo arrived soon after our introductions were finished, having taken the morning off for one of his usual trips to the racetrack. He positively glowed with benevolence; apparently, his chosen horse had come in first, and both the money he'd won and the omen the win represented were enough to put him in a rare good mood.

"Ah, I see the formalities are completed!" he said, lighting one of his foul cigars. "Put the contract on my desk, Willie, and I'll sign it later. Right now, we must move on to more important things—the things that will make our boy here into a star."

He dropped his body into a chair and motioned for me to stand up. "Okay, Jackie, take off your shirt."

I looked at him in confusion. "What?"

Lo creased his brow in impatience. "Don't be stupid, boy," he barked. "When I tell you to do something, just do it. You think people are looking at your *face* in these movies?"

I looked in Madame Lo's direction and flushed slightly. She let out a small giggle and covered her mouth. Oh well, I thought. What did I have to lose? I peeled off my T-shirt and, as an afterthought, flexed my muscles.

Lo nodded. "Not bad," he said. "It ain't Bruce Lee, but you work with what you got. Besides, when I started with Bruce, he was nothing—skinny as a stick. But after *my* special training program . . ."

I looked over at Willie and Madame Lo as Lo babbled on. Willie was rolling his eyes. Madame Lo was laughing affectionately. Maybe that was the secret to their relationship; Ms. Hsu was able to take her husband's excesses with a grain of salt.

Anyway, after Lo finished with his description of how he'd made Bruce into a superman, he returned his attention to me. "Okay, the body checks out. Give me a smile, boy."

I grinned on cue. Lo blanched. "Willie, we gotta fix his teeth. Write that down." Willie was cleaning his glasses and nodded absently.

"While we're at it, we should do something about your eyes. The audiences like big eyes. There's an operation that'll take care of that. Willie, write that down too."

Willie stared at his fingernails, still nodding. I choked. "An operation?"

Lo furrowed his brow again. "Did I tell you to trust me or did I tell you to trust me? Besides, what's a little operation to someone who jumps off buildings for a living, eh?" He had a point.

"Now, the most important thing of all, boy. Your name. What's your name?"

I looked at him like he'd flown in from Mars. "Huh? My name's Jackie," I said.

"No, you dolt, your Chinese name," he roared.

I considered my options. "Well, Kong-sang, I guess."

Lo threw up his hands. "Kong-sang? What kind of name is that for a star? Willie!"

Willie sighed and turned his attention to his boss. "He's been using the name Yuen Lung, Lo."

Lo repeated it to himself under his breath. "Yuen Lung. Yuen Lung. Well, it ain't bad, but it doesn't quite do it for me. A stage name has to have punch. It's gotta say that you're the top of the heap. A hero."

Madame Lo piped up with a suggestion. "How about Yun Lung?" she said. "It *sounds* like Yuen Lung, and it's very pretty—'cloud dragon.' "

The boss waved his hand impatiently. "Pretty ain't what we're looking for here. Besides, a dragon in the clouds can't be seen, right? Doesn't exactly shout success for a movie star."

"How about Zi Lung?" I said. *Zi Lung* means "child of the dragon."

"Forget it," said Lo. "You're a hero, not a kid, kid. We don't want people to think you'll grow up to be a dragon *someday*, we want people to say, 'Hey, this guy's *already* a dragon.' "

Finally, Willie chimed in. "How about Sing Lung?" he said.

Sing Lung means "already a dragon."

Lo snorted and tried to come up with reasons to dismiss that suggestion as well. After a few minutes, however, he conceded that Sing Lung was as good as we were probably going to get.

And that's how I got the name by which I've been known ever since: Jackie Chan Sing Lung—

A new dragon for a new generation.

I was filled with excitement when shooting began on *New Fist of Fury*. I'd woken up early that morning, eaten a big breakfast, and nearly ran over to the set. Willie was already there, deep in discussion with the director of photography. Lo, of course, wouldn't get there until much later in the morning. There seemed to be some agitation in Willie's usually serene features, and I trotted up to him to find out what was wrong.

"Morning, Willie," I said. "What's going on?"

Willie looked up and raised an eyebrow at me. "Good morning, Jackie. Well, it seems that the stunt coordinator that we'd hired for this film has suffered an accident, and of course we'd hate to hold up production to find a new one," he said. "It's a bit of a concern."

I blinked. "Why look for a stunt coordinator when you have the best one in town right here?"

Willie looked surprised, and then nodded in agreement. "Quite right, dear boy!" he said. "You don't mind stunt coordinating in addition to performing?"

It certainly didn't bother me. To tell the truth, I was far more confident about my action direction than my acting. "Do I get more money?"

Willie looked up at the sky as he calculated in his head. "Er, yes, about nine thousand Hong Kong dollars, I suppose."

Nine thousand dollars? "That's three times what you're paying me to be the lead actor!"

He looked at me sheepishly. "Well, yes," he said. "But you're an *experienced* stunt coordinator, and a rookie actor. It's logical, if you think about it."

He patted me on the shoulder again. "*Potential*, Jackie. You have to think potential."

I looked at him, dumbfounded, and then shrugged and headed over to wardrobe. That's Hong Kong showbiz.

My costar in the film was Nora Miao, who played Bruce's girlfriend in the original *Fist of Fury*. She was beautiful and very kind. I'd worked with actresses before, some very big names, but this was the first time I'd worked with a star as a peer. When I had problems with my lines, she helped me out, and as a stunt coordinator, I found her very easy to work with. Though she wasn't a martial artist, she was flexible and athletic, and she carried off her fight sequences quite gracefully.

I, on the other hand, was awkward and stiff as an actor. Part of the problem was my discomfort with the role I was expected to play—intense and angry, a screaming demon with a heart full of vengeance.

Lo Wei wanted me to be the new Bruce Lee, and that went against my whole personality. The experience was frustrating, and I knew that I wasn't doing my best.

"I'm terrible," I said to Willie, after shooting wrapped one evening.

We were sitting in a quiet local bar, drinking beer and trying to release the tensions of the day. Lo had been in a nasty mood from the moment he arrived on the set, screaming at everyone within earshot, even driving poor Nora to the brink of tears with one of his tirades. After several hours of throwing tantrums, Lo left the set in a rage, ordering the cinematographer to finish the day's shooting by himself. Most of the afternoon's sequences were fight scenes anyway, so I found myself in the unusual position of serving as acting director, suggesting setups and camera positions to the bemused D.P. (director of photography).

Willie exhaled a plume of smoke, and stared off into the distance. "It hasn't been a very easy shoot so far, has it, Jackie?"

I leaned my chin on my arms and stretched forward against the bar. "I just don't know if I'm cut out for this, Willie. Lo wants me to be Bruce— you know, a Chinese superman. That isn't my style."

"Mmm," said Willie, taking a sip of his drink. "No, it isn't, is it. Well, the truth is, Jackie, it's not *anybody*'s style—other than Bruce's. It's a sticky situation. Everyone is looking to replace Bruce Lee, not just us. There are producers traveling all over Asia—Korea, Malaysia, China, everywhere— telling people, 'Hello, you look a little bit like Bruce Lee; come on, I'll sign you up.' There are actors out there who are doing nothing but watching Bruce's movies, imitating Bruce, trying to turn into Bruce. I'm sure it's enough to drive someone nuts."

"It's driving *me* nuts." I leaped off my stool and struck a mock ferocious pose. "Here comes the new martial arts hero, Bruce Liu! I mean, Bruce Lai! Bruce Leung!" I hopped from foot to foot, shadowboxing. "Bruce Table! Bruce Lamp! Bruce Chair!"

Shouting a bloodcurdling war cry, I slammed my fist down on the bar, then faked a scream of pain, shaking my hand in mock agony. Stumbling backward, I fell into a chair, tipped it over, and rolled into an upside-down position, then stood up holding the seat of my pants as if I'd ripped them, a mock embarrassed expression on my face.

Then, as if nothing had happened at all, I sat back at the bar and drained my drink. Willie, who'd looked shocked when I began my antics, was now laughing and applauding silently. "And that, I suppose, is your style?"

I shrugged and motioned to the bartender. "I'll have another beer, mister."

"Make that two," said Willie. "Make that two."

We were sitting in the office, our nerves on edge, waiting for Willie to arrive with the box office returns. Lo was puffing madly away on one of his infernal cigars, while I briskly swept the office floor with an old straw broom, working off my anxiety.

It wasn't my job, but I did it out of habit. Despite being away so many years, my training under Master stayed with me, and it probably will for the rest of my life. Even today, when no one's around, I occasionally sweep the floor at the headquarters of the JC Group.

It drives Willie crazy. "What if someone comes in and sees Jackie Chan acting like a janitor?" he always tells me. I don't care. I think it's nice to be tidy.

I'd finished sweeping, and was emptying the wastebaskets when Willie finally arrived. He struggled with the door for nearly a minute before getting it open, then walked in, tossing his coat onto a chair. He didn't look happy.

"What is it?" snapped Lo. "Don't just stand there like a fool; give us the news!"

Willie quoted a figure that sent Lo flying into a fit.

"You gotta be kidding me," he said. Willie stared at Lo without blinking, until the director finally tossed his cigar butt into a nearby trash can—which, fortunately, I'd just emptied—and stomped out the door and down the stairs, slamming it behind him.

I slumped down onto a desk; I'd been through this before. "I guess my luck hasn't changed," I said to Willie. "I should just get my return ticket to Australia now. Before the company goes bankrupt."

Willie sat down next to me. "Don't be ridiculous, Jackie; the company will be just fine," he said. "Despite Lo's little tantrum, the truth is, we'll probably make the film's cost back in Southeast Asia. I'm in charge of sales here, and frankly, I'm pretty good at my job. After all, I'm not just here to decorate the office."

He pulled a pack of smokes out of his jacket pocket, tapped it on one end, removed a cigarette, and lit it. He looked around. "The office *is* looking remarkably nice today." And then he noticed the broom leaning against the wall near my shoulder.

"I thought I told you not to do that, Jackie."

"I know."

"It's not necessary."

"I *know*."

I sighed and picked up the broom to put it away. As I walked toward the closet, I spun it rapidly in my hands, fending off an imaginary attack.

"That's more like it," he said, smiling. "*That's* what you're here for. And don't forget it."

WOODEN MEN AND CHEN

L o, disgusted with the returns from *New Fist of Fury*, decided to farm the directing job for the company's next movie to a young film-maker named Chen Chi-hwa, an earnest and friendly guy with whom I instantly bonded. Chen was just starting out as a director, which meant he was willing to work cheap, which made Lo happy. Chen was also willing to try a few new things—which made *me* happy.

The film we were working on was called *Shaolin Wooden Men*. When a disciple of the Shaolin monks wished to leave the temple and see the world, he'd first have to pass a test to prove that he had the kung fu ability to survive in the dangerous world outside. The test consisted of a long room full of 108 wooden men with arms and legs attached to pulleys that the senior monks would manipulate. They were like puppets—except they were the size of a grown adult, and they moved with lightning speed. To be given the right to leave, the disciple would have to survive a trip through the room of wooden men. Some students died trying. The really good ones—the strongest, quickest, and best-trained—survived, but they would need to use every skill they'd learned from their masters.

In *Wooden Men*, I played a young temple worker who'd made a vow not to speak until I'd avenged my father's death. (Well, it made the job of acting easier, anyway.) To survive the wooden men, and to kill my family's enemies, I had to train in all of the different Shaolin disciplines, from Snake Fist to Crane Style. I also showed off my skills with various weapons, including the staff; I guess my practice with the broom had helped after all!

Without Lo looking over our shoulder, Chen and I experimented with different ideas I had for the action sequences. I jazzed up the animal-style kung fu to make it interesting for the screen—for instance, turning Snake Fist into an elaborate mime of a serpent's attack, with my hands shaped like the open mouths of a striking cobra. It was a lot more entertaining than the stiff traditional styles that Lo Wei demanded in his movies, as far as I was concerned. Sometimes, when we were rehearsing action sequences, I'd clown around, transforming the fights into slapstick routines. Chen even suggested that we include some funny kung fu in the actual movie, but I decided that doing so would probably cause Lo to blow his top. "He's the boss," I said, resigned to my fate and my contract.

While making *Wooden Men*, Chen was still learning about filmmaking, and figuring out what worked and what didn't. Since we saw each other as peers and friends, he often asked me for my opinion. As a result, I myself learned a few things about directing.

In some ways, *Shaolin Wooden Men* was my first "dream movie"—the first film I'd made that felt the way I always thought moviemaking should feel. We weren't just making a product; we were making an experience, and trying to imagine what our audiences would feel while watching the results of our efforts. We made a lot of mistakes—but we learned from our errors and tried to correct them. Lo, on the other hand, had done so many films that he refused to change his style for anyone. His pictures followed a fixed and unchanging formula, one that had been successful for him in the past; his attitude was more or less that if it wasn't broken, why fix it?

But formulas grow stale, and the audiences that had enjoyed the old Shaw Brothers pictures were obviously tired of the same old thing. Bruce Lee should have been a warning, not just to Lo, but to the entire industry: moviegoers wanted something different—a new style of action. The lesson that producers learned from Bruce's success was the exact opposite of the one they should have learned. Instead of looking for something fresh and original, they tried as hard as they could to turn Bruce's style into a *new* formula. And the results were, unsurprisingly, a terrible failure.

Shaolin Wooden Men didn't do all that well in the theaters either. Despite our experimenting, the character that I played was still pretty much a Bruce Lee type—dark, grim, and out for vengeance. By this time, I could tell that Lo was beginning to lose faith in me. On the other hand, Willie told me, the film had gotten me the notice of other producers and actors. "The word is out," he said. "They're saying, 'That Jackie Chan, he can really move.'"

I smiled ironically. "If this keeps up, I'll be moving all the way back to Australia," I said.

A trip was in my future, but it wasn't back down under. In order to save on labor costs, Lo had decided that we'd shoot our next picture in Korea. And to boost the box office potential of the film, which was going to be called *The Killer Meteors*, Lo was hiring a big star to play the lead role— Jimmy Wang Yu, who'd exploded into prominence with his performance in *The One-Armed Swordsman*. After Bruce Lee, Jimmy was maybe the next biggest actor in Hong Kong, following up *One-Armed Swordsman* with a bunch of other films in which he played a martial artist who'd lost one of his arms—*The One-Armed Boxer* and so on. The story was always the same: Jimmy is betrayed by enemies, who cut off one of his arms in order to destroy his fighting ability, and must painfully learn a new, invincible one-armed style, with which he exacts revenge.

Unfortunately for Jimmy, pretty much all of the movies he'd made in which he had two arms were failures, and by the time Lo hired him, his star was beginning to go down. Still, he was much bigger than me—the star of a couple of failed low-budget films—and so I was given the secondary role of villain to play.

Jimmy was a decent guy, but he had been a star for years, and to him, I was just a kid. I hardly got the opportunity to get to know him, despite our weeks together in Korea. The only thing I did find out about him was that he was making a lot more money than I was—HK$50,000, compared to the HK$12,000 I was earning to be both an actor and the stunt coordinator.

I didn't begrudge him his salary. After all, he was a big man. Besides, later on, Jimmy would enter my life again—and I'd end up owing him my life. Compared to that, what's a few thousand Hong Kong dollars?

Despite the presence of Jimmy, *Killer Meteors* was another flop. So was my next film—*To Kill with Intrigue,* a confusing melodrama in which I play the only survivor of a massacre, once again looking for revenge against the murderer of my family. The plot was absurdly complicated, and Lo instructed me to look as tragic and grim as possible throughout the picture even though, halfway through the film, I had lost track of what was going on with the story. Anyone who sees the movie (and I pity you if you do) will understand why. I'm not sure Lo even had any idea where the plot was going, although I have to say, the final fight sequence—which I directed while Lo slept—turned out pretty well.

The next project I was put on, *Snake and Crane Arts of Shaolin,* was something of a relief. Every film in which I had to play a dark and brooding hero was turning into a disaster, so I asked Willie to see whether he'd be able to convince Lo to give me a lighter role to play. *Snake and Crane Arts* wasn't exactly a comedy, but my character—a lone, wandering warrior who is the owner of an ancient martial arts scroll, containing the secrets of a long-dead group of masters—at least gets the chance to show some sarcastic humor. I also was able to play with the action a little bit, adding intricate fights with traditional Shaolin weapons, as well as a somewhat less traditional fight in which I use my female costar as a weapon!

Despite the increased freedom I felt while doing *Snake and Crane Arts,* I still felt trapped by Lo's demands. He hated anything different or original, and he still believed that he could turn me into another Bruce Lee. Every time I tried to lighten up the set, making jokes or doing acrobatic stunts, he became enraged, seeing my attempts at humor as personal mockery of him.

To tell you the truth, joking around was the only way I could relieve my growing bitterness. I was never going to be Bruce, and everyone seemed to know it but Lo.

Sharing another drink with Willie, I finally told him that I was almost at the end of my rope. My two years were almost up, and I still hadn't really gotten anywhere. "I can't do this anymore," I told him.

To my surprise, Willie agreed. "It's a real problem, Jackie," he said. "You're gaining a reputation in the industry as box office poison. If that reputation sticks, the distributors will revolt—and no amount of luck or skill will be able to save your career then."

"What am I going to do, Willie?" I was on the verge of panic.

"Don't worry, dear boy," he said. "Uncle Willie will fix everything."

I hoped he was right. I really did.

FUNNY IS AS FUNNY DOES

I don't know what it was that Willie told Lo, but it must have worked. Lo announced the next day that my next film would be directed by my friend Chen Chi-hwa, and that—unlike the pictures I'd completed for Lo so far—it would be a comedy. The title, he announced, would be *Half a Loaf of Kung Fu*.

"You think you're so clever, boy, we might as well try to use your mouth for something other than just talking back," he grumped. "So laugh all you want. I have more important things to do."

The wheels were already turning in my head. *Half a Loaf* was my big chance to show Lo—and the rest of the world—that kung fu didn't have to be an agonizing journey of revenge. The theaters were more packed with stone-faced warriors than the ancient battlefields of China ever were. It was time to try something different.

And so, Chen and I made *Half a Loaf* into a piece of wild slapstick— turning the martial arts revenge film upside down and inside out. During the opening credit sequences, instead of showing the standard grim kung fu posturing, the camera cuts back and forth between my furious kicks and punches and a wooden practice dummy, the target of my blows. As the credits end, the camera pulls back into a wide shot—showing that the practice dummy I'm attacking is only one foot tall!

I guess the jokes in *Half a Loaf* are pretty broad, like the scene in which I use a villain's toupee as a weapon, twirling it and slapping my opponent with it as if it were one of Bruce's infamous nunchakus. But we had a great time making it, and we were looking forward to the audience's reaction to our ninety-minute-long practical joke.

We didn't get the chance.

According to Willie, when Lo finally got a chance to screen it, he was livid.

"What the hell is this?" he'd shouted. "Is this supposed to be funny?"

Lo never cursed. For all of his faults, he hated profanity. This was a sign that he was very, very angry.

Willie, screening the film with him, replied that yes, indeed it was.

"If he wants funny, *I'll* show him funny," said Lo. "Put this piece of crap in the vault."

And so our movie ended up on a shelf in the office's back closet, unwatched by anyone except for us, Lo, and Willie.

Until 1980, that is.

By that time, I'd gotten to be successful, and Lo decided to release some of my "private" work to the public. And, as usual, Lo's instincts proved to be wrong. When it finally hit the screen, *Half a Loaf* was a hit—among fans who realized that what we were trying to make was the first real martial arts *parody.*

Meanwhile, Lo immediately put me to work on a new project, *Magnificent Bodyguards,* whose only original aspect was that it was shot in 3-D—not that the technology added anything to the movie. (In order to show off the effects, we were instructed to kick and punch toward the cameras. As you might guess, this made my role as stunt coordinator very difficult; usually in a fight, the two combatants are concentrating on trying to hit each *other.*)

Lo refused to talk to me throughout the shoot, directing me by proxy through the D.P. I'm not sure exactly why he was so angry; looking back, I think now that maybe he was offended that Chen Chi-hwa and I hadn't followed in his footsteps, "learning from the master." He was a proud man, and despite all of his bluster, he saw himself as a kind of father figure to me, Chen, and the other young, underpaid people who toiled for his company. And to tell the truth, I did learn a lot from him—a little about what to do, and a lot about what to avoid.

It was only when *Bodyguard* wrapped that Lo finally approached me, a triumphant expression on his face. He announced that he'd commissioned a script for a comedy vehicle of his own, which would show me—and audiences everywhere—what martial arts humor was *really* about.

"It's called *Spiritual Kung Fu,*" said Lo. "I got some great ideas for it already. Just walking up the stairs to get here, I was laughing."

I'd unconsciously edged over to where Willie was sitting, looking in vain for some moral support. Willie had his head buried in some papers, and was trying to appear as busy as possible. It was clear he didn't want to get involved. Lo rolled over to where I was standing and put his arm around my shoulders.

"Now, Jackie, I'm not necessarily saying you aren't funny," he said in a fatherly tone. "See, when you get a little more experience, you'll get an idea what the audience is looking for. This film is going to have 'em *rolling in the aisles.* This is the film that's going to break you into the big time."

I flinched. I had a hint of the kind of stuff Lo thought was funny, and frankly, the whole project sounded to me like a disaster waiting to happen.

Sometimes I'm smarter than I look.

Spiritual Kung Fu was a disjointed mess of bathroom humor and clumsy slapstick, with me stuck right in the middle. Lo's idea of thigh-slapping comic sequences included one scene in which I stuffed a number of small animals into my pants, and another in which I urinated on a midget ghost.

The film was a stinker. Everyone knew it. Even Lo, though he would never admit it. Unable to convince distributors to cough up the funds to get the film released, Lo shelved it and quietly put me into a new film called *Dragon Fist*, which actually had the potential to be a good movie. It had a solid script, with well-written scenes—a rarity for a Hong Kong film. It had nice action. It even had decent characters. As usual, however, none of the characters were suited to *me.*

If Bruce Lee had still been alive, he would have turned the movie into a huge success—burning up the screen with his portrayal of the lead character, a student avenging the death of his master. I did my best, but my best was unconvincing.

Distributors weren't any more interested in *Dragon Fist* than they were in *Spiritual Kung Fu.* Willie's warning, that distributors would begin shutting the door on my movies, was coming true. And without the ability to put films into distribution, Lo Wei Productions was rapidly running out of money.

Somehow, Lo found a way to blame Willie—and me.

After a meeting with his backers, Lo stormed into our office and kicked everyone out, telling us that he wanted a private discussion with Willie. We were hardly out the door when we heard the muffled shouting that was Lo's idea of conversation.

Suspecting that the conversation would have a great deal to do with me, I loitered around the front entrance of the building, waiting for Willie to come out.

The private discussion took several hours. Lo left the building first, chomping on one of his signature cigars, his hat jammed down tight over his head. I ducked around a corner, but Lo would hardly have noticed the queen of England in the state he was in. Then Willie came down, a scarf casually thrown around his neck and a tired expression on his face.

"I know you're waiting for me, Jackie," he called out. I guiltily came around the corner. "Let's go get a drink."

"So what did he say?" I blurted, as Willie downed his vodka tonic in a gulp.

"Well, of course, he reminded me that I'd told him that you would be a star," he said. "I believe he called me a moron and several other unkind words."

I slumped in my seat.

"I told him that you needed more time," he said, tinkling the ice in his glass. "What I didn't tell Lo was that what you *really* need is a different director."

"Now that's news," I said, rolling my eyes.

"Don't you play Mr. Sarcastic with me, boy," sniped Willie. "I wouldn't be saying this to you if I didn't have a solution, would I?"

That got my attention. "What do you mean?"

"Uncle Willie is always looking out for you, don't you know?" He smiled, flicking an imaginary piece of lint from his jacket lapel. "I got a call earlier this week from Mr. Ng See-yuen of Seasonal Films. They're a competitor of ours, small-time, but Mr. Ng is a smart cookie. He's asked us to loan you to them for a few films. They'll pay us sixty thousand Hong Kong dollars for three months, and of course they'll pay you as well."

"What did Lo say?" I asked.

Willie patted himself down, found his cigarettes, and lit a smoke before answering. "He said he'd be willing to pay Ng money to get you out of his hair for a few months. You're off the hook, my dear boy. Now you just go make Uncle Willie proud."

My heart skipped a beat. In a life full of second chances, I was getting yet another. And something told me that this might finally be the one I was waiting for.

SEASON'S TURN

According to Willie, Ng See-yuen, the mastermind of the independent studio Seasonal Films, was known for having a good eye for young talent. Before leaving to start Seasonal, he'd worked as an executive for Shaw Brothers. His coup, and his downfall, was that he'd tried to convince Run Run Shaw to sign Bruce Lee to the monster contract he wanted—and deserved. Shaw, who couldn't imagine that a mere actor was worth that kind of money, suggested that Ng was crazy.

I think the phrase that Americans use is "crazy like a fox." Everyone knows what a mistake Shaw made in missing out on Bruce—even Sir Run Run himself, who told his friends afterward that turning Bruce away was the single biggest error he'd ever made.

After the Bruce fiasco, Ng decided he needed to go off on his own. Seasonal, a well-regarded but small outfit whose films were usually quality projects starring no-name actors, was the result.

The idea to borrow me had originated with one of Seasonal's top stunt coordinators, a man named Yuen Woo-ping. Yuen was actually a Big Brother of mine, though he was old enough that he'd already left the school by the time I got there. I'd met him before through one of his brothers, who'd stunt-coordinated a film I'd worked on some years before, and we'd become friends. When Ng told me that it was Yuen who'd brought up my name, I immediately knew that I could trust him. Any producer who listened to his stunt coordinators was a man worth working for.

"Jackie, let me tell you what I think," said Ng. "I think you have a lot of potential."

I gave him a half-smile. "Yeah, I've heard that," I said.

"I'll tell you what we're going to do," he said. "I don't know you. I don't know much about you. I've seen some of your stuff, and I'm impressed. And *Yuen* believes in you so much that he actually wants to direct you."

That was flattering! Even to this day, I feel good when one of my opera brothers says something nice about my abilities.

"But the truth is," he continued, "no one knows what you can do better than you. So I won't tell you what we have planned for you, because we don't have anything planned for you. I want you to tell *me*. If I put Jackie Chan in a movie, what can Jackie Chan do?"

I was stunned. Lo had gone to great lengths to drum into my head my insignificance. To him, I was just a cog in the movie machine, a part of his grand vision. I was pretty much disposable—cheaper and easier to re-place than a camera, or even a spotlight.

And here Ng was asking me for my opinion. Not on stunt work. Not on martial arts. On filmmaking.

Like an avalanche, it all came out—all of the conversations I'd had with Chen Chi-hwa, with Willie, and even with Samo and Yuen Baio back in my stunt-boy days. I told Ng my likes and dislikes, my dreams, my philosophy about what makes a good action sequence. I said things to him that I never knew I'd thought about before, but that all of a sudden made sense.

"Mr. Ng—"

"N. G., please." For some reason, that was the nickname he preferred.

"N. G., Bruce was the best at what he did," I said. "No one can ever do it better. So why should we try? People want to see living ideas, not dead bones. Bruce was a success because he did things that no one else was do-ing. Now everyone is doing Bruce. If we want to be successful too, we need to be Bruce's opposite."

I leaped off my chair and into a fighting stance, remembering the show I had put on for Willie. "Bruce kicked very high in the air," I said, demonstrating an above-the-head kick. "I say we should kick as low to the ground as possible. Bruce screamed when he hit someone to show his strength and anger. I say we should scream to show how much hitting someone hurts your hand."

I winced and shook out my fist, a comical expression of agony passing over my face.

"Bruce was Superman, but I think that audiences want to see someone who's just a man. Like them. Someone who wins only after making a lot of mistakes, who has a sense of humor," I said. "Someone who's not afraid to be a coward. Uh, I guess that doesn't make too much sense, does it?"

N. G. was stroking his chin, watching and listening to my animated demonstration. "I think it makes all the sense in the world, Jackie," he said slowly. "All the sense in the world. Let's do it. Let's make your movie."

My jaw dropped. I wasn't sure how he'd respond to my suggestions. I guess I was just hoping he wouldn't shout at me. I never thought he'd take what I said seriously.

But he had. And it made me excited and nervous at the same time. Be-cause all this time I'd been telling myself, if only I could make my kind of movies, I'd be a big success.

Now I'd see if I was telling myself the truth.

N. G. decided to give Yuen the directing chance he'd been looking for, and brought him in to flesh out ideas for my first Seasonal project. It was a partnership that was as good as any I'd had in my life; even though

Yuen and I hadn't overlapped during our periods at the school, he knew Master's ways, knew what I was capable of and what would make me look my best. Only Samo knew me better, and at the time, he'd never had the chance to direct.

I showed N. G. and Yuen some of the Snake Fist forms I'd been working on ever since *Shaolin Wooden Men*—showy, silly variations that had less to do with fighting ability than entertainment value. Combined with the acrobatic stunts of my opera training, this kind of Snake Fist would be a good style around which to base the film, we decided.

The other major decision we made was to turn the relationship of master and student upside down. Usually, in martial arts films, the *sifu* is a wise and respected teacher, beloved by his disciples, whose death leads his best student to seek grim vengeance. Maybe as a bit of secret revenge of our own against our old master, Yuen and I suggested that the character of the *sifu* should be a crazy old beggar—but not so crazy that he couldn't teach a young boy a lesson. And, rather than being a noble superman, my character would be a simple bumpkin without manners or ambitions, trapped into learning against my will.

Unlike what Chen Chi-hwa and I had done in *Half a Loaf of Kung Fu*, it wasn't our idea to make fun of kung fu films. With *Snake in Eagle's Shadow*, we wanted to *reinvent* the martial arts movie—to bring humor and humanity to a genre that seemed to have lost its sense of both.

N. G. suggested as my costar and on-screen teacher none other than Simon Yuen Siu-tin, Yuen Woo-ping's father—a veteran Shaw Brothers actor and a former martial arts instructor at my school. Simon lent exactly the right touch of wily malice to his role as the old master, setting off my happy-go-lucky country youth perfectly. In the film, Simon plays the last surviving practitioner of the Snake Fist school of martial arts, which has been under systematic attack by the disciples of the evil Eagle Claw master (played by Korean tae kwon do expert Hwang Jang Lee). When I find the old man lying injured after an attack by Eagle Claw students, I come to his aid and give him food and shelter.

It's a decision I learn to regret, first, because it turns me into a target of the Eagle Claw school, and second, because it leads Simon to take me on as his disciple—and *his* idea of martial arts training features things like push-ups over burning sticks of incense, with him leaning on my back.

Somehow, I survive his instruction techniques and become a Snake Fist fighter.

Unfortunately, in my first battle against the evil Hwang, I realize that Snake Fist is not powerful enough to defeat the Eagle Claw! It looks like the end for me and my master, until I discover my pet cat fighting with a poisonous snake. Even though the snake is fast and venomous, the cat wins the battle with his agility and leaping ability. Once the snake has struck, it is committed; the cat, on the other hand, can twist and turn away from any attack, and land on its feet with any fall. I realize that a cat-style martial arts would be stronger than Snake Fist, and perhaps even stronger than Eagle Claw. After all, cats eat birds, don't they?

And so, in the film's final battle, I defeat Hwang using all of my master's training, combined with the new Cat's Claw kung fu that I've invented. Cat's Claw mostly involves me leaping around and making meowing noises; it's not a real kung fu style. But the acrobatics and tumbling that we incorporated into the style looked wonderful, and the fight was just as exciting as any of Bruce's battles—yet completely unique in look, feel, and tone.

In fact, when we were done with production, we realized that the finished film was different from any kung fu movie ever made. What we didn't know was whether different would translate into popular. Especially since film distributors had warned N. G. in advance that a "Jackie Chan picture" was a recipe for financial heartbreak. Then again, in every way that mattered, this was the first *real* Jackie Chan picture.

We shouldn't have worried.

Snake in Eagle's Shadow was a *blockbuster* hit.

Every week, the three of us gathered in the production office to look over the box office totals, in Hong Kong, and then Taiwan, and Thailand, and Singapore, and Malaysia. The numbers kept going up. And up. And up.

And then, one week, N. G. sat at his desk reviewing the figures, while Yuen and I discussed ideas for the next film we intended to do, occasionally getting up to demonstrate martial arts moves.

"Hey, you two," said N. G., looking up at me and Yuen. "Here's a question: what's the biggest film in the history of Hong Kong?"

We stopped in midspar. *"Fist of Fury,"* I guessed.

"Nah, *Way of the Dragon* was bigger than *Fist of Fury,*" said Yuen. "It's gotta be *Way of the Dragon.*"

N. G. gave us both a broad smile. "You're both wrong." He handed us a slip of paper covered with scribbled numbers. "The answer is *Snake in Eagle's Shadow.*"

Bigger than Bruce!

I whooped and slapped Yuen on the back, sending him sprawling, and then did a backward flip.

Bigger than *anyone!*

As much as I'd fantasized about the possibility of becoming a star, it was always just a dream, something that could never really happen. Fame and success belonged to other people, the beautiful ones, the wealthy ones. Not poor, uneducated, unhandsome boys like me.

"No time to celebrate," said N. G. "We have to prove to the distributors that this thing, this Jackie Chan *phenomenon,* is not a fluke. We have to make them understand that you, my boy, are for real. And that means another movie."

Yuen looked at me, and I grinned back. "No problem, boss," he said. "Listen to this idea. . . ."

The idea we'd been working on would take the successful formula we'd begun with *Snake in Eagle's Shadow* and bring it to the next logical level. It would be faster. Looser. Funnier. And it would throw an even more hallowed tradition for a loop.

One of the greatest legends of Chinese history is a hero named Wong Fei-Hung. He was a doctor and a warrior, a healer of the sick and a protector of the weak. He was one of the most powerful martial artists of his time, one of the Ten Tigers of Canton, a rebel whose skills were feared by the tyrannical Ch'ing emperors and revered by his people. In fact, his story is at the very heart of the Cantonese cinema, because the first hit movies in Hong Kong history were a series of films about his life. (A series so successful, in fact, that it ran for ninety-nine episodes!)

What Yuen and I suggested was that we make a new film about Wong. However, rather than show him as a heroic adult, we would explore what he was like as a young man *before* he grew into his legend—lazy, naive, ignorant, and rebellious.

"I like it," said N. G. "I shouldn't like it, but I like it."

And so we began shooting *Drunken Master,* the film that would change everything for me forever. We took the best stuff from *Snake in Eagle's Shadow*—recasting Simon Yuen as a drunken old master who becomes my mentor. We invented a whole new set of kung fu styles, called Eight Drunken Gods martial arts, based on the drunken-style kung fu that Wong Fei-Hung was supposed to have practiced as his secret weapon. We added wild acrobatics, street brawling, slapstick antics, comic mime, and even some real drama.

It was bigger than *Snake in Eagle's Shadow.*

It was bigger than any of us could possibly have expected.

I had started to see things change for me when *Eagle's Shadow* was released; other actors knew my name, and sometimes people recognized me when I went out. But after *Drunken Master,* I had my first real taste of what it was like being a celebrity.

People ran up to me in public, asking for my autograph. I would see kids playing "drunken master" in the street, weaving and rolling their arms. Newspapers started calling me for interviews, and gossip magazines sent reporters to follow me around. And N. G. wasn't stingy with the money my movie had earned; instead of the HK$3,000 that Lo Wei paid me per film, he gave me HK$50,000—more cash than I'd ever seen in my life.

Instant fame and sudden fortune do things to people. I'm human. And I'm not very proud of the kind of person I became. I was used to eating noodles in the street and sleeping on the floor of my little apartment. Now that I had money, I started to buy things that I'd always envied, big star things, like gold chains and nice clothes. I looked at automobiles, trying to decide whether a Porsche or a Mercedes best fit my new image. I remember walking into the same jewelry shop where I'd bought gifts for my parents; this time, I bought gifts for myself: seven watches, all Rolexes, one for each day of the week. I went into a boutique that I remembered as being very snobbish—one that had warned me that the clothes they sold were too expensive for someone like me. This time, I had them bring out all of their clothes one by one as I sat there, nodding and shaking my head. Finally, I pointed at random items, not even making it particularly clear which ones I wanted, and told the staff to send them to my apartment. I could tell that the salespeople weren't sure which clothes I'd picked, but they were afraid to let me know. It didn't matter; I intended to return some of them anyway, just to make life difficult for them.

Everywhere I went, I was followed by a group of twenty people— stuntmen, acquaintances, and hangers-on. They weren't my bodyguards, and they weren't even really my friends; they were there because I had money and I was willing to spend it. But I was blinded by my ego and pride.

I started acting like a big shot in public, too. There's a hotel in Hong Kong called the Peninsula—the finest, most elegant place on the island. Of course, the rule in Hong Kong is that you must be dressed appropriately. A jacket, a tie, a suit, even a tuxedo. One afternoon, I strolled over to the Peninsula with my gang of followers, and walked through the front door—wearing shorts. It wasn't long before the commotion drew the manager, who recognized me as Jackie Chan, the movie star.

"Mr. Chan," he said, his eyebrows quirking. "We are, of course, honored to have your business, but we cannot allow you to eat here wearing short pants."

"Why not?" I said. My followers clustered around me, nodding their heads and gesturing.

"Well, we have rules about proper attire," he said, sweat beads beginning to appear on his upper lip. "You must wear long pants. . . ."

I looked at him, in his sharply creased black suit, his bow tie, and his crisp white shirt. He was the kind of guy who would have kicked me out if I'd come to the hotel just three months before—the type of patronizing jerk who cared more about how someone was dressed than what kind of a person he was. A well-dressed Triad gangster could be seated here in an instant. Jackie Chan in short pants could not.

"Okay," I said. "I'll wear long pants. Give me a pair of long pants, and I'll put them on."

The manager, flustered, said that it was all very irregular, but soon afterward left and returned with a pair of black slacks in my size. Right there in the Peninsula lobby I pulled them on over my shorts, and then motioned to my people to follow me into the restaurant. I drank one cup of coffee and then motioned to my followers that it was time to leave.

The next day, we came back.

"Mr. Chan, I'm sorry," said the manager again, this time quite agitated.

"What's wrong?" I said, innocently. "I'm wearing long pants."

"But . . . you're wearing a T-shirt," he said. "We have a strict policy—"

I shrugged my shoulders. "You said long pants. You never said anything about what kind of shirt. Let's go, boys."

And we brushed past the manager into the restaurant, where I had my second cup of Peninsula coffee in two days.

It was very immature, but it was the kind of revenge I'd been hungry for all of my life. Somehow, I'd realized that being famous meant I could break the rules without getting punished. I could make my own rules. And even if I was punished, having money meant that I could get away lightly.

It isn't any different here in America. You see teenage idols on drugs, or drunk, or in jail. Too much, too quickly, with no one ever telling them no. I was fortunate to have had my master and my father when I was younger, so I never got into any real trouble. But, as I said, I'm not proud of the way I behaved.

The one thing I am proud of is that I set aside HK$20,000 out of the money N. G. gave me and packed it nicely in a beautiful wooden box. On top of the cash I put an expensive pearl bracelet, and then I wrapped the box myself. The package was delivered to Oh Chang the next day, along with a note telling her that she had my eternal thanks—and more, but that part of our life was over, and we'd both accepted it.

I moved to a beautiful new apartment, nicely decorated with real furniture. I don't know what happened to my handmade junk; I guess it just got thrown out. I wish I'd kept some of it today, just for the memories. But at the time, I didn't want to keep anything from my earlier life.

Unfortunately, there were some things from my earlier life that I couldn't avoid forever.

The phone rang, and I rolled over in my bed to reach for it. It was midmorning, headed toward noon, and I was still dead asleep, having spent most of the previous evening out with my boys.

"Hello?" I said sleepily.

"Jackie, is that you?"

It was Willie, whom I hadn't spoken to since I'd finished my two films with Seasonal. (When I first began working with them, I'd spoken to Willie just about every day, telling him what a joy it was to work with Yuen and N. G., and thanking him for making the "loan" possible. Eventually, though, the excitement of success had taken over, and my communications with Willie had been lost in the noise of the crowd.)

And that's when it hit me.

My work at Seasonal was temporary. I was still under contract to Lo Wei.

All of the success I'd gained could be pulled away just as quickly, if I returned to the box office failures that had haunted my past.

"Hi, Willie," I said weakly.

"Congratulations on your success," he said. "I'm very happy for you, but, I'm sorry to say, it's time for you to come back."

"Isn't there anything you can do?" I said. "I don't care if it's Seasonal or Shaw Brothers or anywhere; loan me out again! I can't make the kind of movies Lo wants me to make."

Willie was quiet on the other end of the line—struggling again between his duty to the company and his friendship with me. "Jackie, let me talk to Lo," he said. "I think I can make him understand that your success is based on your freedom—and that you'll only come back if you can make the movies you want to make, the way you want to make them."

I thought about what Willie said. He was right. I was under contract. And, as my father would have said, it didn't matter if Lo wanted me to put my head in a tiger's mouth. A contract is a contract. My honor was at stake. But if only I didn't have to trade my career for my honor!

My only hope was, once again, to trust Willie.

LO DOWN

"Welcome back, kid!" said Lo, grinning like a bespectacled Buddha. "I knew you had it in you."

I was standing in Lo's office, surrounded by the applause of the company's part- and full-time personnel. Willie had set a vase of fresh flowers on my desk, Madame Lo kissed me on the cheek as soon as she saw me, and in general, people treated me like a conquering hero. I flinched slightly when even Lo gave me a hearty hug.

It was all too much. Just three months ago, I'd been loaned out like an old set of clothes, and now that I'd returned, covered in glory, everyone was acting as if they'd known I was destined for greatness all along. Besides Willie and Madame Lo, who had ever treated me nicely here? Who had ever thought I had a chance of succeeding? Certainly not Lo.

I barely listened as he went on and on about the plans he had in store for me. Finally, claiming to be exhausted, I asked to be excused. Formerly, this kind of impertinence would have sent Lo into a rage: how dare I refuse to listen to his rants!

Obviously, things were different now.

"Whatever you want, Jackie, whatever you want!" he said. "After all, you're *our* star!" The emphasis was on the word *our*, not the word *star*.

I nodded and smiled weakly, shaking hands with some of the proud and happy staffers who saw my return as a chance for the company to finally make some real money.

I was halfway down the stairs when I heard a staccato of footsteps behind me. It was Willie, who evidently had made his own excuse for leaving moments after me.

"Hold up, dear boy," he said. "I think we need to talk. I'll buy you lunch. Though I suppose now that you're such a big star, you should be treating *me*."

Over the slurping of noodles, I told my troubles to Willie: my fear that Lo would take away the freedom I'd found with N. G. and Yuen Woo-ping, that he'd put me in projects that didn't suit my personality and wouldn't appeal to my fans, that a continued connection with Lo would ruin all hopes I had of building on my Seasonal successes.

Willie took off his glasses and polished them with a clean handkerchief. "It's a difficult situation, Jackie," he said. "You *are* under contract for at least one more picture. And, once that contract is finished, Lo will no doubt want you to sign another one."

Replacing his glasses, he rubbed at his mustache and put on an expression of concentration.

"Okay. You have three main problems that I can see," he said, counting them off on his fingers. "The first is that you want to make sure Lo won't interfere with your style. That's the easy one. We'll tell him that *you* want to direct your next film.

"The second is that you want to make sure that any contract you might sign has an out clause—in case someone gives you a better offer. That's no problem, either. I'll make sure the contracts guy puts that into any agreement Lo offers you.

"The last is that you need to find out the market rate for Jackie Chan. And—I shouldn't be doing this, but I will anyway—I'll make some phone calls. There's nothing to worry about, Jackie. The best is yet to come."

Two bowls of noodles later, the world did look quite a bit better. I was going to get a chance to direct my own film. Lo Wei would stay out of my hair. And if my next movie succeeded like the ones I'd done with Seasonal, I'd be able to demand anything I wanted in my new contract. Willie was right.

The best was yet to come.

Unfortunately, by the time we got to Korea, where Lo had decided we'd shoot our next picture, it was clear that Willie's first "no problem" was going to be something of a problem. Lo wasn't about to give up his chance to direct me now that I was hot, and pass up the opportunity to add another million-dollar movie to his résumé.

"Who does this kid think he is?" he raged to Willie, as I sat out of sight but not out of earshot. "He gets lucky a couple of times, and all of a sudden he thinks he's king of Hong Kong. Well, I'm not going to let him screw up a golden opportunity. An *experienced* hand, someone who knows what plays and what doesn't play—"

I wandered out of hearing range of the conversation. *An experienced hand.*

Experienced at what? At making me look like a fool?

My heart jumped up into my throat as I felt myself growing furious at Lo's stubborn pride. I'd rather never make a movie again than walk through another of his stupid attempts to turn me into something I wasn't.

Gathering my resolve, I ran back to my hotel room and packed my travel bag. Lo could do whatever he wanted, but he wouldn't be doing it to Jackie Chan. I didn't speak much Korean, and I had no idea how I could get back to Hong Kong, or Australia, or anywhere where I had friends or family. I was beyond caring. I'd sleep in the streets if I had to, if it only meant a chance to escape the curse of Lo Wei.

I clattered down the stairs, slammed open the door, and drew startled glances from bystanders as I bolted into the hotel lobby. Racing through the streets of Seoul, I ran at top speed, as far as I could, out and away. It felt like hours by the time I stopped, alone in a part of the city I'd never seen before. I wandered through buildings that were beginning to shutter, looking for somewhere to stay, and listening for the sounds of a familiar tongue.

Finally, I found a small place that looked like an inn or boarding-house, and (using cash, sign language, and the few broken words of Korean that I knew) got a place to sleep for the night.

No one knew where I was, least of all me.

On the one hand, this was exactly what I wanted—to be alone and free. On the other, now that I was away from the source of my frustration, my heart had begun to soften, thinking about the people I'd left behind: Willie, my stuntmen, and of course, Madame.

Leaving my small room, I gestured to the boardinghouse manager that I wanted to make a call. After I "convinced" her with some more money, she reluctantly led me to her phone, standing suspiciously behind one shoulder as I dialed the number for one of my stuntmen, who demanded to know where I was. I told him, after getting him to promise not to tell anyone else, and asked him for an update on the situation at the set.

"Bad," he said. "Lo had a fit; he's lying down now, and Madame is worried—about him and about you."

I felt a twinge of guilt as I told him to let them know that I was all right, but that I wouldn't be coming back.

An hour later, as I sat on my lumpy boardinghouse bed, there was a knock on the door.

It was Madame.

She looked heartbroken and sad, and her eyes were red with tears. "Jackie, please," she said. "Don't go."

"It's over," I said. "I'm not going to let him run my life anymore."

She extended her hand, touched me gently on the arm. "Try and understand. He's been in the business so many years, and he's lost so much. First Bruce left him, and now—now you. If he's squeezing too tightly, it's because he's afraid to lose you. And I know he's wrong," she said. "But then, *I'm* afraid of losing you, too."

Somehow, in that instant, I saw Lo as she saw him—a faded star, a man whose youth and greatest success were behind him, hoping against hope that the fire of his career could be relit by mine. I didn't like him, but I could pity him. And for the sake of the woman whom I'd come to think of as a surrogate mother, I realized that I'd have to stay; stay and fight for my rights, perhaps, but not run away, not abandon Lo. Not without giving him another chance.

I hugged Madame Lo, and threw my still-packed bag over one shoulder. Together we walked back to the set.

Willie was waiting for us, smoking a cigarette and wearing a self-satisfied smile. "Welcome back," he said, "director."

And so I made my directorial debut, *Fearless Hyena*. I was working with a smaller budget than in my Seasonal films, but I also had the benefit of knowing more or less what I wanted. As usual, I played a young man who underwent unusual training to learn an obscure martial arts style—in this case, Emotional kung fu. To defeat the villain, played by Yen Shi-kwan, I learned how to get in touch with my feelings, attacking him with joy, anger, and even tears. I still had much to learn about filmmaking, and in a lot of ways *Hyena* is a more uneven movie than *Drunken Master*.

Still, that didn't seem to matter to the audiences, who mobbed the theaters when it came out. *Fearless Hyena* was my biggest hit to date, not to mention Lo's first blockbuster ever since his Bruce Lee days. More and more, he referred to me as the "son he never had," as his pride and joy. He even bought me a sports car to celebrate *Hyena*'s box office success, though I noticed he still paid me only HK$6000 in salary.

"Double what you used to make!" he said, proud of his generosity. I guess he felt that, since the contract required him to pay me only HK$3000, anything he gave me on top of that was an act of amazing benevolence.

And every chance he got, he dropped hints about the future—about the big new contract that he expected to sign with me, tying together Lo Wei Productions and Jackie Chan for decades to come.

"You were right, and I was wrong," said Lo, letting out a strained belly laugh. "It takes a big man to say that he was wrong, eh, Jackie? I'll say it again: *I was wrong*. It's obvious that you know what you're doing. Director, actor, stunt coordinator, everything. You can do it all. Let's just make sure you keep on doing it for *us*."

We were sitting across from one another, Willie and me on one side of the conference table, Lo and his contracts manager on the other side. The seating arrangement wasn't quite coincidence. Even though, as general manager, Willie should have been sitting next to Lo, he'd already made his feelings clear. If Lo Wei Productions was going to keep Jackie Chan, Lo would have to unbutton his notoriously tight pockets.

"It's not just fair, it's good business sense," Willie had said. "Lo, I'm not given to bluntness, but I do believe that other studios are interested in Jackie. Seasonal would love to have him, of course. Shaw Brothers would give him the keys to the studio. And I've heard that Golden Harvest—"

Lo thumped his fist on the table. "Don't talk to me about Golden Harvest."

Willie folded his hands together. "As you wish."

The mention of his former employers never failed to put Lo into a bad temper. But the last thing he wanted to do now was fly into one of his patented fits of rage. Controlling himself with effort, he turned back in my direction. "If it's money you want, money it is. Fifty thousand Hong Kong dollars per movie? No problem."

Willie snorted. "More like a hundred thousand Hong Kong dollars," he said.

"Whose side are you on, anyway?" Lo screamed.

One hundred thousand Hong Kong dollars a movie was already more money than I could imagine. I didn't understand why Willie was taking on Lo the way he was; even if the big boss was not about to fire me, he could probably make life miserable for Willie.

"*And* a reasonable cancellation clause," said Willie. "One movie's worth. One hundred thousand dollars."

Lo's face turned an amazing shade of purple verging on violet. To his left, the contracts manager, an anxious old man who lived in perpetual fear of his employer, was already cringing at the inevitable explosion.

It never came. Reaching deep into some hidden well of self-control, Lo managed to choke off his tantrum before it led to physical violence.

"Okay," he said, breathing hard. "You got it. Just sign on the dotted line, Jackie, and we'll take care of the rest."

The contracts manager pulled out a sheet of lined paper. It was blank.

"What's this about?" said Willie, his lip curled in suspicion.

Lo ignored him. "Sorry, kid, we just got back from Korea, no time to do up all the legalese for a deal as special as this. So, just sign here, we'll get you a copy of the document as soon as it's done, and everyone's happy, right?" He winked at me. "Unless you just want to sign a *standard* contract."

Before Willie could say anything sarcastic, I grabbed his arm and shook my head. Willie might have been acting in my interest, but he had a job to keep, too. I knew that Willie had taken the position with Lo out of necessity. After Cathay had gone under, Willie found himself stuck in Hong Kong with an expensive rent, a fast-paced lifestyle, and a pocketful of debt; Lo's company was the only one hiring. Even going back home wasn't an option, since Willie's mother and brother had moved over from Malaysia to join him here.

I didn't want Willie to fight my battles. And besides, for all of his arrogance, I couldn't imagine Lo would ever do something to hurt me—on purpose, that is. I was a star now, not a slave. I was the one calling the shots.

I took the pen and signed the blank contract.

Lo smiled. Willie glowered. The contracts manager sighed.

I was just glad that the whole thing was finally over, so I could get on with building my new career. Little did I know, of course, that it was *far* from over.

In fact, the battle had yet to begin.

THE JACKIE WAR

The cardinal rule of Hong Kong cinema has always been, "If it works once, do it again." Which is to say that any big hit is sure to result in dozens of quickie rip-offs and at least one or two official sequels.

As a result, it wasn't much of a surprise when Lo Wei announced that my next film for the company would be *Fearless Hyena II*.

We'd already begun shooting when I got an urgent phone call from Willie, who'd decided not to join us on the set.

"Jackie, we need to talk," he said, sounding unusually excited.

"Okay, let's talk," I said, my mind fixated on the movie at hand.

"We need to meet, face-to-face," he said. "As soon as possible."

Something was up. Something big, if Willie didn't want to talk about it over the phone. I told him I'd meet him over at the office as soon as shooting had wrapped for the day.

Willie was at his desk, talking on the phone, when I walked in, still wearing my movie costume. He waved at me, continuing to talk, and motioned at me to sit. I made myself comfortable in a swivel chair—there were no couches in the office—and let my head slump back. Willie's conversation was animated and went on for a while. He was talking about numbers, numbers that sounded vaguely like money, but I was too tired to concentrate on eavesdropping.

Finally, he hung up the phone and swiveled his chair to face mine.

"Who's your favorite uncle?" he said to me, his face lit with a smile.

I opened one eye and looked at him with suspicion. Had he cracked under the pressure? Lo was riding him hard these days, ever since our little contract negotiation, and the two were making a point to stay away from one another—if Lo was at the set, Willie stayed at the office, and vice versa.

"What's going on, Willie?"

Willie laughed and put his hands behind his head, leaning back in his chair. "Only big money, Jackie," he said. "Only big money."

That woke me up. "Huh?"

"Remember I told you I'd make some phone calls?" he said. "I just got off the line with Golden Harvest. They offered you one million Hong Kong dollars to sign an exclusive contract."

My eyes bulged. One million Hong Kong dollars? That could buy my entire apartment building! "What—where do I sign?"

Willie shook his finger at me. "Ah ah ah, you don't sign anywhere. I told them about your loyalty to Lo Wei, and said that a star of your stature wouldn't break a *contract*—"

My face fell.

"—for such a small amount," he finished.

Small amount! I found myself having trouble breathing. "Willie, are you crazy?"

"Don't worry, dear boy, it's a negotiating tactic. Now, the first thing we do is call a meeting with Lo—to give him a chance to beat the offer. Meanwhile, we sit and wait for the next round."

Things were getting beyond me here. "*What* next round?"

He quirked an eyebrow at me in surprise. "You don't think I was silly enough to speak to just one studio, do you?" he said. "I expect Shaw Brothers should be calling shortly with their bid. In the language of the deal, Jackie, you're 'in play.' Now, don't you worry about anything; I've got things under control here, and I'll keep you up to date. In the meantime, isn't it nice to feel wanted?"

One million Hong Kong dollars!

I had to agree with Willie: it felt very nice indeed.

"This is a stab in the back, *traitor!*" shouted Lo, smashing his fists into the table and sending papers flying. I couldn't tell if he was referring to Willie or me, but I suppose that in his eyes, it didn't make a difference.

Sitting in front of him was a check from Golden Harvest for HK$2.7 million, made out to Jackie Chan Sing Lung. That is to say, me.

"I'll rip this up! You have no right to negotiate with other studios," he yelled. "We have a *contract!*"

I looked over at Willie, who was unmoved by Lo's hysteria. "Go ahead and rip it up," he said. "There's plenty more where that came from."

Lo howled.

"The truth is, Lo, Jackie's worth a lot more than you're paying him, and a lot more than you can even afford to pay," Willie continued. "Now, we can make this pleasant, or we can make it difficult—it's entirely up to you."

Actually, my conscience was beginning to nibble at me. I *had* signed a contract with Lo, after all. And I didn't want to abandon Madame.

But the money—well, Willie had said that it wasn't the money, it was the principle of the thing. Although I never imagined that principles could attach to numbers that big.

"I'll sue!" raged Lo.

"Difficult it is," said Willie. "Well, I'd hoped it wouldn't come to this,

I got down and dirty in the line of duty for *Project A*.

With brother-in-arms, Samo Hung.

Twinkle, Twinkle, Lucky Stars allowed me to work with Yuen Biao (on my right) again . . .

. . . and a shot from *Dragons Forever,* which was
the last of our films together. So far.

At a Japanese
TV appearance
alongside my
brothers—fellow
action stars Yuen
Biao (center) and
Samo Hung
(right).

Trying to catch up with some crooks,
1) I snag with an umbrella the back
of the bus they've hijacked . . . 2) only
to have them hit the gas! 3) Up to the
second tier of the bus, dodging oncoming
traffic . . . 4) and hanging on for dear life.
For the rest of the stunt, you'll have to
rent the video.

A shot from the movie that almost killed me (although you could say that about all of my movies): *Armor of God.*

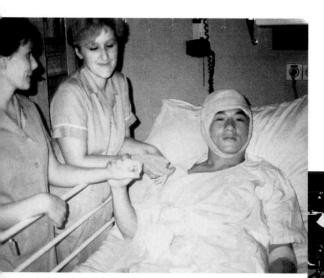

A simple stunt gone awry led to my getting emergency brain surgery in a hospital in Yugoslavia. Ever since then, I've had a hole in my head.

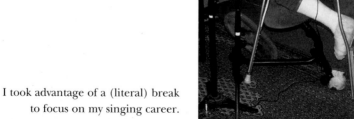

I took advantage of a (literal) break to focus on my singing career.

AIR JACKIE—
AS MUCH AS I
PREFER KEEPING
MY FEET ON
THE GROUND,
I ALWAYS END
UP JUMPING,
SLIDING, OR
FALLING FOR
THE SAKE OF
ACTION.

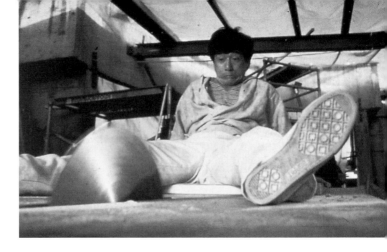

Mr. Nice Guy

First Strike

Supercop

HERE I AM, GETTING
MY KICKS . . .

Mr. Nice Guy

First Strike

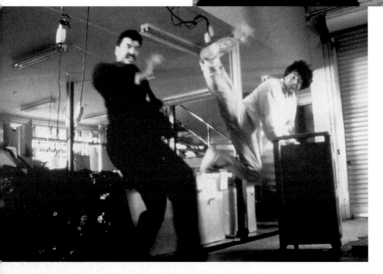

Scenes from *Rush
Hour,* costarring
Chris Tucker. He's
a hilarious guy.

Looking cool in New York City's Washington Square Park.

My fans come in all shapes and sizes. I met this
one during the filming of *Wheels on Meals*.

seeing as how Jackie is in the middle of shooting a picture, but I believe it's time for us to go."

Lo pointed a fat index finger directly at Willie. "*You* go! You're *fired*! And as for him, *he* ain't going nowhere!" Lo called to his contracts manager, who was trying to be invisible behind the divider. The manager walked slowly over to his boss, carrying a handful of papers. "Read 'em and weep." He spread them in front of Willie, who adjusted his glasses and began reading. After a few minutes, he pulled off his glasses and slapped them onto the table.

"Lo, this is revolting," he said, his voice icy. "You have broken Jackie's trust and turned your back on any honor you might have remaining in your tiny soul. He should have left you years ago, instead of waiting to find out what a villain you truly are."

The words coming out of Willie's mouth were the hardest things I'd ever heard him say. The contracts manager had turned as pale as paper. Lo, on the other hand, didn't seem to care at all.

"He can leave anytime he wants," said Lo. "As long as he pays me HK$10 million."

"What?!" I shouted, jumping up. Willie let the papers falls to the desk. The number was there, exactly as Lo had said—right above our signatures. Lo had taken advantage of my naïveté, changing the terms of our agreement after I'd already signed a blank contract. Instead of the HK$100,000 we'd agreed upon, my buyout was a hundred times higher—and four times what Golden Harvest had offered me as a signing bonus.

"Now get the hell out of here, my *former* general manager, before I call the police," snarled Lo. "And as for you, Jackie—let's put this whole ugliness behind us and get back to making movies, okay?"

"You can't fire me, Lo—I won't give you that satisfaction," said Willie. "I *quit*." He pushed back his chair and walked out, grabbing his coat and slamming the door. I turned my back on Lo and ran to follow my friend.

My worst nightmare had come true. Willie had lost his job. I'd lost my chance at the big money. And any kindness in my heart toward Lo, the man who called himself my godfather, well, that was gone too.

Which didn't leave me with very much at all.

"I'm sorry, Willie," I said, as we sat at our usual bar, surrounded by an air of gloom. "I was stupid to sign that blank contract."

Willie sighed. "No, Jackie, you weren't stupid," he said. "Just young. And who could have known Lo would pull a stunt like that? It's beyond belief. It's beneath anything I thought he might be capable of."

We stared at our drinks, as if some happy resolution to our mess might emerge from a glass of cocktails.

"If only we could prove that Lo changed the contracts," said Willie.

"Right now, it's our word against his. And unfortunately, he does have your signature on those papers."

I slapped my head, as if to punish myself. *Stupid!*

"Hello, Willie . . . Jackie," said a voice behind us. We both turned toward the sound. It was the contracts manager, looking nervously in all directions. "I need to talk to you."

Willie patted the bar stool next to him, and the manager, a somewhat creaky older gentleman, hopped up with difficulty.

"Can I get you a drink?" said Willie. There was a sourness to his tone, since Willie obviously considered the manager to be one of Lo's tools, but the look on the old man's face suggested that he had something to say that was worth hearing.

He shook his head, declining the offer. "I just needed to talk to you quickly; Lo will wonder where I've gone. Listen, Jackie, you've been good to me, and I'm ashamed at the way Lo has treated you. I remember how you lent me money for my daughter."

The manager's daughter, who still lived on the mainland, had been ill, and I'd given him some cash to send to her, even though at the time I didn't have much myself.

"Well, I'm not one to repay a favor with a bad turn, so I want you to know this: Lo told me to change the contracts. I have a memo he signed that tells me exactly what to do—turn one hundred thousand Hong Kong dollars into ten million Hong Kong dollars. And if this goes to court, I'll be your witness, even if it means losing my job." He placed a folded piece of office paper on the bar, nodded to Willie and me, and then left.

Willie unfolded the paper, read the note, and Lo's signature at the bottom. And then he let out a whoop—nearly causing me to spill my drink, since Willie was not given to public displays of emotion.

"Jackie, my dear boy, we're back in business," he crowed. "This is all we need to prove that Lo acted in bad faith. Don't worry about me—I'll be making phone calls from home."

He drank the rest of his drink and slapped a handful of money on the counter.

"Let the bidding begin!"

A week later, Willie called me at Lo's office.

"You shouldn't be calling me here, Willie," I whispered.

"It's all right, Lo never answers the phone, and the receptionist is hardly going to turn me in, is she?" he said, sensibly. "I was quite nice to her."

"What's the news?"

"Are you sitting down?"

I sat down. "Yeah."

"Golden Harvest has upped its bid to four-point-two million Hong Kong dollars," he said.

I kicked out my legs and spun around in my chair. In two weeks' time, they'd doubled their initial offer, and then doubled it again.

"That's not all, Jackie," he said. "Shaw will go as high as five million."

My head began spinning. Four million, five million, two billion; all the numbers were too high to count, and more than I could imagine spending in a lifetime. There really didn't seem to be a difference anymore.

"What—what should I do, Willie?" I said.

Willie paused, as if to think. "Take the Golden Harvest offer. Raymond Chow and Leonard Ho are good people. Run Run Shaw—he's something else," he said. "Besides, Leonard is guaranteeing you all the major markets. You're the biggest thing in Asia since steamed rice, Jackie. But how would you like to be big in France, Germany, and Spain? How about *America?*"

The U.S.A.! Bruce had been the only Chinese star ever to conquer the States. Golden Harvest had put him there. And now they were promising to send me on a journey to the West as well.

"Where do I sign?" I shouted, causing people around me to look in my direction, startled from their chores.

I didn't care. I was gone.

I'd stayed with Lo out of loyalty and innocence, and I was leaving in disgust. I would miss Madame, and I knew she would miss me. But I would leave her a note, explaining what had happened, and I thought she would understand.

Lo's chains were broken, and the future was bright. And America— the home of Hollywood, where filmmaking began—awaited. I had long watched American films with envy, wishing I had the budgets and resources they boasted with every frame; I'd danced along with Fred Astaire, hummed to Frank Sinatra and Julie Andrews, laughed at Chaplin and Keaton and Lloyd, the great comics of the silent classics.

Now, someday soon, I'd join them in Hollywood's galaxy of stars.

Nothing could stop me now.

GOLDEN BOY

Coming back to Golden Harvest was like coming home. I felt a shock of recognition as I walked through the gates. I'd spent so many days here—sweating in the half-shade while waiting for the stunt coordinator's call, testing my limits in countless death-defying feats, hanging out with my brothers on the studio lot, kicking around a soccer ball. Now I was returning, the keys to the studio in my hand.

The Golden Harvest offices were more crowded and in better shape than I'd ever seen them. After recovering from the shock of losing Bruce, the studio had found new life in comedies and romance dramas. They'd discovered a fresh set of stars in Michael Hui and his brother Sam. Michael was a bespectacled Everyman whose character Mr. Boo had been featured in dozens of rollicking farces, while Sam was a singer and teen idol, beloved by young Asian girls everywhere.

They were at the top of their game, the Hui brothers. But even with all of their success, neither of them was being paid the kind of money I was getting. Golden Harvest was making an investment in me, assuming that I would become a superstar. An action king.

I wouldn't let them down.

Willie was pacing in the reception area, waiting for my arrival. When he saw me, he gave me a warm hug, which I happily returned. The door to my future had opened because of him, and I'd already decided that Willie was my secret weapon. I might be able to direct a movie or a stunt, but it took a different set of skills to direct a career. Willie had told me to trust him; my trust had been rewarded. From this point on, my life was in his hands.

The man we were going to see was Leonard Ho, Golden Harvest's vice president and head of production. He and Raymond Chow had built the studio together, with Raymond as the flamboyant dealmaker and front man and Leonard as the soft-spoken nuts-and-bolts professional. They'd worked as journalists together at the Voice of America, and then left to work for Run Run Shaw. Raymond quickly rose to a position as Shaw's right-hand man, while Leonard became a prominent executive in Shaw's publicity and marketing department. When Raymond left to start his own studio, it was only natural that he'd bring Leonard with him; their partnership had produced nothing but success since then.

One thing that struck me about Golden Harvest as we waited in the reception area was the fact that among the new faces I saw among the staffers were a number of foreigners—Americans, by the sound of their accents. Ever since their success with Bruce, Chow had decided that Golden Harvest's future was as an international film company, producing films in both English and Chinese, and releasing them in both the East and the West. No other Chinese studio had as much of a global presence. If any company could bring me to the attention of the world, Golden Harvest could.

"Come this way," said the receptionist, motioning toward us. "Mr. Ho will see you now."

We followed him down a hall, pausing briefly to examine posters from some of Golden Harvest's movies—featuring Bruce, the Hui brothers, and other top stars. The posters were in English, Japanese, Korean, and languages that I didn't even recognize. When I walked through the gates, I'd felt like I was coming home. Now I felt like I was stepping into another world.

Leonard's office was neatly and richly decorated, and dominated by an elegant wooden desk. The chairs, unlike the ones in Lo's office, were upholstered in leather. I couldn't resist bouncing lightly in my seat, testing the depth of the cushion. Willie nudged me in the shoulder and gave me an annoyed look.

Then Leonard entered the room, and I met the man whom I would learn to respect and love like a father.

He was immaculately groomed, and his black hair was streaked with gray. He wore a dapper tailored suit and an expensive but tasteful watch. I had enough money now to wear nice clothes, but next to him, I felt like I was still a ragged kid.

"You must be Jackie," he said warmly, and walked over to press my hand. "And of course, the illustrious Willie Chan—it's good to see you again, Willie."

Willie smiled and greeted his old acquaintance.

"I'm so glad you decided to join us. We're very excited to have you on our team," he said, seating himself at his desk. "Now, I'm here to listen, not to talk, so let's get down to business. Tell me your ideas."

I didn't have any ideas! I was still trying to digest all of the new changes in my life. My stomach churned as I tried to come up with something to say to this important gentleman.

Willie noticed my discomfort and jumped into the conversation. "Leonard, Jackie is certainly very excited to be here as well, and I know that he'll be happy working with you and Raymond," he said. "As you know, he's experienced some good success in his recent films; perhaps you might tell him some of the things that you like about his work, and what you'd like to see him do in the future."

Leonard leaned back in his chair and smiled. "Well, of course, we've admired his abilities for a good while," he said. "Even as a stuntman, he's had a tremendous reputation. But we feel the films he's done so far haven't fully stretched his potential. The imagination in your choreography, Jackie, and the comic element—they make your work different from anything we've seen. The important thing to us is that you be yourself—and that you constantly strive to reach new ground. Try fresh things. Original ideas. It's all very well to follow in the footsteps of past successes, but we feel that every movie should leave audiences feeling like they've seen something they've never seen before."

I was amazed. I'd never heard a Hong Kong production executive say that he wanted to see anything new; new things are risky, and in an industry as fast-paced and competitive as Hong Kong's, it was almost always seen as better to repeat the past than chance the future.

"Mr. Ho—"

"Call me Leonard," he said.

"Leonard," I said awkwardly. "I just want to make *good* movies. My kind of movies. Good action, good comedy. I want to show people what martial arts films can really be, if enough time and effort are spent to make them look and feel proper."

Leonard spread his hands in reassurance. "Jackie, we run a business, and we're as interested in making money as the next person," he said. "But do you know what the biggest star in Hong Kong is making per movie—the biggest star after you?"

Well, I had no idea.

"Michael Hui and his brother make one hundred thousand Hong Kong dollars per picture," he said. "We didn't give you a bonus of four million because we don't believe in you. I know this is our first meeting, but I swear to you that as long as you make movies for Golden Harvest, you'll be able to make them exactly the way you want. No need for budget approvals. No month-by-month deadlines. You make the movies, and *we'll* concentrate on making money."

And with that, I was struck mute. What else could I say? It was like a fairy had appeared and told me that all of my wishes were granted at once. Wealth, fame, and freedom to create.

Willie continued the small talk with Leonard, but the real reason for the meeting was finished. If I hadn't been sure about Golden Harvest before, I was sure about it now.

Yes, I was home.

And Willie, an I-told-you-so gleam in his eye, gave me a broad and knowing wink.

Charged up with enthusiasm, it wasn't long before I got back to work. After some discussion with Willie and Leonard, I decided that what I wanted to do was to make a film that would showcase *classical* kung fu in a new and fresh way. No crazy master, lazy student. No secret and obscure training sequences. I knew people were expecting me to do something similar to my Seasonal films, but then again, everyone had already copied that style—in fact, even Seasonal was making movies, starring other actors, that used the same formula.

If anything, I wanted to do a story that was simple but had strong moral value, without falling back on the tired old revenge plots of the Shaw Brothers heyday. The message I wanted to send would be the importance of friendship and brotherhood. And while it would use traditional martial arts styles, I also wanted to make a point about the limitations of tradition: if my career had proved anything so far, it was that sometimes you have to do the unexpected, break out of the mold, in order to achieve victory.

So, in *The Young Master*, I'd play a young martial artist whose school is betrayed by its best student. But rather than seeking to defend my school's honor by killing my brother student, I'd go out to try to save him—and end up being mistaken for him by the police. In the end, I'd face the rival school's master, played by Whang Inn-sik, a Korean tae kwon do expert. All of my techniques would prove to be too weak to defeat him. Finally, I would beat him up using a wild, furious flurry of attacks, showing no skill at all. And even if the result was that I'd be terribly injured—the final scene ended up showing me waving good-bye in a full-body cast!—it would demonstrate that emotion and self-expression are sometimes more important than tradition and pure skill.

In some ways, I saw *The Young Master* as the end of a phase in my life, one where I was surrounded by barriers put there by history and other people's expectations. From now on, the only expectations I worried about were those of my fans and myself.

I wanted everything to be perfect for this film. It would be my first movie for Golden Harvest, and I knew everyone would be watching to see if I could keep up my string of successes. Taking Leonard's promise to heart, I'd shoot and reshoot scenes until I felt that I'd gotten them right. For one shot, in which I was to kick a fan into the air and catch it nimbly with one hand, I shot over five hundred takes!

But as the extended shoot continued, strange things began to happen on the set. A fire broke out unexpectedly in front of the studio; police later determined that it was arson. And then a Golden Harvest executive found a bloody, severed dog's head in his car.

These events were too unusual and too close together to be a coincidence. It seemed that there was some unfinished business at hand.

My suspicions would soon be proved correct. One night, as I was leaving the studio, I walked out of the front gates only to realize that I was being followed by three ugly men, none of them taking the trouble to seem innocent.

I figured that anything that was going to happen would happen whether I caused trouble or not. If there was a fight, I could handle myself; my martial arts is mostly for performance, not brawling, but I wasn't afraid of a few thugs. Of course, it would all change if they had knives or guns. It's not so easy to beat an opponent with a gun if you aren't his stunt coordinator and his boss.

"Jackie Chan!" shouted out the tallest one, pointing at me. He didn't sound like a fan.

"That's me," I said, turning to face them.

"You're coming with us," said the thug to his left. "We don't want any trouble."

I shrugged. I didn't want any trouble either, so I raised my palms to show I'd go peacefully. I wasn't particularly scared, but I *was* curious. There was only one person who could have arranged this, and if he'd gone to this much effort to bring me to a meeting, I supposed it was in my best interest to play along.

I was escorted by the three bullyboys to a late-model Mercedes, whose license plates had been covered with gray gaffer's tape. If I'd had any doubt about what kind of people I was dealing with before, I didn't anymore.

I mentioned the Triads before, in discussing the three promises my father had asked me to make. I think I should go into a little more detail about these gangsters, and their involvement in Hong Kong entertainment.

The Triads have been a part of Hong Kong performing arts since the turn of the century, when secret society members joined wandering opera troupes to disguise their movements. Since many early film stars came from the opera, there was always something of a tie between the Triads and the movies. But that alone wouldn't have led to the problems we have today.

The biggest fault can be laid at the feet of Shaw Brothers—which basically controlled the movie industry until the rise of Golden Harvest. Shaw Brothers was the biggest employer in cinema, and without serious competition, they were able to pay slave wages. I thought the money I was getting as a freelance stuntman was bad, but at Shaw's, even contract stars got almost nothing.

To survive, some actors and stuntmen turned to the Triads—acting as small-time muscle for mob operations in exchange for a level of pay they couldn't get from their legitimate jobs.

When Shaw Brothers went into television, they brought their absurdly low pay scales with them, and another part of the entertainment industry soon became infected. And since music in Hong Kong is so closely linked to film and television, it shouldn't be a surprise that the Triads soon had a great deal of control over music as well.

In fact, it's sad to say, but it's almost impossible to do business in any of these industries without running into gangsters. Some of them have a lot of power, running production companies, talent agencies, and music labels. Others are much more small-time. But even a small-time thug can cause big-time trouble.

There are always reports of actors and actresses who are threatened with death (or worse) unless they agree to star in a Triad producer's movies, of singers caught in wars between competing Triad record moguls and forced to announce world tours just to get out of Hong Kong, of models and beauty queens pushed into acting as escorts for Triad bosses.

In fact, the Triad hold on Hong Kong entertainment is so strong that it's now become almost an accepted part of the business. Many directors and stars now speak of "good" Triads and "bad" Triads—good Triads being the ones who take money without threatening violence. I suppose the implication is that, if you have to work with gangsters, you should pick only the best.

It's an awful situation. My feeling is that we shouldn't have to do business with gangsters at all—good, bad, or indifferent. Hong Kong's entertainers have never had much power, compared to Hollywood stars. But working together, we should be able to make a difference!

A few years ago, after a series of very ugly public Triad incidents, I rounded up many of my friends and colleagues, and we staged a protest march against Triads in the entertainment industry. The march was covered by the media, and our demands to the government got heard. A special police team was put together to investigate organized criminal activities, and promises were made that the abuses we were being subjected to would be curbed.

I guess we'll see what happens in the future.

At the time of my capture and involuntary Mercedes ride, of course, I had no power to do anything at all, and knew very little about the Triads and how they operated. I did know that there were some people who had the reputation of being "connected guys," knowing or having a relationship with Triad bosses.

For instance, my former boss, Lo Wei.

The Mercedes pulled up outside of the offices of Lo Wei Productions, and the three men helped me out of the car and up the stairs.

"I'm sorry it has to be this way, Jackie," said Lo. "As I've told you time and again, I think of you as a son. But every so often, when a son is disobedient, discipline is necessary."

I was sitting in my usual position, in a swivel chair facing Lo's cluttered desk. The bullyboys had exited for the hallway at Lo's request, leaving the two of us alone.

"Do you really need three thugs just to give me a spanking, 'Dad'?" I said, sarcastically.

Lo laughed. "Please, Jackie, I don't want you to get the wrong idea. These . . . *friends* of mine are just here to make sure that you don't still have hard feelings over how we last parted. Actually, our, ah, failure to communicate hurt me deeply. I just wanted the chance to talk things out with you, one on one—without outside interference."

It wasn't hard to guess that Lo meant he wanted Willie out of the way. I suppose he thought that, without Willie, I was a soft touch—that I'd easily be rolled into a sucker deal.

Lo pulled out our old contract. The buyout clause had been scratched out. So had the old salary figure, of HK$100,000 per film.

"No funny business, Jackie," he said. "You just write in whatever number you want there, 'cause I know I can trust you to be reasonable. And then we can go back to the way things were always meant to be. Lo Wei and Jackie Chan. And you won't be working for me, you understand. It'll be Lo and Chan, *partners*. A team, see?"

I stared at the contract, and then at Lo's face. There was a damp sheen to his face under the flickering fluorescent bulb. He didn't look too good. Losing me must have hit the company pretty hard. And for him to reach out to his "connections" probably put him in a dangerous position. If I didn't sign up with Lo again, it wouldn't just be me in the wringer. The Triads never helped anyone out without a promise of a piece of the action.

A very difficult situation had developed—an uneasy balance of forces, between Lo, me, Golden Harvest, and now the Triads. For the situation to be resolved, something would have to give—and "giving" could be very unpleasant indeed.

"Listen, Lo," I said, keeping my voice as calm as possible. "I'll need a little while to think about this. After all, I'm in the middle of shooting a film over at Golden Harvest, and it wouldn't do for me just to disappear, would it?"

Lo frowned. "Being in the middle of shooting didn't stop you from jumping ship here," he said. "Well, all right, Jackie, but, ah, don't take too long. I can't guarantee the actions of my colleagues beyond a certain point, okay? You take your time, but not *too* long."

I nodded in understanding. Lo's hold on the Triads would last only until they decided that I might be about to slip away. At that point, they'd be motivated by the need to protect their own investment. By any means necessary.

"Can your three little friends give me a ride home?" I asked. "I heard it isn't safe to walk around alone at night in Hong Kong anymore."

Lo flinched, looking almost as if he had a conscience. "Sure, Jackie. Sure."

I rode home with the three Triad boys in silence.

None of them asked for my autograph.

The next day, I went to work as usual. We were about two-thirds complete on *The Young Master,* and I wanted to get the film done as quickly as possible, before any further disruptions occurred. I guess I seemed a bit on edge. Sitting in the production office that Golden Harvest had provided for me, Willie expressed concern at the way I was pushing myself and my team.

"What's wrong, Jackie?" he said. Willie wasn't officially a part of the production team, but as my chief adviser and career consultant, he was a constant presence. In fact, I'd talked to him about setting up a special arrangement—forming a company, which he would help me run. The name would be Jackie and Willie Productions; Willie would be CEO, and I would be chairman. J&W Productions would handle my career and manage any business interests I might develop. At the time, there was no such thing as a talent agent or manager in Hong Kong, but I hardly knew anything about that. I only knew that Willie, as I said before, was my secret weapon.

Which didn't mean that I didn't have my own secrets. I hadn't told him about Lo's bullyboys, or the threat he'd made if I didn't go back. I guess I didn't want to put him in any danger—but, come to think of it, he was probably already in danger.

I had to tell him. And so I did.

Willie put his head into his hands and cursed under his breath. "Damned thugs," he said. "And to think that Lo would sink so low."

"He seems kind of desperate," I said, thinking back to his pale, sweaty appearance.

"No excuse. Well, let's take a look at our situation," said Willie. "First, you have to finish this movie. It's very important that your career continue strongly; you can't afford to lose any momentum. Second, we have to find a way to appease Lo. And then, of course, there's the Triads. I don't have any 'connections,' and I'm not sure that I know anyone reliable who does. I'm going to have to go to Raymond with this."

Raymond was the boss, Golden Harvest's president. Though I'd met with him frequently since I'd been signed, most of my studio dealings were through Leonard, who was chief of production. Raymond was the big negotiator, but Leonard handled day-to-day business.

"Why Raymond?" I said.

Willie gave an ironic smile. "Because this may involve a lot of money, Jackie, and Raymond is the one who approves Golden Harvest's investments."

I moved quickly toward completion of *The Young Master*, not knowing whether Lo's ultimatum was measured in days or weeks. The answer came in an unsubtle fashion. One day, when I arrived at work, there were an unusual number of strangers hanging around the front gate. Most of them were wearing sunglasses, and all of them watched me as I came up the road.

I waved cheerily to them, and tried to press on through the gates. Like a blob of honey, they oozed around me and blocked my way.

"What seems to be the problem?" I said, my eyes flickering around for the security guards.

The tall bullyboy who'd escorted me on my midnight ride stepped forward. "We're just here looking for some answers," he said.

"And what would be the question?" I said, seeing the guards running over from the distance.

"Don't try to be smart with us, Jackie," he said. "Are you going to make movies for Lo Wei, or not?"

I crossed my arms. "What if I say no?"

"That would be a bad career decision," he said, "and probably a bad life decision."

The security guards arrived and whistled at the crowd to disperse. The Triads jostled one another and moved off the walk, allowing me to pass, but not before the tall one made it clear that they weren't going very far.

The gates closed behind me, shutting my problems outside. Unfortunately, I couldn't live at the studio. And neither could my friends and coworkers.

I hoped Willie had another solution in his bag of tricks.

Unfortunately, I didn't see Willie all day. Night fell, and I wrapped the shoot, steeling myself for another confrontation with the boys at the gate.

I wasn't disappointed.

"Out late tonight, guys?" I said, as the Triads took their positions along the sides of the gate walk. They glowered at me and said nothing.

"Listen," I said. "I don't want to waste any more of your time, and I'm sure you don't want to waste mine. So here's what I suggest, okay?"

I told them that I'd agree to do Lo Wei's next film, as long as they let me finish production on my Golden Harvest film. We were going into postproduction on *Young Master* anyway; it wouldn't be too hard to get away to work on another set. I certainly wouldn't be the first Hong Kong star to work on back-to-back productions.

The leader of the bunch talked it over with his colleagues, and finally they agreed. "No funny business," he said. "I'll be here to pick you up tomorrow afternoon, and you'd better be ready to go when I arrive."

I assured him I'd wait with open arms.

At least this bought us some time. With any luck, Willie and Raymond could figure a way out of this mess that didn't involve watermelon knives and mayhem.

Sometimes life is even stranger than the movies, isn't it?

I spent the next few days commuting between postproduction on *Young Master* and preproduction on the movie that Lo Wei's company was supposed to be making. I noticed that Lo was nowhere in sight, however, and that the Triad boys were everywhere. There was no script. The equipment was shoddy even by Lo's standards. The crew was minimal— subminimal, really. In fact, I wouldn't have used the setup I'd been provided for shooting home videos, much less a feature film.

It didn't matter; I had to make it look like I was making a movie, even if I had no idea what the Triads expected. "Is there a particular kind of movie you guys are looking for?" I asked.

The head Triad boy looked at me like I was an idiot. "An action movie," he said.

"Oh," I said. "That kind of movie."

I shrugged my shoulders and did my best to prepare my inexperienced crew to shoot *Action Movie: The Feature Film*. Starring Jackie Chan and a cast of nobodies.

It was probably an idea ahead of its time.

"Okay, Jackie, I think we finally have things under control," said Willie, walking into my production office to find me slumbering on my desk. "Jackie?"

I lifted my head and groaned. I'd been working double days for a week, editing and looping *The Young Master* during the day, while working on preparations for *Action Movie* in the evening and at night. I was exhausted. "What took you so long?"

Willie looked irritated. "You cannot expect us just to wave a wand and make all the Triads in Hong Kong disappear, dear boy."

So *that* wasn't the solution, then. "Well, what did you do?"

Willie sat down and lit a cigarette. "Okay, we had three problems, correct?"

I nodded.

"First, there was finishing *Young Master*, and you're very close to doing that."

Even if it was killing me.

"Then, there's the problem with Lo Wei, who still has a contract that says you owe him ten million Hong Kong dollars, even if you and I know it's a fraud," said Willie. "Let's just say that Raymond has agreed to take care of that."

I didn't ask for details, but Willie had said that Raymond was responsible for Golden Harvest's investment decisions, and this was an investment if I'd ever heard one.

"Lastly, there's the problem with the Triads. Which is actually our biggest problem, as I'm sure you've noticed." I gave Willie a glare. "Yes, I see you have. Well, it seems that someone has volunteered to be a moderator between the various parties involved here: our old friend Jimmy Wang Yu."

If you remember, Jimmy was my costar in *Magnificent Bodyguards*. He knew Lo, and he knew Raymond—he'd been at Golden Harvest for years after leaving Shaw Brothers. Most important, he knew the Triads. He was based in Taiwan, and there were rumors that he was something of a big man in shadowy operations on that side of the water.

"Jimmy is going to try to broker a peace agreement between the Sun Yi On—that's the Triad group we're dealing with—Lo Wei, and Golden Harvest. If he succeeds, we're off the hook. If he fails, it really doesn't matter, because you won't be around to find out."

I blinked. That was a more fatalistic comment than I expected out of Willie, usually quite the optimist.

"Do you mean I'll be dead?" I said.

He laughed. "No, Jackie, you'll be in Hollywood," he said. "Although there are some people who'd say that's pretty much the same thing."

JOURNEY TO THE WEST, PART ONE

J ust days after my conversation with Willie, the two of us were on a plane, leaving Hong Kong. We spent a short time in Taiwan, getting updates by phone from Leonard Ho. From there we went to South America, where we flew from country to country—"like refugees," joked Willie, which in a way we were.

"Here's some good news," said Willie, as we sat on a hotel sundeck in Rio. "I received a telegram from Leonard saying that *Young Master* just broke ten million Hong Kong dollars at the box office. You have another hit, Jackie."

I took a sip of iced tea. It was nasty—Brazilians just didn't know how to make proper tea, that is to say, Chinese tea—and I was in a rotten mood anyway. "When do we go to America, Willie? I want to get back to work."

Willie snapped the newspaper he was reading, and turned the page before answering. Somehow, Willie was always able to get Chinese-language newspapers, no matter where in the world we went. "Well, Jackie, think of it as a vacation," he said. "Golden Harvest wants to make sure your 'situation' is resolved before it puts you on a new project. Besides, the script isn't ready, and I'm sure you want your first American film to be as good as possible, don't you? Finish your tea and go out on the beach. It's lovely here, and both of us deserve a little bit of rest."

And then Willie leaned back in his deck chair, covered his face with his newspaper, and went to sleep.

I threw up my hands in disgust. I didn't know how Willie could be such a cool customer, considering the situation. What would happen if things didn't work out? Would we be on the run forever?

I was bored out of my wits, and I hated being bored more than anything. It almost made me want to go back and face the Triads. At least I'd see some action.

My prayers were finally answered a few days later. Willie knocked on the door to my room, waking me from a deep slumber. I shook the sleep from my head, and opened the door, still in my shorts. "Morning, Willie,"

I mumbled. As usual, he'd woken early and was already dressed in a tropical blaze of color.

"Morning, Jackie," he said, good-naturedly. "Time to pack up. We're checking out today."

I blinked. "Another country?"

He nodded. "Several, actually. That is to say, I'm going back to Hong Kong, while you, dear boy, are headed north—to America."

"What? How come you're not coming with me?"

Willie shrugged and walked into my room, tsking at the discarded clothing that lay in heaps on the floor. "You're usually neater than this, Jackie. Vacationing doesn't bring out the best in you, does it?" he said. "Well, it seems that Leonard and Raymond feel that you should go alone—you'll have to learn to fit in, you see, and I'd only act as a crutch. This time, you're on your own, I'm afraid."

I dove back into bed, hiding my head under a pillow. "What am I going to do, Willie?" I said, my voice muffled by the fabric. "I've never been to the States; I don't know anyone there. I don't know any English. I wouldn't even know how to order *breakfast* in America!"

Willie sat down on the bed and patted me on the leg. "Well, of course, I can tell you how to say some simple things!" He laughed. "And there's a Golden Harvest office in America—you won't be completely alone. Besides, if you have any troubles, you can always just call Hong Kong. Just remember that there's a thirteen-hour time difference; I don't want to be woken up in the middle of the night, okay?"

He stood up and headed for the door. "And Jackie," he said, as he left the room. "Remember to write!"

As we sat in the airport waiting for our respective flights, Willie filled me in on what had happened in Hong Kong. The summit meeting between Lo, Jimmy Wang Yu, and the Sun Yi On had apparently not gone well. The news wasn't clear, but there had been some sort of altercation that had ended with the gathering being broken up by the police.

Luckily, calmer heads eventually prevailed. Lo's contract with me had been bought out by Golden Harvest, and Lo had settled his arrangement with the Triads. He retained the rights to the movies I'd made under that contract (including the unfinished *Fearless Hyena II* and the undistributed *Half a Loaf of Kung Fu*), but agreed to release me to Golden Harvest without restrictions and without further harassment.

"In short, Jackie, there shouldn't be any further problems with anyone," said Willie. "Although there is the matter of owing Jimmy Wang Yu a few favors. It got somewhat sticky for a while there, I imagine."

That was probably an understatement. Later, I ended up returning the favors to Jimmy Wang Yu by appearing in two of his films—*Fantasy Mission Force* and *Island of Fire*. They were both awful, but I'd been raised to believe that nothing was as important as repaying a debt.

Still, in the end everything had worked out for the best. And all that was left now was for me to start earning back Golden Harvest's investment.

Hollywood, I thought to myself, *ready or not, here I come!*

COMING TO AMERICA

os Angeles International Airport was extremely crowded and very noisy, even by Hong Kong standards. I had never been around this many foreigners in my life—that is to say, Americans. I had to remember to start thinking of myself as the foreigner!

It was very unnerving, being on my own in a place where I didn't know a soul and had no knowledge of the language. Of course, I'd been in the same situation in Australia—but at least I'd known my parents were going to be there to meet me. Here, in America, I truly was on my own.

Willie had told me that a Golden Harvest representative would come to meet me at the airport—an overseas Chinese guy named David Chan. (He wasn't related to Willie or to me. I know, it seems strange, but Chan is a very common Chinese name.) I looked around, pausing to examine the occasional Asian face for signs of recognition, but no one approached me. Finally, I walked out toward the concourse on my own.

Just as I was beginning to think I'd been abandoned in America, a breathless voice shouted out, "Mr. Chan!" in Chinese. I turned and saw a man about my age, dressed in jeans and a sports shirt, holding a cardboard sign that said my name—Sing Lung.

"I'm sorry, I thought you'd be at the baggage claim," said the young man, who I assumed was David.

"I don't really have any bags," I said. "I've been traveling around—I guess I packed light."

David nodded and smiled. "Well, welcome to Los Angeles, Mr. Chan. I'll be driving you to your hotel. You'll be staying at the Westwood Marquis; it should be very comfortable."

I had no idea what the "Westwood Marquis" was, and so I tried to memorize the syllables, in case I needed to ask directions in the future. Of course, I wouldn't understand the directions anyway, so what was the use?

The prospect of being in America was starting to look a little less rosy.

In the car on the way to the hotel, David chatted on about my films, all of which he'd seen. "I'm actually a big fan, Mr. Chan," he said. "*Drunken Master* is one of my favorites. I'd show you my own drunken style, but you know, I'm driving. We could get arrested." David laughed at his own joke. "Seriously, Mr. Chan—"

"Call me Jackie, David," I said. "We're the same age; you're making me feel old."

"Sorry, Mr. Chan. I mean, Jackie. I was just saying, I saw the script they've written for your debut, and it looks pretty good," he said. "And they've hired the director and producer from *Enter the Dragon.* Top of the line all the way. I'm sure it'll be a big hit."

I winced. Although I was sure it was well intentioned, the idea of once again stepping into Bruce Lee's footprints was a little troubling.

"Here we are, Jackie," said David, pulling the car into the driveway and signaling the valet. "I'll check you in. You'll get to meet the rest of the L.A. staff tomorrow. In the meantime, you can get some rest."

I got my bag out of the trunk and walked into the lobby of the Westwood Marquis, my home away from home while I embarked on my conquest of America.

It was exciting, of course.

But I found myself wondering what time it was in Hong Kong.

The next morning, I woke up late—around 11 A.M. I was hungry, and my very first thought was to get some breakfast.

Luckily, Willie had taught me exactly what to say if I wanted to order in a restaurant—a real American breakfast. "Eggs, bacon, milk, and toast," he'd said, repeating each word with me until he was confident I'd gotten my pronunciation correct.

I threw on some clothes and took the elevator down to the lobby coffee shop. I noticed that people in Los Angeles smiled a lot, so I simply smiled back at them. When the woman at the front asked me a question in English, I just nodded, and she took me to a table. So far, I was doing just fine.

Soon a waitress came over, a pretty blond woman in a pink outfit. She said some things in English that I assumed was a question about my order.

I responded with a grin: "Eggs, bacon, milk, and toast."

The woman returned my smile, and wrote down the order. Then, unexpectedly, she asked me another question. (Later, David explained that she was probably asking me how I wanted my eggs. I hadn't realized that there were so many different options. I figured they'd just bring me fried eggs, which was what I imagined Westerners ate for breakfast.)

At the time, I was puzzled; had she misunderstood my order? So I repeated it, very slowly: "Eggs, bacon, milk, and toast."

She blinked at me in confusion, and repeated her question.

I was beginning to sweat! Not knowing what else to say, I just repeated my order one more time. "Eggs, bacon, milk, and toast."

For some reason, the waitress seemed annoyed and walked away.

Maybe she thought I was making fun of her, or maybe she thought I was stupid. I couldn't tell. All I knew was that I wasn't hungry any longer. I pulled out my wallet, counted five dollars in American money, and left it on the table as a tip.

It was going to be a long day.

My troubles continued when I went back into the lobby. A bellboy came up to me and said something very fast, pointing toward the front desk. I didn't know what he wanted, but I went over to the desk anyway. The lobby clerk smiled at me—everyone was smiling, but I was beginning to run out of smiles—and handed me a slip of paper.

It had a message on it, written in English. The only words I recognized were my name, at the top, and David's name, at the bottom. The gibberish between the two names was just a bunch of letters.

I groaned, and decided I had to get some help.

"Hello, Willie?" I said hesitantly, when the international call went through.

"Oh my, Jackie, what is it?" There was a fumbling noise, as Willie put on his glasses and looked at his clock. "Do you know it's after midnight here? I'm still jet-lagged from the plane. I've been asleep. I hope it's something important."

I gulped, and then burst into an explanation of my situation, apologizing for waking him up. After he heard my story, he was sympathetic as usual. "Jackie, I feel terrible for you, but you're not going to be able to make a transpacific call every time you need a translation!" he said. "I know it's difficult, but you're going to have to take English lessons. Leonard has arranged for a good Chinese tutor to take you on. I'm sure you'll be fine. Now, spell out the message for me and I'll tell you what it says."

Luckily, the message wasn't very long: it told me to meet David in the lobby at 7 P.M. for dinner.

"Oh no," I said. "Seven o'clock!"

"What's wrong? Do you have a previous engagement?"

"No, it's just that I'm starving," I said. "If I have to wait until seven to eat, I'll die. Willie, please, if you're my friend, tell me how to order lunch!"

We both broke up in laughter.

I spent the next half hour practicing the words in front of the bathroom mirror, until I was sure I had them perfect. Then I went down to the restaurant and was shown right to the table I'd abandoned. The waitress seemed surprised to see me, but was probably quite happy about my tip.

Before she could say anything, I quickly recited my order: "Burger. French fries. Coke."

And this time, she smiled and went off to bring me my food.

———

I had a lot of time before I had to meet David, and I didn't want to wander around and get lost. I spent most of my time watching TV, which was much better in the U.S. than it was in Hong Kong. The production values on American television shows were better than on Hong Kong feature films!

I probably learned more from television while I was in the States than from anything else. I'm not sure if that's a good thing or a bad thing, but it's true.

That evening, I met David, and was introduced to his boss, Andre Morgan. Andre had started out as Raymond Chow's assistant in Hong Kong, and was eventually promoted all the way up to the head of Golden Harvest's international division. When he met me, he greeted me in fluent Cantonese, which probably shouldn't have surprised me, since he'd worked with Raymond for twelve years! Still, it was amazing hearing an American speak Chinese so well.

Andre told me more about the film I'd be starring in, *Battle Creek Brawl.* It would be a period film, set in the 1930s. My character would be a happy-go-lucky young man, forbidden to use my kung fu by my father. But when mobsters attack my father's restaurant, I'd be forced to go into action, effortlessly defeating three thugs all by myself. Impressed, the mob boss would recruit me to be a contestant in an anything-goes fighting contest, held in a backwater town called Battle Creek, Texas. The contest, Andre assured me, would give me a chance to display my skills, just as Han's contest gave Bruce Lee a chance to shine in *Enter the Dragon.* And the budget would be $4 million—tremendous, by my standards; about HK$20 million.

"We think it'll be big," said Andre. "We'll do publicity, put you on talk shows, everything. You, my friend, will be a star."

"The next Bruce Lee?" I said, a little sarcastically.

"Bigger, pal," he said, digging into his steak. "Bigger. Of course, you'll have to do something about your English. Unfortunately, you won't have as much time for lessons as we'd like; shooting begins in two weeks. Time to hit the books, Jackie!"

I stared at my food glumly. Two weeks to learn an entirely new language! And I hadn't been in a classroom since I was twelve years old. "Eggs, bacon, milk, and toast," I muttered under my breath.

"What was that, Jackie?" said David.

"Nothing."

So for the next week, I spent my days going to a tutor, doing my best to squeeze the English language into my head, and my evenings watching television.

It was a terrible time. I still had no friends, and after a week of classes, my English was not much better than it was when I'd arrived—although I made sure I learned the right phrases to order food.

When the weekend came, I decided I needed a break, and took a trip to the beach. David wrote down the address of the hotel on a card for me, so I could show it to a cabdriver if I had trouble getting back. He also suggested that I try something new while I was down by the boardwalk— roller-skating, a skill I'd have to know for *Battle Creek Brawl.* I wasn't a very good skater, but the script called for a scene in which I demonstrated my roller-skating expertise. It made sense to practice as much as possible.

The sun was beating down furiously by the time I got to the beach, and most of the people walking around on the boardwalk were wearing very little clothing. It was eye-opening; Hong Kong is a pretty sophisticated city, but in California, girls—and guys—wore things in public that you wouldn't even see at a gentleman's club. There were a lot of roller skaters, so I supposed I wouldn't look out of place if I strapped on my skates and joined them. Even if I wasn't wearing a thong or a string bikini.

I learn new things—physical things, anyway—pretty quickly. I went from stumbling around to cruising lightly up and down the boardwalk in a few hours, but it was definitely hot work. Some of the other skaters were doing tricks, dancing and performing acrobatic stunts to the beat of disco music, so I decided to sit down, get a drink, and watch them for pointers.

I skated over to a beachfront snack bar, wiggling my butt to the rhythm, and drawing some appreciative laughs from passersby, then finished off with a flashy toe stop that almost sent me spinning into the arms of a surprised young woman in sunglasses. Unlike the other tanned, blond boardwalk denizens, this girl had dark hair and pale skin, and she was fully clothed. In fact, she was Asian—and she somehow seemed familiar.

"Gosh, I'm sorry," I said to the girl, who seemed a little shaken up. "I shouldn't be showing off in such a crowded place, I guess."

The girl looked up at me and smiled. "That's all right."

It was then that I realized—I'd spoken to her in Chinese, and she'd responded in Chinese! And then I realized why she seemed so familiar, and I let go of her shoulders with a start.

The girl I'd happened to bump into was Teresa Teng Li-jun, one of China's most famous and beloved singers! I hadn't recognized her with sunglasses on and her hair pulled back, but there was no mistaking her features.

"Teresa Teng!" I said, sputtering and nearly falling back off my skates. "What are you doing here in Los Angeles?"

She held a finger to her lips and shushed me, looking around at the crowd of patrons around the snack bar. "Please, let's not make a scene!" she said. For a big star, she seemed remarkably shy. On an impulse, I took her hand and pulled her away from the snack bar, skating over to a bench facing the ocean. She let out a giggle as I awkwardly dropped myself onto the seat, my skate-footed legs sticking out in front of me, and then delicately sat down next to me.

"It's nice to meet a fellow Chinese," she said, shaking my hand before letting it go. "I really don't know anyone out here."

"I don't know anyone either," I said. "Wow, I can't believe I just ran into you! I'm a big fan. . . ."

It was then that I noticed that she was staring at me strangely. I self-consciously realized that I was sweaty, and that I probably looked like a mess. "I, ah, I've been exercising—if I knew I was going to run into you, I'd have taken a shower. Or, well, I guess there's nowhere to take a shower around here, but . . ." I trailed off, afraid I was beginning to sound like an idiot.

But she didn't seem to be listening to my babbling. "Excuse me, are you *Jackie Chan?*" she said.

My mouth dropped open. I don't know why, but it was still a surprise to me when someone recognized me. Especially an idol like Teresa. "You know who I am?" I said.

She laughed. "Well . . . I'm a big fan!" she said.

The situation was a little ridiculous—two Chinese stars who'd never met each other in China, running into each other, literally, in the United States. I started laughing too, and soon we were leaning on each other, wiping the tears of hilarity from our eyes.

"We could exchange autographs," I suggested. That set off another round of laughter.

As crazy as the situation was, it was also almost perfect. Both of our families were from Shandong in China. Both of us were strangers in Los Angeles, trying to learn English. And we were living just minutes apart— me in Westwood, she in Santa Monica.

We began getting together in the evenings to study, which led to nights of dinner and dancing. We talked about our hopes and dreams, and about the good things and bad things that came with success. I taught her how to roller-skate; she gave me vocal lessons, after I'd confessed to her that singing had always been my secret love.

All too soon, however, a week had gone by. It was time for me to leave for San Antonio, to begin shooting my American debut. Teresa was leaving too, heading for Taiwan and a return to her recording career. "I guess we've both spent enough time on vacation," she said philosophically, as we studied together one last time. "It's time to get back to work."

"It was nice getting to know you," I said.

She smiled, a mischievous sparkle in her eyes. "Did you really have to cross an entire ocean just to meet me?"

I took her hand and squeezed it. "It was worth it," I said. "Will I see you again?"

She squeezed back. "Come to Taiwan after you're finished shooting your movie," she said. "I'll be waiting."

Waiting for what? I thought. Were we friends, or—well, more than friends?

I'd dated other girls since Oh Chang, but no one seriously. Teresa, with her sweetness and generosity of spirit, was the first woman I'd met who made me feel the kind of joy I felt when I was with my very first love.

And I'd never even had the nerve to try to kiss her!

I walked her to the door of my hotel room, wondering what I should say. "Um . . ."

She turned and looked at me. "Hmm?"

Suddenly, I was too embarrassed to tell her how I felt. I found myself saying the first thing that came to mind: "Remember to practice your English."

She burst out laughing, as I cursed myself as an idiot. Then, carefully and slowly, she said:

"Eggs, bacon, milk, and toast."

And she leaned over and kissed me gently on the lips.

"See you in Taiwan," she said. And then she was gone.

I grabbed my English text off my desk and threw it into the air.

Waaahooo!

BRAWLING FOR DOLLARS

I don't know why I thought that making Hollywood films was any more glamorous than making Hong Kong films. Trust me, there's nothing more boring than being on location for a movie shoot. Especially if you're one of the only people on the set who can speak your language.

David had brought me down to San Antonio, complimenting me on my newfound grasp of English the whole way. "You speak like a native, Jackie!" he said.

Well, *that* was an exaggeration. I could make my way through simple conversations, and I wouldn't die of hunger or thirst if I were left alone in a strange city, but I wasn't going to be engaging in any debates on philosophy.

"Do they have Chinese food in Texas?" I asked gloomily. The truth was, I was still thinking about Teresa and our dinners together. Los Angeles had some great Chinese restaurants.

"They have Chinese food *everywhere*," he promised.

He wasn't lying; there was a Chinese restaurant just a few blocks away from the hotel where we were staying. Unfortunately, the food there was terrible, and it was the *only* Chinese restaurant in the entire city. Every time I finished eating, I swore to myself that I wouldn't come back. And, of course, every day I'd end up returning, hungry less for the food than for a taste, however awful, of home—and a memory of my moments with Teresa.

It kept my mind off my troubles on the set.

Not that it was so awful; it was better than working with Lo Wei. But rehearsing the script, I felt my jaw tighten as I said each line. I was concentrating so hard on speaking the words properly that I could barely hear what I was saying. Any emotion, any passion or feeling, was blocked by a rocky wall of unfamiliar syllables.

And then there was the action.

I was used to directing my own stunts. Even if someone else was the actual coordinator, I'd always had the freedom to shape the intricate dance that made up a fighting sequence, adding my own unique spin. Improvisation was at the heart of all my performances. Even a scene that just called for me to run down a street, if I saw a way to do it that would add a burst of humor or adrenaline, I'd reshape the scene to incorporate the move.

But that wasn't the American way. The director, Robert Clouse, had scripted and storyboarded every scene in advance, deciding exactly where the cameras would be placed and how the action would move. This worked when he was directing Bruce Lee; Bruce's martial arts were tightly controlled, a compact whirlwind of energy that could be captured in a single master shot. But my style was wilder, more open, and acrobatic. As my films became more sophisticated, I found myself running through fight sequences in two, three, and four separate takes, shot from different angles, to get every facet of the intricate choreography on screen.

We ran through one scene in which I was supposed to move from a car to the door of my father's restaurant, which was being held up by mobsters. As I walked around the set, I saw in my mind how the scene could go. Through broken English and physical demonstrations, I showed Clouse my idea: I'd leap forward out of the car, roll into a somersault to stay beneath the line of sight, and then backflip to a position near the door.

"No, Jackie," he said. "Just get out of the car and *walk*."

"Just walk?" I said, in disbelief.

"Walk."

Reining in my frustration, I slowly walked from the spot where the car would be to the restaurant entrance. Then I turned around to face the director, and summoned up all of the English at my command:

"No one will pay money to see Jackie Chan walk!"

It was a prediction that would later prove tragically correct.

The shoot seemingly went on forever.

Now, these days, I'm known in Hong Kong for taking a long time on my productions; usually, the best I can do is turn out a movie a year, because I want everything to be perfect. It takes twenty years to raise a child, right? So one year to make a movie isn't that bad.

But at this point in my career, I was used to productions that started, ran, and wrapped in less than a month. Sitting for weeks on end in San Antonio, eating bad food, and walking through the same boring scenes was driving me crazy.

And I still had Teresa's face floating in my mind. I imagined what it would be like to see her again, and thought about our one and only kiss. I was a little afraid that she'd have forgotten me after all our time apart, or that she'd have realized that I was just a silly kid, too ugly or unsophisticated to think of as a boyfriend.

I looked different, too: to go with the 1930s period look of the film, I'd had to cut my hair, which was one of my most prized features. As I sat in the barber chair, David told me that I looked like I was losing my best friend. Well, in a way, I was; at the opera school, all of us boys had to shave our heads, so as soon as I had the chance, I grew my hair as long as possible. It was like making up for lost time. I guess it's silly when I think about it now, but back then, it felt like a disaster.

Still, it didn't kill me, and hair always grows back. I figured that by the time I had the chance to get back to Asia, I'd have my good old shaggy look back again.

And I was right.

The weeks on the set of *Battle Creek Brawl* passed like dripping water, but they were just the tip of the iceberg. I didn't find out until I was back on the plane to Los Angeles, but my stay in America would be a lot longer than I expected.

"Another movie?" I exploded.

Battle Creek Brawl—now titled *The Big Brawl*—was in postproduction, and Golden Harvest was eagerly awaiting its release. I was looking forward to getting back to Asia and seeing Teresa.

It wasn't in the cards.

"Well, you have to stick around to do publicity anyway," said David. "You know, let the American public meet Jackie Chan. And besides, this film is different—a lot of other big stars will be in it, too. Hollywood stars."

That got my interest. "Really?"

"And it's about an auto race, so you get to drive in a fast sports car," he added. "Very exciting."

I decided I could wait just a little while to go back. *Cannonball Run* sounded like it might be fun.

"Of course, first you'll have to face the most terrifying challenge of all," he said, adopting a mock tone of fear. "American reporters!"

I scoffed at his joke. I'd survived a childhood under my master's stick. I'd jumped off buildings for a living. I'd even faced down Triad gangsters.

Why should I be scared of American reporters?

MEETING THE PRESS

"How do you pronounce your name?"
"Do you really know karate?"
"Are you the new Bruce Lee?"

I sat at a long table in a conference room facing a small mob of interviewers, all of them shouting out questions too quickly for me to understand. David sat next to me, trying to bring the room to order. "Please, one at a time," he said, looking at me anxiously as I slumped down in my seat.

"My name is Jackie Chan," I said, slowly. "I do kung fu, not karate. And I am not Bruce Lee."

A woman with a notepad raised her hand and David gestured in her direction. "Can you break boards with your hands?"

I had no idea what she was talking about. "Why would I want to break boards?"

"So you can't break boards?"

David took a deep breath and tapped his watch. "Speaking of breaks, Jackie is very tired, and I think he could use a rest. He'll be available for interviews for the next few weeks; please just call the offices of Golden Communications if you want to schedule a session." Golden Communications was Golden Harvest's U.S. subsidiary.

Muttering in annoyance, the reporters got up from their seats and left for the corridor, where there were refreshments and snacks.

"They're crazy," I said. "In Hong Kong, when I say something, the press just says, 'Yes, Jackie!' Here they all want me to show them how to do karate. I don't know any karate. But I'd like to show them some kung fu."

I punched at the air, gritting my teeth in irritation. David patted me on the shoulder. "Now, Jackie, don't be angry, you're doing fine. This is just newspapers, anyway. Save your energy for the big stuff. I got a call from the publicist in New York, and she says that they want you for TV!" And he named one of the top national morning talk shows.

I'd watched a lot of television while I was here in the U.S., but I usually didn't get up early enough to watch morning programs. I had no idea what show David was talking about, except that he, and everyone else, seemed to think it was very important.

That night, I gave Willie a call.

"Hello?" he said, in his familiar morning voice—not quite awake, but still trying to sound alert. "Oh, it's you, Jackie. How are things in America?"

I told him my story about being thrown to the media wolves. "It's really terrible," I said. "I have no idea what to say to these people. They all look at me like I'm an animal in a zoo."

Willie made sympathetic noises. "There's a price to pay for success, Jackie," he said. "The bigger you get, the more pieces of you people want. Now, there's a secret to dealing with the media—all you have to do is plan out in advance what you want to say. We'll just work out all the questions that they might possibly ask, and figure out answers for them, right? And really, you'll be just fine."

We talked late into the night, and when my head finally hit my pillow, I felt almost confident about facing the TV cameras. I had a script; I had my lines. How different could it be from acting in a film?

"Okay, the interview is going to be taped, not live, so relax, Mr. Chan. If you have trouble with anything, we'll just edit around it." The producer was putting a body mike on my shirt, and having a little trouble because I'd chosen to wear a T-shirt. I never wore dress shirts if I could help it, and besides, for my first broadcast interview, I wanted to be comfortable.

"Okay, I think you're set. Do you want some makeup?"

I shook my head. "No makeup," I said. "Not a girl, I don't have to look pretty."

The producer, a balding man with horn-rimmed glasses, gave a perfunctory grin in return and then escorted me over to the set, where I was seated in a comfortable chair. The host soon joined us and gripped my hand, making a face and shaking his fingers as if I'd crushed it. "You must be very strong," he joked. "All that martial arts stuff—really builds you up, huh?"

I nodded, smiling, and drummed my fingers on the arms of my chair, trying to remember the things I'd talked about with Willie.

"Okay, are we ready to roll?" he said. "Great. Wonderful. Let's go."

"On three . . . rolling!" called the cameraman.

"Hello, and we're back!" said the host, his face shifting into a plastic grin. "With us now we have the next great star of martial arts. His first film, *The Big Brawl*, is coming soon to a theater near you. Let's welcome the man who's going to make you forget all about Bruce 'The Dragon' Lee—Jackie Chan!"

I waved to the camera, keeping my smile fixed on my face.

"So, Jackie, I hear you've spent most of your life training in karate."

"No, no, kung fu. Not karate," I said. "Karate is Japanese; kung fu is Chinese."

"But basically, they're the same thing, right?"

"Not the same thing!"

"Can you smash a brick with your fist?"

I shrugged. He was speaking very fast, and I was starting to get nervous. "I'm sorry?"

The interviewer's smile became brittle. The producer, offstage, made some hand motions and pointed to his mouth and ear. "Okay, uh, well, there's that old saying about letting your fingers do the walking, right? Why don't you show us a little of your kung fu? You know, do a demonstration?"

I'd completely lost track of what he was saying by this point. I looked off-camera and saw the producer throw up his hands, as someone called out, "Cut!"

The host pulled off his mike, walked off the set, and began whispering to his producer. The publicist came over and tried to reassure me that things were going to be all right. "They want you to show off your kung fu, Jackie," he said, striking a martial arts pose. "Can you do that?"

I was aghast. Here I was, the biggest star in Asia, and the host was asking me to perform like a trained dog! What was I supposed to do—sit up and beg? Roll over? I'd spent hours the previous night going over the things I wanted to say about my film, and all they wanted me to do was kick and jump around.

The publicist saw my face turn red, and he stepped back. "Don't be angry, Jackie," he whispered. "Listen, everyone wants to see what you can do. You're the best in the world, right? Just let 'em see it, and they'll be happy."

I thought about what Willie told me, about the price of success. "Okay," I said finally. "If they move that table, maybe there's room to do something." I stepped off the set to stretch out. Behind me, the producer had returned and was speaking to the publicist.

When I came back, the publicist had a resigned expression on his face. "Forget it, Jackie," he said. "It's . . . it's okay. They'll, ah, they'll just get some footage of you in Los Angeles. You won't have to go on camera today."

I felt the tension go out of my body. The whole trip was a big waste of time—six hours from L.A. to New York, and now another six hours back again—but at least I didn't have to do stupid things in front of that grinning host. And I was sick of speaking English. I resolved not to say another English word for the rest of the day, and I didn't, communicating only in nods and shakes of my head.

Some months later, I found out the truth: the show had decided my English wasn't good enough for broadcast and had cut my segment. There wouldn't be any "footage in L.A." The publicist had just wanted to spare my feelings.

The day I found out, I threw myself down on my bed and cried. It had built up inside me for months, my rage at being a permanent stranger, a foreigner in a foreign land. How could I go from being a prince in Hong Kong to being a beggar in America? Where was my pride?

I had an interview with a big magazine later that day, and I showed them a different side of Jackie Chan.

The first thing the reporter said was that even though I was famous in Asia, he'd never heard of me. "Is it strange not to be recognized as a star here in the States?" he asked.

"It's okay that you don't recognize me," I said, shrugging at him in disdain. "Everyone in Asia recognizes me."

Irritated, the reporter prodded me again. "Mr. Chan, it seems like you need to work harder to get into the U.S. market," he said.

"I'm not interested in the U.S. market," I responded. "What I'm interested in is Asia. There are billions of people in Asia, and how many millions in the U.S.? America is a very small market."

The interview didn't go very well, and when it was printed, some people found my lack of humility shocking. But my take-it-or-leave-it attitude had an effect: after the interview ran, dozens of TV and radio stations began asking for interviews, telling the publicist that people were writing and calling in, wanting to know more about this high-handed new guy from China. Was he really that big of a star? Who did he think he was, anyway? Who *was* he?

Even that morning show called me for another interview. I agreed, on one condition: the host would have to fly out to L.A. to meet *me*.

And you know what? They agreed to my demands. And the show was a big success—without my having to do silly things to show off. (I only show off when I *want* to.)

I'd made my point. I wasn't going to jump through any more hoops for patronizing reporters or feel any shame for being Chinese.

I've done a lot of talk shows in America since then. My English is a lot better now, but the important thing has been the adjustment in my attitude. I know who I am; I'm Jackie Chan. I may not have perfect English, but tell me, how many talk show hosts can speak Chinese? Can Jay Leno? David Letterman? I can guarantee that I know more of their language than they know of mine!

There are billions of people in China, and millions of Chinese people around the world. Someday, everyone will have to learn Mandarin, just like most people have to learn English today.

Unfortunately, despite all the advance publicity, *The Big Brawl* was small at the box office. Most viewers who weren't kung fu fans just didn't bother to go see the film.

I guess I wasn't that surprised. The acting wasn't very good, and the story was boring—but not as boring as the action. Part of it was the stiff choreography, which was still a source of resentment for me. Part of it was the fighters who were cast to play my opponents. They were big, beefy guys whose fighting skills were very limited.

"In Hong Kong, I can hit my stuntmen, bam, bam, bam, and they'll block every punch," I complained to David. "American stuntmen are so slow! If I hit them, they'll still be blocking the first punch by the time I'm swinging my third."

David nodded, agreeing. "Well, as I said, the next film is different. It's not a kung fu film, so you won't have to worry about that kind of action. You can just be yourself."

That statement was about as wrong as you could get. In *Cannonball Run*, I played a race car driver who was Japanese! Because I wasn't supposed to be American, I didn't really have to speak any lines, at least not any English ones. All I had to do was make funny faces. There was a little bit of fighting, but nothing interesting; it could have been anyone playing my role. It certainly didn't have to be Jackie Chan.

Except for the fact that Golden Harvest was trying to cover all of its bases. My costar in the film was Michael Hui, Mr. Boo himself—Golden Harvest's other big superstar. With him and me in the cast, they could guarantee that the film would sell in Asia, and it did very well in Japan, billed as JACKIE CHAN and MICHAEL HUI in *Cannonball Run*, with Burt Reynolds.

In America, it was advertised as BURT REYNOLDS in *Cannonball Run*, with Jackie Chan and Michael Hui. Way at the bottom.

They were using the American stars to introduce me to the American audience; it was another strategy, the opposite of what they were doing with *The Big Brawl*. If I couldn't become a Hollywood star on my own, they thought, at least I could ride to success on other stars.

And I had heard of some of the big American names before—Dean Martin, Burt Reynolds. They talked nicely to me, but they had no idea who I was. It was all very phony—"Oh, hi, yeah, good morning, guy, great to see you." Very Hollywood, in the bad sense of the word.

I remember that Sammy Davis Jr., who was partnered with Dean Martin in the movie, came up to me and said, "Gozaimas!" every day. Which I later learned he thought meant "good morning" in Japanese. "You're a famous cat in Japan, right, man?" he'd say. And I'd tell him, "No, I'm not Japanese— I'm Chinese." And then he'd say, "Right, babe, Chinese. Sayonara!"

It got so that I stopped wanting to talk to anyone. If someone approached me and spent more than three minutes chatting, I tried to find an excuse to get away. Eventually, people got the idea.

The film turned out to be a very big hit in America, and also in Japan. (As a result, they made a sequel, which unfortunately I was obligated to appear in, according to my contract.)

In Hong Kong, however, it was a big flop.

My Hong Kong audiences didn't want to see me as part of an ensemble of American stars, and they certainly didn't want to see Chinese people being made to look ridiculous.

In my world, I was a star. In fact, I was *the* star—the boldest, brightest one there was.

Why couldn't Americans understand?

COMING HOME

I came back home an angry young man.

I had something to prove, which I could do only in Hong Kong. Hollywood had rejected me and turned me into something silly and shameful.

I had to show the world that Jackie Chan was still the biggest star—in Asia, if not in the West.

Willie met me at the airport and was surprised at the way I acted: curt, arrogant, and mean. I think I hurt his feelings. After all, I hadn't seen him for a while. But our friendship had seen harder days before, and he was willing to give me the benefit of the doubt.

"Do you want to go home and get a rest, Jackie?" he asked. "You seem quite out of sorts."

"Forget it," I said. "I want to go to the studio."

He went silent and drove on.

"I know you're unhappy about the way your trip to America turned out," he said. "But really, you shouldn't let it get under your skin. Just a matter of bad timing, I think. And of course, you're still the big man here in Hong Kong."

Once we got to the studios, I brushed my way past reception to go to Leonard's office, with Willie in my wake. Leonard seemed surprised to see me, but welcomed me with his usual good grace. I shook off his attempts to make polite conversation about my trip and instead told him about my idea for my next movie. It would be a big picture, an epic martial arts film, with stunts that would put American films to shame. I'd film in Korea, in Hong Kong, and Taiwan. I'd shake up the entire genre of kung fu cinema and show people that Jackie Chan was really back in town.

Leonard was silent throughout my monologue, simply nodding here and there at points I made. When I was done, he looked over at Willie and raised an eyebrow. Willie shrugged.

"Jackie, it sounds like an ambitious project," he said. "Of course, anything you want, we'll support you. But I feel like you need to think things over a little bit—relax, perhaps look up some of your friends, take a vacation. You're young; you should live life, right?"

I shook my head angrily. "I've had enough time off. I'm a filmmaker, and I want to make films. I've had enough of being a trained monkey in other people's circus shows."

Leonard sighed. "Well, Jackie, do as you choose. Get started immediately, if you like. But I just want you to remember: there are important things in life besides work. Don't put them aside, and don't forget about them, because you never know when it might become too late."

I wasn't in a mood for lectures, so I just thanked him and left the room.

Recently, just this past year, Leonard Ho passed away—disappearing suddenly out of my life and the lives of all those he'd touched with his generosity, kindness, and wisdom. I attended his funeral and burned incense in his memory, surrounded by his friends and family—many of them people who had shaped my life as well.

He had adopted me as his godson, treating me as he would his blood—better, in many ways, than any father figure I ever had.

Looking back, I think that lecture he gave me may have been the wisest words I've ever heard; yet somehow, throughout my life from then on, I managed to ignore Leonard's precious piece of advice.

Time passes on, and people pass on. Work will always be there. I've spent most of my life at work, and I've missed out on important things—including my family and my friends. In some ways, I wonder if I'm too old to change; the momentum of my career carries me on from project to project, with little time in between to hold on to the golden moments. But now, as I grow older, Leonard's words still haunt me, and I think each year: this will be the year I slow down to enjoy the important things in life.

Some year. Sometime soon.

A few weeks after my conversation with Leonard, I'd already pulled together my stunt team, cast my actors, and set off for Korea. Unfortunately, I'd made the mistake of not really preparing a script or even thinking through a story line. All I knew for sure was that the movie would be a semisequel to *The Young Master*—it even started out under the title *Young Master in Love*—and that it would feature the most spectacular kung fu action sequences ever filmed.

Haste makes waste.

We stayed three months in Korea, spending over HK$1 million of Golden Harvest's money, and at the end of our time there we had almost nothing to show.

I brought the whole crew back to Hong Kong, refusing to admit defeat. Then we shipped off for Taiwan, virtually starting over from scratch.

The picture ultimately took almost a year to finish—almost forever, by Hong Kong clocks. To his credit, Leonard hardly pressured me at all, checking up on me more out of concern for my emotional state than the amount of time and money I was spending. (Besides, Southeast Asian distributors had already put up plenty of cash for release rights, so Golden Harvest wasn't likely to lose any money regardless of how much I spent.)

Willie, on the other hand, could barely keep himself from pulling me aside and giving me a spanking. The truth was, I was out of control, and no one was in a position to put me back in line.

Well, there was one person.

Someone I'd almost forgotten about, in my obsession with correcting my American failures.

And one day, she just showed up on the set, looking like a dream.

"Hello, Jackie," said Teresa. "I hope you've been practicing your English."

YOUNG MASTER IN LOVE

The next few weeks were the best of times. I renewed my friendship with Teresa, and it blossomed quickly into a full romance. We spent evenings together, eating at fine restaurants and attending fancy parties. The gossip columns buzzed with rumors about our relationship—"China's most beloved pop singer seen with young action superstar! Could it be love?"

It could have been.

She was sweet, and smart, and funny, and beautiful. Her taste in fashion and food alike were wonderful; she never failed to choose precisely the right dress, the right accessories, and the right place to show them off.

About the only bad decision she ever made was in her choice of men.

The truth is, she was too good for me.

Or at least for the me that I was at the time.

She was a living, breathing symbol of class and elegance, and I was raw and rough, a boy living his dreams of being a man. I talked tough, lived fast, and strutted when I could have walked. I was still burning from my experiences in the U.S. and eager to show off in front of my adoring public.

She would wear lovely designer dresses, cut exactly right. I would hit the town wearing short pants, a T-shirt, and as much gold as my wrists and neck could carry.

She was a wonder of politeness, a miracle of manners. I thumbed my nose at authority, laughing in the faces of hotel managers and haughty waiters, putting my feet up on tables.

And, while she was content to go out alone, with no one but me as her gentleman escort—not that I was much of a gentleman—I refused to be seen anywhere without my boys: a gang of stuntmen in sunglasses, taking my coat when I walked into restaurants, pulling out my chair when I decided to sit.

I was young, rich, and spoiled by fame.

I was making more money than any star in Hong Kong and spending like it was going out of style.

I loved her, but I loved myself more. And no heart can ever serve two masters.

"So you're finally finishing the movie?"

I was on the phone with Willie, lounging on a sofa in my hotel suite, watching my boys play cards and drink expensive scotch.

Willie had gotten disgusted with my new way of life and had returned early to Hong Kong. He had better things to do than watch me act like a clown, he'd said. I wouldn't take those kinds of words from anyone else, but Willie had earned the right to tell me anything. And besides, it wasn't like I listened to him.

"We wrapped shooting today," I said, shouting over the sounds of the noisy game in progress. "Leonard can start breathing again."

Leonard had kept to his promise that I'd never have to get budget approval for my films, but *Dragon Lord*—the latest title for *Young Master in Love*—had set a new record for money spent and wasted. I'd hired dozens of stuntmen, partly because of my ambitious cinematic vision, and partly because everyone and his brother, lured by the sweet smell of money, was now asking to join my team. I'd shot entire sequences, only to change my mind about the story line at the last minute, sending miles of footage into the garbage bin. And for one scene alone—a martial arts contest that had dozens of stuntmen scrambling up a rickety pyramid, battling one another all the way to the top—I actually set a Guinness world record for the most takes used in a single film sequence: over 2,900!

"Well, will you be coming back to Hong Kong?" said Willie. "More important, will you be coming back to your senses?"

I ignored Willie's sarcasm. A fight had developed at the card table. "You guys shut up; I'm trying to talk here!" I yelled. "Yeah, I'll be flying back tomorrow for editing and some reshoots."

On the other end of the line, Willie fell silent.

Then, slowly and softly, he asked me a question that he'd obviously been thinking about for a while. "And will Teresa be coming back with you?"

"What's it to you?" I retorted.

"Well, what's it to *you*?" he said, matching my irritated tone. "Listen, Jackie, she's not only a very nice girl, she's also a *very* famous, *very* high-profile, and *very* well-liked entertainer. Now, recently, you've been letting my advice pass right through your head, but let me suggest a few thoughts you might consider: first, if you keep on treating her the way you do, you will hurt her. Second, if you hurt her, you stand a good chance to become one of the most unpopular individuals in Asia, not to mention wherever Chinese people are found around the globe. So please—try not to be a fool."

My angry response was drowned out by the fight among my boys, which was threatening to turn into an open brawl. Willie hung up on me.

I swore, and tossed the phone onto the floor, wading into the melee and pulling the two wrestlers apart. "You idiots keep it up, and you're all fired," I shouted. The fighting stopped, as everyone put ingratiating smiles on their faces and began apologizing for their behavior.

"Sorry, *dai gaw*," said one.

Dai gaw means "big brother." It was what they called me, and I liked it.

"Don't like cheating," said another.

"Who's cheating? *You're* cheating."

"Ah, shut up."

"Come on over here and make me."

"Quiet!" I said, slapping the heads of the two squabblers, who were about to go at each other again. "You want to fight, you fight somewhere else." I picked up a bottle of cognac that had luckily managed not to be broken and handed it to the taller of the two. "You want to drink, drink to each other like brothers."

The party was just getting back into swing when my phone rang again. Probably Willie, calling to apologize for calling me names. Half of me wanted just to keep him hanging, letting the phone ring on and on until he gave up; the other half of me, the half that was feeling hurt at my friend's harsh words, wanted to find a way of making up.

The hurt half won out. "So you realized you were wrong, huh?" I said as I picked up the phone.

"Wrong about what?" It was Teresa, sounding puzzled.

I waved at the boys to quiet down; immediately guessing that it was Teresa, they began making rude faces and smooching gestures.

"Nothing, nothing," I said, throwing the guys a glare. "I thought it was someone else."

"All she does is call and *dai gaw* is like this," one of them whispered, putting a hand on his head and pretending to faint.

"Well, I'm sorry to disappoint you," she said, sounding miffed. "I just wanted to come see you; I know you're leaving for Hong Kong tomorrow, and I thought you might want to get together."

I did want to see her, but the taunting of my boys had gotten me riled up. I knew it was immature, but I needed to act like a *da nan ren*, a big man.

"All right," I said. "You want to come over, come over." And then I hung up the phone.

As soon as I did it, I thought to myself, *What kind of a guy am I to be so rude to my girlfriend—especially when it's possibly the last chance we'll get to see each other for a while?*

But the guys clearly were impressed at how cool I could be. Teresa was a big star and a beautiful woman, and I was dismissing her like she was just a girl off the street. That took guts!

Guts—and an ice-cold heart.

There was a soft knocking at the door.

I knew it would have been the right thing to get up and answer the door, but the boys were looking at each other, expecting a big romantic scene. Instead, I just shouted, "It's unlocked. Come in!"

And she did . . . turning every head in the room.

She looked incredible. She was dressed in a white silk dress and heels, and carried a small leather pocketbook. Accents of pearl and gold were at her neck, her ears, and wrists. Even the boys were too stunned to make rude comments and simply resumed playing in silence.

Smiling, she walked over to the sofa where I sat with my feet up on a cushion. Gently pushing my feet onto the floor, she sat down next to me.

"Hello, Jackie," she said. "I thought we might go have dinner at that new French restaurant—a 'bon voyage' celebration."

I made a big show of groaning. "You always want to go to these places where I can't read the menus," I said. "I hate it! I don't know what to order; I never know what color wine to choose. And they make you sit there for hours waiting for your food."

"Well, I think it would be nice to do something special," she said, looking hurt. Guilt briefly overwhelmed my need to be macho.

"Okay," I said sulkily. "Let me just round up the guys."

She threw her purse onto the ground. "What?"

"The boys," I said, pointing at my stuntmen, still playing cards and drinking. "Gotta let them know it's time for dinner."

"We are *not* going out with the boys," she said angrily.

I threw up my hands in exasperation. "What do you mean? I don't go anywhere without my boys."

"It's our last night together," she shouted. "Don't you want to be alone?"

"We can be alone later," I said. "Why do we have to be alone when we eat? Eating doesn't require any privacy."

She looked at me with a blank expression, as if she were going over something in her mind. And then: "It's either them or me," she said. "If you want to spend the evening with your boys, fine. I'll be leaving, then." She stood up, and I put my feet back onto the cushion where she'd been sitting.

I was annoyed that she was making a scene in front of my stunt guys. What did she expect me to do, anyway? Let her walk all over me in public? I wasn't about to lose that kind of face.

"Good-bye."

"Good-bye."

And she picked up her purse and left.

The boys had stopped playing and gone quiet when they saw her head for the door alone. I kept up my look of studied coolness, hoping that she'd turn around and come back.

Then one of the guys said, "*Dai gaw,* don't you think you should walk her to the elevator?"

I nodded and then slowly got up and walked into the hallway. Seeing it empty and the elevator door closed, I ran to the stairwell and bolted down ten flights at top speed.

I burst out into the lobby, spinning around and looking everywhere for a petite white silhouette. Nothing. Without hesitating, I charged through the revolving door and out onto the sidewalk.

She was just stepping into her private car, a big black Cadillac. I shouted out her name, but either she didn't hear me or she didn't care. The car door closed, and she drove out of the driveway, leaving me standing alone in a puff of exhaust.

Later on, after my boys had left for the evening, I called her on the phone. I was ready to throw myself at her mercy. She had none to give.

"I'm sorry, Teresa," I said. "I acted like a jerk."

"What do you have to be sorry about?" she said. "When we were together in Los Angeles, we had no one but each other. Now you have your friends, your boys. You don't need me anymore. And I don't need you."

And she hung up the phone.

I listened to the dead line in shock. I'd been dumped. Of course, I deserved it, and worse. But for her to walk out of my life, just as Oh Chang had—no, *worse* than Oh Chang had, because Teresa was making her own decision . . .

Didn't she know I loved her?

Then again, how could she? When had I ever shown her what was in my heart, or told her what I really felt?

The truth was that I was not capable of treating her, or any woman, the way she deserved. I had so little experience with romance, and I was so driven by the need to prove myself to others—to my fans, to the Hong Kong movie industry, to the world.

A quarter of a century later, I wonder how much I've changed.

Maybe a lot.

Maybe not so much.

I don't have anything to prove anymore. I've accomplished just about everything I've ever wanted to, and more. But I say this as someone who knows from experience: the farther you run in a certain direction, the harder it is to go back and start over.

I wonder to myself sometimes, if I could turn back the clock, whether I'd make different choices in my life. Would I spend more time and energy with my loved ones, my family?

Or would I follow the path I took—the one that led me here, fulfilling my hopes and dreams, at the expense of my heart?

I'm married. I have a teenage son. But working as I do, I haven't ever been able to fulfill my duty as a father or as a husband. I spend two-thirds of my time abroad, and even when I'm in Hong Kong, my schedule is so full that I can barely find time to be with my wife and child. They understand—but I know they wish I could be with them, and I know my son would have loved to have had his father with him growing up. I've been able to provide for them well, but I know I owe them so much more.

I've always tried to live my life without regrets.

I've done what I set out to do, and I've had to make sacrifices to get there.

But still—sometimes I wonder.

There's a sad postscript to the story of my brief romance with Teresa. If you're a fan of Teresa's, and she had many millions of fans, then you already know what I'm about to say.

On May 8, 1995, while on a trip to Thailand, Teresa suffered a sudden asthma attack and passed away, without warning.

She was still beautiful, still popular, and still beloved by Chinese people throughout the world.

She was only forty-three years old.

We'd gotten to be friends, some years after our romance. Her heart was too big to stay angry at me, and one day she'd called me, out of the blue. Her excuse for telephoning was that she was looking for a health club in Hong Kong and needed my advice. I think she just wanted to speak to me, to let me know that she forgave me for the way I'd treated her.

From then on, we talked every so often, and when she came into town, we'd have dinner—and I always let her choose the restaurant, and I never complained.

On the day she died, her secretary called me with the news even before it was released to the media. I was shocked, because she was so vibrant, so *alive*, and because I'd never even known about her condition.

In some ways, it was just another example of how little I'd gotten to know her. Then again, I guess she kept it hidden from everyone. To her fans, she was Little Teng, the bright and innocent flower of China, and they wanted her to be perfect, especially in a time when China itself was having so many troubles.

Teresa is buried in a large and peaceful garden, in the beautiful region of Taipei County known as West Lake Village, on Chinpao Mountain, overlooking Hsi Shih Lake. Throughout the memorial are monuments that celebrate her, as a person and as a musician. At the entrance to the park is a CD machine that automatically plays one of her songs—in Mandarin, English, Japanese, Cantonese, or Taiwanese—as soon as a visitor steps through the gates. At the center of the park is an enormous piano keyboard that plays musical notes when stepped on.

Even though it has been several years since her death, her grave is visited by hundreds of mourners a day, many of them bringing gifts and tokens of their affection. It's a tribute to how much she was loved and always will be loved.

I wasn't able to attend her funeral. I was away shooting a film, and it might not have been appropriate for me to be there anyway.

But I did find a way to remember her, in my own way. When I had some quiet time to myself—the kind of time that, in our brief period together, I might have shared with her—I put on one of her old albums and listened again to her voice, singing the song that some consider to be her masterpiece: "When Will You Come Back Again?" The lyrics of the song include the following lines:

> *Missing you brings tears to my eyes . . .*
> *When will you come back again?*

You will never be forgotten, Teresa.

LOST AND FOUND

Months late and hundreds of thousands of dollars over budget, I finally finished *Dragon Lord*.

The triumph of completing the film was a cold one. My break-up with Teresa put me into a state of depression; suddenly, the original title of the film, *Young Master in Love*, seemed bitterly ironic.

But at least the movie was finished, and I had every hope that it would restore whatever shine my star had lost with my American failures.

I was wrong. Though it did all right in Japan and elsewhere in Asia, in Hong Kong, *Dragon Lord* was a box office disaster.

When the truth became obvious, I spent almost a week at home, sleeping, staring at the walls, and leaving only to eat. I wouldn't take anyone's calls. When my stuntmen invited me to join them on our usual nighttime bar crawls, I told them curtly to leave me alone.

It finally took Willie to snap me out of my funk. As I sat on my couch, listening to a record album, I heard an insistent knock. I just turned up the music and paid no attention, until finally the sound grew too annoying to ignore.

Dragging myself to the door, I mumbled to my unexpected guest that I didn't want any visitors. To my surprise, there was the sound of a lock opening and the doorknob turned by itself. In strolled Willie, a duplicate set of my keys in his hand.

"If you recall, you told me to watch your apartment while you were in Taiwan," he said, tossing the key ring onto my coffee table and seating himself on the couch.

"Go away, Willie," I said. "I'm busy."

He picked up the album sleeve, which had been carelessly dropped to the floor. "This is one of my favorites, too, Jackie," he said, humming along. *"When will you come back again . . ."*

I grabbed the album out of his hands and put it on the table. "Why are you here?"

Willie rolled his head back onto the couch cushion. "To help you, as usual," he said. "Only to help."

I sat on the couch and put my head in my hands. "You can't help this time," I said. "I've lost her. I've ruined my career. It's over. Everything."

He patted me on the shoulder consolingly. "Jackie, you have a right to be upset—you've made mistakes," he said. "But everyone makes mistakes; mistakes are just the way life teaches you lessons. Which, if you don't mind my saying so, you were rather overdue in learning."

A month before, I'd have blown up and told him to get out of my apartment. Instead, I nodded slowly. "I've been a jerk," I said. "To you. To Leonard. To Teresa. To everyone."

He smiled, and he could have been cruel—he could have flashed me a triumphant I-told-you-so look—but he didn't. Well, my head was still down, so I don't know for sure, but he's not that kind of guy. I'll give him the benefit of the doubt.

"Jackie, I want you to close your eyes and think for a moment," he said. "Think back ten years into the past, and tell me what you were doing then. Tell me what you see."

I did what he asked, without questions. "I guess I'm a stuntman," I said. "I'm hanging out on the set at Golden Harvest; I'm waiting for the coordinator's call. Just talking with the other guys. Hoping that I'll get a chance to work today."

He nodded. "Okay, now think back another ten years."

"I'm at the school," I said. "I've only been there a while. I don't really know anyone, and I'm afraid of Master."

Willie nodded again. "Now open your eyes and look around."

I rubbed my eyes and scanned my apartment. It was a terrible mess, but it was large and well furnished, with everything I'd ever dreamed of having: television, stereo, a nice kitchen, exercise equipment. There was a large picture window with a spectacular view. And here and there, there were mementos of my movies—posters, souvenirs I'd picked up from abroad, old props.

"Jackie, think of how far you've come," he said. "Twenty years ago, you were nothing—a kid in rags scrounging for extra food. Today, you're the biggest star in Asia."

He was right. Almost. "Well, I *was*," I said. "Before I destroyed my career."

Willie snorted. "What are you talking about? One or two bad movies doesn't destroy anyone's career. Let me remind you, you had many more disasters before, when you were working with Lo Wei," he said. "The truth is, you haven't lost your talent, or your health, or your drive, or your imagination. All of the tools that brought you this far are still yours. But there's something else that you've been missing, Jackie, something that made you different and special."

I turned toward him, searching his expression in an attempt to see what he was trying to say. And then I understood.

I'd been thinking only about myself. About what I wanted, about my own success. After my sudden rise to the top, I'd somehow forgotten my heart—my ability really to care about other people. My friends. My loved ones. My family.

This was why I'd lost Teresa, and it was why, I realized, I'd been so unhappy, even when I was playing at being the big man.

I thought back to the closest and oldest ties I had in my life and career. And then I realized what it was that I needed most, not just as a filmmaker, but as a person.

I needed my brothers.

HE AIN'T HEAVY . . .

"I've been meaning to call you," said Samo, shifting uncomfortably in his upholstered chair. It had been a little while since we'd actually had a chance to talk, what with my long stay in Taiwan and my subsequent disappearance from the face of the earth.

"Me too," I said. We were sitting in Samo's office at Golden Harvest; while he hadn't achieved my level of success as an actor, he'd become one of the studio's most trusted directors and producers, with a number of solid successes under his substantial belt. "It's been a while since we've gotten together," I said. "Been longer since we've worked together."

Samo nodded. There was a certain awkwardness in the situation. The last time we'd really worked together closely, he'd been on top and I'd been his assistant; now, despite my recent flop, I was a big star, and he was best known for his work behind the camera. "You haven't had the time, huh, Little Brother," he said. It was as much an accusation as a question.

I nodded, slowly. "I have time now," I said. "And I'm sorry."

He began to say something harsh, but stopped himself before speaking. A smile spread across his wide face—a genuine one. "Every time you get knocked down, you always come back to Big Brother, huh, Jackie?" he said.

He meant it as a joke, and I took it as one, laughing along. "Guess so," I said.

"Well, if you *really* want to work together . . ."

"If you think it's something *you* want to do . . ."

And he told me an idea that he'd been kicking around with Leonard, one that would hopefully bump Golden Harvest back to the top of the box office charts. Rather than showcasing a single star, why not take a hint from the American successes of films like *Cannonball Run*—bringing together a group of well-known names in one movie? If one star was good, a whole galaxy should be even better.

The idea turned into *Winners and Sinners*, a fast-paced action comedy that featured Samo, journeyman comedians Richard Ng, John Shum, and Stanley Fong, and veteran hunk Charlie Chin (whose wedding I'd worked at, years before). The five of them played crooks trying to go straight, and failing when they get mixed up in a Triad war. Sibelle Hu was the ingenue, the love (and lust) interest of the whole motley crew; I was a childhood pal of the five ex-cons and had grown up to become a cop. To complete our set, Samo even brought in Yuen Biao for a cameo; the last time I'd worked with him was in *Young Master*—I'd given him his first acting part, a small supporting role, and then he'd gone on to be the lead in a couple of films that Samo had directed, *Knockabout* and *The Prodigal Son.*

It was the first time all three of us had worked together since we were stuntmen.

It was the first time we'd acted together since our days in the opera.

The magic was still there. It was the most fun I'd had working on a movie since I'd left Lo Wei. And the film was a tremendous success, blowing away all the competition, and producing a bunch of sequels, which were dubbed the Lucky Stars series.

As for me, I was lucky both to have such friends—and to feel like a star once more. Any doubt I'd had in myself was erased by the experience of working again with my closest, oldest friends in the whole wide world.

THE THREE AMIGOS

While *Winners and Sinners* was rocketing to the top of the box office charts, I'd been working diligently with Edward Tang, my
screenwriter, on ideas for my next project.

Edward had been assigned to me by Leonard when I'd first signed
on with Golden Harvest, and the partnership had just felt right from
the start. Since then, Edward has scripted nearly all of my films; no
other writer I've ever worked with has had his amazing ability to take my
stray thoughts or suggestions and spin them into full-fledged cinematic
epics.

He'd been as upset as I was when *Dragon Lord* failed. However, while
I'd been sulking at home, Edward had spent his time watching other
movies, especially American blockbusters, trying to find fresh inspiration.

The film that finally excited him enough to get back to work was
Raiders of the Lost Ark, Steven Spielberg's blockbuster homage to Hollywood's action history.

Eager to do something similar—a period piece full of guns and goons
and swashbuckling stunts—Edward came to me with a story he called *Pirate Patrol*, in which I'd play a turn-of-the-century Hong Kong coast guard
captain forced to work as a land cop after buccaneers destroy my fleet.
Despite the disapproval of the by-the-books chief of police, I manage to
unravel a conspiracy, discover the secret location of the pirate hideout,
and take care of the pirates once and for all.

I liked the idea. The script was set in a more modern era than any
of my previous films, so the look of the movie would be unique—like
a classic Hollywood film, only with a Chinese cast and a Hong Kong
setting.

I think I mentioned earlier that I've always loved Hollywood's
black-and-white silent classics—the comedies of Keaton and Lloyd and
Chaplin that, even after decades, continue to make people smile,
scream, and laugh. The early silent greats were comic pioneers, setting
a gold standard in screen humor for everyone else who's followed
since.

What people forget sometimes is that they were also, in some ways, the
first action heroes. Without special effects and without stunt doubles,

they did amazing things, falling and flying, climbing and tumbling, using their bodies to make miracles on screen.

I'd gotten hooked on the old silents because much of the story was told physically, which meant that, despite my limited English, their antics were as funny to me as they must have been to their original audiences. Maybe funnier, because I understood what it took to make them happen.

Well, Edward's story seemed like a perfect opportunity to bring the comic sensibility of the old Hollywood silents to Hong Kong cinema. In late-night brainstorming sessions, we worked to add sequences that would celebrate the great stunts of silent comedy—like Harold Lloyd's high-altitude tango with a clock tower from *Safety Last*, and Buster Keaton's intricately choreographed chase sequences.

Actually, I'd already included an homage to Keaton in *Dragon Lord*, with a scene where a large ornamental facade collapses onto me and I survive being crushed because I'm standing in the exact space where an opening in the facade exists. My inspiration was Keaton's *Steamboat Bill, Jr.*, in which he misses being crushed by the falling wall of his house because he happens to be standing in the doorway. (I did an even bigger version of this stunt later in the sequel to *Pirate Patrol*—but that's getting ahead of myself.) But that was an exception; in *Pirate Patrol*, the action style of the silent classics would be the rule.

For our ambitious ideas to work, the film's other principal roles—a straitlaced police officer and a local con man—had to be played by actors who understood action in the same way I did, martial artists who could speak the language of my choreography with perfect fluency.

Deciding who to cast was hardly a problem. I'd known from the very beginning that there was one thing that would make this movie complete.

Well, two things, really.

Or, actually, two *people*:

My Big Brother Samo and my Little Brother Yuen Biao.

"To old times," said Samo, raising a bottle of beer in a toast to me and Yuen Biao.

It was the final day of production, and after we'd wrapped, he and Yuen Biao and I had celebrated by going back to the same bar where we'd spent so many evenings back in our stuntman days. The bar was the site of countless rounds of beer and games of pool, and even years after we'd gone on to bigger things, it still felt like home.

"And old friends," I added, returning Samo's toast.

Yuen Biao made a difficult shot on the billiards table and crowed as the ball dropped. "We should come back here more often," he said. "Best table in town."

There were a lot of things we should do more often, I realized. Working with my brothers had been the best experience in my film career so far. Our different personalities balanced one another out and brought a special warmth to our on-screen characters. And their martial arts skills complemented mine perfectly—Yuen Biao the agile acrobat, Samo the strong and surprisingly nimble brawler. When we worked out fight scenes, we could almost read one another's minds, we knew one another so well.

Of course, we had our differences: Samo was Biggest Brother, and he always demanded respect from us. "Your voice may be loud, Jackie," he'd say, "but my voice is louder." I knew that secretly, and sometimes not so secretly, he resented the fact that I'd become a big star. That alone meant that we couldn't work as a trio forever; they needed their space, to make careers and identities beyond being "Jackie Chan's brothers."

But still, I knew that as a team, we were stronger and better than any of us were alone. And for as long as it could last, I wanted us to stick together.

I was right about how good we were as a team.

Pirate Patrol, which was eventually released as *Project A*, was a huge success on every level. It was critically acclaimed. It made tons of money at the box office. And in many ways, it was a groundbreaking film in martial arts cinema: it showed that it was possible to make period films that didn't feature the Shaolin Temple or wandering warriors, while keeping the dynamic fight sequences and thrilling stunts that give kung fu movies their appeal.

I think that a lot of the success of *Project A* was a result of the three of us working as one. On the other hand, *Project A* was also the first film in which I did something that has since become my signature:

The really, really, really dangerous stunt.

The superstunt has become the thing that makes a Jackie Chan movie unique. People come to see my films in part because they expect a fast-paced and funny experience. But the truth is, lots of films are exciting and hilarious. A Jackie Chan movie has something else: the thrill of high risk.

No blue screens and computer special effects.

No stunt doubles.

Real action. Real danger. And sometimes, real and terrible injury.

In shooting my stunts, I've hurt myself in hundreds of ways and nearly died dozens of times. People have called me crazy, and maybe they're right, because you need to be a little crazy to do the things I do. Which isn't to say that I don't know the meaning of the word fear. I'm terrified every time I have to put my body on the line, but somehow, I still manage to do it anyway.

The big stunt in *Project A* was a sequence in which, after a wild chase through back alleys and then up a flagpole, I leap to the top of a clock tower. From there, I drop from the face of the clock to the earth, more than fifty feet down.

We didn't have any special technology to do the stunt. It would simply have to be done, by a real live human being, and I remembered the words of the stunt coordinator, long ago, who'd told me not to make a stuntman do anything that I wasn't willing to do myself. The chase ended with me on top of the tower; at the end of the scene, I had to be at the bottom. There was only one way to get from the top of the tower to the bottom, and that was for me to fall.

To prevent me from smashing into the ground and bursting like a watermelon, there was a series of cloth awnings, which I'd hit and rip through one by one—hopefully slowing the speed of my drop and making it nonfatal.

"Are you sure this is even possible, Jackie?" Yuen Biao had asked me, looking at me like I was some kind of idiot for even suggesting the stunt.

"Uh, sure," I said. "No problem. We'll just test it first."

My stuntmen were not eager to try the fall themselves, and so we worked out a compromise: a bag of dirt was dropped from the tower, through the awnings, and to the ground.

The first time we did it, the bag exploded when it hit, sending dirt everywhere.

"Not good," said my head stuntman, shrugging.

That was an understatement. We tightened the awnings and tried it again. This time, the bag survived the fall.

Maybe I would, too.

So the next morning, I climbed to the top of the tower, and a stuntman helped me out onto the clock face, where I dangled from one of the hands of the clock, hanging out in space as the cameras rolled. Minutes went by, the metal of the clock hand cutting into my palms. And then, finally, I shouted for the stuntman to pull me back inside.

I kept on imagining the exploding bag of dirt and thinking, *That could be me!*

I know that the movie posters all say that I have "no fear," but that's just marketing. Anyone who really thinks I'm not scared out of my wits when I'm about to do one of these stunts is nuttier than I am.

The next day, I tried again. And again I let myself get pulled back in. And again. And again. And again. For six days, every morning began the same way, with me climbing up to the top of the tower, dangling for a few minutes, and then bailing out.

"This is ridiculous," I said finally, on the seventh day.

"I told you that a long time ago," said Samo, who by now was thoroughly tired of watching me not do the stunt. Though I was the film's director, Samo was far more experienced than I was, and throughout the shoot he helped me make decisions on where to place cameras and how to frame shots. "Let's just cut the stunt and move on."

I waved him off. "That's not what I'm saying," I snapped. "The stunt is good. *I'm* the one that's bad. No more excuses; today I'll do it for real."

This time, I told the stuntman to leave as soon as I was out hanging on the clock hand. There was no choice for me now; without someone to help me back into the tower, the only way for me to get down was to let go and fall.

And I did.

Free fall.

The rip of fabric as I hit the first awning, and then the next, and then finally, the hard-packed dirt, rolling to muffle the impact as much as possible.

I'd survived, even though I'd landed hard on my neck. After a little ice was placed on my injury, I told the crew to set the stunt up again.

"What?" shouted Samo, his eyes wide. Yuen Biao looked just as shocked. I explained to them that we hadn't had enough cameras rolling to get the effect I wanted. We had just four at the time; later, I'd use as many as ten in order to capture the angles I wanted all at once.

This time, however, I figured that I'd have to repeat the stunt—and again, for a total of three completed takes.

We needed the takes, but I'll tell you the truth: I was a little irritated with myself for chickening out so often earlier, and I wanted to prove to Samo and Yuen Biao, and everyone else, that I had successfully conquered my fear.

All three of the successful falls were combined in the final cut of the film. I didn't let the footage from some of my uglier attempts go to waste either; I added it to the end of the movie, running under the credits.

This was something I'd started to do with *Dragon Lord*: show the "no goods" of stunts and fight sequences under the final credits, to make it clear that what we were doing was real, and really dangerous. *Dragon Lord* had some difficult stunts, such as the "bun pyramid" scene in the opening action sequence, but nothing as wild as the stuff in this movie. For *Project A*, we had so many "no goods" from different scenes that I could have made an entire feature-length blooper reel if I'd wanted to. As my movies got bigger, and the stunts more and more complex, our "no good" footage files ballooned. To be honest, sometimes the "no good" footage is a lot more spectacular than the regular footage! But I run a family operation; if kids saw some of the things that happen to me and my stuntmen and fellow cast members during our shoots, I don't think they could sleep at night.

A HITCH IN TIME

Speaking of family operations, it was around this time that something happened that would in some ways change my life completely, and in other ways, not at all.

I hadn't fully recovered from my breakup with Teresa, or at least that's what I told myself. As a result, I put most of my energy into my work, hardly ever going out. When I did go out, I went with my brothers or with stuntman friends.

I'd pretty much decided that romance was not a priority in my life, and despite all the gossip that still went on in the Chinese newspapers—they're never happy unless they're reporting that someone is having an affair with someone, or breaking up with someone else—the truth is, I was leading a pretty boring existence.

Well, relationshipwise, anyway.

Now, back in 1981, when I was on my way back from the U.S., I'd stopped off in Taiwan, thinking that I might have the chance to see Teresa. Unfortunately, she was on tour at the time, so I used my layover to visit other people instead. While I was there, a friend of mine named Zhou Xianglin invited me to attend a party. Despite my objections—I wasn't all that interested in making cocktail party chatter, and I didn't have that much time before I had to go back to Hong Kong—I eventually bowed to my friend's wishes and came to his house.

Zhou greeted me like a lost brother at the door, and quickly escorted me into his living room, which was filled with beautiful, well-dressed men and women. I recognized most of them as actors and actresses; some of them were big stars in Taiwan.

"Attention, attention," said Zhou, briskly getting the room's notice. "Does everyone know who this is? This is Jackie Chan—Hong Kong's second Bruce Lee!"

I groaned to myself at Zhou's introduction—first, because it put me on the spot in front of all these beautiful people, and second, because I'd just come back from months and months of being labeled the next Bruce Lee by ignorant American reporters.

It made me want to sink into the floor, out of sight, and away from possible humiliation. No such luck. Zhou then went around the room, introducing me to each of his guests in turn.

"Hello," I said. "Jackie Chan. Nice to meet you. Hello." The faster I could go through the crowd, the sooner I could leave, I figured.

And then Zhou came to a woman whose introduction stopped me in my tracks.

"And Jackie, this is Lin Feng-jiao," he said. "Have you ever heard of her?"

Who hadn't? She was one of Taiwan's top actresses, reputedly the most beautiful woman in the country. It was often said in Taiwan's movie industry that "the two Chins and the two Lins divide the world." The two Chins were handsome male actors (one of them was Charlie Chin, whose wedding I'd assisted with and who would soon be my costar); the two Lins were beautiful female actresses. One of the Lins was Brigitte Lin Ching-hsia, who later became a screen icon in Hong Kong. (She later appeared in one of my movies, too—*Police Story,* one of my most successful films ever.)

The other was Lin Feng-jiao. And her looks put even Lin Ching-hsia's statuesque beauty to shame.

"Of course I've heard of you," I said to her, stammering slightly. "I'm a big fan of yours—I've seen several of your movies."

Lin's personality was sweet and demure; she was described by the Taiwanese press as the perfect "girl next door," if you happened to live next door to a beauty queen. Her cheeks turned rosy at my compliment, and she looked away in a charmingly shy manner as she responded. "I've seen many of your movies, too," she said. "Your martial arts are so impressive. I wish I could do something like that."

"Really?" I said earnestly. "I could show you some moves—it's not always as hard as it looks."

Lin smiled, and bunched up her fists in a mock kung fu stance. I gently corrected the position of her arms, saying, "Be careful—you could really hurt someone this way, you know." She burst into giggles.

Seeing us occupied with one another, Zhou slipped away to rejoin his other guests, leaving us to talk late into the evening—almost too late for me to make my plane.

"It was nice to meet you," I said.

She nodded. "It was very nice to meet you, too."

"Maybe I'll see you again."

"Maybe if I come to Hong Kong."

"Or maybe when I come back to Taiwan."

We shook hands, and I got into my car and raced to the airport.

I never thought I'd see her again.

I couldn't have been more wrong if I'd tried.

After the completion of *Winners and Sinners,* while I was working with Edward on the script to *Project A,* I found myself in Taiwan again, checking out locations for possible shoots. The thought crossed my mind that maybe Lin Feng-jiao might be around; despite my vow to avoid romance, any opportunity to be with a girl as lovely as she was was not to be missed. I called her up, out of the blue, and was surprised and happy when she was as enthusiastic about seeing me as I was about seeing her.

Our dinner together was fantastic. In addition to being lovely and gentle, she was very down to earth and had not much interest in the kind of luxurious things that Teresa had always loved. Despite the fact that I was still very rough and immature, she went out of her way to put me at ease, never correcting my pronunciation or grammar or etiquette, and ordering the same thing that I ordered, even when I had no idea what the fancy menu said.

Something about her just made me feel comfortable. She let me be myself, and she seemed to like me for who I was. I think that on her side she found me different from the guys who usually asked her out— the handsome, suave actors and businessmen who always knew exactly what to say, how to dress, and how to act. Even though I'd improved a lot from when I was with Teresa, I was still full of wild stories and crazy ideas. We had several dinner dates together before I headed back to Hong Kong, and each one was more fun than the last. When I realized it was finally time to go, I felt my heart sink into my stomach. But Edward was finishing the script for *Project A*, and work, as always, came first.

"I still haven't had a chance to give you those kung fu lessons," I joked to her as I said good-bye.

She playfully punched me in the shoulder, and it felt like a butterfly's kiss. "Well, I guess I know who to call if I ever need to learn how to fight," she said. "Or other things."

I smiled. "Or other things."

So we went our separate ways again, still not knowing when we'd see each other next. But I couldn't get the thought of her out of my mind. It wasn't the way it had been with my first love, or with Teresa—I didn't dream about her in a passionate way. It just felt as if there was something missing when we were apart. Like something about her completed me.

I threw myself into preproduction for *Project A*, putting Feng-jiao out of my mind. Samo had heard I'd gone on some dates with her and bugged me for more information. Every time he asked, I told him that nothing had happened, that she was very sweet, but not my type.

"We're just friends, okay?" I said, as he made moon-eyed faces in my direction. "I probably won't even see her again."

He made a rude noise. "Sure, Little Brother. Whatever you say."

Then one day, I got a phone message at our production office. "It's your girlfriend," said Samo, his eyes dancing with mischief. "She wants you, oh, she wants you."

I kicked in his direction and he dodged my foot. "Gimme the message."

The note said that Feng-jiao had called me looking for help. I immediately dropped what I'd been doing, which was talking with my stuntmen about some ideas I had for the movie, and called her back.

"Hi, Feng-jiao?" I said, as I was transferred to her line. She was at her studio, about to begin a new movie, so I had to navigate through a couple of different receptionists before I finally got to her.

"Hi, Jackie," she said. "Remember what you promised me before?"

My mind went blank. What had I promised her? "Uh . . . which promise?"

She laughed. "To teach me how to do martial arts," she said. "*Sifu*, I need help!" She went on to explain how the film she was doing had some action sequences—not fighting, but stunt work—and that she was going to be doing them herself. They weren't very dangerous stunts, but she knew she'd need training in how to use protective padding and how to keep from getting hurt.

"Is that all?" I said. "Don't worry, you've called the right guy. I'll see you tonight!"

Before she could protest that she didn't want to cause me trouble, I said good-bye and hung up. Samo had drifted over to where I was talking on the phone and was looking at me with disapproval. "You'll see her tonight? What about the stunt meeting?" he said.

I shrugged at him coolly. "We'll have it on the plane," I said. "Come on guys, pack up; we're going to Taiwan."

Samo exploded. "What? You're taking the stunt team with you?"

I ignored him and started instructing different stuntmen on what equipment we'd have to bring. Finally, Samo threw up his hands and helped the stunt team gather their things. "All I can say, Brother, is that if this is the kind of thing you do for your friends, I can only imagine what you do for your girlfriends," he grumbled.

That evening, the entire Jackie Chan Stuntman Organization and I showed up on the set of Lin Feng-jiao's movie, without warning or notice.

The director had a fit. "What are you doing here? How come you didn't let us know you were coming?"

I was the biggest star in Asia, and my arrival anywhere was newsworthy. To descend suddenly on a movie being shot by a studio I had no connections to, *with* my entire stunt team—well, it was like an invasion from another planet.

But who was going to stop me?

My guys and I took over the production for several days, showing Feng-jiao exactly what to do in her stunt sequences, and lending her and the other actors our equipment.

And then it was time for us to leave.

"Thank you very much," she said. "You kept your promise."

I grinned. "I do my best."

"Does that mean I won't see you anymore?" she said. "I mean, now that you've done your job?"

"It wasn't such a bad job," I said. "And don't bet on not seeing me again."

Well, let's just say that I did see her again. A lot.

Though I was shooting in Hong Kong, I'd take off on weekends, fly to Taiwan, and spend time with Feng-jiao.

It was almost perfect.

That is to say, it was perfect for me, and nearly perfect for her. We enjoyed each other's company when we were together, and at the end of each weekend, I went back to Hong Kong and back to work—free and happy. But even though she wasn't the kind of girl to complain, it slowly dawned on me that our relationship wasn't enough for her. She was a very traditional woman, with traditional expectations. And the Taiwanese papers were beginning to write rumors about our relationship: was I seeing her seriously, or just playing around? Would I marry her, or was I simply having fun? What were my intentions?

She was one of Taiwan's most popular actresses, and as much as they liked me there, they also knew my reputation, as a wild boy who worked too hard, who didn't know the meaning of the word commitment. I knew the rumors were hurting her, but she never said a word.

Finally, I surprised her one day by leaving the production of *Project A* behind and flying to see her in the middle of the week. When I walked onto the set, she was filming a scene; as soon as she saw me, she ran to embrace me, before the director even had the chance to say, "Cut."

"Get him off the set!" the director shouted, enraged that I'd interrupt while the cameras were rolling.

I held up one hand and looked sternly in his direction. "I'm sorry about making trouble, sir, but I have to borrow your star for a few minutes."

The director shook his fists at me. "You can't do this!"

"Hmm. Well, just watch me," I said, grabbing Feng-jiao's hands and pulling her away and out of the soundstage.

Her eyes were huge and a little bit frightened. "Jackie, what are you doing here?" she said, wondering if something were wrong. "I didn't expect you until Saturday—is there trouble on your set?"

"I have something important to ask you," I said.

Her eyes widened even further. I'm sure she thought I was going to tell her that our relationship was over. I guess, if I could do it all over again, I would have tried to make things more romantic. But it was difficult for me, the decision I'd made. I'd agonized for weeks about what to do, and finally I'd realized that if I were going to be a real man, I had only one choice. As soon as I came to that realization, I'd headed for the airport—knowing that the longer I waited, the harder it would be.

"What is it, Jackie?" she said, her lip trembling.

I let go of her hands and faced away. "Feng-jiao," I said, my throat feeling dry. "You know I'm not a very good guy. I don't think I can ever be good enough for a woman as nice as you. . . ."

I heard her sob, and I turned back toward her, to see her put her hands to her face. Tears were making her makeup run, and she looked as if she were about to run away at any second.

"No! Don't cry, Feng-jiao," I said, beginning to panic. "Just listen to what I'm saying!"

She continued to sob, and I reached over to try to wipe away her tears. "Feng-jiao, all I'm trying to say is, do you think I have to change? Be a different kind of guy?"

She shook her head. "Why should you have to change?" she said. "You never fooled me about the way you are; I just wanted to be with you anyway."

It was true. I hadn't tried to be anything I wasn't around her, and still, she cared about me. What other woman would be so kind? Who else could deal with my personality and lifestyle?

When I'd started to see her, I'd opened a certain door in myself—one I'd never really shown to anyone else. And she, in turn, had not held back anything, remaining devoted to me despite my absences and despite my wild reputation.

If you start a movie, you have to finish it. All things change eventually, and all phases in life must pass. She'd said to me when we first started seeing each other that she'd never try to change me, and even now, with the whole world gossiping about her, she was holding to her vow.

It was time for me to change myself.

Even if I couldn't be the man of her dreams, at least I could stop being the irresponsible wild boy. I could give her the security and the comfort and the commitment that a traditional girl like her wanted from her man.

"Feng-jiao," I said, taking both of her hands again. "Marry me."
She let out a gasp.
I went down on one knee.
"Marry me!"

And so, the following weekend, in 1983, under a veil of extreme secrecy, Feng-jiao and I flew to Los Angeles, California, and got married. The only person to attend the ceremony was Willie, who served as my best man and gave Feng-jiao away.

Soon after completing her film, Feng-jiao announced that she was retiring from acting, sending waves of anger and distress through the media. Many people thought, somehow, that it was my fault, and I guess in some ways it was.

We'd thought about making our marriage public, but were warned by Willie and Leonard that any such announcement could have unusual consequences. They were right: when a publication in Japan finally printed the rumor that I'd gotten married, a young Japanese girl threw her body in front of a subway and killed herself. Another girl flew to Hong Kong and came to the offices of the JC Group, taking poison in front of Willie and a horrified bunch of staffers. She was rushed to the hospital and saved.

I'd never thought of myself as a marquee idol, like a pop singer or a romantic leading man. Still, I had a lot of fans, and it was impossible to say what people's reactions would be. Besides, Feng-jiao had no interest in being a part of the celebrity love scene, with photographers following us around and making trouble. When, a year later, our son Jackson was born, we decided that we would raise him outside of the media spotlight and do our best to keep our personal lives personal.

Of course, what this has meant is that some people have continued to talk about us. The gossip columns always print rumors that I was seen kissing this actress, or fooling around with that singer. It's ridiculous. If I actually did all of the things that the newspapers say I do, I wouldn't even have the time or energy to make movies.

The truth is, fifteen years after we got married, Feng-jiao and I are still together, and still happy, and our son is devoted to both of us. Our marriage may seem nontraditional, at least by American standards, but what matters is that it works. We don't see each other as often as we'd like, but when we're together, we're a family.

I've been in Hollywood and I've been in New York and I've been in places all around the world. I've seen how many couples are. In America, people marry, spend one passionate year together, and then get a divorce.

Feng-jiao and I spend months and months apart from one another, and lead very independent lives. On the other hand, we've been together fifteen years, and I believe we'll be together for the rest of our lives.

So you tell me:

Which is better?

BROTHERS ABROAD

After the success of *Project A*, Golden Harvest was eager to green-light more adventures of the Three Brothers, and we quickly found ourselves with Leonard's blessing to increase our expected budget to an unexpected level—about U.S.$3.5 million, which seems like nothing compared to Hollywood spending (just one fifty-seventh of a *Titanic*). To us, though, it was a blockbuster amount. Leonard had told me that I'd never have to approve a budget for one of my movies, but he still got increasingly nervous as the money added up, especially after the failure of *Dragon Lord*. This time he was saying, "Go ahead and spend; I trust you." It probably helped that the director for our next project was Samo, who had a good reputation inside Golden Harvest for making films on time and under cost.

Unlike me, I guess.

But Samo had some big ideas of his own for *Meals on Wheels*, our next film project. Instead of filming it in Hong Kong—or even elsewhere in Asia—he wanted to bring a crew to Spain, to shoot on location there.

"Chinese people in Spain?" I asked him, confused as to his logic.

"Hey, Bruce shot in Rome, right?" he said. "There are Chinese people everywhere. It's a pain in the ass to shoot in Hong Kong anyway—too crowded, too many bureaucrats. Think of it as breaking new ground. We're bringing Hong Kong cinema to the world!"

Samo was right about one thing: by using new and different locations, not to mention non-Asian costars, we were able to make a film that looked like more than just a Chinese picture. It looked and felt like an international film, something that anyone could watch and understand, with a little translation.

The worldwide success of *Wheels on Meals*—a superstitious executive had made us reverse the words, claiming that movies beginning with *M* had always failed for the studio—made Golden Harvest sit up and take notice.

Golden Harvest had made English-language films for the U.S. market, and sometimes featured Asian stars (like me) alongside American ones. It had made Chinese films for the Asian market, and distributed these films in a small way in the U.S. and in Europe. But it had never made Chinese films that were intended from the very beginning to be released around the world.

The appeal of Cantonese cinema was considered to be limited, due to its low production values, the difficulty of translation, and its lack of internationally recognized stars.

Samo's movies showed a way we might be able to get around these barriers. And, even though I knew that our major market would be Asia for a very long time, it started me thinking about the future and what it might hold. Hong Kong's movie industry had been considered a little cousin to Hollywood too long, I thought. If America could export its product around the world, why couldn't Hong Kong do so, too?

We didn't have the money, or the technical expertise, or the marketing and distribution clout of the American studios, but we had things that Hollywood didn't have—including the kind of raw, yet beautifully choreographed action that required intense training and "unacceptable" risks to create. The training Yuen Biao and Samo and I went through would be considered child abuse in the U.S. And the risks that we take on the set, day after day, would cause us to be shut down by the unions or by insurance companies. (No one has been willing to insure a Jackie Chan film since *Dragon Lord*. Whenever someone gets hurt on one of my sets, I pay for all of the treatment myself, out of my own pocket.)

But that's what makes our movies unique.

Ten years later, take a look at Hollywood today. Every major Hong Kong action film director has been recruited to shoot American pictures—from John Woo to Tsui Hark to Ringo Lam, and more. Chow Yun-fat, Michelle Yeoh, and I, we've all recently done Hollywood films. And even the pictures that aren't shot by Hong Kong directors and that don't feature a Hong Kong star—every frame, every sequence, every choreographed turn, twist, and leap—you couldn't copy a Hong Kong film more closely if you used a Xerox machine.

Things sure do change, don't they?

Samo and Yuen Biao and I continued to make films together—some more installments in the Lucky Stars series, until it ran out of gas, and then a dramatic change of pace called *Heart of Dragon*, in which I played a Hong Kong police officer and Samo played my retarded older brother. Samo's relationship with me in the movie was similar in some ways to the relationship between Dustin Hoffman and Tom Cruise in *Rain Man*. Of course, *Heart of Dragon* came out two years earlier—not that I'm saying that Barry Levinson copied me and Samo!

But *Heart of Dragon* was as risky a project for Hong Kong as *Rain Man* was for Hollywood. Compared to our other films, it had very little action. Golden Harvest wasn't sure that people wanted to see me as a dramatic actor. I wasn't so sure they did either. But Samo was insistent—the film was a way for us to break new ground, he maintained. *Wheels on Meals* proved that a real Hong Kong film could be made on foreign soil using a mixed cast. *Heart of Dragon* would prove that a rich, powerful story and complex characters could coexist with action—unlike most other movies, where the martial arts came first and the dialogue and characters were usually added later.

The film did moderately well in Hong Kong, though it was a disappointment compared to our other films. Golden Harvest even made Samo shoot additional fight scenes, which were added for the film's release in Japan. The movie's failure to take off left Samo morose and irritable, and he and I soon fell back into our squabbling ways.

It was time for a break, a chance to give us time away from each other.

Coincidentally, time away from my brothers—and Hong Kong in general—was exactly what Golden Harvest had planned for me. Having proven that my star was still bright in Asia, they wanted me to try one more time to break through to a new set of audiences.

Well, not so new, actually. I'd tried, and failed, to succeed there in the past. And I wasn't enthusiastic about returning, especially in the middle of my successful run in Hong Kong.

"I'm sorry, Jackie," said Willie as he broke the news. "I can understand why you're reluctant, but there's no help for it. You're going to have to go back."

Back to America.

JOURNEY TO THE WEST, PART TWO

S ometimes mistakes teach you lessons.

Sometimes they teach you the wrong lessons.

I was sitting back in the offices of Golden Communications, the U.S. subsidiary of Golden Harvest. David Chan and Andre Morgan were sitting across from me, telling me about their idea for my latest attempt to break into the U.S. market.

"The problem we had last time, as far as we can tell, is that we were trying to make you look too, uh, cute, you know?" said Andre. "Cute doesn't fly in America. Americans don't want cute action heroes; they want hard guys. Tough guys. Look at Clint Eastwood. 'Make my day,' right? We're going to make you make our day, Jackie."

The only thing this new idea was doing was making me feel a little sick. No one expected Jackie Chan to be a "tough guy" in Hong Kong. Well, maybe tough in the sense that I could take a punch or a kick or a fall and get up again, but not tough in the sense of mean, vicious, or hard-boiled. And certainly not in the Clint Eastwood sense. I didn't enjoy hurting people. I wasn't a killer. I fought only to defend myself or to protect my friends.

Even when I *was* forced to punish someone, it was only when I was driven to the end of my rope—and it never ended the way Eastwood's movies did, with a smoking gun, a corpse, and a cool one-liner.

But in *The Protector*, which would costar Danny Aiello and be directed by James Glickenhaus, that's the kind of Jackie Chan they were looking for.

I play a New York City cop. Danny Aiello is my partner. A wealthy man's daughter is kidnapped and we're assigned to the case. The plot thickens, as the trail leads us to Hong Kong, where we discover that the father may be involved in a Triad drug-trafficking scam. The script included all the typical Hollywood action clichés—swear words, casual nudity, and barrages of bullets. The action was stiff, slow, and predictable.

If *The Big Brawl* was a mistake, *The Protector* was a catastrophe.

Halfway through the production, I even called Leonard in Hong Kong and told him that either Glickenhaus would have to go, or I would.

"Now, Jackie, I'm sorry, it doesn't look like things are going so well," said Leonard, sounding sympathetic. "But we can't do anything about this right now; James has an iron-clad contract, and we can't simply replace him."

"He's destroying me," I said curtly. "You know how long his fight sequences take to shoot? Four days. Four days! I've never shot a sequence that took fewer than twenty days. Even when a scene looks terrible, Glickenhaus just says forget it, let's move on. This film is making me look like an idiot."

Leonard sighed. "Jackie, it's obvious that we made an error," he said. "But we need to finish this production. Just finish the shooting in America and come back to Hong Kong. If you're still upset, we'll figure something out."

I never hang up on people in the middle of conversations, and I certainly wouldn't do that to Leonard, to whom I owed so much. But I was tempted this time. I knew it wasn't that he didn't understand what I was going through. It wasn't that he didn't care. But it wasn't just his call on this. The U.S. subsidiary thought it knew what American audiences wanted, and they had made a lot of the decisions on the casting, the script, and, of course, the director.

When I'm doing a movie in Hong Kong, I make sure that every shot is perfect—that it follows the rhythm of the fight, that it properly captures the flow of the choreography. I plan the action. I supervise the editing. I hire the fighters and stuntmen. I can make sure that what I see in my head comes out on the screen. In my Hollywood movies, I never had that kind of freedom or that kind of control.

So even if the films starred Jackie Chan, they weren't Jackie Chan movies. And when someone pays ten dollars for a ticket to one of my films (the price keeps on going up and up), they expect to see a Jackie Chan movie.

Let the American audiences watch their American-style film, I said to myself. I wasn't about to give my Asian fans something less than first-class. And so, when I got back to Hong Kong, I demanded what I should have asked for from the very beginning: the chance to do the film the right way—the Jackie Chan way. For the version of *The Protector* that was released in Asia, I brought back Aiello and Bill "Superfoot" Wallace—the American martial artist who played one of the main villains—and reshot the final fight, making it longer, more dynamic, and more exciting. I had Edward Tang write a subplot to the film featuring a new character played by Sally Yeh, the popular singer and actress. And I cut out all of the crude nonsense that Glickenhaus had squeezed into the film, including the scene in which I walk into a drug laboratory full of nude women!

Compare his version and mine side by side, and tell me which is better. To me—and my fans in Asia—I think the answer is clear. And as for the audiences, well, in the United States the film was a complete bust. But in Hong Kong and Japan, my version held its own.

In any case, I told Leonard that I didn't care about the American market anymore and that I didn't want to make any more bad films just to try to break through.

"I still think there's a great deal of potential there, Jackie," he said.

"I'm sick of the word *potential,*" I retorted. "If I ever go back to America again—and I'm not saying I will—I'm not going as Bruce Lee, or Clint Eastwood, or John Wayne. I'll go back as *Jackie Chan,* or I won't go at all."

Leonard knew I was right.

There was nothing left to say.

MAKING MOVIES

I realize now that I've talked a lot about making Jackie Chan movies, without really explaining what it's like actually to make a Jackie Chan movie.

If you've seen one of my films, and you probably have if you're reading this book, then you may have some idea of the things that make my movies different from American action movies. (If you haven't, put this book down and go rent one now! You can find them at your local video store.) (Hopefully.)

In most action movies, the hero is usually a perfect fighting machine— a killer who never loses a battle and who hardly ever gets hurt.

In my movies, I get beaten up all the time. It's not that I like looking like a loser; it's just that that's the way life is. You lose, and lose, and lose, and then, with any kind of luck, you eventually find a way to win. Life isn't about winning every battle; it's about winning the ones that count. It's like the difference between martial arts tournaments and real fighting.

In a tournament, the winner is the person who tallies up the most points.

In real fighting, the winner is the person who throws the last punch. You can be beaten to a pulp and about to fall over, but if you can reach inside yourself for the energy to throw the final blow that knocks your opponent out before you're knocked out yourself, you win.

My characters aren't perfect, and usually they don't even like to fight. But they fight when they have to, and they win when they have to. That's what counts.

The second thing you'll notice is that American movies always cut away from the action during stunts. Someone will be falling out a window, and then the camera will go to a reaction shot—"Oh, my god, you threw him out the window!"—and then down to the ground, to show the broken body. It's obvious why they're doing this: no Hollywood actor is really going to jump out a three-story window for the sake of a movie. Every stunt is done with doubles, or special protective equipment, or computer animation. It's safer that way, but it's fake—and no matter how good the effects are, people can tell.

In my movies, the camera shows the fall. All the way down. There's no way of faking it, and no way of switching in a stunt double. What you see on the camera is exactly what we did. Even if it almost killed us to do it!

And American fight scenes are quick and deadly. Someone like a Steven Seagal will kill or maim dozens of people in one scene, bang bang bang, one after the next, like he's eating candy. Not even Bruce Lee went through opponents that quickly. But in America, the idea seems to be that the longer it takes to beat someone, the weaker the hero seems to be; a hero has to be a superman, able to take out normal people in the wink of an eye.

Compared to that, in my movies, the fights go on forever! Part of the reason for this is reality—fights are hardly ever decided by a single punch; they keep going until someone gets lucky or wears the opponent down. But most of the reason is that the fighting in my movies isn't just a means to an end. People watch my films to see good fights, not to see people get knocked out. I do with my fistfights what my old friend John Woo does with his gun battles—make them into a thing of beauty, an intricately choreographed dance.

And this leads to another important difference between American movies and my movies. As I mentioned earlier, the action scenes in American films are pretty much scripted out every step of the way. Every punch and kick and tumble has to be storyboarded in advance, because the stuntmen or special effects people have to be prepared for what's going to happen.

In the scripts for my films, the fights are barely described—it's just, "Jackie fights the henchman as they climb the scaffolding." How the fight goes is completely up in the air, because it's all decided right before the cameras roll. I think of different props I want to use, and my stuntmen suggest different fighting stunts to incorporate. We'll stand and brainstorm around the location, trying out different techniques. It's slow work, maybe, but the results are worth it—every screen fight that I've ever shot is completely integrated with the scenery, the props, and even the bystanders. It's like jazz: I never know what's going to come out until the mood and the environment come together.

A garden rake can be used to pull out someone's legs or to vault up to a ledge, can be spun like a staff or swung like a club. A rope becomes a whip, a restraining device, a tangling net. A barrel, a ladder, a chain-link fence—all can be thrown together in a dozen different ways, and until I'm actually there with my stunt team, weaving the scene together, I don't know which way will look best on screen.

You can see how difficult this would be to do on a Hollywood set, where every second lost is a hundred dollars wasted. There isn't much room for inspiration, and even less for innovation.

I'm in the middle of making my first Hollywood film in over a decade right now—*Rush Hour*, which costars a young comedian named Chris Tucker. He's very good, definitely coming up fast. He gets the funny lines, but I get the big action scenes, so I guess it's pretty even.

The studio is sparing nothing to make me feel like I'm a star. I have a beautiful rented mansion, a luxurious trailer on the set, a personal trainer, and a car standing by at all times. Even my stuntmen have their own private rooms. In my Hong Kong movies, we squeeze together, share what we have to, and eat lunch together all out of the same big pot. I do everything and anything I want to—I'm the director, the producer, the cameraman, the prop guy, the janitor. Anything. Here, they won't let me do anything except act. They won't even let me stand around so they can check the lighting—they have a stand-in, my height, my color, wearing my clothes, come in, and they check the lighting off of him while I sit in my trailer.

Dialogue scenes seem to take forever. Fighting scenes go by very quickly. We spend ten days doing dialogue, and two days doing action. In Hong Kong, we spend twenty days doing action, and two days doing dialogue.

I guess it's because Americans like to talk so much. But at least this time, I can do the stunts and fights my way. Or as close to my way as I can, in one-tenth the time, and under all of Hollywood's rules.

The first day of the production, we went to a location to examine how it might be used in a later scene. There was a window on the second story that I was supposed to climb into, and the director wanted to know how I'd be able to do it. Luckily, there were a few trees around the house, so I pointed out that I'd run up one tree, jump to another tree, and then jump from there to the window, about twenty feet off the ground. The director didn't understand, so I took off my shoes and showed him—up the tree, over to the other tree, and over to the window.

Well, that caused the director's jaw to drop open. Once he realized I could do it, he penciled in the location as a shooting site. A day later, we did a rehearsal, and I did the stunt again and again to frame the shot for the cameras. And then, a day after that, the actual day of shooting came. I went over to the first tree, got about halfway up, and then someone shouted out, "Cut! Stop filming!"

Three insurance guys were standing around the director, shouting at him. "He can't do that," they were saying. "What if he falls and gets hurt?" The director tried to explain to them that I'd already done it five or six times, but they wouldn't listen.

It took several hours for them to rig padded mats so that they'd catch me if I fell, and all the camera angles had to be changed to hide them from view.

I'm not saying it's wrong to take precautions, especially when actors' lives are at stake. But in Hong Kong, we trust our training to protect us even where a padded mattress won't. No one's ever gotten killed on one of my movies—there are always injuries, but never anything that's ended a life or a career. We just have different systems, and going from the Hong Kong way to the Hollywood way has taken some getting used to.

The really great thing about the Hollywood way, of course, is that you can get just about anything you need—equipment, locations, props—without worrying about cost or time. If you need a Steadicam, it's yours. When we need that kind of a shot on my movies, we rig something up with bungee cords and try to walk in as smoothly as possible. What about a crane for a sweeping overhead shot? No problem. In Hong Kong, we take a ladder, put one guy on top with the camera, and get ten people to lift the ladder and turn it around.

The quality of our results is worse than Hollywood films, but not by as much as you'd think. And besides, look at what that means for Hollywood: *Speed 2. Batman and Robin. Titanic.* $100 million, $200 million budgets. Out of all three, only *Titanic* made money, because it's a good film. But in most of Asia, my latest film beat *Titanic* at the box office.

I just wonder what kind of movie I'd make if someone gave me $100 million to play with. My most expensive film cost U.S.$20 million to make. If I had $100 million, I bet I could make a movie that looked like $300 million. No private jets, no mansions, no luxurious trailers, no fancy food. Everything up on the screen. Nothing but ideas and pictures.

And action.

Some of my best movies have begun with just a strange offhand idea. When I began *Police Story*, it was right after finishing *The Protector*. I'd decided that I wanted to do a movie about a cop—my way. And I wanted to make it as spectacular as possible. While walking around Hong Kong, which has gone from being a city of small, almost suffocatingly cramped buildings into a city of giant skyscrapers, I noticed how much of the landscape had become dominated by steel—and glass.

I immediately arranged a meeting with Edward Tang, and told him I wanted to do a film in which the action played with glass—breaking it, smashing through it, falling onto it.

It sounds a little silly, but that was how *Police Story*, which my stuntmen nicknamed *Glass Story*, began. There are lots of amazing stunts in the film—the opening sequence, which features a breakneck car chase down a mountainside and *through* a shantytown composed of old shacks; the scene that follows right after, in which I use an umbrella to hook onto the back of a speeding double-decker bus, and then use it to pull myself up and into the bus after a hectic flying ride around the city.

But the scene that was most dangerous and most memorable was the final battle, which took place in a crowded shopping mall. Glass is every-where, being shot up, being shattered by fists and bodies.

To make it look as real as possible, I ordered special breakthrough glass from a supplier in America, asking that it be made twice as thick as ordinary "sugar glass." This made it twice as dangerous, of course; people were getting bruised and cut all the time, and at one point, Willie was go-ing back and forth from the set to the hospital every day, taking over new injured people and checking on the ones who were already hurt. But any-thing less would not have had the same effect.

The movie's last stunt—the superstunt—was the pièce de résistance. To try and catch the boss gangster, who's trying to escape with the evi-dence of his crimes, I have to make a desperate leap from five stories up, grabbing onto a chandelier made of twinkling lights, strung along a se-ries of thick wires. I slide down the wires, sending sparks and broken glass flying on my way down, and then crash through a series of glass over-hangs, before finally hitting the ground.

We could use the shopping center only after it closed in the evening, so we had to work fast; there were only so many hours in the night. By the time the construction team had hung the wires and set up the layers of glass, the sun was about to rise, so we had to hang black cloth over the mall's atrium roof to block out the early rays of dawn. The shops opened at 10 A.M., and we had to be finished, cleaned up, and out of there by 9:30. There were two hundred extras and twelve cameramen standing around waiting all night, not to mention my costars, Brigitte Lin, who played a witness I was assigned to protect, and Maggie Cheung, who played my longtime girlfriend.

We had only one chance to make the stunt work, because otherwise we'd never get the place put back in order by our deadline. The cameras started rolling, and the mall went quiet. I leaped from the third-story bal-cony, and slid, and slid, and fell, and crashed. Glass exploded in all direc-tions, and there I was, flat on my back on the hard floor of the ground level. Everyone held their breath, not knowing if I was hurt, and if so, how badly. And despite the pain throughout my body, especially my hands, I managed to stand up.

And the whole mall, all the extras and the cast and crew, began to clap, even without hearing the word "cut" that would tell the cameras to stop rolling. Brigitte and Maggie ran over to me, tears running down their faces. The stunt was a success.

While sliding down the light wires, I burned all the skin off my fingers and palms. I had blood running down my face and glass sticking into my legs and torso. But still . . . the stunt was a success.

Every time I make a new film, I'm thinking about how to push the envelope—to surprise the audience, to do something different. Sometimes it's in the stunts; how do I make them bigger, faster, harder, riskier? Sometimes it's in the stories; what can I do that goes against the trends? If everyone is doing period films, I want to do a modern film. If everyone is using guns, I want to use fists. There's a formula to my films—people expect certain things out of a Jackie Chan film—but within those expectations, I want to give people a shock.

After I'd done *Project A*, a period piece, I did *Police Story*, which was set in the present day. Then, since *Police Story* took place in Hong Kong, I decided I wanted to do something in a foreign country, so I made *Armour of God*, teaming up with pop singer Alan Tam and Lola Forner, the Spanish model who'd been my costar in *Wheels on Meals*.

This time, my character was a daredevil treasure hunter named Asian Hawk, hired by a wealthy man to recover the pieces of a mystical artifact. The character and story line were inspired by Steven Spielberg's Indiana Jones, but the action was Jackie Chan action—fists and flying bodies, not guns and flying bullets.

I'll always remember *Armour of God* as the movie that brought me closer to dying than I've ever been. As you might guess, the stunts in the film were pretty spectacular, but the one that almost killed me was actually a very simple one, jumping from the top of a wall onto the limb of a tree. The branch wouldn't hold my weight, and I ended up falling to the ground, smashing my head against a rock so hard that blood began pouring from my ears.

We were filming on location in Yugoslavia, and the hospitals there were not as advanced as one might hope. Luck, as usual, was on my side, however: it just so happened that the city we were closest to was also the home of the country's most famous brain specialist.

After having surgery to remove the piece of bone that had been pushed into my cranium by the rock, I spent six weeks recovering, and was soon ready to begin filming once more. Determined to conquer my fears, I went back and did the jump again. This time, the stunt was a success—as was the movie, which became the third biggest grossing film in the history of Hong Kong cinema.

Maybe the news stories about my near-death experience helped to sell the film; I don't know. (If that's true, I want to go on the record as saying that, as dedicated as I am to making movies, there are *some* things I don't ever want to go through again, even for the sake of success.)

After *Armour of God*, I reunited with my brothers again for the sequel *Project A II*, and then for a film called *Dragons Forever*—an ironic title, considering that it was the last film in which we three "dragons" have appeared on screen as costars.

In some ways, it was our finest cinematic moment, with memorable characters and terrific fight sequences, including the first-ever battle royal involving all three of us fighting one another. In other ways, it was a sad sendoff: the tensions that lay just beneath the surface of our relationships finally exploded during that production, and when the shoot wrapped, we went our separate ways. It was a few years before we talked again, and a few more years before we worked with one another again—I did a cameo appearance in Yuen Biao's directorial debut, *The Kid from Tibet,* and asked Samo to be my action director for the movie *Thunderbolt.* He followed that up by directing me in *Mr. Nice Guy,* one of my most recent films.

I think that, after a decade of being irritated and resentful toward one another, Samo and Yuen Biao and I have finally come to a point where we're past the differences that pulled us apart. We've even talked about projects that might put us together again, in front of the cameras. Still talking. Still waiting for the right time and the right project.

Our awkward breakup and our recent reconciliation is just more proof to me that *things change.* Even the best friendships occasionally run aground. Tastes and trends and fashions are always shifting. And, at forty-four years old, I can't afford to let myself feel too comfortable, too trapped in my habits.

I've always said that all I want to do is make Jackie Chan films, but I've reinvented the Jackie Chan film over and over again during my career. I don't like to think about it too much—it hurts more than all of the injuries I've suffered over the years—but there will eventually come a time when I physically won't be able to do what Jackie Chan does, at least this version of Jackie Chan.

Can a fifty-year-old man still jump off buildings? At fifty-five, will I be fast enough and nimble enough to move and fight the way I want to, and the way my audiences expect me to? What kind of stunts could a sixty-year-old Jackie Chan perform?

I know that eventually I'll have to start a new phase in my life, one in which I'll actually need to get medical insurance!

Over the years, I've tried to prepare myself for that time. Through Golden Way, the production company I created under the mantle of Golden Harvest, I've produced dozens of films—from action movies like *Naughty Boys* and *The Inspector Wears Skirts,* to romances and historical dramas like *Rouge* and *Centre Stage.* I've helped to launch the careers of other performers—giving my good friend Anita Mui a chance to step from singing into the movies with *Rouge;* providing a platform for Michelle Yeoh to make her action comeback in *Supercop;* showcasing new, young talent in most of my recent films, from *Rumble in the Bronx* to my just-completed *Who Am I?*

And I've also put my efforts behind businesses and pursuits that have nothing to do with movies at all. Through the JC Group, the company that I founded with Willie as managing director, I've bought real estate, launched clothing lines, opened coffee shops—and given millions of dollars to charity.

I'm even a partner in the restaurant chain Planet Hollywood, along with American stars like Bruce Willis and Sylvester Stallone. I'm the only Asian performer they asked to join their group, which seemed kind of unfair; that's why I recently agreed to invest in a new theme restaurant chain, Star East, which will showcase Chinese entertainers in the same way that Planet Hollywood showcases American actors and actresses. The visionary and lead investor in Star East is Alan Tam, my old costar in *Armour of God*. Many of my good friends in the industry are part of the group as well, as we've already opened restaurants in Shanghai and in Pasadena, California. Who knows? We could be opening one in your neighborhood sometime soon.

All of these activities will probably keep me busy long after I've stopped doing action films—but I'm not ready to give up making movies anytime soon. A couple of years ago, I had a talk with Willie about my career, in which he told me how worried he was about the pounding my body had gotten over all these years.

"Jackie, you can't keep this up forever," he told me.

I laughed at him. "Forever is a long time," I said. "I'm not going to be around that long anyway."

"Be serious, Jackie," he said, puffing on a pipe I'd bought for him while I was scouting locations for my newest movie. The doctor had made Willie quit smoking cigarettes some years before, so he'd switched over to pipe tobacco—still not a very good habit, but one that was easier on the lungs and heart. "I'm saying this not because I want to be depressing, but because I'm tired of visiting you in the hospital all the time. And I can't imagine you don't think about this yourself."

Well, I did think about it ... once in a while. "Look, Willie, I know that eventually, I'll have to change my life and my career," I said. "But I've got a lot of good years left in me yet."

Willie puffed and smiled. "Of course you do, Jackie," he said. "Of course you do. The secret is to extend your action years as long as possible. And, as much as you're not going to like this solution, your old Uncle Willie has an idea about how you can keep on making movies and cut down on wear and tear."

The Hong Kong style of filmmaking, which was the only one I really knew, depended too much on physical ability and personal risk, he pointed out. "The answer is that you need to start learning another style," he continued. "Not to replace your style, but to *add* to it."

I leaned back in my chair and nearly fell over backward as it hit me what he was suggesting. "You mean go back to Hollywood!" I said, almost as an accusation.

Willie nodded. "Whatever you may think about American movie-making, Jackie, the truth is, an action star's career lasts longer in Holly-wood," he said. "Look at Harrison Ford—in his fifties, still doing action movies. Sylvester Stallone and Arnold Schwarzenegger both are older than you, and they can still make action movies. You learn special effects, you learn how to use blue screens, and bingo! Ten, fifteen more years of action. And I'm not saying you can't keep putting yourself in the hospital whenever you want to. This just gives you an option."

Thoughts raced through my mind. I'd promised myself that I wouldn't try to jump blindly into the American market again—that I wouldn't let myself suffer those kinds of humiliations. But then again, Golden Harvest was already in negotiations to sell my current films to studios in the U.S., and Raymond was dropping not-so-subtle hints that an extended trip to America for publicity purposes was somewhere in my future. And the main reason I'd vowed not to go back was because I didn't want to be shaped into someone I wasn't. Now that my style and reputation and image were known throughout Asia (and much of the rest of the world), maybe I could finally return and make a Hollywood film my way. As Jackie Chan.

Besides, I'd always had two lingering dreams that my previous American adventures had not fulfilled. The first was to have a big, glitzy, gala opening night premiere, with photographers and velvet ropes and celebrities, just like on TV. The second was to get my hands and name printed in the cement outside of the famous Mann's Chinese Theater in Hollywood. By every other measure, I guess I could consider myself a star—but somehow, those two things seemed to make all the difference in the world.

"I suppose it can't hurt to explore the possibility," I said, finally.

"Beautiful, Jackie," said Willie. "Once more into the breach! Or, more precisely—third time's the charm."

JOURNEY TO THE WEST, PART THREE

It turned out that making the decision to try Hollywood again was the easy part.

Finding the right project—

Well, that was another thing entirely.

I got offers to do American movies all the time, but hardly ever in a way that I thought made sense. Michael Douglas, for instance, had invited me to play the part of a Japanese killer in his movie *Black Rain*. Well, not only did the film make Asians look bad, but why would my fans want to see me as a bad guy?

To go from being a hero in Asia to being a villain in America didn't make any sense. If I was going to make a movie in Hollywood, it had to be one that would appeal to my fans in China, Japan, Thailand, and the rest of the world as well. Asians may want to see Mel Gibson or Tom Cruise, but they don't want to see them beat up one of their own idols. That's kind of insulting, don't you think? (Especially when you and I know that just about any trained Hong Kong martial arts star could make an American actor look pretty bad in a fight. This isn't boasting. Just the facts.)

Then Sylvester Stallone talked with me about a project in which I'd play a drug dealer who'd have a change of heart and turn into a good guy. I still didn't like it; I didn't want to play a pusher on screen, even one who gets reformed. Stallone knows that I've always enjoyed his movies, and that I admire him very much, and over time, we've gotten to be friends. But I couldn't compromise my values, even to work with a friend.

It got so I was beginning to think I'd never find a project that was right for me. Bruce Willis suggested we make a movie together, but there wasn't a script around that fit our personalities. Wesley Snipes wanted me for a film called *Confucius Brown*, in which we'd play long-lost brothers. (He and Woody Harrelson also played "brothers" in *Money Train*. Wesley's family is starting to look like the U.N.!)

I had problems with the script, and my schedule and Wesley's ended up getting crossed up, so *Confucius Brown* never happened, although I heard that it might be back on track again—with Michelle Yeoh playing the role I was supposed to play. I guess the script's been rewritten.

(Coincidentally, another film Stallone had offered me was *Demolition Man*, a movie with Sandra Bullock from *Speed*. He wanted me to play a supervillain running loose in the far future, chased by a supercop, played by him. I didn't feel right about that role either. It ended up going to Wesley Snipes—so the two people I'd wanted to work with, and couldn't, ended up working with each other.)

"This isn't working, Willie," I said. "All of the scripts we've seen so far have been pretty lousy."

"Oh, come on, Jackie, we've only just begun," he said, trying to cheer me up. "Besides, we haven't even had any real meetings yet—I'm sure once we start getting together with producers in Hollywood, things will get better. That's when we'll start seeing some *substance*, dear boy."

The whole time that we were searching for the right Hollywood project, I continued making movies in Hong Kong: *Crime Story,* a dark and somewhat grim police thriller directed by Kirk Wong; *Drunken Master II,* a sequel to my first big hit (and the first traditional-style kung fu movie I'd made in more than ten years); and *Rumble in the Bronx,* directed by Stanley Tong Kwei-la, my good friend and one of my favorite collaborators. Stanley is a former stuntman himself, and Leonard had introduced him to me as someone whose style he thought would mesh well with mine. As usual, Leonard was right; Stanley has made possible some of my most spectacular action scenes ever, beginning with *Supercop.*

In *Rumble,* Stanley and I took the idea of making an "international" Hong Kong film—one that would be as accessible to Western audiences as for Eastern ones—as far as it could go.

I'd cast European model Lola Forner in *Wheels on Meals* and *Armour of God,* and both were shot on location abroad. In *Armour of God II: Operation Condor,* I had *three* lovely costars—Carol Dodo Cheng from Hong Kong, Shoko Ikeda from Japan, and Eva Cobo de Garcia from Spain—the idea being to cover as many markets as possible. Most of that film was shot outside of Asia, too, in Spain and Morocco.

But the setting of *Rumble* was completely Western. The villains and background characters were all non-Asian. And much of the dialogue was in English.

From the very beginning, Raymond Chow and Leonard Ho believed that *Rumble* would be my ticket West. They were on the verge of selling a package of my earlier films to U.S. distributors. A movie set in America would seal the deal—and make for a terrific lead-in for a return to Hollywood . . . my way.

And that's why, rather than *Showdown in Macao* or *Gang War in Kowloon,* my second film with Stanley Tong became *Rumble in the Bronx.*

Even though it was supposed to be set in New York, we shot the movie in Vancouver, Canada—I'm no stranger to taking risks, but making a movie on location in the Bronx seemed crazy even to me. (Anyone who knows what New York looks like can tell that it's not actually the Bronx, anyway. The architecture is wrong, the streets are different, and there are mountains visible in some of the backgrounds. But then again, if you're staring at the scenery while I'm fighting, I'm doing something wrong.)

In early 1995, the deal was closed for New Line Cinema to bring *Rumble in the Bronx* to the United States. The money they paid wasn't that big, just a couple of million dollars. But as part of the agreement, New Line was going to put their entire publicity machine behind it—and behind me.

"The idea we have isn't just to introduce people to the movie," their marketing guy said. "It's to introduce them to Jackie Chan."

"I've been here before," I said. "I think people already know me."

The marketing guy laughed. "Yeah, some people may have seen your American films, and you've certainly got a big cult following," he said. "But seriously, do you think that America—middle America, shopping mall America—knows Jackie Chan? The *real* Jackie Chan? Do they know you're the biggest action star in the world?"

I looked over to Willie, who raised an eyebrow at me. The marketing guy had been speaking in English, of course, and even after all these years, my English wasn't perfect.

It didn't matter.

This guy was talking in a language I could understand.

Rumble in the Bronx would be the film that would show audiences in the U.S. the *real* Jackie Chan. And New Line's publicity push would put me on the covers of magazines, in newspapers, on talk shows. Not as some kind of strange animal, or Bruce Lee clone, or one-hit wonder who'd just gotten off the boat from Hong Kong. As the biggest star in the world.

"Biggest star in the world, I don't know," I said. "Biggest star in Asia, yes."

That drew a shrug from the marketing guy. "So you're the biggest star in the biggest continent in the world. Billions of people love Jackie Chan. Let's not get hung up on the details."

That's when I remembered something. I leaned over and whispered in Willie's ear, and then smiled at the marketing guy a little sheepishly.

"Jackie has a small request," said Willie. "Rather simple, I believe, but really, it means a lot to him . . ."

And so there I was, some months later, standing on a burgundy red carpet, as flashbulbs popped and video cameras whirred and the crowd squeezed against the restraining ropes, shouting my name and asking for autographs. Hundreds of people lined the walkway, most of whom had probably never heard of me half a year before—but who'd decided to wait for hours on this warm Los Angeles night, just to see me walk into my first-ever gala premiere.

It was everything I ever imagined on all those long-lost evenings; the nights I spent watching films from Hollywood's glorious past, slouched in cramped Hong Kong theaters with terrible sound.

This was the way that Hollywood was supposed to be.

This was being a star in America.

Rumble in the Bronx made $9.8 million on its opening weekend, becoming the first Hong Kong film ever to make it to number one at the U.S. box office. It went on to make over $30 million—a spectacular hit for New Line, an indie studio whose movies usually earned a third of that, or less.

And Hollywood sat up and took notice.

I'd gotten an American agent, Brian Gersh, who was with the William Morris Agency. He set up meetings for me and Willie to take—in Hollywood, people always "take" meetings; they don't "have" them. I got an avalanche of offers—although I have to say, I wasn't used to the way showbiz works here in the States. It's all talking, talking, talking; everything seems to be happening, but nothing is real. Nothing can be trusted until the movie starts shooting—and even then, you should probably wait until it actually arrives in the theaters, just to be safe. One producer even claimed to have four scripts for me, all with famous directors and actors attached to them. I was impressed, until he admitted that none of the directors or actors had actually agreed to do the movies yet. And then he asked me for an autograph for his daughter!

"In Hong Kong, if I say I want a movie to happen, it happens," I said to Willie, pacing around my hotel room one day. "I can't even believe they make movies in this city. All they seem to make is conversation. What do you think the ratio is here—ten meetings equals one project?"

"More like a thousand meetings," said Willie philosophically. "But please, Jackie, did you think just one meeting would be enough to iron out a deal? You've waited for fifteen years to come back to Hollywood; you can wait a few more months."

John Hughes wanted me to star in a film called *The Bee*, in which I'd play a guy trying to catch a bee that seemed to have a mind of its own. The movie would have given me the chance to do some very funny stunts, but to tell the truth, I wasn't sure that I wanted to make my return to Hollywood in a film where I was stupider than a bug.

Between all the meetings, Willie and I returned to Hong Kong, where I kept on making films: *Thunderbolt, Police Story IV: First Strike,* and *Mr. Nice Guy.* All three were also bought by U.S. studios for American release.

I was in the middle of making *Mr. Nice Guy*—which was directed by none other than Biggest Brother Samo—when I got a call from Willie, who told me that my agent in America had exciting news for me.

"A movie with Spielberg?" I said, a little sarcastically. Nothing ever came out of Hollywood but "exciting news," and it almost always bored me to death.

"Mmm, no, but that *would* be exciting," said Willie. "Of course, if you're going to be so testy, perhaps I won't tell you the news at all."

If it were anyone else, I could have put him in a headlock and made him tell me, but instead I said, "Please," which works better with Willie anyway.

"Well, Jackie, remember your second Hollywood wish?"

If you walk down Hollywood Boulevard, between Highland and La Brea, you'll see Mann's Chinese Theater—formerly Grauman's Chinese Theater.

It's not very Chinese at all, actually; all the decoration is cheesy and fake, or it would be, if it weren't such a famous and historic showbiz spot.

But I helped make it a little more Chinese that day, on January 5, 1997—putting my handprints, my footprints, my signature, and even my nose-print into the cement outside, in a ceremony that fulfilled my second big Hollywood wish.

And while I was out there to do the ceremony, I finally got a deal started on a movie that should be out in the theaters right now, *Rush Hour*—my return to America, not as Bruce Lee, not as Clint Eastwood, not as John Wayne . . . but as Jackie Chan.

If it fails, I have many more movies to make in Hong Kong. If it does okay, I have many movies I want to make in Hollywood. I'd like to work with James Cameron. With Steven Spielberg. With Stallone, and Bruce Willis, and Robert DeNiro. There are so many of us Chinese stars here in Hollywood now, maybe we could all do a project together—my old friend John Woo directing, my old costar Michelle Yeoh as female lead, Chow Yun-fat and Jet Li and me as a team!

Maybe that isn't possible in Hollywood today. The studios wouldn't know how to market a movie with so many Chinese in it. But oh, imagine how much money that movie would make in Asia!

I've been on David Letterman and Jay Leno.

I've gotten an award on MTV.

I was a presenter at the Academy Awards. While I was there, Robin Williams, Tom Hanks, John Travolta, they all came up to me and told me they were fans.

The other day, one of my favorite singers, Lionel Richie, came to visit me on the set. Yesterday, Michael Jackson gave me a call.

Hollywood has opened its doors to me and made me feel at home. But even if Hollywood turns me away in the future, I've already gone farther than I imagined, far beyond my dreams.

I was a useless child.

A ragged boy.

A reckless teen.

And now—

Look who I am now!

EPILOGUE:
A LEAP OF FAITH

The blue of the sky and the sound of applause.

I'm on my back, looking up at a Rotterdam day, surrounded by a crowd of cheering extras. In the minutes after a stunt, after the adrenaline has surged and drained away, sometimes I see faces—faces and ghosts.

My father and mother, in their home a continent away. Are they thinking of me? Are they worrying that this will be the time I won't come home?

My wife and son, leading their separate lives, wondering perhaps if this husband, father, stranger will ever really be a part of their world, or always lost to the larger world outside.

Leonard Ho, who believed in me when few people did, who supported me, taught me, and helped me grow up.

Willie Chan, who has stood by me in good and bad, and been all the guide, mentor, and friend that anyone could ask for and have the fortune to receive.

My brothers and sisters, big and little, with whom I ate and slept and fought and argued and grew and learned.

And Master!

You made this leap possible, and all the ones before it. Without you, there would never have been a Jackie Chan.

I hated you.

I feared you.

I love you, Master.

Some things change.

And some never will.

MY TOP TEN STUNTS

1. "Shantytown Stakeout," *Police Story*

As far as action is concerned, *Police Story* is my favorite movie I've ever made, a real whirlwind of slam-bang stunts and wild fights from beginning to end. To start things off right—that is to say, in an insanely exciting and dangerous way—Edward Tang King-sang and I scripted this opening sequence. My character and my fellow cops have been assigned to an undercover stakeout in an attempt to nab a notorious mobster. We set our trap along a winding mountain highway, taking up hidden positions throughout a rickety village of old tin and wood shacks. When our trap is sprung too soon, the dragnet turns into a disaster, as the gangsters try to escape by driving through the mountain village. Not "through" as in "zigzagging around the buildings," but through as in smashing into, over, and *through* the buildings. I quickly commandeer a car and begin a crazed chase down the slope after them. The car is smashed (as is the village), so I chase the crooks on foot. When they hijack a double-decker bus, I grab an umbrella, take a running leap, and hook its handle onto the rim of an open window! Hanging desperately onto the umbrella, I try to pull myself into the bus, but am eventually thrown clear. Scrambling down to a lower part of the highway, I draw my pistol, order the speeding bus to stop . . . and it does, just inches away from my body.

2. "The Great Glass Slide," *Police Story*

This is where I finally put the drop on the gangsters once and for all. Of course, I had to put the drop on myself in order to do it—literally. After a glass-shattering fight inside a shopping mall, I spot my target several floors below, on the ground level of an open atrium. The only way to get down from my perch in time to do my policeman's duty is to take a flying leap into the air, grab ahold of a pole wrapped in twinkling Christmas lights, and slide a hundred feet to the ground—through a glass-and-wood partition, onto the hard marble tile. We had to do this in one take, so I crossed my fingers and prayed that I'd hit the stunt the first time (and that I'd hit the ground softly). I made my jump, grabbed the pole, and watched the twinkling lights crack and pop all the way down, in an explosion of shattering glass and electrical sparks. Then I hit the glass. And then I hit the floor. Somehow I managed to survive with a collection of ugly bruises . . . and second-degree burns on the skin of my fingers and palms.

3. "Clock Tower Tumble," *Project A*

After a wild bicycle chase through Hong Kong's back alleys, I find myself high in the air, dangling from the hands of a giant clock face. With no other way to get down than fall, I let go—and crash through a series of cloth canopies before smashing into the ground. I had to do this one three times before I was satisfied with the way it looked. Trust me, I wouldn't want to do it a *fourth* time.

4. "An Aerial Tour of Kuala Lumpur," *Police Story III: Supercop*

By this time, all of you probably know Michelle Yeoh from *Tomorrow Never Dies*, the James Bond film. She resurrected her action career by costarring with me in *Supercop*, my first film with Stanley Tong. Michelle isn't a fighter; she never formally trained in martial arts, beginning her career as a ballet dancer. But one thing you can say for her is that she has the heart of a lioness. She did all of her own stunts in *Supercop*, because she threatened to beat me up if I wouldn't let her! Her most dangerous sequence in the movie was a scene in which she rides a motorcycle up a ramp, into the air, and onto the roof of a moving train. I have to admit that after I saw her do that stunt, I felt like I had something to prove. That's why we added this sequence, in which I jump from the roof of a building to a rope ladder swinging from the bottom of a hovering helicopter. The crooks flying the chopper try to knock me off the ladder by swinging me back and forth through the air and into buildings, moving at high speed above the streets of Malaysia's capital. They don't succeed—lucky for me. And the stunt looks *almost* as dangerous as it really was—lucky for all you action fans out there.

5. "Going Down . . ." *Who Am I?*

This scene was billed by my producers as the "world's most dangerous stunt." They were probably telling the truth—although just about any stunt is dangerous, if you do it wrong. (The stunt that nearly killed me took place less than fifteen feet off the ground, after all.) Luckily, I did it right. Eventually. Even though one of my stuntmen proved it could be done (from a lower level, of course), it took me two weeks to get up the nerve to try it myself. The sequence begins with me fighting it out with some thugs on the top of a very tall building in Rotterdam, Holland. After battling with them around the roof, and nearly falling off once or twice, I finally take the quickest possible trip to the sidewalk below—sliding down the side of the building, which is slanted nearly forty-five degrees, all the way to the ground. Twenty-one stories. If I ever have an amusement park, I'll be sure to turn this stunt into a ride.

6. "The Walls Come Tumblin' Down," *Project A II*

I saw Buster Keaton do this in *Steamboat Bill, Jr.*, so of course I had to do it too. After running down the face of a ceremonial facade that's in the process of falling over, I narrowly escape being crushed by standing in the right place at the right time—with my body going through an opening in the facade as it crashes down right over me. It's all in the timing.

7. "No Way to Ride a Bus," *Police Story II*

Another chase sequence—this time running along the tops of moving buses, while narrowly dodging signs and billboards that pass overhead and around me. At the end of the chase, I leap through a glass window. . . . Unfortunately, I chose the wrong window as my target, and instead of hitting prop glass, I smashed through a real pane. Which left *me* in real pain.

8. "Down, Down, and Away," *Armour of God*

I did this stunt just weeks after recovering from my near-fatal fall and serious brain surgery. The show must go on. My character, Asian Hawk, is an adventurer who specializes in daredevil escapes. The most daring one happens near the end of the movie, when I take a wild leap off of a sheer cliff . . . and land on top of a huge hot air balloon, safe and sound. I did this stunt by parachuting from a plane. Which didn't make it any safer.

9. "Roller Boogie," *Winners and Sinners*

I'm not really the star of the "Lucky Stars" movies—I did the films mostly because of Samo. (Well, it helped that the movies were box office hits.) As a result, I don't get much screen time, which is fine, because the rest of the cast is talented and hilarious. This scene gave me a chance to shine, though—using the roller-skating skill I learned for *The Big Brawl* in a chase sequence on a crowded highway. The wildest part of the sequence has me rolling over a Volkswagen Beetle, and then under an eighteen-wheeler truck rig. That's one way of beating rush hour traffic.

10. "Cycle Thriller," *Armour of God II: Operation Condor*

We intended *Operation Condor* to be epic in every way: big fights, big budget, and, of course, big stunts. There's a chase sequence toward the beginning of the movie that stands as one of my best ever. After racing through the streets of Madrid on the back of a motorcycle, I find myself headed for the waterfront with nowhere to go but into the sea. Luckily, I spot a cargo net hanging from a crane at the edge of the docks—so I gun the engines and head full-speed toward the end of the pier in a deadly game of chicken with my pursuers. They're forced to veer off and crash into stacked piles of crates, while I ride my cycle off the pier and into the air, leaping up to grab hold of the net at the very last minute. What a waste of a good bike.

MY TOP TEN FIGHTS

1. "Jet Fighter, Part One," *Wheels on Meals*
This was my first face-off with American champion kickboxer Benny "The Jet" Urquidez. He's a great fighter—good enough that he tested my skills to the limit. In fact, throughout the filming of this scene, I teased him that we should fight a real match, not just a movie brawl. "Come on, Benny, let's do it," I'd say. And he'd say, "Any time, Jackie, any time." Well, the time was always "sometime soon," and by the time the film was finished, he finally caught on that I was just joking. To be honest, I don't know who would have won if we did fight. He's that good.

2. "Mall Brawl," *Police Story*
Well, I said that *Police Story* was my favorite movie for action, didn't I? Leading up to the Great Glass Slide was a fight that just didn't let up, with shattering shop windows and display cases everywhere, and nearly everyone getting cut or bruised as the glass flew. Even Brigitte Lin Ching-hsia—poor Brigitte!—got into the action, with her body being thrown through a glass table. I have to say, she really took the punishment like a trouper.

3. "Factory Fight," *Drunken Master II*
A lot of my fans feel this is the best film I've made in the past five years—and it really was a big hit—but I'm still a little disappointed with the way *Drunken Master II* turned out. It was a sequel to my first real blockbuster, of course, so maybe I'm just holding it to a higher standard. Anyway, the film began with veteran Shaw Brothers director Lau Kar-leung at the helm, but he and I had different ideas about action. It's pretty obvious how our philosophies contrast if you look at the fights at the beginning of the film and the one that ends it, which I choreographed and directed by myself. His ideas are very traditional, almost like classical music; mine are more like jazz. My main opponent in this fight is Kenneth Lo, who's my friend and bodyguard in real life. He was a champion kickboxer before going into the movies, and you can tell from the lightning speed of his leg work. To face Kenneth's Thai boxing, I use Choy Li Fut, a hybrid kung fu style that blends Northern and Southern techniques—as well as some of the "Drunken kung fu" that everyone expects to see in a movie called *Drunken Master II*! In fact, at the very end of the scene, I actually drink industrial-strength alcohol, which gives me the strength (and tolerance for pain) to finally win the fight.

4. "Come Drink with Me," *Drunken Master*
I face off in the finale of my first big box-office smash against Hwang Jang Lee, a Korean martial artist who is one of the greatest kickers in the history of kung fu cinema. It's an intense and unusual fight, featuring my comical "Eight Drunken Fairies" drunken-style fighting against Hwang's tae kwon do: fast, funny, and furious.

5. "Jet Fighter, Part Two," *Dragons Forever*
In my opinion, the final fight of this movie is one of the best-shot action sequences that Samo has ever directed. The pacing of my second battle with Benny "The Jet" Urquidez is wonderful, too, beginning slow with each of us sizing up the other while we take off our shirts and circle warily, and then building tremendous momentum into a whirlwind of kicks and punches. Truly a classic kung-fu moment. If I say so myself.

6. "Child's Play," *Police Story II*
An example of intricate prop fighting, in which I use playground equipment to take out a gang of thugs. Think of a complicated dance with a whole bunch of partners, over, under, through, and around swingsets, jungle gyms, and seesaws, and you'll get a small piece of the picture here.

7. "Monks and Amazons," *Armour of God*
A bizarre battle between me and a mob of angry monks, with a few warrior women thrown in for good measure. I developed my "one-man-against-the-world" fighting style in this crazy fight, battling outward in a spiral while using circular kicks to keep the cassock-wearing combatants at a distance.

8. "Bar Bash," *Project A*
It's us Coast Guard sailors against our hated rivals, the police squad, in a sensational bar-room brawl. The action is so fast, and there are so many combatants, that it's a little hard to follow everything that's going on. But this is as close as it gets to filming a real bar fight (even though we weren't actually out to kill each other); me and my stuntmen really were bouncing off the walls and furniture in this scene!

9. "No Pain, No Gain," *The Young Master*
In this epic, extended battle, I fight hapkido expert Whang Inn Sik. I was very impressed with his martial arts, and was determined to show the audience the power and beauty of this Korean fighting style. As a result, I shot the entire scene at a wide angle with relatively few cuts. To finally defeat the master, I throw out all of my traditional techniques, and just go at him like a lunatic, flailing my arms and smashing into him with my head, my fists, and every other part of my body. I do win in the end, but at a price: the last scene of the movie shows me in a complete body cast, waving goodbye with my fingers!

10. "Turbo Charged," *Armour of God II: Operation Condor*
I feel like I've got to include this fight just because it was so much trouble to stage, and because the idea behind it was so bizarre. Me and Vincent Lyn, an American mar-

tial artist (he's half-Chinese), battle in a giant wind tunnel—flying through the air, smashing against the back wall of the tunnel, and tumbling to the ground when the turbine is turned off. We did the whole thing wearing wires and harnesses, which were a pain to deal with (but how else were we going to pretend to be flying?). It's a campy scene, but it's a lot of fun. Especially when I fly at Vincent with my fist outstretched, shouting "Superman!" and use the thrust of the wind to punch him out.

"IT ONLY HURTS WHEN I'M NOT LAUGHING": MY ACHES AND PAINS

Anyone who's a fan of my movies knows that if you watch my films to the very end, you'll get a sort of ghoulish treat: a selection of my "no-goods," outtakes from stunts and fight sequences that just didn't work out right. A lot of times the result is an injury, and sometimes a bad one. My very worst injury ever, the one that almost killed me, actually occurred on a very routine stunt. I was shooting *Armour of God* in Yugoslavia, and was still recovering from the jet lag of flying twenty hours to get there. The stunt was simple—just jumping down from a castle wall to a tree below. The first time I tried it, the stunt went perfectly, but I wasn't satisfied with the take. I tried it again, and the second time, I somehow missed the branch I was trying to grab. Whish! I fell past the tree and onto the ground below. Actually, there was a cameraman down there trying to capture a low angle, and if he hadn't scrambled out of the way, I would have probably landed on him. We would both have been hurt, but not badly. Instead, I hit the rocky ground head first. A piece of my skull cracked and shot up into my brain, and blood poured from my ears. The production team quickly got on the phones to try to find the nearest hospital that could do emergency brain surgery, and eight hours later, I was going under the knife. The operation was successful, and I recovered quickly—even though there's a permanent hole in my head now, with a plastic plug there to keep my brains in.

Here are some of my other serious injuries (though none of them were as serious as that one):

HEAD: Other than the brain hemorrhage I suffered on *Armour of God*, I've hit my head and injured it many times. I was actually knocked completely unconscious while working as a stuntman on *Hand of Death*.

EARS: The *Armour of God* fall also left me hard-of-hearing in one ear.

EYE: On *Drunken Master*, my brow ridge was injured, and I nearly lost an eye.

NOSE: You'd think that someone Up There had it in for me and my nose! It's bad enough that it's so big to begin with, but I've actually broken it at least three times—on *The Young Master*, *Project A*, and, most recently, *Mr. Nice Guy*.

CHEEK: While making *Supercop*, I dislocated a cheekbone. I didn't even know you could do that.

TEETH: Hwang Jang Lee is a tremendous kicker . . . as I found out when he kicked out one of my teeth (accidentally) while we were making *Snake in Eagle's Shadow*.

CHIN: I injured my chin on *Dragon Lord*. It was painful even talking for a while. Which made it hard to direct, not to mention act.

THROAT: During *The Young Master*, I was almost suffocated when I injured my throat.

NECK: I've hurt my neck a lot, but my worst neck injuries happened during the clock-tower fall in *Project A*, and after I messed up a flip during *Mr. Nice Guy*.

SHOULDER: I dislocated my shoulder while making *City Hunter*.

HAND: During *The Protector*, I hurt my hand and finger bones—adding injury to insult.

ARM: While I was shooting a fight scene in *Snake in Eagle's Shadow*, my arm was accidentally slashed by a sword that should have had a blunted edge. Blood went everywhere, and I fell down screaming . . . and the camera kept rolling! That's real pain you see in the movie!

CHEST: On *Armour of God II: Operation Condor*, I dislocated my sternum after falling from a hanging chain. That's another bone I didn't know you could dislocate, but somehow I managed to do it.

BACK: I've had a lot of back injuries doing my movies, but the pole-slide scene in *Police Story* almost paralyzed me when I nearly broke the seventh and eighth vertebrae in my spine.

PELVIS: Also during the pole-slide stunt, I dislocated my pelvis. I guess you're wondering just how many weird bones a person can dislocate. Sometimes it seems like I've dislocated them all.

LEGS: I crushed my legs while shooting *Crime Story*, after getting caught between two cars.

KNEE: I've hurt my knees so often that I wonder whether there's even any cartilege left in them. (If you think I run a little funny, that's part of the reason why.) It makes any stunt in which I have to jump harder, but I do my best anyway. Would you expect anything less? One of my worst injuries occurred during *City Hunter*, while I was shooting a skateboard chase.

FOOT: I broke my ankle while jumping onto a hovercraft in *Rumble in the Bronx*. After the bone was set and a cast was put on, I was told to stay off my feet until it healed. But I had a movie to finish! I went back to the set and put a sock on my broken foot, painted to look like a sneaker.

MY FILMS

Big and Little Wong Tin-Bar (1962)

My very first movie—I was just eight years old when I was cast for this role. At that time, it was common for film companies to come to opera schools to pick out kids to play child roles, and even though I'd only been there for a year, something about me must have impressed the director. (Samo also had a small part in the film.) A very famous Taiwanese star, Li Li-hua, played my mother. I guessed I impressed her too, because after *Big and Little*, Li Li chose me to play her son in a few other films. No action scenes yet, though!

Even back then, I loved being on the set. It wasn't because I dreamed of being a movie star; that came later. I liked doing movies because it meant I didn't have to wake up at 5 A.M. I didn't have to practice. Sometimes, people even treated me to snacks. Of course, at the end of the day, Master would take any money I earned. But after being treated like a little prince all day, it was worth it.

The Love Eternal (1963, *Love Eterne*)

Another child role with Li Li-hua.

The Story of Qui Xiang Lin (1964)

Yet another child role.

Come Drink with Me (1966, also: *The Girl with the Thunderbolt Kick*)

A very famous film, directed by one of the great directors of Hong Kong cinema, King Hu. I was just playing a kid role again, but it was still great working with Cheng Pei-pei, the leading martial arts actress at the time. (Later, Cheng would appear in *Painted Faces*, a docudrama telling the story of our lives in the opera school. Cheng played a character based on the real-life opera teacher Fan Fok Fa; Samo played *Master*! Frankly, though, the movie didn't come anywhere close to showing how bad it was at the school.)

CAST: Cheng Pei-pei

A Touch of Zen (1968)

Another famous King Hu film, which gave Samo his first major role, playing a Japanese swordsman. He was only sixteen at the time. My own part is just a tiny cameo.

Fist of Fury (1972, also: *The Chinese Connection* [USA])

In this film—probably the best-loved of Bruce Lee's movies, at least in Hong Kong—Lee plays a kung fu student who returns from a trip abroad to discover that his

328 • I AM JACKIE CHAN

teacher was murdered by a rival martial arts school run by the Japanese. Lee then goes on a mission of vengeance, using disguises, detective work, and his amazing fighting skills. The film is based on a real-life folk hero from the 1930s named Chen Zhen, whose own legendary teacher was killed by a Japanese master.

I was just a stuntman on the film, but I doubled for the head villain himself, Mr. Suzuki. During the final fight scene, Bruce kicks me through a wall, my body flying fifteen feet before hitting the ground—at the time, that was the longest distance a Hong Kong stuntman had ever been thrown without some kind of safety device. I can also be seen, very briefly, in the opening scene, as one of the sparring students. Another of my opera school brothers, Yuen Wah, was fortunate enough to be picked as Bruce's stunt double, performing most of his acrobatic scenes. (Yuen can also be seen as the Japanese man who mocks Lee at the park entrance, referring Lee to the infamous No CHINESE OR DOGS ALLOWED sign.)

CAST: Bruce Lee, Nora Miao, Tien Feng, James Tien, Lo Wei
DIRECTOR: Lo Wei
PRODUCER: Raymond Chow
WRITER: Lo Wei
MARTIAL ARTS DIRECTOR: Bruce Lee

The Little Tiger of Canton (1971, also: *Little Tiger from Canton, Cub Tiger from Kwang Tung, Stranger in Hong Kong, Marvelous Fists, Ten Fingers of Death*; with additional footage, *Master with Cracked Fingers, Snake Fist Fighter* [USA])

This was my first chance at playing a lead role, even though the film wasn't released until long after, when I finally became a star. In the movie, a feud between Triad gangs leads to the death of my father, leaving me orphaned. After I grow up and learn how to fight, I return to avenge his death. In 1978, after I hit the big time with *Drunken Master*, some shifty producer added footage using a Jackie Chan "lookalike," and put together a "new" movie called *Master with Cracked Fingers*—also known in the United States as *Snake Fist Fighter*.

CAST: Jackie Chan (aka Chen Yuen Lung), Juan Hsao Ten, Shih Tien, Han Kuo Tsi, Yuen Bill, Chang Chin, Kuen Yung Man.
DIRECTOR: Chin Hsin
STUNT COORDINATOR: Chan Yuen Long, Se Fu Tsai
PRODUCER: Li Long Koon

The Heroine (1971, also: *Attack of the Kung Fu Girls, Kung Fu Girl* [UK])

My first adult role on-screen, and my first chance to be a stunt coordinator. (This was also my first-time meeting Lo Wei—not that he remembered who I was, of course. Even if he does say that this was the film in which he "discovered" my talents.) In the story, Cheng Pei-pei plays a woman who comes to Beijing to assist the resistance movement against the Japanese. I played the Japanese villain, if you can believe that.

CAST: Jackie Chan (aka Chen Yuen Lung), Cheng Pei-pei, James Tien, Jo Shishido
DIRECTOR: Lo Wei
STUNT COORDINATOR: Jackie Chan

Police Woman (1972)

In this film, I play the sidekick of the female lead, appearing onscreen with a huge and unsightly clump of hair on one side of my face! The only good thing to come out of this flop was my friendship with the film's male lead, Chun Cheung Lam. During the production, he gave me acting lessons in return for me teaching him kung fu.

CAST: Jackie Chan (as Chen Yuen Lung), Chun Cheung Lam

Hapkido (1972)

Samo starred in this film—his first lead role—while I had a small cameo appearance. He plays one of three Chinese friends who travel to Korea to study hapkido, then return to China to open their own school. When one of the friends is killed by a rival Japanese school, the remaining two seek revenge. Angela Mao Ying, who is also in this film, was one of Golden Harvest's first stars. She had a black belt in hapkido, which gave stunt coordinators like myself a lot of room for creativity when we worked with her. In fact, in some ways, I identified strongly with her. At the age of five, she was enrolled in Taiwan's Fu Shing Academy, where she received hard training similar to my own. Later on, she became one of Hong Kong's top martial arts actresses, before retiring in 1980.

CAST: Samo Hung, Angela Mao, Carter Wong, Wei Ping
DIRECTOR: Huang Feng
PRODUCER: Raymond Chow

Not Scared to Die (1973, also: Eagle's Shadow Fist, Eagle Shadow Fist)

This movie is based on the true story of a group of Chinese performers who put on patriotic plays during the Japanese occupation of China; behind the scenes, the performers are resistance fighters who use their martial arts to strike back against the oppressive Japanese masters. My part is just a supporting role, and I even die in the end. At the beginning of the movie, though, I get to reexperience my school days, appearing in the opening scene in full Beijing opera costume and makeup. After the success of Snake in the Eagle's Shadow, this film was rereleased as Eagle's Shadow Fist.

CAST: Wang Qing, Lin Xiu, Jackie Chan (aka Chen Yuen Lung)
DIRECTOR: Zhu Wu (aka Heng Tsu)
PRODUCER: Hoi Ling
WRITER: Su Lan
STUNT COORDINATOR: Jackie Chan

Enter the Dragon (1973, also: The Deadly Three)

In this most famous of Bruce's movies, an evil drug lord stages a kung fu tournament on his island retreat in order to recruit the best fighters for his criminal purposes. Bruce plays an undercover operative sent to gather evidence against the evil Mr. Han, while also seeking to avenge his sister's death at the hands of Han's henchmen. Again, I'm just a stuntman in this film. In the tunnel fight scene, I grab Bruce from behind, only to have him pull me back by my hair and snap my nack. Samo, on the other hand, gets to fight Bruce in the opening scene!

CAST: Bruce Lee, Shek Kin, John Saxon, Jim Kelly, Yang Tse, Bob Wall, Peter Archer, Samo Hung

DIRECTOR: Robert Clouse
PRODUCERS: Paul Heller, Fred Weintraub
WRITER: Michael Allin
STUNT COORDINATOR: Bruce Lee

The Young Dragons (1973)
I was stunt choreographer for this film.

Golden Lotus (1974)
In this movie, I played a very small supporting role.

The Himalayan (1975)
A man and woman study kung fu with a holy lama in Nepal, then return to their native village to exact revenge against an oppressive town leader. I play a small role, and work as a stuntman on this film.
CAST: Angela Mao, Chen Sing, Tan Tao Liang, Samo Hung
DIRECTOR: Huang Feng
PRODUCER: Raymond Chow
WRITER: I Kuang
STUNT COORDINATOR: Han Ying Chieh, Samo Hung

All in the Family (1975)
This is a very silly movie, and I'm lucky that not many people bothered to see it. Samo and I both had supporting roles—me as a rickshaw driver who tries to seduce both a mother and her daughter. I actually have a sex scene in it, and if you do manage to watch this film, you'll see why I decided never to do one again.
CAST: Linda Chu, Dean Shek, Samo Hung, Jackie Chan
DIRECTOR: Chu Mu
PRODUCER: Raymond Chow
WRITER: Ken Suma

The Dragon Tamers (1975)
I was stunt coordinator for this film.

Hand of Death (1976, also: *Countdown in Kung Fu, Countdown in Death, Shaolin Men*)
In this film—John Woo's debut as a director!—Samo, Yuen Biao, and I all have small parts. I play lead actor Dorian Tan's trusty sidekick; the two of us are given the job of protecting a courier, bearing a top secret message, from death at the hands of the evil Manchus. Samo was the film's martial arts coordinator, and he does a great job. The movie wasn't a wild success, but it did have the distinction of being the first time all three of us brothers acted in a movie together.
CAST: Dorian Tan, James Tien, Jackie Chan
DIRECTOR: John Woo
WRITER: John Woo
STUNT COORDINATOR: Samo Hung

New Fist of Fury (1976)
My first film with Lo Wei was a sequel to the original *Fist of Fury* (which was called *The Chinese Connection* when it was released in the United States). I play the brother of Chen Zhen, Bruce's character from the original *Fist*. Unlike Chen Zhen, my character doesn't enjoy fighting, and has no interest in the martial arts—until a Japanese school begins to terrorize the local Chinese kung fu school. Then I go into training mode so I can defeat the Japanese. I felt very uncomfortable stepping into Bruce Lee's fighting shoes, but it was nice working with Nora Miao, one of the biggest martial arts actresses at the time.
CAST: Jackie Chan, Nora Miao, Lo Wei, Han Ying Chieh, Chen King, Chang Sing
DIRECTOR: Lo Wei.
STUNT COORDINATOR: Han Ying Chieh

Shaolin Wooden Men (1976, also: *36 Wooden Men, Shaolin Chamber of Death, Young Tiger's Revenge*)
I play a young man who has vowed not to speak until I have avenged my father's murder. In order to learn kung fu, I go to the Shaolin Temple, where I find work as a handyman. The master eventually takes pity on me and begins training me in martial arts. I become very skilled, and I'm eager to leave so that I can take my revenge. But for a student to leave the temple, he must first pass the ultimate test of the Wooden Men—a room full of clockwork robots, controlled with chains and pulleys. In order to defeat these nonhuman opponents, I must use several different forms of kung fu, proving that the best fighter is a well-rounded fighter. The film allows me to show off my mastery of all five "animal styles" of kung fu, as well as my skill with the staff. Unfortunately, it was a commercial flop.
CAST: Jackie Chan, Kam Kan, Simon Yuen, Lung Chung-erh
DIRECTOR: Lo Wei
WRITER: Chen Chi-hwa
STUNT COORDINATOR: Li Ming-wen, Jackie Chan

Dance of Death (1976, also: *The Eternal Conflict*)
I was stunt coordinator for this story of a young woman who learns kung fu from two rival masters in order to defeat the villain responsible for killing her clan.
CAST: Angela Mao, Dean Shek, Chin Pei
DIRECTOR: Chen Chi-hwa
PRODUCER: Yen Wu Tun
STUNT COORDINATOR: Jackie Chan

Iron Fisted Monk (1977)
Samo hired me as assistant stunt coordinator for this film, his directorial debut. Samo also plays the lead role, as a young man who learns kung fu at the Shaolin Temple to avenge his father's death at the hands of the Manchu. If the plotline sounds familiar, that's because this same basic plot was used hundreds of times in movies dating back to the beginning of the Shaw Brothers era. In fact, it's basically the same plot as my film *Shaolin Wooden Men*.
DIRECTOR: Samo Hung
STUNT COORDINATOR: Jackie Chan, Samo Hung

Killer Meteor (1977, also: The Killer Meteors, Jackie Chan vs. Wang Yu)

I play the *villain* in this film—an evil warrior named "Immortal Meteor," who terrorizes a small town. As in American Westerns, this means that I eventually go head-to-head with the Good Guy, "Killer Weapon," played by Jimmy Wang Yu, who was a big star back then. Even though *Killer Meteors* was made in 1976, it would be two years before it was actually released. I wish it had never been released at all!

CAST: Jackie Chan, Jimmy Wang Yu, Chu Feng
DIRECTOR: Jimmy Wang Yu
PRODUCER: Hsu Li Hwa
WRITER: Ku Lung
STUNT COORDINATOR: Jackie Chan

To Kill with Intrigue (1977, Jackie Chan Connection)

Hong Kong actress Chu Feng leads the Killer Bee Gang on a revenge mission to destroy my family. She kills everyone but me, falls in love with me, and later, saves my life by putting me through a torturous training regimen so that I can defend myself against some two-faced "friends"! We filmed this in Korea, where it was terribly cold. Our trampolines and film equipment froze, and the chill generally ruined everyone's mood. It was no fun making this movie. It's not that much fun watching it, either. A side note: The name of my girlfriend in the movie, Chin Chin, had to be changed for the Japanese version, because "Chin Chin" is the slang term for "penis" in Japanese!

CAST: Jackie Chan, George Wang, Chu Feng (aka Hsu Feng)
DIRECTOR: Lo Wei
PRODUCER: Lo Wei
WRITER: Ku Lung
STUNT COORDINATOR: Chin Hsin, Chen Wen Lung

Snake and Crane Arts of Shaolin (1978)

Eight kung fu masters get together to write a book containing the secrets of each of their styles. When they are murdered, somehow I end up with the book. Everyone wants it, but of course they have to fight me first. I've mastered the techniques from the book, using Snake Style with one hand and Crane Style with the other, so I beat them all pretty easily. I consider this film my first dream project. My friend Chen Chi-hwa directed, so I was allowed more freedom in terms of character development and fight choreography. In the fight scenes, I used everyday objects as combat props—a martial arts style that I use even today. Even though this movie wasn't a box office hit (mostly because of lack of advertising), it did earn me more respect in the film industry, which I needed badly!

CAST: Jackie Chan, Nora Miao, Kam Kan
DIRECTOR: Chen Chi-hwa
PRODUCER: Hsu Li Hwa
STUNT COORDINATOR: Jackie Chan, Tu Wei Ho

Half a Loaf of Kung Fu (1978)

I play a hapless wanderer who dreams of one day becoming a kung fu master. In the course of my journeys, I befriend a man and his daughter, and agree to help them fight off villains who are in search of their precious "jade and soul pills." In the process, I learn how to fight—reading the pages of a kung fu manual while dodging the attacks of my opponent!

In this film, Lo Wei finally gave me creative control, mostly because he was fed up with me. As a result, the entire film is a parody of elements found in most kung fu movies. For instance, the opening credits of a kung fu film is usually a time for the hero to showcase his talents. In my film, I mock that tradition with oddball editing and gratuitous slow motion. You see two fighting Jackies coming from either side of the screen, edited so it looks like I'm under a strobe light; the two figures meld into one, and then split into two again. A sequence in which it looks like I'm attacking a combat dummy is revealed when the camera is pulled back to be me kicking and punching at a dummy that's only twelve inches high. Later in the movie, a gang of thugs beat me up, throwing me to the ground. I see a spinach plant growing next to me, get excited, and stuff handfuls of it into my mouth. The "Popeye" theme song comes on, and suddenly I'm transformed into a fighting machine, flexing my muscles and pounding on my opponents. Lo hated this film and refused to release it until much later, but I swear that this film is worth a rental. To quote a line from the film: "If I'm lying to you, I'm a son of a bitch."

CAST: Jackie Chan, James Tien, Lung Chung-erh, Kam Kan
DIRECTOR: Chen Chi-hwa
PRODUCERS: Lo Wei, Hsu Li Hwa
WRITER: Tang Ming Chi
STUNT COORDINATOR: Jackie Chan

Magnificent Bodyguards (1978)

A woman hires me to escort her sick brother to the doctor, but in order to get there, we must pass through Stormy Hills, an area controlled by bandits. Imagine my surprise when I learn that the sick brother is actually a bandit too. The only thing that's halfway interesting about this film is that it was Hong Kong's first movie filmed in 3-D. It was obvious that Lo Wei was beginning to run out of ideas. (He even used the *Star Wars* theme as for the soundtrack music for the final fight scene—displaying an absence of originality, not to mention a lack of concern for copyright law.) There are some funny moments, though, even if they're not intentional. At one point in the film, unable to fight off our attackers, we flee into a temple and ring the temple bells to knock them out: "Well, all of them were pretty tough fighters, but none of them could survive my bells!"

CAST: Jackie Chan, James Tien, Dorian Tan (aka Bruce Leung)
DIRECTOR: Lo Wei
PRODUCER: Hsu Li Hwa
WRITER: Ku Lung
STUNT COORDINATORS: Jackie Chan, Luk Chuen

Spiritual Kung Fu (1978, also: Karate Ghost Buster, Karate Bomber)

A meteor crashes to the earth, releasing five spirits who teach me "spiritual" kung fu, also known as the "Five Fists" style. I use these otherworldly techniques to retrieve a stolen kung fu manual for the Seven Fists style—a technique that's two whole fists deadlier than the Five Fists style. With this film, Lo tried to prove that he could make a comedy, but much of the humor was vulgar rather than funny. The only laughs in the film come from the special effects: the so-called meteor was a sparkler being waved around in front of a black backdrop, and the five spirits are actors in brightly colored wigs and shining hoop skirts.

CAST: Jackie Chan, James Tien, Shih Tien
DIRECTOR: Lo Wei
PRODUCER: Lo Wei
STUNT COORDINATOR: Jackie Chan

Dragon Fist (1978)

My master is killed, so his wife, his daughter, and I set off to seek revenge on his murderer. When we find him, we discover that he's repented his sins, and even cut off his leg as penance. Then the one-legged master and I come together to defeat an evil lord who has poisoned my master's widow. By this time Lo was running out of money, so Spiritual Kung Fu and Dragon Fist didn't even get released until after the success of Snake in the Eagle's Shadow.

CAST: Jackie Chan, Nora Miao, James Tien
DIRECTOR: Lo Wei
PRODUCER: Hsu Li Hwa
STUNT COORDINATOR: Jackie Chan

Snake in the Eagle's Shadow (1978, also: The Eagle's Shadow, Bruce vs. Snake in Eagle's Shadow, Snaky Monkey)

I play a poor boy who works at a kung fu school; my only friend is my pet cat. I don't know any kung fu myself, but that doesn't stop the guys at the school from trying out their moves on me. One day, I come to the rescue of an old man who is being bullied by the mean-spirited students of the rival Eagle Claw school. It turns out he is the last living master of the Snake Fist Style, and he agrees to be my teacher. Unfortunately, the evil Eagle Claw master is on a mission to wipe out the Snake Fist Style, and he plans on killing both myself and my master. Eventually, I use Snake Fist, combined with tricks learned from watching my pet cat, to destroy him.

This movie was my first big hit! At this point, Lo Wei had directed me in so many flops that he had just about lost all faith in me ever becoming the star he had hoped. He loaned me out to Seasonal Films, glad just to be rid of me for a while. My favorite line in the movie comes when I'm using my newly learned Snake Fist against my opponent: "I'm a poisonous snake," I shout, and then give him a quick punch to the groin: "*That's* called finding the snake!"

CAST: Jackie Chan, Hwang Jang Lee, Simon Yuen Siu Tin, Roy Horan
DIRECTOR: Yuen Woo Ping
PRODUCER: Chen Chuan
WRITER: Ng See-yuen, based on my story

Drunken Master (1978, also: *Drunken Monkey in a Tiger's Eye; Drunk Monkey; Eagle Claw, Snake Fist, Cat's Paw*)

Wong Fei Hong is one of China's most famous folk heroes, beloved for his fighting ability, his treatment of the sick, and his nobility in the face of danger. That's why it was shocking when I suggested making this movie, in which I play Wong as a mischievous young man. Audiences were surprised to see me portray Wong in such a disrespectful light, but they also found it funny and refreshing. In my version of the legend, Wong—punished by his father for disobedience—is sent to an old, eccentric master to learn martial arts. I decide that the master is crazy and the training too difficult, so I run away. But when I get beaten up by an evil martial artist, played by Hwang Jang Lee, I return to the old master, determined to learn the skills necessary to defeat Hwang's powerful kicking style. And so my master, played by Simon Yuen Siu Tin, teaches me the secrets of the "Eight Drunken Fairies," a set of ultimate boxing techniques that mimic the moves of a drunkard . . .

In this movie, we built on the things we'd learned from the success of *Snake in Eagle's Shadow*, keeping the most important elements (like the relationship between me and Simon Yuen Siu Tin and the deadly presence of tae kwon do master Hwang), while adding even more humor and acrobatic fighting. The result was phenomenal: *Drunken Master* earned HK$8 million at the box office. And, after nearly a decade of slaving away in the movie business, I was finally a star.

CAST: Jackie Chan, Simon Yuen Siu Tin, Hwang Jang Lee, Dean Shek Tien
DIRECTOR: Yuen Woo Ping
PRODUCER: Ng See-yuen
WRITER: Hsiao Lung

The Real Wong Fei Hong

Born in Canton in 1847, Wong Fei Hong was sort of a Chinese Robin Hood—a master of Hung Gar boxing, a teacher, and a physician, dedicated to helping the poor and downtrodden. He died in 1924 at the age of seventy-seven. Wong's story has dominated Cantonese entertainment since the turn of the century, first in Beijing operas, and later on film. In fact, a ninety-nine-episode black-and-white film series about Wong ran from 1949 through 1970, and many cast members from this series would go on to train the next generation of Hong Kong cinema stars. In the early 1990s, producer Tsui Hark revived the Wong Fei Hong legend for another very popular set of films, the *Once Upon a Time in China* series, starring Jet Li as Wong. I didn't appear in any of these movies, of course, but I did sing the closing theme music for the first sequel.

Fearless Hyena (1979)

After my "loan" to Seasonal was over, I returned reluctantly to Lo Wei, who after all still held on to my contract. At least Lo finally decided to make a film that fit my personality this time (and, after I demanded more control, even let me direct). In *Fearless Hyena*, I play a young man who accidentally leads a gang of evil villains to my grandfather, the last of the Hsin-yi fighters, and he is killed in the resulting battle. In order to deal with my guilt—and get my revenge—I learn "Emotional Kung Fu," which is powered by the body's reaction to positive and negative emotions. Together with the old master who taught me Emotional Kung Fu's secrets, I defeat the murderous villains.

This was the first movie I ever directed, and audiences loved it! While production values were lower under Lo Wei than with Seasonal Films, I was given the freedom to try out some really unusual things. For example, I made up "Emotional Style" kung fu just for the movie. I also included sequences in which I fought under different personas—dressed as a girl and fighting in a feminine style, and disguised as a cross-eyed bum. This is also the last complete movie I did with Lo Wei, although he later took footage I'd done for a sequel and completed *Fearless Hyena II* with a lookalike. *Fearless Hyena* was even more successful than *Drunken Master*; for a while, it was the second-highest grossing film in Hong Kong cinema history.

CAST: Jackie Chan, Yen Shi-kwan, Li Kuan, James Tien, Shih Tien
DIRECTOR: Jackie Chan
PRODUCER: Hsu Li Hwa
WRITER: Jackie Chan
STUNT COORDINATOR: Jackie Chan

The 36 Crazy Fists (1979, also: Blood Pact, Master and the Boxer)

This was a "comedy" about an orphaned boy taken in by monks, who teach him kung fu to avenge his father's death. I'm not even supposed to be in this movie, since I was just the film's stunt coordinator, but the unscrupulous producers put together a documentary of the film, *The Making of 36 Crazy Fists,* that included behind-the-scenes shots of me working. Later, they edited this footage into the movie and released it as a "Jackie Chan movie." You can believe I was furious, especially since the footage showed me smoking a cigarette! (I quit this filthy habit a long time ago—it was something I picked up in my roughneck days as a young stuntman.)

CAST: Liu Cha Yung, Ku Feng, Chin Pei
DIRECTOR: Chen Chi-hwa
PRODUCER: Chiang Kit
STUNT COORDINATOR: Jackie Chan

The Odd Couple (1979, also: Dance of Death)

My Big Brother Samo and Liu Chia-yung star as two masters who teach each other their own patented techniques—Samo is a master of the spear, and Liang is an expert swordsman. Then they join forces to defeat some evildoers. I was stunt coordinator for the film.

CAST: Samo Hung, Liu Chia-yung, Shih Tien (aka Shek Kin)
DIRECTOR: Liu Chia-yung
PRODUCER: Karl Maka
STUNT COORDINATOR: Jackie Chan

Fearless Hyena II (1980)

This was my final, unfinished film for Lo Wei. The story is about two brothers who get together to avenge the murder of their father at the hands of a local gang. I only shot a few scenes before I left the production for good. That didn't stop Lo from cashing in by combining these scenes with scrap footage from *Fearless Hyena*, hiring a double to pretend to be me, and making a patchwork sequel. Lo even goes out of the way to insult me in the dialogue, which was recorded in postproduction! A storeowner, describing my features, tells me I have small eyes, a big nose, and long hair "like a monkey." The end product was so bad that I tried to prevent it from being released by going to court. I dropped the case after Golden "settled" with him, giving him the rights to release my old work.

CAST: Jackie Chan, Shih Tien
DIRECTOR: Lo Wei

The Young Master (1980)
In this film, which tries to continue in the spirit of the films I did with Yuen Woo Ping, I play a young kung fu student who discovers that my martial arts brother Tiger is secretly betraying our master. However, when Tiger is framed for a murder he didn't commit—and I get mistaken for Tiger—I'm forced to prove my innocence and his, while at the same time fighting off my would-be captors. This was my first movie for Golden Harvest, so I had to make it better than anything I had done before. I started filming immediately after escaping Lo's clutches, even before the script was finished, so the film has some continuity problems, but the fighting and humor make up for that, I hope! For the first time, I also sing on the movie's soundtrack—something that I'd do in most of my later films. (The funny thing is that I sang the song for *Young Master* in English, and back then, my English was really terrible. Since then, I've stuck to singing in Chinese. I think my listeners appreciate this decision.)

CAST: Jackie Chan, Shek Kin, Yuen Biao, Chiang Kam, Lily Lee, Whang Inn Sik
DIRECTOR: Jackie Chan
WRITERS: Lau Tin Chee, Tung Lio, Edward Tang King-sang
STUNT COORDINATOR: Jackie Chan

The Big Brawl (1980, also: Battle Creek Brawl)
My first American movie, and not a very easy experience. I play an immigrant who comes to the United States to help protect my grandfather's restaurant. When the local gangsters kidnap my sister-in-law, I'm forced to enter a fighting tournament to win her back. It's surprising that *Brawl* didn't turn out as well as we expected. Raymond Chow brought in Robert Clouse and Fred Weintraub, the same people who helped make *Enter the Dragon* so successful. The most frustrating part of making this film was that I had so little control over the stunt design. I'd been choreographing fights in Hong Kong for almost ten years, and now they were telling *me* what to do!

CAST: Jackie Chan, José Ferrer, Kristine De Bell, Mako
DIRECTOR: Robert Clouse
PRODUCERS: Raymond Chow, Fred Weintraub, Terry Morse Jr.

Cannonball Run (1981)
A silly movie about a wild cross-country race, featuring a huge cast of American celebrities, plus me and Michael Hui, one of Hong Kong's top comedians. (It's based on the *real* "Cannonball Sea to Shining Sea" Race, which starts in Connecticut and ends in California.) Michael and I play bumbling Japanese race car drivers with a gizmo-filled supercar. It isn't exactly a film that shows off my best skills, but the guys at Golden Harvest felt that putting me in a small role in this film would help to introduce me to the American public. (And it *was* a hit: *Cannonball Run* made $100 million worldwide,

though it bombed in Hong Kong.) One thing I did pick up from this film: The use of bloopers and outtakes under the final credits, which I've done in all of my movies since. Of course, *my* "no-goods" are very different from Burt Reynolds's no-goods . . .
CAST: Burt Reynolds, Roger Moore, Dean Martin, Sammy Davis Jr., Farrah Fawcett, Don DeLuise, Jackie Chan, Michael Hui
DIRECTOR: Hal Needham
PRODUCER: Albert Ruddy
WRITER: Brock Yates

Dragon Lord (1982)

This film was originally supposed to be a sequel to *Young Master*, but the continuity between the two films got thrown out and we changed the movie's name to *Dragon Lord* (from *Young Master in Love*). The movie begins with me sending a love note to my girlfriend on the other side of a wall via balloon; unfortunately, the wind sends it in the wrong direction! I go after the balloon, only to find myself inside the headquarters of a gang of thieves who are smuggling precious artifacts out of China. *Dragon Lord* didn't do as well as we hoped in Hong Kong, but the Japanese market loved it. They seem to love everything "Jackie"!
CAST: Jackie Chan, Mars, Whang Inn Sik, Chan Wai Man, Tien Fun
DIRECTOR: Jackie Chan
WRITERS: Jackie Chan, Barry Wong, Edward Tang King-sang
ACTION DIRECTOR: Jackie Chan
STUNT COORDINATORS: Fung Ke-an, Corey Yuen Kwai
• Nominated for Best Action Design, Hong Kong Film Awards, 1982

Fantasy Mission Force (1982, also: *The Dragon Attack*)

I did this movie because I owed Jimmy Wang Yu a favor. I appear in only a few stunts, but I'm billed as the lead. Jimmy stars as a hero who is called in to rescue a group of world leaders kidnapped by the Japanese. He and his troupe of crazy cohorts succeed in doing so, but not without first battling aliens, Nazis, vampires, and Amazons. If it sounds ridiculous, that's only because it was.
CAST: Jimmy Wang Yu, Chang Ling, Brigitte Lin Ching-hsia, Sun Yuen, Jackie Chan
DIRECTOR: Chu Yen Ping
PRODUCER: Shen Hsiao Yi

Ninja Wars (1982)

A young man avenges the death of his girlfriend. I have only a cameo here, but did it because I wanted to work with Japanese martial artist Sonny Chiba, who starred in the popular *Street Fighter* series of the 1970s.
CAST: Henry Sanada, Noriko Watanabe, Sonny Chiba, Jackie Chan
DIRECTOR: Mitsumisa Saito
PRODUCER: Masao Sato
WRITER: Ed Ogawa

Winners and Sinners (1983, also: Five Lucky Stars)

This film, about a group of ex-cons who try to go clean after being released from prison, was the first of the very successful *Lucky Stars* series. It's the first time that Samo, Yuen Biao, and I acted together on screen, although Yuen Biao and I were only in supporting roles.

CAST: Samo Hung, Richard Ng, Charlie Chin, John Sham, Jackie Chan, Yuen Biao
DIRECTOR: Samo Hung
PRODUCER: Leonard Ho
WRITERS: Samo Hung, Wong Pin Yiu
STUNT COORDINATORS: Yuen Biao, Chan Wui Ngai, Lam Ching Ying
• Best Action Design, Samo Hung's Stuntman Association, Hong Kong Film Awards, 1983
• Nominated for Best Actor, Richard Ng, Hong Kong Film Awards, 1983

Cannonball Run II (1983)

Okay, so why did I agree to appear in yet another *Cannonball Run* movie? The answer is simple: It was in my contract. As soon as they decided to make a sequel, I was doomed to repeat history. The format and plot of this film was basically the same as the first, only this time, the mob is after us. Also, instead of Michael Hui, my copilot is Richard Kiel (the giant who played "Jaws" in the James Bond movie *Moonraker*).

CAST: Burt Reynolds, Sammy Davis Jr., Dom DeLuise, Susan Anton, Jackie Chan, Richard Kiel
DIRECTOR: Hal Needham
PRODUCER: Albert Ruddy
WRITERS: Harvey Miller, Hal Needham, Albert Ruddy

Project A (1983, also: Pirate Patrol and Karate Pirates)

This is the first time all three of us brothers starred in a movie together. I play a Coast Guard officer named Dragon Ma, who gets assigned to the police force when a pirate gang destroys my fleet. Despite being stuck on land, I'm still intent on capturing the pirates. Frustrated by the lack of support from my superiors, I join forces with a gambler played by Samo and a rookie cop played by Yuen Biao. In this film, I really begin to focus on big stunts as well as martial arts, and as a result *Project A* is packed full of dangerous action, like the famous clock tower jump. I've long been a fan of the stars of America's silent film era, like Buster Keaton, Harold Lloyd, and Charlie Chaplin; the clock tower jump is an homage to a similar stunt in Lloyd's *Safety Last* (although he did his stunt with the help of lighting and mirrors, while I actually fell several stories in mine!). I was in the middle of shooting *Project A* when some friends said they had just seen *E.T.*, and that it had a breathtaking bicycle scene! I got scared because I had been planning a bicycle scene in *Project A* too. How could I compete with Hollywood with all their fancy special effects? Of course, the bicycle scene in *E.T.* is very different from the bike chase in my movie. On the other hand, if you look at the motorcycle chase in Spielberg's *Indiana Jones and the Temple of Doom*, you might think that Steven was inspired by *Project A*!

On a historical note, this movie takes place at the turn of the century, a time when the harbors of the South China Sea were filled with pirates and other unsavory types.

Project A is the name of a real plan the Chinese government implemented to try and get rid of them. Each time Samo, Yuen Biao, and I have worked together, we've had great success. This film made HK$14 million in its first week of release.

CAST: Jackie Chan, Samo Hung, Yuen Biao, Mars, Dick Wei
DIRECTOR: Jackie Chan
PRODUCER: Leonard Ho
WRITER: Jackie Chan
STUNT COORDINATOR: Jackie Chan

• Best Action Design, Jackie Chan's Stuntman Association, Hong Kong Film Awards, 1984
• Nominated for Best Actor, Jackie Chan, Hong Kong Film Awards, 1984

Wheels on Meals (1984, also: *Spartan X, Million Dollar Heiress, Weapon* X)

In this film, the second big collaboration between the Three Opera Brothers, Yuen Biao and I play two guys running a fast-food truck based in Barcelona called Everybody's Kitchen. We both fall in love with a pickpocket, played by Lola Forner (a model who was a former Miss Spain). In our attempts to protect the object of our affections, we run up against a shady character who seems to be following her. Her stalker—played by Samo—turns out to be a private eye, hired to follow Lola because she's actually an heiress to a great fortune. When the heiress gets kidnapped by terrorists disguised as monks, it's up to the heroic trio to storm the medieval castle where she's being held and save her!

This is the first time I shot a movie in Europe. It was Samo's idea to do the production in Spain, in order to give the film an international feel. We also brought in two Americans—kickboxing champion Benny "The Jet" Urquidez and karate champ Keith Vitali—to make the movie even more universally accessible.

As for why the movie's called *Wheels on Meals*, chalk it up to Hong Kong superstition. Two Golden Harvest films whose English titles had begun with M, *Megaforce* (1982) and *Menage-á-Trois* (1982) had recently flopped, so they reversed the original title—the far more sensible *Meals on Wheels*.

CAST: Jackie Chan, Samo Hung, Yuen Biao, Lola Forner, Benny "The Jet" Urquidez, Keith Vitali, Herb Edelman
DIRECTOR: Samo Hung
WRITERS: Edward Tang King-sang, Johnny Lee, Samo Hung
STUNT COORDINATOR: Samo Hung
PRODUCER: Leonard Ho

• Nominated for Best Action Design, Jackie Chan's Stuntman Association, Hong Kong Film Awards, 1984

Two in a Black Belt (1984)

I made a small cameo appearance in this film.

My Lucky Stars (1985, *The Lucky Stars*)

In the sequel to the smash hit *Winners and Sinners*, Yuen Biao and I play police officers tracking down a drug lord. When Yuen Biao gets kidnapped, I enlist my childhood buddies, the Lucky Stars, to help me save him. Even though my role is pretty small, the film is full of comedy, and has some pretty exciting fights. My big fight scene takes place in the amusement park where the crooks have their secret hideout; dressed in a silly disguise, I have to fight my way through a dimly lit chamber of horrors, not knowing which direction I'll be attacked from next. There's also a great fight scene between Michiko Nishiwaki, a Japanese women's bodybuilding champion, and Sibelle Hu, who plays a female cop assigned to supervise the Lucky Stars. It was Michiko's first movie in Hong Kong; she didn't speak any Chinese, and no one on our crew knew Japanese. But she sure could communicate with her fists!

My Lucky Stars made HK$10 million in its first week, and finished with a record-breaking HK$30 million, which at the time was Golden Harvest's biggest box office ever. Raymond Chow even treated us to a gala dinner for our good work, complete with an ice sculpture shaped into the characters for "$30 million," which we smashed, just for fun.

CAST: Jackie Chan, Samo Hung, Yuen Biao, Charlie Chin, Eric Tsang, Fung Shui Fan, Richard Ng, Sibelle Hu, Michiko Nishiwaki, Dick Wei
DIRECTOR: Samo Hung
WRITER: Barry Wong
PRODUCER: Leonard Ho
STUNT COORDINATORS: Samo Hung, Yuen Biao, Yuen Wah
• Nominated for Best Action Design, Samo Hung's Stuntman Association, Hong Kong Film Awards, 1985

Twinkle, Twinkle, Lucky Stars (1985, also: My Lucky Stars II, The Target)

In Hong Kong, if something works, you try, try again. A successful movie series might have six or seven sequels—more, if the series remains popular. This film takes place right after *My Lucky Stars*, with the Lucky Stars going on a vacation to Thailand to celebrate their success in capturing the drug lord.

There's a lot of good action in this one, which makes up somewhat for the less-than-stellar story line. *Twinkle* was a success as well, but it was during this period that Samo and I began to feel a resurgence of our old Big Brother–Little Brother rivalry. We kept on working together for a while, but we knew that the good times wouldn't stay good forever. Michelle Yeoh (who would later costar with me in *Supercop*) makes a brief appearance here as a judo instructor.

CAST: Jackie Chan, Andy Lau, Samo Hung, Yuen Biao, Richard Ng, Fung Shui Fan, Charlie Chin, Ching Ying, Dick Wei, Rosamund Kwan, Michelle Yeoh
DIRECTOR: Samo Hung
WRITER: Barry Wong
PRODUCER: Eric Tsang
STUNT COORDINATOR: Samo Hung

Pom Pom (1985)

Twinkle was basically the end of the *Lucky Stars* series, prompting Samo to produce this film in an attempt to start a new hit franchise. Yuen Biao and I make cameo appearances, playing our roles from *Twinkle, Twinkle, Lucky Stars*. The film is about a pair of wacky detectives, played by John Sham and Samo; despite their clumsiness, they eventually triumph in the end. *Pom Pom* wasn't as big a hit as *Winners and Sinners* had been, but it was enough to start another successful chain of films (which went on without me and Yuen Biao).

CAST: John Sham, Samo Hung, Richard Ng, Dick Wei, Mars, Jackie Chan, Yuen Biao
DIRECTOR: Cheung Cheung Joe
PRODUCER: Samo Hung

The Protector (1985)

In one more disastrous attempt to break into Hollywood, I play a New York City cop partnered up with Danny Aiello. A wealthy man's daughter is kidnapped, and we're assigned to the case; as the plot thickens, the case takes us to Hong Kong, and we discover that the father may be involved in a Triad drug trafficking scam.

It's no secret that the director James Glickenhaus and I did not get along. He didn't let me fight in a way that showed my skills; he tried to make me act like Dirty Harry, speaking softly and carrying a big gun. I tried to get him replaced, but he had an ironclad contract.

Because the original American version was so poorly done, after Glickenhaus left Hong Kong I took over production and made extensive changes—cutting out the swearing and gratuitous nudity, while adding a subplot that featured pop singer Sally Yeh to give the story depth. Most importantly, I reshot fight scenes, including the final fight with Bill "Superfoot" Wallace. Glickenhaus's version of the finale is short, slow, and predictable, and the editing is sloppy. In my version the choreography is faster and more complicated, and true to my style of combat.

The only good thing to come out of *The Protector* was that it gave me the inspiration for *Police Story*—the movie that changed the face of Hong Kong action films.

CAST: Jackie Chan, Danny Aiello, Roy Chiao, Bill "Superfoot" Wallace, Victor Arnold
DIRECTOR: James Glickenhaus
WRITER: James Glickenhaus
STUNT COORDINATORS: Billy Lai, Stanley Chow

Heart of Dragon (1985, also: First Mission)

This film was a real challenge for me—a movie with serious dialogue, complex characters, and rich drama. It was a very interesting experience, and I think it's a quality film. Unfortunately, it also made me realize that my audiences aren't all that interested in seeing me in a dramatic role.

I play a police officer burdened by the responsibility of taking care of my retarded brother, played by Samo. When Samo accidentally gets involved in a robbery, he is kidnapped by thugs and I'm forced to come to his rescue. There's some great fight choreography in the final sequence (designed by Yuen Biao), but much of the movie deals with my resentment and guilt over my brother's condition and the sacrifices it has forced me to make. Western audiences have described it as a martial arts *Rain Man*. (Considering that the movie is about the relationship between brothers, it's interesting that this production featured not just me, Samo, and Yuen Biao, but also Yuen Wah and Yuen Kwai, who are also in the film!)

As interesting as it was to film *Heart of Dragon*, we had to listen to reality: the box office take for my big dramatic turn was just HK$1 million, a real disappointment. Luckily, my next film more than made up for it—both in terms of action and in terms of box office.

CAST: Jackie Chan, Samo Hung, Emily Chu, Mang Heoi, Liu Chia-yung, Wu Ma, Dick Wei
DIRECTOR: Samo Hung
WRITERS: Barry Wong, Samo Hung
FIGHT COORDINATORS: Yuen Biao, Samo Hung
- Best Song, Hong Kong Film Awards, 1985
- Nominations, Hong Kong Film Awards, 1985: Best Actor, Jackie Chan; Best Action Design, Samo Hung's Stuntman Association; Best Music, Lam Man Yi

Police Story (1985, also: *Jackie Chan's Police Force, Jackie Chan's Police Story, Police Force*)

Some people call this the greatest action film of all time, and while I have to be humble and say that I disagree, it's definitely the favorite action film I've ever made. It was a huge hit with audiences, too—so big that I've made three sequels . . . so far.

I play a Hong Kong cop who's part of an elite team of officers assigned to fight organized crime. In the process of convicting a powerful crime boss, I get framed for the murder of a fellow officer. I have to clear my name and rescue a witness who's been kidnapped by his henchmen to prevent her from testifying—the boss's girlfriend, played by Brigitte Lin Ching-hsia. Unfortunately, all of this mistaken identity and chasing after a lost girl puts my relationship with my longtime girlfriend in danger. The role of my girlfriend is played by Maggie Cheung, who became a good friend and frequent costar; at this time, she was also being represented by my manager and partner, Willie, so working with her was like working with family.

Even I am amazed when I watch this film again; the stunts and the action choreography really set an entirely new level for me, and though I've had many hits since then, I don't think I've ever completely matched it. It's also the first time I played an action hero as a complete person, with a complex personality, a private life, and even a romantic relationship. I even got nominated for Best Actor at the Hong Kong Film Awards that year for the first time—a real coup, since all of my previous nominations were for action.

But the success of *Police Story* didn't come without a price. The amazing hillside car chase that opened the movie cost HK$500,000 to shoot, and left four stuntmen badly injured: one with a cut earlobe, one with a slashed foot, one with a twisted ankle, and one with two broken ribs. And when I did my final slide down a seventy-foot pole wrapped in Chistmas lights, I burned all the skin off my hands. Later, I found out that the production electrician hadn't plugged the lights into a low-voltage car battery like he was supposed to, but used a wall socket instead—giving me twice as much of a jolt as anyone had anticipated. I could have been electrocuted!

Police Story is the first of my films to use Bill Tung, who would appear in many of my films as an older and wiser voice of reason, in counterpart to my youthful spontaneity.

Meanwhile, I think this movie has made something of an impression on American action stars: Sylvester Stallone copied the through-the-bus-window chase scene from *Police Story* in his film *Tango and Cash* practically shot for shot. And Brandon Lee—Bruce Lee's son, who died tragically while shooting *The Crow*—used *Police Story*'s shopping mall–motorcycle chase scene in *Rapid Fire*, again, almost shot for shot. Which I think is flattering.

CAST: Jackie Chan, Chu Yuen, Brigitte Lin Ching-hsia, Bill Tung, Kenneth Tong, Maggie Cheung
DIRECTOR: Jackie Chan
PRODUCTION COORDINATOR: Willie Chan
SUPERVISOR: Edward Tang King-sang
STUNT COORDINATOR: Jackie Chan

* Best Picture, Hong Kong Film Awards, 1985
* Best Action Design, Jackie Chan's Stuntman Association, Hong Kong Film Awards, 1985
* Nominations, Hong Kong Film Awards, 1985: Best Actor and Best Director, Jackie Chan; Best Actress, Brigitte Lin Chiang-hsia; Best Cinematography, Cheung Yiu Cho; Best Editing, Cheung Yiu Chung

Armour of God (1986, also: Thunderarm)

I've always been a fan of Steven Spielberg's movies, as has Edward, my screenwriter. That's why he and I cooked up this "homage" to Spielberg's *Raiders of the Lost Ark*, in which I play Asian Hawk, an Indiana Jones–type treasure hunter and adventurer. At the start of the movie, I'm introduced in a sequence that shows me recovering pieces of the magical Armour of God, which I then sell at a high-stakes auction. But when an old friend (and former bandmate!), played by pop idol Alan Tam, needs my help, I put aside all thoughts of monetary gain and jump into action. A religious cult has kidnapped his girlfriend (who happens to be my ex-girlfriend); they say that they'll kill her unless Alan and I obtain for them the pieces of the Armour of God that I've just put up for sale.

I convince the wealthy man who bought the Armour to lend it back to me—on the condition that we bring back not just his pieces of the Armour, but the ones that the cult owns as well. To keep an eye on me and the Armour, the tycoon sends along his daughter, played by Lola Forner (whom you may remember from *Wheels on Meals*).

This movie almost killed me! In a sequence shot in Yugoslavia, I fell from a tree while attempting a routine stunt and landed on some rocks, which punctured my skull. I was rushed to the hospital, they did some surgery, and now I have a plastic plug in my head. (See "The Injury List" for details.)

This later caused one very obvious lapse in continuity. The original director, Eric Tsang (my costar from the *Lucky Stars* series), made me trim my signature mane. The film starts off with me sporting a shorthaired do. After the accident, however, I grew my hair back long, to cover the hole in my head. So my hair suddenly changes length, without explanation, during the movie! Since then Raymond Chow has not let me touch my hair. I mentioned to you that Hong Kong people are superstitious: he thinks that after I cut it off, I lost my power!

Despite all of the trouble and suffering I went through, not to mention the near-death experience, *Armour of God* was worth making—it ended up becoming Hong Kong's third-highest grossing film of the 1980s.
CAST: Jackie Chan, Alan Tam, Lola Forner, Rosamund Kwan
DIRECTORS: Eric Tsang, Jackie Chan
WRITERS: Edward Tang King-sang, Szeto Choek Hoin, John Sheppard
STUNT COORDINATORS: Lau Kar Wing, Yuen Chung Heung, Jackie Chan

PRODUCERS: Leonard Ho, Chua Lam
- Nominated for Best Action Design, Jackie Chan's Stuntman Association, Hong Kong Film Awards, 1987

Naughty Boys (1986)

Upon his release from jail, a crook goes on a hunt for the money he hid before he was sentenced. Unfortunately, other former members of his gang are looking for it too—even if they have to go through him to get it.

I produced this movie for my production company, Golden Way; I have only a small acting cameo, though you'll see me in the outtakes. I'm also the stunt coordinator.

This is the first movie that Kenneth Lo, my future bodyguard and on-screen opponent, did for Golden Harvest, though his part is a small one. Ken, a former kickboxing champion, fights Kara Hui Ying-hung in the film's finale. Impressed by Ken's easygoing personality and fighting ability, I recruited him for my stuntman association, and then as my bodyguard (there are some crazy people out there, and even I don't have eyes in the back of my head!).

CAST: Kara Hui Ying-hung, Carina Lau, Clarence Ford, Mars, Ken Lo, Lo Mang
DIRECTOR: Wilson Chin
PRODUCER: Jackie Chan
STUNT COORDINATOR: Jackie Chan

Project A II (1987, Project B)

After all of the stress of *Armour of God*, I wanted to do something a little more familiar and close to home, and so I decided to make a sequel to *Project A*, returning to the role of marine-turned-cop Dragon Ma. The film is set right before the 1911 revolution, a time of great political tension; being a simple and rather innocent guy, I do my best to make sense of all the opposing factions—revolutionaries, pirates, British colonialists and Ch'ing imperial loyalists—and to stay out of their way, until injustice forces me into action.

Though it was tough to top the clock-tower jump from the first *Project A*, there are still some great stunts here. In one scene I run down the side of a falling ceremonial wall and narrowly miss being crushed, passing through a paper window with the rest of the wall falling all around me. I got the idea for this stunt from Buster Keaton's *Steamboat Bill, Jr.* (1928). In another scene, I perform a wild chase, and must fight off my attackers—while handcuffed to another man. But my favorite scene in the movie was inspired by Marx Brothers. In it, Maggie Cheung must hide five different sets of people in her apartment, while keeping all of them from knowing about the others, and with some of them handcuffed to the furniture! It took me almost a month just to figure out the slapstick logistics of this scene. It was worth the extra time, because the end product is hilarious.

Another hilarious scene—that I didn't find so funny at the time: While fighting off my enemies in the finale, I defend myself by chewing a mouthful of chili peppers, spitting the juice onto my hands and rubbing them into my attacker's eyes. Unfortunately, when the time came to shoot the scene, the art department hadn't made up prop peppers yet. As a result I had to use *real* ones! You can see me guzzling jugs of water in the outtakes, trying to stop the burning sensation.

We did a lot of research to make sure all the scenes looked authentic. All the period costumes were imported from Great Britain, and we built a huge set on the old Shaw Brothers studio lot, so authentic-looking that they still use it today.

CAST: Jackie Chan, Maggie Cheung, David Lam, Rosamund Kwan, Carina Lau, Bill Tung, Regina Kent

DIRECTOR: Jackie Chan

WRITER: Edward Tang King-sang

PRODUCER: Leonard Ho

STUNT COORDINATOR: Jackie Chan

- Best Action Design, Hong Kong Film Awards, 1987
- Nominated for Best Editing, Cheung Yiu Chung, Hong Kong Film Awards, 1987

I Am Sorry (1987)

I was coproducer of this film.

Dragons Forever (1987, also: *Cyclone Z, Three Brothers*)

This is the third and, so far, last movie that I and my opera brothers Samo and Yuen Biao starred in together. The title *Dragons Forever* is a kind of tribute to us and our friendship. Unfortunately, after the production was completed, we went our separate ways; Samo, as Big Brother, was unhappy about being in my shadow, while Yuen Biao also needed his own space to create an image and a career of his own. The plot features me as a somewhat sleazy lawyer, hired to defend a chemical company that is polluting a local waterway. When the owner of an adjoining property sues the company, I hire my buddies Samo, a weapons dealer, and Yuen Biao, a slightly crazy technology specialist, to help me. But after I meet the lovely woman behind the suit—and after I find out that the chemical company I'm representing is actually an illegal drug factory—I have a change of heart. Literally.

Yuen Wah, another one of our brothers, plays one of the evil villains in the final battle in the factory. I also called Benny "The Jet" Urquidez (from *Wheels on Meals*) to come back to Hong Kong to play the deadliest of the bad guys. One thing of note: This is the only film in which you can watch Samo, Yuen Biao, and I fight each other.

CAST: Jackie Chan, Samo Hung, Yuen Biao, Yuen Wah, Dick Wei, Deannie Yip, Kao Fei, Pauline Yeung, Benny "The Jet" Urquidez, Lo Lieh, Billy Chow

DIRECTOR: Samo Hung

PRODUCER: Leonard Ho

- Nominated for Best Action Design, Samo Hung's Stuntman Association, Hong Kong Film Awards, 1988

Police Story II (1988, also: *Police Force II*)

I play the same officer from *Police Story*, but because of all the trouble I caused during the first movie, I've been demoted to traffic cop. Still, when bad guys strike again, randomly bombing buildings, I'm reinstated to my former position—until I get kidnapped and tortured. Of course, the good guys win in the end.

There are a lot of great fight scenes and stunts in this film. In one scene, I'm walking with my girlfriend (again played by Maggie Cheung) in the park, and we're attacked by thugs. The park playground becomes a battleground, and the swings and slides turn into weapons. In another scene, I cross the street by jumping from a balcony, to a truck going one way, then to a double-decker bus going the other way—all while managing to stay clear of threateningly low street signs. At the end of the scene, I crash through a billboard and then dive through a glass window, into the bad guys' headquarters. The stunt resulted in my scalp getting riddled with glass shards; I felt like a porcupine.

Another scary part of the movie occurred on the highway. Because of our schedule and our fear of what the Hong Kong bureaucracy would say, we didn't arrange shooting permits with the city's transportation department in advance; we just went out there and started filming. As a result, I didn't know which of the cars on the highway were ours, and which were civilians going to work. I spent the morning dodging oncoming traffic, hoping the car zooming toward me was being driven by a stuntman who knew when to stop! One of the stunt drivers kept stopping too soon; he was supposed to stop as soon as he reached me. The next time he tried the stunt, though, he stopped too late, and pushed me ten feet along the road! If I had slipped I would have found myself under the car.

Maggie was hurt on this one. She gets thrown down a chute in the final fight scene, but she couldn't control her speed going down the chute, and she landed on her head, which put her in the hospital. Stitches were required to sew up the horseshoe-shaped cut on her head. As a result, any shots of the back of Maggie's head were taken using a double.

CAST: Jackie Chan, Maggie Cheung, Bill Tung, Lam Kwok-hung
DIRECTOR: Jackie Chan
PRODUCER: Leonard Ho
WRITERS: Jackie Chan, Edward Tang King-sang
STUNT COORDINATOR: Jackie Chan
PRODUCTION COMPANY: Golden Way
• Best Action Design, Jackie Chan's Stuntman Association, Hong Kong Film Awards, 1988

Rouge (1988)

Something of a Chinese *Romeo and Juliet*, this film is about two lovers who vow to commit suicide rather than be separated; the woman (played by my good friend Anita Mui) goes through with the suicide, while the man (played by pop idol Leslie Cheung) does not. As a result, Anita becomes a heartbroken ghost; Leslie lives a normal life, and then dies—but, fifty years later, is reincarnated. And that's when phantom Anita decides to renew their acquaintance . . .

I'm proud of this film; it was critically acclaimed and did fairly well at the box office too, even though it's not an action flick. I wanted to prove that my production company, Golden Way, had what it took to make quality dramas. Anita, who started out as a pop star (they called her the "Madonna of Hong Kong"), won Best Actress at the Hong Kong Film Awards for her role, establishing herself as a serious artist.

CAST: Anita Mui, Leslie Cheung, Alex Man
DIRECTOR: Stanley Kwan
PRODUCER: Jackie Chan
WRITERS: Li Pik Wah, Yau Tai On-ping

- Best Actress, Cinematography, and Art Direction, Golden Horse Awards, Taiwan, 1988
- Best Picture, Screenplay, Editing, Music, and Song, Hong Kong Film Awards, 1988

Inspector Wears Skirts (1988, also: *Top Squad*)
After *Rouge*, it was back to action for Jackie the producer. For this film, American kickboxer Cynthia Rothrock plays the leader of an all-female police unit, known as the Top Squad. The movie is about their rivalry with their male counterparts, which is half about fighting and half about flirting. In the end, male and female cops come together in order to defeat a gang.

Rothrock is a rarity in Hong Kong cinema, a kung fu superstar who has made a name for herself in a mostly Asian, mostly male industry. I was so impressed with her skills that I agreed to produce the film, after she was introduced to me by Ng See-yuen, the same man who "discovered" me during my early and unfortunate days with Lo Wei.
CAST: Cynthia Rothrock, Sibelle Hu, Jeff Falcon, Billy Lau, Kara Hui Ying-hung, Bill Tung
DIRECTOR: Wilson Chin
PRODUCER: Jackie Chan
WRITER: Cheng Kam Fu
STUNT COORDINATOR: Jackie Chan

Inspector Wears Skirts II (1989, *Top Squad II*)
In this sequel, Sibelle Hu takes over Cynthia's role as head of the all-female Top Squad. She falls in love with the head of the male unit, played by Billy Lau. But there's no time for romance when the bad guys from the first movie break out of jail.
CAST: Sibelle Hu, Billy Lau, Jeff Falcon
DIRECTOR: Wilson Chin
PRODUCER: Jackie Chan
STUNT COORDINATOR: Jackie Chan

Outlaw Brothers (1989)
I was stunt coordinator for this film.

Miracles: Mr. Canton and Lady Rose (1989, also: *Miracle, Mr. Canton and Lady Rose, The Chinese Godfather, The Canton Godfather*)
Out of all the films I've done, this is my favorite. It doesn't match *Police Story* for action, but it has so much more that I'm proud of, both as an actor and, especially, as a director. The film is set in the 1930s, and I play a country bumpkin who comes to the big city for the first time, only to have everything I own stolen from me as soon as I arrive. But this is just the beginning of my adventure: after receiving a lucky rose from a poor flower woman, I find myself unwittingly being put in charge of a large gang of mobsters. Despite my basic honesty, I find myself forced to lead the thugs, and use my charm and fighting skills to turn them toward the path of goodness. Throughout it all, I remember the flower lady—and when her daughter and her daughter's wealthy in-laws-to-be announce that they're coming to Shanghai, I decide to turn her into a refined and aristocratic lady, so that the in-laws will allow the marriage to go on.

I got the idea for this movie from Frank Capra's classic *Lady for a Day* (1933), which he later remade as *Pocketful of Miracles* (1961). I saw both films when I was a kid; though I couldn't understand the English, I loved the story anyway. Of course, I had to make a lot of changes—including adding fight scenes. If it wasn't for the fighting and stunts, Golden Harvest would have vetoed the whole idea.

As director, I used this film to experiment with my technique, using wide angle shots and panning camera. One of my favorite shots—which took three days with a Steadicam—is a smooth, gliding tracking shot of Anita Mui, my love interest, walking into a grand hotel through various richly decorated rooms.

Miracles took HK$64 million and nine months to shoot, and Golden Harvest wasn't too happy about that. It also didn't make much money, considering the cost. But for me, it will always be special.

CAST: Jackie Chan, Anita Mui, Gloria Yip, Jackie Cheung, Billy Chow
DIRECTOR: Jackie Chan
WRITER: Jackie Chan
PRODUCER: Leonard Ho
STUNT COORDINATOR: Jackie Chan

- Best Action Design, Jackie Chan's Stuntman Association, Hong Kong Film Awards, 1989
- Nominations, Hong Kong Film Awards, 1989: Best Actor, Jackie Chan; Best Editing, Cheung Yiu Chung; Best Art Direction, Eddie Ma

Stagedoor Johnny (1990)

Like *Miracles*, this film is also set in 1930s Shanghai. Anita Mui stars as one of a group of female performers who band together to defeat a Triad boss.

CAST: Anita Mui, Kara Hui Ying-hung, Chan Yuk-lin, Lai Yin-san, Wu Ma
DIRECTOR: Wu Ma
PRODUCER: Jackie Chan

Armour of God II: Operation Condor (1990, also: Operation Eagle, Project Eagle)

After *Miracles*, it was time to go back and recoup some box office. As a result, I dusted off one of my biggest hit characters—adventurer Asian Hawk, now calling himself Asian Condor. In this film, I'm recruited by the government to lead a team through the Sahara Desert, to recover a lost treasure in gold bars hidden by the Nazis during World War II. The team consists of myself and two women, played by Carol "Do Do" Cheng and Eva Cobo de Garcia. Later, we're joined by yet another woman, Shoko Ikeda. With one Cantonese, one European, and one Japanese, I figured I had my various international markets covered.

This movie was full of trouble, but it was also full of action! One of my favorites is the fight in the wind tunnel. Inspiration came from Buster Keaton's *Steamboat Bill, Jr.* (1928), which has a scene in which he's fighting to walk against the wind, and from a visit I took to the Mitsubishi Motors test grounds. We spent close to HK$1 million dollars to build our mock wind tunnel; the propellers were so heavy that they'd break off when the turbine spun, so wires were put on them to hold them in place for each shot. The final result is amazing to watch, as my enemy (American martial artist

Vincent Lyn) and I try to use the shifting winds to our advantage. At one point I lunge at my enemy, using the force of the wind to carry me, and yell, "Superman!" before hitting him with my outstretched fist.

Much of the film was shot in Morocco, a beautiful place, but one that led to no end of headaches. Somehow, the prop money we made for the movie ended up getting circulated off the set and used by natives as actual currency, even though it was clearly printed with the Golden Harvest logo! The Moroccan authorities called me in for questioning and confiscated my film footage, and I had to call lawyers in Hong Kong and Great Britain before I could get my film back. What's worse, the production manager was arrested for distribution of counterfeit money and held in prison for three months, which meant we had to leave him behind when we went onto the Sahara.

Working in the desert was crazy; the sand got into the equipment, the camels wouldn't listen to us, and a crew member got bit by a scorpion. The production was delayed for two months, as over fifty crewmembers fell ill. Eventually, we returned to Hong Kong to film the rest of the desert scene, bringing ten tons of sand back with us.

This movie took us through Asia, Africa, and Europe, and cost HK$115 million— about U.S.$15 million, the most expensive Hong Kong movie ever at the time, though still a small sum in comparison to U.S. movie budgets.

CAST: Jackie Chan, Carol "Do Do" Cheng, Eva Cobo De Garcia, Vincent Lyn, Ken Lo, Shoko Ikeda.
DIRECTOR: Jackie Chan
PRODUCER: Jackie Chan
WRITER: Jackie Chan
STUNT COORDINATOR: Jackie Chan
- Nominated for Best Action Design, Jackie Chan's Stuntman Association, Hong Kong Film Awards, 1990

Island of Fire (1991, also: Island on Fire, Burning Island, The Prisoner)

A cop goes undercover in a prison to find out who ordered the assassination of his father-in-law. What he finds instead is a prison system so fraught with abuses that it's hard to tell who's more delinquent, the prisoners or the wardens. I play a prisoner who is also part of an elite group of assassins, recruited by the prison warden.

I did this film as a favor to Jimmy—in fact, pretty much everyone in the cast, who are all stars themselves, owed a favor to Jimmy. I'm in it only briefly, though I'm listed as starring in it. I was doing Armour of God II: Operation Condor at the same time; needless to say, those were busy days.

CAST: Tony Leung Kar Fei, Jackie Chan, Samo Hung, Andy Lau, Jimmy Wang Yu
DIRECTOR: Chu Yen-ping
PRODUCERS: Jimmy Wang Yu, Ka Chuen Hsing
WRITERS: Fu Lee, Yen Yun Chiao

Twin Dragons (1991, also: Double Dragons, Brother vs. Brother, When Dragons Collide, Duel of Dragons, Dragon Duo, When Dragons Meet)

In this film, which was a benefit for the Hong Kong Director's Guild, I play identical twins separated at birth. One brother, Ma Yu, becomes a famous orchestra conductor;

the other brother, Wan Ming, becomes a gangster. We accidentally bump into each other at a restaurant, where we've arranged to meet our respective girlfriends. When rival gangsters mistake Ma Yu for Wan Ming, total chaos ensues. Wan Ming winds up conducting the orchestra, while Ma Yu fights for his life. Luckily (or is that unluckily?) we have a psychic connection that allows one to feel what the other is going through.

All the profits from this movie were supposed to go toward the building of the Director's Guild's new headquarters, but as of early 1998, the office hasn't been built. Still, the film was something of an achievement. A slew of Hong Kong celebrities were enlisted to make the film; it was even codirected by top filmmakers Tsui Hark and Ringo Lam.

Compared to Hollywood special effects, Hong Kong special effects are not that good. The action remains as impressive as ever, though; the final fight in the car factory is fantastic.

CAST: Jackie Chan, Teddy Robin Kwan, Maggie Cheung, Nina Li Chi, Philip Chan, David Chiang, Anthony Chan, Alfred Cheung, Wang Lung Wei, Lau Kar-leung, Tsui Hark, Ringo Lam, Wong Jing, Eric Tsang, Chu Yuen, Jacob Cheung, Ng See-yuen
DIRECTORS: Tsui Hark, Ringo Lam
PRODUCER: Teddy Robin Kwan
STUNT COORDINATOR: Jackie Chan

A Kid from Tibet (1991)
Yuen Biao plays a monk with magical powers, destined to overthrow an evil sorceror. This was Yuen's directorial debut; I have a small cameo appearance.
CAST: Yuen Biao, Jackie Chan
DIRECTOR: Yuen Biao

Police Story III: Supercop (1992, also: Police Story III, Supercop)
The biggest, most over-the-top installment of my *Police Story* series yet. My character, who's jokingly called the Supercop by his buddies after busting the gangs from the first two movies, is assigned the unpleasant job of going to the Mainland in order to bust a drug operation. My partner in this project is a beautiful, by-the-book mainland cop named Hana Yang, played by Michelle Yeoh. Together we pose as bad guys to infiltrate the drug gang, and go undercover to destroy the operation from the jungles of Thailand to the city streets of Malaysia, battling the gangsters in some of the most spectacular stunt scenes I've shot to date. I won Best Actor award in Taiwan for this film—a first for an action film star. It was nice being acknowledged for more than my fighting and stuntwork.

The most frightening stunt in the movie for me was when I jump from a building to a rope ladder hanging from a helicopter. The camera pulls back to show how very high up in the sky I am; there's no net, and if I'd fallen, there would have been no way to save me. Michelle, the toughest woman I know, also did some impressive stunt work, her biggest stunt being a motorcycle jump up a ramp and onto a moving train. (The stuntman who tested the stunt broke his leg!)
CAST: Jackie Chan, Michelle Yeoh, Maggie Cheung, Tsang Kong, Yuen Wah, Lo Lieh, Bill Tung

DIRECTOR: Stanley Tong
EXECUTIVE PRODUCERS: Leonard Ho, Jackie Chan
PRODUCERS: Willie Chan, Edward Tang King-sang
WRITERS: Edward Tang King-sang, Fibe Ma Mei-ping, Lee Wei-yee
STUNT COORDINATOR: Stanley Tong
• Best Actor, Jackie Chan, Golden Horse Awards, Taiwan
• Nominations, Hong Kong Film Awards, 1992; Best Actor, Jackie Chan; Best Action
Design, Stanley Tong

Once Upon a Time in China II (1992)

While I don't appear in this movie (the second of Tsui Hark's own remakes of the
Wong Fei Hung legend, starring Jet Li), I sing the final theme song for the movie's
soundtrack.

Actress (1993, also: Center Stage)

Another dramatic vehicle, produced by my company Golden Way. Maggie plays Hong
Kong's first movie star, the real-life actress Ruan Ling Yu, who lived fast and died
young, before the age of thirty. It won Maggie great critical acclaim, as well as a Best
Actress award; it didn't make much money, though.
CAST: Maggie Cheung, Tony Leung, Waise Lee, Carina Lau
DIRECTOR: Stanley Kwan
PRODUCER: Jackie Chan
WRITER: Yau Tai On-ping
• Best Actress, Maggie Cheung, Hong Kong Film Awards

City Hunter (1993)

This was an attempt to reach out to my Japanese market, as I took on the role of an
extremely popular Japanese comic book and cartoon character named Ryu Saeba,
the "City Hunter." I'm a womanizing private eye, hired by a wealthy tycoon to locate
his runaway daughter. I track her to a cruise ship, and end up on board myself (along
with my pretty, and very jealous, assistant). Before I can grab the girl, though, the ship
gets hijacked and I'm distracted by having to save the passengers, not to mention
finding time to flirt with a beautiful undercover operative and her partner. . . .

  This movie is okay, but not one of my favorites. The humor is very broad, which is
typical of the film's director, Wong Jing; one of the best gags is one in which, in a tribute to the popular arcade game, Gary Daniels and I fight it out while transforming
from one Street Fighter character to another! (I even don drag as the woman warrior
Chun Li.) Another good gag has me getting advice on how to fight from Bruce Lee as
I fight two incredibly tall villains: a movie screen happens to be showing Bruce's fight
with Kareem Abdul-Jabbar in Game of Death (1972/78).
CAST: Jackie Chan, Gary Daniels, Richard Norton, Chingmy Yau Shuk-ching, Joey
Wang, Kumiko Goto, Leon Lai, Michael Wong
DIRECTOR: Wong Jing
PRODUCER: Chua Lam
STUNT COORDINATOR: Ching Sui Tung

Project S (1993, also: *Police Story IV, Once a Cop: Supercop II*)

Michelle Yeoh plays her Mainland cop character from *Police Story III: Supercop*, Hana Yang, in this semi-sequel. She's sent to Hong Kong to stop a gang, but what she doesn't know is that it's her own boyfriend who is the leader of the gang. As a result, she's torn between love and honor—and ends up going with honor, of course, as befits a Supercop. I make a cameo appearance in the movie, appearing as my *Police Story* character, busting a jewel robbery while in very bad drag.

CAST: Michelle Yeoh, Michael Wong, Emil Chow, Dick Wei, Yu Rong-guang, Jackie Chan
DIRECTOR: Stanley Tong
PRODUCER: Jackie Chan

Crime Story (1993, also: *Police Story IV, The New Police Story, Serious Crimes Squad*)

This movie is based on the true story of the kidnapping of a Hong Kong businessman. I play a no-nonsense cop whose emotional state is shaken by a recent bloody encounter with terrorists. When I'm assigned to bring back the kidnapped businessman, it's a test of my emotional stability and my skills as an officer.

This is a very serious story, and I didn't like it at first, but now I think it was good for me to play such an intensely dramatic role—the first time I did one since *Heart of Dragon*, years before.

CAST: Jackie Chan, Kent Cheng, Poon Ling-ling, Ng Wing-mie, Blackie Ko Shou-liang, Stephen Chan, Chung Fa, Mars, Ken Lo
DIRECTOR: Kirk Wong
PRODUCER: Chua Lam
WRITER: Chan Man Keung
STUNT COORDINATOR: Jackie Chan

- Best Actor, Jackie Chan, Golden Horse Awards, Taiwan, 1994
- Best Editing, Cheung Yiu Chung, Hong Kong Film Awards, 1994
- Nominations, Hong Kong Film Awards, 1994: Best Actor, Jackie Chan; Best Director, Kirk Wong; Best Action Design, Jackie Chan's Stuntman Association

Drunken Master II (1994, also: *Drunken Monkey II*)

This is a sequel to my very first super-hit, continuing the adventures of the hero Wong Fei Hong. While traveling with my father, I somehow get mixed up in a scam by the British to smuggle ancient treasures out of China. With the help of an old Manchurian officer, as well as my stepmom (played by Anita Mui), I manage to thwart the plan.

It's funny that Anita and Ti Lung play my parents in this film; Ti Lung is only seven years older than me in real life, and Anita is much younger than me! But it all hangs together on film, and Anita almost steals the show with her performance.

The fight scenes in this film include some of my favorite choreography. In the first scene in which I use Drunken Fist, Anita actually tosses bottles of wine at me to drink so that I can fight off the bad guys better; the audience gets its first taste of the fluid motion that is the foundation of drunken boxing. The timing for this had to be perfect: I'd have to throw the bottles into the air, swing some very fast punches, catch the bottles and take a swig, and then fight some more! Of course, it's the final fight with Ken Lo where my character really gets to let loose. I accidentally drink grain alcohol instead of wine, and my fighting style becomes furious, bordering on crazy. The scene took four months to film, although every second was worth it when I saw the final cut.

Drunken Master II grossed over HK$22 million, a new Hong Kong record. The film's director, Lau Kar-leung, was a Shaw Brothers star long before I came onto the cinema scene. Although he and I ultimately disagreed on the direction of the film, he did some wonderful work on the movie, as both director and actor, and I'm indebted to him for his veteran skills.

CAST: Jackie Chan, Lau Kar-leung, Anita Mui, Ti Lung, Ken Lo
DIRECTOR: Lau Kar-leung
STUNT COORDINATOR: Jackie Chan
- Best Action Design, Lau Kar-leung and Jackie Chan's Stuntman Association, Hong Kong Film Awards, 1994
- Nominated for Best Editing, Cheung Yiu-chung, Hong Kong Film Awards, 1994

Rumble in the Bronx (1994, also: Red Bronx)

In this, the film with which I made my big comeback to the United States, I play Keung, a Hong Kong cop who travels to New York to help my uncle with his grocery store, which is located in a seedy section of the Bronx called "Fort Apache." When I get there, I find out that Uncle is getting married, retiring, and selling the store to an unassuming woman named Elaine, played by Anita Mui. As soon as the sale goes through, however, a gang of thugs descend upon the store, stealing from Elaine and demanding "protection" money. Feeling responsible, I stick around to help her fight off the brutes; this leads to us getting mixed up in a mobster's diamond-smuggling scheme.

Because of production concerns, Vancouver doubled as the Bronx. And yes, I know there are no mountains in New York City! At first we tried to maintain the illusion, avoiding shooting angles that would show the mountains. We even hired people to paint graffiti on the walls. But then we had to paint over it all at the end of the day. In the end, I decided to forget about trying to simulate New York, figuring that people shouldn't be watching the scenery so much as the action anyway. . . .

In Hong Kong, *Rumble* was the top movie of 1995. When it was released in the States in 1996, it made $10 million in its first week.

CAST: Jackie Chan, Anita Mui, Bill Tung, Francoise Yip
DIRECTOR: Stanley Tong
WRITER: Edward Tang King-sang
PRODUCER: Barbie Tung
STUNT COORDINATORS: Samo Hung, Jackie Chan
- Best Action Design, Hong Kong Film Awards, 1996
- Nominations, Hong Kong Film Awards, 1996: Best Actor, Jackie Chan; Best Actress, Anita Mui; Best Supporting Actress, Francoise Yip; Best Editing, Cheung Yiu-chung; Best Action Design, Stanley Tong and Jackie Chan

Thunderbolt (1995, also: Dead Heat)

I love cars, and always dreamed of doing a movie that let me play a race car driver. This was my chance. My character is an auto mechanic turned police informer who helps track down illegal drag-race drivers. When a gang kidnaps my two sisters, I'm forced to enter a high-stakes auto race in order to free them. Former Miss Hong Kong Anita Yuen, now a very popular actress, plays a reporter who's eager to get my story—and who ends up falling for me (though the romantic angle never really goes anywhere).

This film cost HK$2 billion, or U.S.$25 million—the most in Hong Kong film history. The demolished cars alone cost U.S.$2 million! This wasn't my favorite film, but on opening day it took in a record-breaking HK$4 million.

CAST: Jackie Chan, Anita Yuen, Michael Wong, Ken Lo, Chor Yuen, Thorsten Nickel
DIRECTOR: Gordon Chan
PRODUCER: Leonard Ho
WRITERS: Gordon Chan, Chan Hing Ka, Kwok Wai Chung
STUNT COORDINATORS: Jackie Chan, Samo Hung, Frankie Chan
CAR STUNT DIRECTOR: Frankie Chan

Police Story IV: First Strike (1996, also: Jackie Chan's First Strike)

The Supercop is back, and this time I'm fighting for America! At least, that's what all the posters say. Assigned to a special international mission, I get caught in the middle of a nuclear scam between a former CIA agent and the KGB, and then framed for murder. Bill Tung is back as my superior, though Maggie, my character's long-standing girlfriend, doesn't appear. (Maybe next time.)

The movie has the feel of a James Bond film—I even jokingly say that I feel like James Bond in one scene. One early chase scene was inspired directly by a Bond flick: I'm sliding down a mountain slope on a snowboard, pursued by bad guys on skis and snowmobiles. Of course, my scene ends better than Bond's did—I jump off a cliff and grab onto a helicopter, only to have the copter get shot down. I quickly let go of the copter just in time to avoid being blown to bits, and fall through the ice into a frozen pond. I nearly died of hypothermia.

CAST: Jackie Chan, Jackson Lau, Annie Wu, Bill Tung, Yuri Petrov, Terry Woo
DIRECTOR: Stanley Tong
PRODUCER: Barbie Tung
WRITERS: Stanley Tong, Nick Tramontane
STUNT COORDINATORS: Stanley Tong, Jackie Chan

Mr. Nice Guy (1997, also: A Nice Guy)

I'm the nice guy of the title—a chef with my own talk show. One day I find a strange tape mixed in with my own videos, and it turns out to be a video of a mobster killing his rival. Suddenly, I find myself on the run from the gangsters who want the tape back. This is the first film Samo directed me in since way back in the '80s, and the reunion felt good.

CAST: Jackie Chan, Richard Norton, Gabrielle Fitzpatrick, Karen Mclymont, Peter Lindsay
DIRECTOR: Samo Hung
WRITER: Edward Tang King-sang

Burn Hollywood Burn: An Alan Smithee Film (1997)

I had just a cameo in this satire about the dark and dirty world of Hollywood

...making. The film seemed silly, but I did the appearance because it gave me a chance to work with one of my friends, Sylvester Stallone.

CAST: Sylvester Stallone, Eric Idle, Coolio, Whoopi Goldberg, Jackie Chan
DIRECTOR: Arthur Hiller
WRITER: Joe Eszterhas
PRODUCERS: Joe Eszterhas, Ben Myron, Andrew Vajna

Who Am I? (1999)

I play an agent attempting to bust some smugglers, who have obtained a set of stones that can be used as the key ingredient for a new kind of weapon of mass destruction. While trying to hunt them down, I get dropped from a plane, and I find myself lost in a jungle without my memory. While trying to figure who I am, I get mixed up with the smugglers again, and follow them from South Africa to Holland.

The most spectacular stunt in the movie, of course, is my twenty-one-story slide down the side of a building in Rotterdam, but there're some other great scenes in this movie, particularly during the safari sequence, where I end up playing around with a bunch of wild animals, dressed in full tribal war paint. One of the messages I wanted to send with this film was that we need to preserve nature and protect the environment, and so the jungle sequences were very important to me. The movie was a big success, even beating out *Titanic* in some Asian countries! I guess Jackie Chan can stop a $200 million juggernaut as well as any iceberg . . .

CAST: Jackie Chan, Michelle Ferre, Mira Yamamoto
DIRECTORS: Benny Chan Muk Sing, Jackie Chan
WRITER: Edward Tang King-sang

ABOUT THE COAUTHOR

JEFF YANG is the publisher and founder of A. *Magazine: Inside Asian America,* which he launched upon graduating from Harvard University in 1989. Since then, A. has grown into the nation's largest publication for English-speaking Asian Americans.

Before embarking on his collaboration with Jackie, Yang cowrote A. *Magazine's* first book, *Eastern Standard Time: A Guide to Asian Influence in American Culture, from Astro Boy to Zen Buddhism* (Houghton Mifflin, May 1997). Yang has also been a columnist for *The Village Voice,* and a featured contributor for *Vibe.*

He lives in New York City, where he *always* does his own stunts.

ACKNOWLEDGMENTS

Jeff Yang would like to gratefully acknowledge the following persons for their support, hard work, and patience: My research assistant and translator, Fon-Lin Nyeu; agent extraordinaire Ling Lucas; Lisa Kennedy and Andy Hsiao, who gave me my first break, and made this one possible too; the staff of A. *Magazine;* Seaton Chang; Peter Borland, Judith Curr, and Emily Grayson at Ballantine; David, Bailing, and Christine Yang; Norman Wang, Willie Chan, Solon So, and, of course, Jackie.

IT'S OFFICIAL, IT'S ENDORSED BY INTERNATIONAL
ACTION MARTIAL ARTS MOVIE SUPERSTAR JACKIE CHAN
AND IT'S HERE FOR YOU TO READ NOW!!!

SCREEN POWER
THE OFFICIAL JACKIE CHAN MAGAZINE

Each issue is packed with exclusive interviews with Jackie, his directors,
co-stars, stuntmen, bodyguards and staff, on-set reports from current movies,
reviews, detailed articles, past and present projects profiled, worldwide letters
page, competitions (with top prizes!), worldwide pen-pal service, full colour
official merchandise catalogue, and all the new and happenings in the
Jackie Chan world.

GUARANTEE YOUR COPIES –

SUBSCRIBE NOW WHILE

STOCKS LAST!!!

For a magazine subscription form or more information on Jackie
Chan's films, schedule, and personal appearances write to:

Mr. Richard Cooper
Screen Power Magazine
Subscription Dept.
P.O. Box 1989
Bath, BA2 2YE
United Kingdom

CHECK OUT THE OFFICIAL WEB-SITE NOW AT:
http://www.jackie-chan.co.uk